'The book provides a roadmap for teachers who want to provide their students with the knowledge and skills they will need to thrive in the 21st century.'

- Allan Collins, Professor Emeritus of Learning Sciences, Northwestern University, US

DEEPER LEARNING, DIALOGIC LEARNING, AND CRITICAL THINKING

Deeper learning, dialogic learning, and critical thinking are essential capabilities in the 21st-century environments we now operate. Apart from being important in themselves, they are also crucial in enabling the acquisition of many other 21st-century skills/capabilities such as problem solving, collaborative learning, innovation, information and media literacy, and so on. However, the majority of teachers in schools and instructors in higher education are inadequately prepared for the task of promoting deeper learning, dialogic learning, and critical thinking in their students. This is despite the fact that there are educational researchers who are developing and evaluating strategies for such promotion. The problem is bridging the gap between the educational researchers' work and what gets conveyed to teachers and instructors as evidence-based, usable strategies.

This book addresses that gap: in it, leading scholars from around the world describe strategies they have developed for successfully cultivating students' capabilities for deeper learning and transfer of what they learn, dialogic learning and effective communication, and critical thought. They explore connections in the promotion of these capabilities, and they provide, in accessible form, research evidence demonstrating the efficacy of the strategies. They also discuss answers to the questions of how and why the strategies work.

A seminal resource, this book creates tangible links between innovative educational research and classroom teaching practices to address the all-important question of how we can realize our ideals for education in the 21st century. It is a must read for pre-service and in-service teachers, teacher educators and professional developers, and educational researchers who truly care that we deliver education that will prepare and serve students for life.

Emmanuel Manalo is a professor at the Graduate School of Education of Kyoto University in Japan. He teaches educational psychology and academic communication skills to undergraduate and graduate students. His research interests include the promotion of effective learning and instructional strategies; diagram use for communication, problem solving, and thinking; and critical and other thinking skills.

DEEPER LEARNING, DIALOGIC LEARNING, AND CRITICAL THINKING

Research-based Strategies for the Classroom

Edited by Emmanuel Manalo

First published 2020
by Routledge
2 Park Square, Milton Park, Abingdon, Oxon OX14 4RN

and by Routledge
52 Vanderbilt Avenue, New York, NY 10017

Routledge is an imprint of the Taylor & Francis Group, an informa business

© 2020 selection and editorial matter, Emmanuel Manalo; individual chapters, the contributors

The right of Emmanuel Manalo to be identified as the author of the editorial material, and of the authors for their individual chapters, has been asserted in accordance with sections 77 and 78 of the Copyright, Designs and Patents Act 1988.

The Open Access version of this book, available at www.taylorfrancis.com, has been made available under a Creative Commons Attribution-Non Commercial-No Derivatives 4.0 license.

Trademark notice: Product or corporate names may be trademarks or registered trademarks, and are used only for identification and explanation without intent to infringe.

British Library Cataloguing-in-Publication Data
A catalogue record for this book is available from the British Library

Library of Cataloging-in-Publication Data
A catalog record for this book has been requested

ISBN: 978-0-367-33958-6 (hbk)
ISBN: 978-0-367-26225-9 (pbk)
ISBN: 978-0-429-32305-8 (ebk)

Typeset in Bembo Std
by Cenveo® Publisher Services

To my parents, Antero and Cecilia, for their constant love, support and encouragement

CONTENTS

Acknowledgements   *xiii*
List of contributors   *xv*

Introduction: Establishing a case for sharing
research-based instructional strategies   1
Emmanuel Manalo

PART 1
Structuring dialogue   15

1   The Playground of Ideas: Developing a structured
approach to the Community of Inquiry
for young children   17
Laura Kerslake

2   The *Thinking Together* approach to dialogic teaching   32
Neil Phillipson and Rupert Wegerif

3   Compare and Discuss to promote deeper learning   48
*Bethany Rittle-Johnson, Jon R. Star, Kelley Durkin,
and Abbey Loehr*

PART 2
Facilitating meaning construction 65

4 Refining student thinking through scientific
  theory building 67
  Hillary Swanson

5 Extending students' communicative repertoires:
  A culture of inquiry perspective for reflexive learning 84
  Beth V. Yeager, Maria Lucia Castanheira, and Judith Green

6 Transforming classroom discourse as a resource
  for learning: Adapting interactional ethnography
  for teaching and learning 105
  W. Douglas Baker

PART 3
Cultivating questioning 121

7 Question Based Instruction (QBI) promotes
  learners' abilities to ask more questions and express
  opinions during group discussions 123
  Yoshinori Oyama and Tomoko Yagihashi

8 *AugmentedWorld:* A location-based
  question-generating platform as a means
  of promoting 21st-century skills 141
  Shadi Asakle and Miri Barak

9 Effective ways to prepare for deeper learning
  of history 160
  Keita Shinogaya

PART 4
Promoting engagement and reflection 175

10 "Laughter is the best medicine": Pedagogies
   of humor and joy that support critical thinking
   and communicative competence 177
   Jean J. Ryoo

Contents **xi**

11 Improving college students' critical thinking
through the use of a story tool for self-regulated
learning training 193
*Pedro Rosário, José Carlos Núñez, Paula Magalhães,
Sonia Fuentes, Cleidilene Magalhães, and Kyle Busing*

12 Debugging as a context for fostering reflection
on critical thinking and emotion 209
*David DeLiema, Maggie Dahn, Virginia J. Flood,
Ana Asuncion, Dor Abrahamson, Noel Enyedy,
and Francis Steen*

PART 5
Training specific competencies 229

13 Showing what it looks like: Teaching students
to use diagrams in problem solving, communication,
and thinking 231
*Emmanuel Manalo, Yuri Uesaka, Ouhao Chen,
and Hiroaki Ayabe*

14 Class design for developing presentation skills
for graduate research students 247
Etsuko Tanaka and Emmanuel Manalo

15 Online written argumentation: Internal dialogic
features and classroom instruction 263
*Naomi Rosedale, Stuart McNaughton, Rebecca Jesson,
Tong Zhu, and Jacinta Oldehaver*

16 Cultivating pre-service and in-service teachers'
abilities to deepen understanding and promote
learning strategy use in pupils 279
Tatsushi Fukaya and Yuri Uesaka

PART 6
Program/course teaching 297

17 Cultivation of a critical thinking disposition
and inquiry skills among high school students 299
Takashi Kusumi

18 Using task-based language teaching in the second language classroom: Developing global communication competencies 321
Chris Sheppard

19 Collective reasoning in elementary engineering education 339
Christine M. Cunningham and Gregory J. Kelly

Index 356

ACKNOWLEDGEMENTS

This book has only been made possible because of the generous help of many people. I would like to sincerely thank the following colleagues who freely gave of their time and knowledge to read and provide constructive comments on the chapters during the review process. All chapters were double-blind peer reviewed, except for the two that I co-authored and the Introduction section (which were also peer reviewed, but not blind).

Mohammad Javad Ahmadian, University of Leeds, UK
Susan Carter, University of Auckland, New Zealand
Monaliza Chian, University of Hong Kong, Hong Kong
Ban Heng Choy, National Institute of Education, Singapore
James E. Corter, Columbia University, USA
Rachel Dryer, Australian Catholic University, Australia
Hanna Dumont, DIPF/Leibniz Institute for Research and Information in Education, Germany
Junya Fukuta, Shizuoka University, University
Andrea Gomoll, Indiana University, USA
Alexandria Hansen, California State University, Fresno, USA
Huili Hong, Towson University, USA
Takamichi Ito, Kyoto University of Education, Japan
So-Hee Kim, Korea University, Korea
Po Yuk Ko, Education University of Hong Kong, Hong Kong
Masuo Koyasu, Konan University, Japan
Chris Krägeloh, Auckland University of Technology, New Zealand
Kristiina Kumpulainen, University of Helsinki, Finland
Richard Lehrer, Vanderbilt University, USA
Debora Lui, University of Pennsylvania, USA

Adam Maltese, Indiana University, USA
Richard E. Mayer, University of California, Santa Barbara, USA
Yasushi Michita, University of the Ryukyus, Japan
Ai Mizokawa, Nagoya University, Japan
Kou Murayama, University of Reading, UK
Ryo Okada, Kagawa University, Japan
Michael Paton, University of Sydney, Australia
Helena Pedrosa-de-Jesus, University of Aveiro, Portugal
Paula Pinto, Polytechnic Institute of Santarém, Portugal
Alina Reznitskaya, Montclair State University, USA
J. Elizabeth Richey, Carnegie Mellon University, USA
Ronald Rinehart, University of Northern Iowa, USA
Ryan Rish, State University of New York at Buffalo, USA
Albert D. Ritzhaupt, University of Florida, USA
Lisa Scharrer, Ruhr-University Bochum, Germany
Déana Scipio, IslandWood, USA
Robert Stebbins, University of Calgary, Canada
Pat Strauss, Auckland University of Technology, New Zealand
Jan T'Sas, University of Antwerp, Belgium
Yuri Uesaka, University of Tokyo, Japan
Stan van Ginkel, HU University of Applied Sciences Utrecht, Netherlands
Amy Vetter, University of North Carolina at Greensboro, USA
Abeer Watted, Technion, Israel Institute of Technology, Israel
Ian A. G. Wilkinson, University of Auckland, New Zealand
Emma Williams, University of Warwick, UK

In addition to the above colleagues, I would like to thank Ayano Tsuda and Becki Paterson (Kyoto University, Japan) for carefully proofreading and checking the readability of all the chapters prior to submission. Thank you also to Agustina Yohena (Kyoto University, Japan) for assisting with the compilation of the index.

The work I have undertaken in producing this book was supported by a grant-in-aid (15H01976) I received from the Japan Society for the Promotion of Science. Any opinions, findings, and conclusions or recommendations expressed in this book are those of the authors and do not necessarily reflect the views of the Japan Society for the Promotion of Science.

CONTRIBUTORS

Dor Abrahamson, PhD, is a professor at the Graduate School of Education, University of California, Berkeley, where he directs the Embodied Design Research Laboratory. With training in cognitive psychology and the learning sciences, Abrahamson develops theory of mathematical cognition, teaching, and learning through engineering, implementing and evaluating pedagogical resources. Email: dor@berkeley.edu

Shadi Asakle is a PhD student in the Faculty of Education in Science and Technology, Technion, Israel Institute of Technology. His doctoral dissertation is about promoting scientific thinking and motivation through situated, online, collaborative and interactive learning. Led by Asst. Prof. Miri Barak, Shadi developed *AugmentedWorld,* a collaborative, location-based, question-generating platform. He is currently Head of Software Department of Practical Engineering at Ort Braude College. Email: as.shadi@campus.technion.ac.il

Ana Asuncion is a Learning Designer at 9 Dots, a Learning technology nonprofit organization in Los Angeles, California. Her interest is in transforming the classroom into a space where students are engaging in fun, rigorous problem solving through accessible computer science curriculum. Email: ana.asuncion@9dots.org

Hiroaki Ayabe is a doctoral candidate at the Graduate School of Education of Kyoto University in Japan. His research examines the design and implementation of effective learning and instructional strategies, student diagram use, and cognitive load – from the perspectives of educational psychology and brain science. Email: ayabe.hiroaki.56c@st.kyoto-u.ac.jp

W. Douglas Baker, PhD, is associate dean of the College of Arts & Sciences and professor of English Education at Eastern Michigan University in the USA. His research adapts an ethnographic perspective to explore discourse processes and interactions in classrooms and other educational settings. Email: wbakerii@emich.edu

Miri Barak, PhD, is a professor at the Faculty of Education in Science and Technology, Technion, Israel Institute of Technology. She is Head of the Science and Learning Technologies group, and her research involves the design and implementation of web-based environments for the advancement of 21st-century education. Her studies examine cognitive and sociocultural aspects of online learning and the constructs of innovative and flexible thinking. She is a principal investigator (PI) and co-PI of national and international projects on location-based learning and massive online open courses (MOOCs). Email: bmiriam@technion.ac.il

Kyle Busing, PhD, is the Director of Academic Innovation and Development at Schreiner University in the USA. His interest is in conducting and using research to develop and implement best practices to improve student learning, success, and retention. Email: jkbusing@schreiner.edu

Maria Lucia Castanheira, PhD, is a professor in the School of Education, Federal University of Minas Gerais, Brazil. She is also a researcher in a literacy research center in the same institution, *Centro de Alfabetização, Leitura e Escrita*. Her research interests focus on the examination of literacy practices in and out of school and university. She is particularly interested in examining the social construction of opportunities for learning through exploring discourse analysis and interactional ethnographic approaches. Email: lalucia@fae.ufmg.br

Ouhao Chen, PhD, is a lecturer/research scientist at the National Institute of Education, Nanyang Technological University in Singapore. He teaches primary mathematics and educational research skills to pre-service teachers and graduate students. His research interests include cognitive load, working memory, math education, and drawing to learn. Email: ouhao.chen@nie.edu.sg

Christine M. Cunningham, PhD, is a professor of engineering and education at the Pennsylvania State University in the USA. Her work focuses on making engineering and science more relevant and understandable, especially for populations underrepresented and underserved in these disciplines. Her interest is in developing research-based curricular materials that foster equity and access and engage children with engineering and science knowledge and practices. Previously, Cunningham was the Founding Director of Engineering is Elementary (EiE). Email: ccunningham@psu.edu

Contributors **xvii**

Maggie Dahn is a doctoral candidate in the Urban Schooling Division of UCLA's Graduate School of Education & Information Studies and a 2018 NAEd/Spencer Dissertation Fellow. Her research focuses on how students learn in and through the arts, and the development of voice and identity through art making. Email: maggiedahn@gmail.com

David DeLiema, PhD, is a postdoctoral researcher at the University of California, Berkeley, where he studies collaborative storytelling about failure, specifically in the context of debugging computer code. His research also investigates play-based learning, viewpoint and spatial reasoning in gesture, and epistemic cognition. Email: deliema@berkeley.edu

Kelley Durkin, PhD, is a research assistant professor in Teaching and Learning and in Psychology and Human Development at Vanderbilt University in Nashville, Tennessee, in the USA. Her research focuses on evaluating educational programs and how ideas from cognitive science and psychology can be applied in educational settings to improve learning. Email: kelley.durkin@vanderbilt.edu

Noel Enyedy, PhD, is a professor at the Department of Teaching and Learning, Vanderbilt University's Peabody College, where he studies how people learn through social interaction. In particular, he studies how mixed reality environments, play-based learning, and embodied learning spark conversations between students and support instructional conversations in productive ways. Email: noel.d.enyedy@vanderbilt.edu

Virginia J. Flood is a PhD candidate in education at UC Berkeley and a 2018 NAEd/Spencer Dissertation Fellow. Her research investigates the role embodied meaning making resources like gesture play in technology rich STEM learning environments. Email: flood@berkeley.edu

Sonia Fuentes, PhD, is a postdoctoral researcher in self-regulation of learning in the Universidade do Minho, Portugal. She is also a trainer in cognitive mediation at ICELP (International Center for the Enhancement of Learning Potential) in Israel, Director and founder of the Center for Self-Regulated Studies of Mediated Learning, and professor and university researcher in educational psychology. Her research interests include learning strategies for effective and autonomous learning, cognitive mediation, critical thinking development, and promotion of self-regulated learning processes. Email: sofu2028@gmail.com

Tatsushi Fukaya, PhD, is an associate professor at the Graduate School of Education of Hiroshima University in Japan. His research interests include metacognition and teacher education. He conducts practicing-based research such as cognitive counseling and explores how it could change teachers' way of teaching students. Email: fukaya@hiroshima-u.ac.jp

Judith Green, PhD, is Professor Emerita and Founding Director of the Center for Literacy and Learning in Networking Communities at the University of California, Santa Barbara, in the USA. Her research draws on theories of culture and learning from anthropology, sociolinguistics, and discourse studies to examine how linguistically, culturally, socially and academically diverse students socially and discursively construct knowledge and ways of learning in and across times in classrooms and community settings. Email: judithlgreen@me.com

Rebecca Jesson, PhD, is Associate Director of the Woolf Fisher Research Centre, senior lecturer and Associate Head of School: Research, at the School of Curriculum and Pedagogy, Faculty of Education and Social Work at the University of Auckland in New Zealand. Her research interests involve applying theories of learning and teaching to achieve acceleration in literacy learning. Email: r.jesson@auckland.ac.nz

Gregory J. Kelly, PhD, is senior associate dean and a distinguished professor of science education at the Pennsylvania State University in the USA. His research draws from history, philosophy, and sociology of science to study the construction of knowledge through discourse processes in educational settings. Recent work examines epistemic practices in science and engineering education. Email: gkelly@psu.edu

Laura Kerslake is a researcher in the Faculty of Education, University of Cambridge, in the UK. Her research interests include Philosophy with Children, classroom dialogue and dialogic interaction. Recent work includes *Theory of Teaching Thinking: International Perspectives* (Routledge). Email: lsk30@cam.ac.uk

Takashi Kusumi, PhD, is a professor at the Graduate School of Education of Kyoto University in Japan. He teaches cognitive and educational psychology. His research interests include the promotion of critical thinking, inquiry skills, multiple literacies, practical knowledge, and wisdom in school and the workplace. Email: kusumi.takashi.7u@kyoto-u.ac.jp

Abbey Loehr, PhD, is a postdoctoral researcher in education at Washington University in St. Louis in the USA. She aims to understand and develop ways to support learning, primarily within academic domains such as mathematics. Her research examines how incorrect knowledge changes as people learn, and how misunderstandings affect the construction of correct knowledge. Email: abbey.loehr@wustl.edu

Cleidilene Magalhães, PhD, is an associate professor in the Department of Education and Humanities of the Federal University of Health Sciences of Porto Alegre, Brazil. Her research interests include education and health promotion in formal and informal contexts, psycho-pedagogical support for college students, teaching in health, and the training of teachers to promote critical thinking and student autonomy. Email: cleidilene.ufcspa@gmail.com

Paula Magalhães, PhD, is a postdoctoral fellow at the School of Psychology at the University of Minho in Portugal. Her research interests include self-regulation of learning and academic procrastination among university students, the promotion of self-regulation strategies for health across the lifespan, and the use of gamification strategies and "serious games" in educational interventions. Email: pmagalhaes@psi.uminho.pt

Emmanuel Manalo, PhD, is a professor at the Graduate School of Education of Kyoto University in Japan. He teaches educational psychology and academic communication skills to undergraduate and graduate students. His research interests include the promotion of effective learning and instructional strategies; diagram use for communication, problem solving, and thinking; and critical and other thinking skills. Email: manalo.emmanuel.3z@kyoto-u.ac.jp

Stuart McNaughton, PhD, is Director of the Woolf Fisher Research Centre, Faculty of Education and Social Work at the University of Auckland, and Science Advisor to the Minister of Education, in New Zealand. His research work informs explanations of teaching, learning and development, and the design and evaluation of large-scale interventions in literacy and 21st-century skills. Email: s.mcnaughton@auckland.ac.nz

José Carlos Núñez, PhD, is a full professor in the Departamento de Psicologia at Universidade de Oviedo, Spain. He is the Director of the Department of Psychology and one of the editors of the journal, *Psicothema*. His research interests include approaches to learning and learning strategies among secondary and university students. Email: josecarlosn@uniovi.es

Jacinta Oldehaver is a PhD student and a professional teaching fellow at the Faculty of Education and Social Work at the University of Auckland in New Zealand. She is also a researcher/facilitator on the *Developing in Digital Worlds* project at the Woolf Fisher Research Centre. Jacinta's doctoral research seeks to investigate patterns of "dialogic talk" in primary schools with high numbers of Pacific students in Aotearoa, New Zealand. Email: j.oldehaver@auckland.ac.nz

Yoshinori Oyama, PhD, is an associate professor in the Department of Education at Chiba University in Japan. He is in charge of teacher education for students training to become teachers in elementary through to high schools. His main research areas include teachers' questioning skills training, and development of students' questioning skills to enhance spontaneous use. Email: y_oyama@chiba-u.jp

Neil Phillipson, DPhil, has 20 years of experience as a teacher, a consultant and a trainer. He is a Sapere-registered trainer in Philosophy for Children (P4C) and works closely with schools to develop their practice in P4C and dialogic teaching. He co-authored the book *Dialogic Education: Mastering Core Concepts through Thinking Together* with Rupert Wegerif and is a facilitator of international dialogues with Generation Global. Email: phillipson7@gmail.com

Bethany Rittle-Johnson, PhD, is a professor in psychology and human development at Vanderbilt University, in Nashville, Tennessee, in the USA. Her research focuses on how people learn and how to improve their learning, especially in mathematics. She collaborates with teachers and educational researchers to apply and test her research in classroom settings. Email: b.rittle-johnson@vanderbilt.edu

Pedro Rosário, PhD, is an associate professor with tenure in the Escola de Psicologia at the Universidade do Minho, Portugal. His research interests include students' self-regulation of their learning and procrastination. Dr. Pedro runs projects to enhance self-regulation in Portugal, Brazil, and Chile. He is the Director of the Research Centre (CiPsi) at the Escola de Psicologia. Email: prosario@psi.uminho.pt

Naomi Rosedale is a senior researcher on the *Developing in Digital Worlds* project and is in her final year of PhD studies at the Woolf Fisher Research Centre, Faculty of Education and Social Work at the University of Auckland in New Zealand. Her research examines school and wider community influences on students' 21st-century skills in online digital contexts and student creation of digital learning objects. Email: n.rosedale@auckland.ac.nz

Jean J. Ryoo, PhD, is the Director of Research of the Computer Science Equity Projects in Center X at the University of California, Los Angeles, in the USA. Her work focuses on building research-practice partnerships that support equity-oriented science and computing learning experiences/research valuing the wealth of knowledge and cultural backgrounds youth bring to the table. Email: jeanryoo@ucla.edu

Chris Sheppard, PhD, is a professor at the Faculty of Science and Engineering at Waseda University in Tokyo, Japan. He teaches on an ESP (English for specific purposes) program designed to develop the academic communication skills of science and engineering students. His research interests are in task-based language teaching, curriculum design, and second language acquisition. Email: chris@waseda.jp

Keita Shinogaya, PhD in education, is an associate professor in the College of Economics at Nihon University, Japan. He teaches educational psychology to undergraduate students who aspire to become school teachers. His main research interest is in developing and evaluating effective ways of connecting learning at home and at school to improve students' self-regulated learning skills. Email: shinogaya.keita@nihon-u.ac.jp

Jon R. Star, PhD, is a professor of education at the Harvard Graduate School of Education in the USA. Star is an educational psychologist who studies children's learning of mathematics in middle and high school, particularly algebra. Star's current research explores instructional and curricular interventions that may promote the development of mathematical understanding. Email: jon_star@harvard.edu

Francis Steen, PhD, is an associate professor at the Department of Communication, University of California, Los Angeles, where he studies how we learn from mass media. His research addresses how people use the multimodal information in mass media to form complex and integrated models of reality, using language, images, gesture, and emotion. Email: steen@comm.ucla.edu

Hillary Swanson, PhD, is a research assistant professor of learning sciences in the School of Education and Social Policy at Northwestern University in the USA. Her research examines the productive role of prior knowledge in learning and how classroom science instruction can be designed to refine students' everyday thinking through theory-building practices. Email: hillary.swanson@northwestern.edu

Etsuko Tanaka, PhD, is an assistant professor in the Doctoral Education Consortium of Nagoya University in Japan, where she contributes to fostering young professionals to becoming global leaders. Her research interests include class design for the development of interest in learning, and effective collaborative learning. Email: tanaka.etsuko@h.mbox.nagoya-u.ac.jp

Yuri Uesaka, PhD, is an associate professor at the Center for Research and Development on Transition from Secondary to Higher Education, the University of Tokyo, Japan. Her interest is in using psychological approaches to develop effective instructional environments for enhancing the quality of student learning. She also participates in studies focused on practical applications of research in real school settings. Email: yuri.uesaka@ct.u-tokyo.ac.jp

Rupert Wegerif, PhD, is professor of education at the University of Cambridge, where he teaches educational psychology. His research focuses on education for dialogue in the context of the Internet age. He researches dialogic theory in education and ways of teaching through dialogue and teaching for dialogue in classrooms with and without technology. He is co-lead with Sara Hennessy of the Cambridge Educational Dialogue Research group (CEDiR) and founder and co-convenor of the Educational Theory Special Interest Group of the European Association of Research on Learning and Instruction (EARLI). Email: rw583@cam.ac.uk

Tomoko Yagihashi holds a bachelor's degree in social welfare and has been an elementary school teacher for 26 years. She currently teaches at Chiba University's Faculty of Education-affiliated elementary school, in Japan. Her main research area is ethics education through role-play and discussion.

Beth V. Yeager, PhD, is a consultant with Rio School District in Oxnard, California, USA. She draws on an interactional ethnographic perspective to focus, at the nexus of research/practice, on practitioner inquiry, literacy, disciplinary practices and identities, and transdisciplinary inquiry-based instructional design, with/for linguistically, culturally, socially, and academically diverse students. She was a bilingual pre-K-6 teacher. She is retired as a researcher from California State University, East Bay, and University of California, Santa Barbara, where she was also Executive Director of the Center for Literacy and Learning in Networking Communities. Email: eyeager76@gmail.com

Tong Zhu is a PhD student and a research fellow at the Woolf Fisher Research Centre, Faculty of Education and Social Work at the University of Auckland in New Zealand. His research interests include the analysis of hierarchical structured data (with particular application to New Zealand primary and secondary student achievement data), categorical data analysis, applied statistics, and data visualization. Email: t.zhu@auckland.ac.nz

INTRODUCTION

Establishing a case for sharing research-based instructional strategies

Emmanuel Manalo

Preamble

As its title indicates, this book is about promoting deeper learning, dialogic learning, and critical thinking. Very briefly, "deeper learning" refers to profound (rather than superficial) understanding of knowledge, "dialogic learning" means learning through dialogue, and "critical thinking" pertains to careful and reflective thinking about what to believe or do. More detailed explanations of each of these will be provided later in this Introduction.

Deeper learning, dialogic learning, and critical thinking can all be considered as being both *processes* (i.e., ways of achieving a particular goal or purpose) and *outcomes* (i.e., results or consequences of actions taken). For example, where critical thinking is concerned, we can approach a task by taking the necessary steps to think critically about it (i.e., this is the process we follow), and the result of our effort can be described as critical thinking (i.e., the outcome we get, which in this case is the quality of our thinking). All three are also *capabilities* in that they refer to abilities to carry out certain processes and/or achieve certain outcomes (e.g., the ability to think critically). For the sake of simplicity, and to avoid potential confusion as a consequence of using multiple descriptors, from here onward in this Introduction they will simply be referred to as *capabilities*.

This Introduction will first describe the pressing challenge that is addressed in this book: that of providing education to meet some of the essential requirements of the 21st century. It will then explain these three capabilities, and why equipping teachers with the ability to promote them in their classrooms is particularly crucial in addressing that challenge. Finally, an outline of the structure of this book and the 19 chapters it contains will be provided.

The challenge addressed in this book

We are now well into the 21st century, and by all accounts the provision of education should now be different compared to how it was provided in the previous century, during which it was usual for the teacher to stand in front of the class and tell students what they needed to learn, for the students to listen quietly and diligently learn from the teacher, and for the teacher to test students on their retention of what had been taught. Education should by now have evolved so that it is addressing the requirements of learners in the current century's fast-changing environments, where information is ubiquitous (we no longer need to keep everything in our heads), and the many facets of technology have advanced and continue to advance in leaps and bounds. In those environments, the emphasis is no longer on how much people know but on how well they can acquire knowledge and use the knowledge they possess – especially in new and novel situations (e.g., Ananiadou & Claro, 2009; Griffin, McGaw, & Care, 2012).

But has education really changed adequately to meet the current century's requirements? The short answer to this question is "no." Of course, there will be some exceptions, and most of us can probably think of at least a few examples of classrooms we have observed that would be "near enough" matches to how we might imagine education provision in the 21st century ought to be. (We might even conduct our own classrooms in such a manner.) However, for the vast majority of classrooms around the world, not a lot has changed. The blackboard might have been replaced by a whiteboard or even an electronic board/screen. A lecture management system might be used so that records are now stored electronically, and teachers and students can distribute/submit information (e.g., reading materials, lecture notes, assignments, opinions) online. But in most classrooms around the world, the teacher still stands in front of the class to impart knowledge to students, who still by and large listen quietly so that they can learn what they need to know from the teacher, and the teacher tests the students' ability to retain what they have been taught. The teacher may now emphasize to students the importance of understanding what they learn (something which had always been important, even prior to the 21st century, but which had previously been largely overlooked in favor of retention). But what teachers require students to do, and how they assess students, remains heavily focused on retention of information – whether it be to define and explain concepts (according to the teacher and/or the textbook), or to execute problem solving or some other procedure (again, according to the teacher and/or the textbook). As the US National Research Council's *Committee on Defining Deeper Learning and 21st Century Skills* noted, "current educational policies and associated accountability systems rely on assessments that focus primarily on recall of facts and procedures, posing a challenge to wider teaching and learning of transferable 21st century competencies" (National Research Council, 2012, p. 11). "Understanding" in such assessment more or less equates to whether you can remember what you have been told or shown to learn (facts, procedures, etc.). The problem is that such "understanding" is far from adequate in terms of the knowledge, skills, and competencies that most people would need to successfully operate in the real world outside of school (i.e., at work, in personal life, in family and social situations, and so on). In fact, it is very unlikely that recall of much of those facts, definitions, explanations, and procedures that students have memorized at school would ever be required once they leave school – and yet, that is how most of our education systems continue to evaluate the achievement and merit of students.

The question of why most systems of education delivery have changed little compared to how they were in much of the previous century is a pressing and important one. However, answering it is not easy – and it is outside of the scope of this book to consider this question in any extensive manner. Suffice it to say, there are many factors that conspire against change. It has been known for a long time that change generally causes people a lot of stress (e.g., Holmes & Rahe, 1967; Rabkin & Struening, 1976). So, irrespective of what the change is, it is bound to encounter some resistance in society, especially when the change required is of this magnitude. Andreas Schleicher, the OECD's (Organisation for Economic Co-operation and Development) Director of Education and Skills, expressed the view that it is difficult to implement the educational reforms required in the 21st century because there are many interests, beliefs, motivations, and fears of people involved in educational decision-making that act against them. This happens because the vast structure of established education providers entails extensive vested interests. If changes are made to the current systems, there would be many stakeholders who would lose some power or influence, and so they feel it necessary to protect the status quo (Schleicher, 2018).

One crucial point that Schleicher (2018) made when considering the question of "what successful reform requires" is that capacity development is indispensable. This means that we need to ensure that those who will be responsible for implementing the reforms – most importantly, the educational administrators and teachers – will actually have the required knowledge, skills, and resources for doing so. We cannot, for instance, expect teachers to modify their current approaches to teaching or to cultivate new sets of student capabilities if they lack the corresponding know-how and instructional resources.

How teachers are provided with training and professional development is an area that requires attention. At present, much of pre-service and in-service training tends to focus almost exclusively on subject instruction (i.e., how to teach particular subjects like math, science, English, history, and so on). While cultivation of subject/disciplinary knowledge remains an important component of 21st-century education (OECD, 2018), there are many other forms of knowledge, skills, capabilities, attitudes, and values that teachers need also to be able to cultivate and guide students toward development. For instance, we know that students need to develop effective learning strategies that will serve them not only while they are in school but also afterward, at work, as well as generally in their everyday life as self-regulated, lifelong learners. However, as Dunlosky (2013) observed, many students are not learning about such strategies, and one of the reasons he attributed this to was inadequacy in teacher knowledge about how to teach or cultivate such strategies in their students. While most pre-service teachers are introduced to the notion of effective learning strategies through their training and in educational psychology textbooks, the coverage of those strategies is usually minimal and insufficient. As Dunlosky noted, textbooks for example tend to leave out discussion of the most effective strategies, and they do not deal with the practicalities of how to actually teach students to use those strategies.

The same problem concerning the instruction of effective learning strategies that Dunlosky (2013) identified applies to the development of the broad aims/objectives of 21st-century education, including the capabilities that the present book deals with. Pre-service teachers get introduced to concepts such as deeper learning, effective communication[1], and critical thinking in their training and textbooks, but they receive limited instruction or guidance on how to actually teach to promote their achievement. Like the educational psychology textbooks that Dunlosky referred to, most academic books dealing with 21st-century education *contain* the relevant theories and research about what such education needs to provide, but they rarely address the question of *how* we can actually teach to meet those requirements. Thus, most teachers for example would be well informed about critical thinking and its importance in modern societies, but would be limited in their ability to describe specific strategies they use – or could use – for cultivating critical thinking in their students. Part of the problem is that there is a widespread but erroneous belief that teachers already know how to teach to promote 21st-century skills and capabilities (Rotherham & Willingham, 2010), so insufficient effort is being placed on ensuring that they would have the necessary professional development and instructional materials for such purposes.

It should be noted here that "strategies" for promoting 21st-century skills and capabilities are actually not hard to find. There are many how-to books and other publications for teachers and students – both in print and online (e.g., on Internet websites) – focusing on the improvement of teaching and learning, and dealing with various aspects of 21st-century education. However, more often than not, such publications are written *not* by education experts but by professional education writers, and the strategies they describe are usually based only on common sense and intuition, the authors' personal experiences, and/or their personal views and opinions about what teachers and/or students should do. Often, the strategies described have not been evaluated by research, and there is usually little or no evidence provided to demonstrate their effectiveness.[2]

At the same time, there are many educational researchers who are undertaking studies relating to the promotion of skills and capabilities considered important in 21st-century environments. However, they usually publish their findings in academic books and journals, using language and reporting formats that are largely inaccessible to the majority of classroom teachers. Hence, their valuable findings about effective strategies often fail to make their way into the reading lists of teachers and consequently the conduct of teaching in real classroom settings.

Addressing the above problem is essentially the purpose of this book. In other words, this book is intended to contribute to bridging the gap or disconnection between what educational researchers are finding in their studies and the guidance/materials being provided to teachers about the cultivation of crucial student capabilities. Although, as Schleicher (2018) pointed out, there are many hurdles that need to be overcome in order to achieve all the educational reforms necessary, one aspect that educational researchers can directly address is making research-based strategies for promoting 21st-century skills and capabilities available to teachers. If research reveals that a particular form of instruction or intervention is effective, then teachers should know about it. Information needs to be shared with teachers in such a way that they would be able to understand the applicability (or otherwise) of the strategy to classrooms such as their own, and how they might be able to find out more should they wish to try using that strategy.

Another important objective of this book is to convey the value of sharing strategies – so that we are learning from each other for the purposes of developing and enhancing classroom practices (i.e., educational researchers learning from each other, teachers learning from researchers, and researchers learning from teachers). We need to acknowledge that many researchers are working on developing effective learning and instructional strategies, and that there is not going to be one "right" approach that would suit all teachers and students in all situations: there are far too many factors that would influence what could be deemed suitable. Hence, instead of promoting only the strategies we favor, we should be alerting teachers to the range of potentially useful strategies that are available and educating them about how they can appropriately decide which strategy to use (e.g., based on the learning objectives and requirements of their classroom, availability of resources, evidence for effectiveness, etc.). Furthermore, as education increasingly becomes global, it would likely be beneficial to consider not only strategies originating from places near us, but also from further afield, so that we are sharing with and learning from international – rather than just local – experts and practitioners in education.

Deeper learning, dialogic learning, and critical thinking

Deeper learning, dialogic learning, and critical thinking are by no means the only capabilities that are important in 21st-century environments, but they are being focused on here because they also play crucial roles in facilitating or enabling the acquisition of various other important capabilities (e.g., problem solving, collaborative learning, information and media literacy). Hence, they are not only important in themselves, but are also important for the sake of other processes and outcomes – as will be explained. The 19 chapters in this book describe research-based strategies that can be used to promote one or more of deeper learning, dialogic learning, and critical thinking, along with the other capabilities that are consequently also facilitated.

Deeper learning

Deeper learning, as noted earlier, refers to *profound understanding of knowledge* (including knowledge in particular domains) so that the person who is learning is able to grasp not only what that knowledge is (including its meanings and significance), but also how, why, and when that knowledge can be used. It incorporates what Marton and Säljö (1976, p. 9) referred to as "deep-level processing," during which the person manages to apprehend "what is signified (i.e., what the discourse is about)." It can be considered as the opposite of superficial learning, where the person can only recite, recall, or reproduce knowledge, but is not able to understand much more about it or how it can be used.

Take the arithmetic operation of multiplication, for example. A person could memorize and recite multiplication tables without understanding much more about the process of multiplication itself: that would be learning about multiplication superficially. To more deeply learn about multiplication, the person needs to understand how multiplication is similar to addition, and how it is the inverse of division. He or she would be able to use the knowledge about multiplication not only to answer test questions in arithmetic at school, but also to solve problems in other knowledge domains (e.g., statistics, science, geography) and in his or her everyday life – such as at home (e.g., when cooking) and at work (e.g., when planning and budgeting). Another example would be learning vocabulary in a foreign language. A person could just superficially learn by memorizing definitions and model sentences to pass school exams. But deeper learning would entail greater understanding about the words being learned, including how those words can be used to access knowledge and to communicate, with materials and in contexts that have never been encountered before.

Important features of deeper learning include not only the abstraction of general principles, patterns, and rules, but also the apprehension of interconnections or relationships between various strands of knowledge, ideas, and information. Hence, the US National Research Council defined deeper learning as "the process through which an individual becomes capable of taking what has been learned in one situation and applying it to new situations (i.e., transfer)" (National Research Council, 2012, p. 5). This is an important definition as it provides us with one means for determining when deeper learning has occurred.

Transfer is of course essential for most if not all of the skills and competencies that are generally deemed important in 21st-century education, including problem solving, creativity and innovation, and all the intrapersonal (e.g., decision making, initiative and self-direction) and interpersonal (e.g., communication, collaboration) competencies (see, e.g., Ananiadou & Claro, 2009). In fact, the National Research Council (2012, p. 8) concluded that "the process of deeper learning is essential for the development of transferable 21st Century competencies … and the application of 21st Century competencies in turn supports the process of deeper learning, in a recursive, mutually reinforcing cycle." What this suggests is that to develop competencies like effective collaboration, deeper learning of knowledge and skills about, say, "questioning" is necessary (i.e., to the extent that the person understands not only the facts about questioning, but also why, how, and when it might be useful in collaborative situations; see, e.g., McTighe & Wiggins, 2013; Oyama, 2017). In turn, the application of questioning in collaborative contexts would contribute to the person's deeper learning about questioning (e.g., the experience would give the person greater understanding of how various factors like individual differences, culture, and purpose could affect the way questioning is used in collaboration).

Dialogic learning

Dialogic learning, again as noted earlier, essentially means *learning through dialogue* – ideally where the dialogue between participants is egalitarian (i.e., conducted between equals rather than in a hierarchical manner). Dialogic learning is used in this book to represent communication, in acknowledgement of the fact that dialogue comprises much of the communication in teaching and learning contexts. Furthermore, where 21st-century skills and capabilities are concerned, many can be facilitated most effectively in the egalitarian manner by which dialogic learning is meant to proceed.

But when can we consider learning to be "dialogic" instead of, say, "monologic"? According to Wegerif (2017), monologic conveys the idea that "everything has one correct meaning in one true perspective on the world." Thus, in monologic learning the aim for the learner would be to acquire that one correct meaning of whatever is being learned, and there would be little or no room for considering alternative perspectives (except perhaps to eliminate or demote them in the process of arriving at the "correct one") or to negotiate variations to that one correct meaning. The learner is *not* an active participant in the construction of knowledge: he or she is only a recipient or consumer of predetermined, more-or-less fixed knowledge. In contrast, an essential characteristic of dialogic learning is that the learner is an active participant in the construction of knowledge, as he or she engages in dialogue. That dialogue can be in the form of interactions with teachers and other students – as well as of course other people – in one-to-one or group situations. It need not be face-to-face, as it can occur via text or other forms of messaging, in virtual space or online. In fact, when we consider the broad meaning of dialogue, as Wegerif (2007) noted, even texts (i.e., written works like essays, reports, and books) can be considered as being *in dialogue* with other texts as they contain references to each other, thereby contributing to that process of knowledge construction.

In dialogic learning, the meaning of something – such as what a person says to us (e.g., a teacher saying, "Well done") – can only be understood in context. That context may include what that person had said previously (e.g., the instruction that the teacher provided for the task), what you have previously talked about with that person (e.g., about how to undertake the task in a particular way), as well as other things you know that may bear on what was said (e.g., that the teacher wants you and other students to do this task quickly, so you can move on to some other task). Thus, you as the recipient of the utterance, contribute to constructing what it might mean (e.g., "the teacher is happy I have finished this task quickly"). For another student – or even the teacher – the meaning may somewhat be different (e.g., "the teacher is trying to hurry us up by praising those who have already finished" – for another student, and "good to see she has been able to follow the method I showed earlier" – for the teacher). By saying something yourself and contributing to the dialogue (e.g., "Thank you. What should I do now?"), you add to the construction of the meaning that is evolving (e.g., that a student should take initiative *in consultation with the teacher*).

A key point is that knowledge never exists in its final form – it is all the time being constructed and developed as a consequence of the dialogues taking place. As Wegerif (2017) pointed out, in dialogic learning we do not conceptualize knowledge as something to be grasped or understood of a world that is external to ourselves, but rather as something that emerges in dialogue as part of the dialogue itself. As he explained, "knowledge has to take the form of an answer to a question, and questions arise in the context of dialogue ... since the dialogue is never closed the questions we ask will change and so what counts as knowledge is never final."

When we consider the requirements of 21st-century education, including all the skills and competencies that ought to be cultivated (see, e.g., Ananiadou & Claro, 2009), the importance of dialogue – and the effective communication it enables – as a means not only to apprehending knowledge, but also to becoming an *active contributor* to the construction of that knowledge, becomes apparent. It would be very difficult to cultivate students' capacities for flexible and adaptive thinking, creativity and innovation, and learning to learn, if all we require them to do is learn and be able to reproduce what the teacher tells them. But with dialogic learning, the mere concept of knowledge not being fixed or final opens up possibilities for flexibility and adaptation (e.g., what I know will change, and I will need to change), as well as of course creativity and innovation (e.g., I can modify or adapt this, or use it to make something else new). Students' essential role in the construction of meaning necessitates communication with others – which in turn requires taking of responsibility for sharing and finding out – and hence, for learning to learn.

Critical thinking

Critical thinking is consistently included in lists of skills and capabilities that 21st-century education is meant to promote. Although numerous ways of defining it exist, the essence of it being *careful and reflective thinking that is deliberate and goal-directed* is contained in most definitions. For example, Ennis (1985, p. 45) defined it as "reflective and reasonable thinking that is focused on deciding what to believe or do," while Fisher and Scriven (1997, p. 21) described it as "skilled and active interpretation and evaluation of observations and communications, information and argumentation." There are broad and narrow conceptions of critical thinking, and the broader ones often incorporate other thinking skills, such as problem solving and decision making, and even creative thinking (e.g., Bailin, 1987). The focus of this book is on critical thinking, but many of the chapters also deal with other thinking skills, highlighting the interconnectivity of these skills. For instance, engagement in appropriately designed problem solving tasks can help learners develop capabilities for both critical and creative thinking, which in turn can enable them to make better decisions, innovate, and generate higher quality solutions to the tasks.

Critical thinking has both a predisposition aspect (i.e., it can be a habit of mind, or tendency to think in a particular way) and an ability aspect (i.e., a competence to think in a particular way when required) (e.g., Halpern, 1998; Paul & Elder, 2006). And it is not one skill but a set of skills and sub-skills. For example, Facione (1990), using the Delphi method with a panel of experts, produced the following consensus list of cognitive skills at the core of critical thinking: interpretation, analysis, evaluation, inference, explanation, and self-regulation.

The particular value of critical thinking in 21st-century education perhaps becomes most apparent when we consider that, in modern societies, there is a largely uncontrolled proliferation of unvetted information through the Internet and other forms of social and mass media (e.g., Glassner, Weinstock, & Neuman, 2005; Thomm & Bromme, 2011). We are constantly required to distinguish between what might be true and what might be misinformation, and to decide what and how to think – and behave – in response to all the information we get exposed to. But it is not only in responding to our environment that critical thinking is of value: it is also indispensable in thinking ahead about what may be needed in the future and how our actions today could impact that future (e.g., OECD, 2018; Schleicher, 2018).

Apart from being valuable in itself, critical thinking is also important in facilitating the development of other 21st-century skills and capabilities, including innovation, decision making, and problem solving – as previously noted; but also of communication, information literacy, and media literacy. For instance, through critical thinking we may be able to construct better argumentation and thus communicate in a more persuasive and convincing manner. Likewise, both information literacy and media literacy require competence in making decisions about choice and use of information – which relies to a large extent on the application of critical thinking skills. Furthermore, as evident in many of the chapters of this book, critical thinking has a co-facilitative role with the other two capabilities of deeper learning and dialogic learning. Thus, for example, the application of critical thinking skills (e.g., interpretation, analysis, evaluation) would facilitate deeper learning, but deeper learning would also bring about the capacity to think – and perhaps behave – more critically.

Structure of the book

The 19 chapters of this book have been organized into six sections according to the kinds of strategies that are described in each chapter for promoting deeper learning, dialogic learning/communication, and/or critical thinking. Those strategies are by no means the only ones that are pertinent in considering the promotion of these capabilities. There are likely to be many others: the ones included here are only those that emerged from the chapter manuscripts that have been included this particular volume.

Part 1: Structuring dialogue

The strategies described in the three chapters included in this section promote the target capabilities primarily by providing a means for *structuring* the language used in classroom interactions and learning. In Chapter 1, Laura Kerslake describes the "Playground of Ideas" approach, which provides a structure or framework, based on play equipment commonly found in children's playgrounds, to support the development of children's critical thinking skills and predispositions through collaborative dialogue. In Chapter 2, Neil Phillipson and Rupert Wegerif explain the value of dialogic teaching approaches in promoting deeper learning, and they demonstrate this through their description of one particular approach – the "Thinking Together" approach – including its use of ground rules, focus on reflection, structuring and grouping of lessons, and techniques for dialogue facilitation to ensure quality of talk in the classroom. Chapter 3, by Bethany Rittle-Johnson, Jon R. Star, Kelley Durkin, and Abbey Loehr, deals with math learning and the use of the "Compare and Discuss" method which provides a structure for developing deeper learning of math strategies and communicative competence in students.

Part 2: Facilitating meaning construction

There are also three chapters in Section 2, all of which describe strategies that promote the target capabilities by guiding learners to find meaning. In Chapter 4, Hillary Swanson explains how getting students to engage in scientific theory building in the classroom (which mimics what scientists do in real life) can help them develop deeper scientific understanding by refining everyday concepts and ideas they possess. Chapter 5 is about a classroom practice developed by Beth V. Yeager, Maria Lucia Castanheira, and Judith Green, in which students and teachers become co-ethnographers[3] in the process of developing a culture of inquiry to support deeper learning, critical thinking, and communicative capabilities in the students. In the final chapter in this section, Chapter 6, W. Douglas Baker describes another ethnographic approach in which two university instructors and their graduate students (who were also teachers of literature) examined selections of their classroom discourse to cultivate deeper learning and understanding about how to interpret and teach literature.

Part 3: Cultivating questioning

The three chapters that comprise Section 3 focus on the cultivation of effective questioning to promote the target capabilities. Chapter 7 by Yoshinori Oyama and Tomoko Yagihashi, introduces "Question Based Instruction," a method in which classroom instruction revolves around student-generated questions, with the aim of promoting deeper understanding and better engagement in students. In Chapter 8, Shadi Asakle and Miri Barak provide details of *AugmentedWorld*, a web-based platform that teachers and students can use to generate location-based, multimedia-rich questions, for the purposes of promoting contextualization, creativity, critical thinking, and ICT (information and communications technology) literacy. Finally, in Chapter 9, Keita Shinogaya explains how deeper learning in the subject of history can be achieved by assigning students preparatory learning tasks for upcoming classroom lessons: at the center of such preparation is the generation and answering of pertinent questions.

Part 4: Promoting engagement and reflection

The three chapters under Section 4 describe the use of various techniques that promote student engagement and reflection, which lead to deeper learning, better communication, and critical thinking. In Chapter 10, Jean J. Ryoo describes how teachers can use humor in the classroom to more effectively get students to engage in critical thinking and communication practices. Pedro Rosário, José Carlos Núñez, Paula Magalhães, Sonia Fuentes, Cleidilene Magalhães, and Kyle Busing describe in Chapter 11 the use of a story tool, "Letters from Gervase," for promoting both self-regulated learning and critical thinking in students. And in Chapter 12, David DeLiema, Maggie Dahn, Virginia J. Flood, Ana Asuncion, Dor Abrahamson, Noel Enyedy, and Francis Steen explain how various activities for facilitating debugging (i.e., the process of finding and fixing problems or errors in computer programming) – student journaling and art making, and teacher modeling and prompting – promote reflection and critical thinking in students.

Part 5: Training specific competencies

There are four chapters in Section 5, all of which describe methods for training specific competencies that in turn lead to the promotion of the target capabilities. In Chapter 13, Emmanuel Manalo, Yuri Uesaka, Ouhao Chen, and Hiroaki Ayabe describe methods they have developed for teaching and encouraging diagram use for the purposes of problem solving, communication, and thinking. Etsuko Tanaka and Emmanuel Manalo then describe in Chapter 14 the research-based design, implementation, and evaluation of a workshop for developing graduate research students' presentation skills. In Chapter 15, Naomi Rosedale, Stuart McNaughton, Rebecca Jesson, Tong Zhu, and Jacinta Oldehaver provide details of an online tool they designed and used to support students' development of argumentation skills considered important for reasoning, critical thinking, and perspective taking. Then, in Chapter 16, Tatsushi Fukaya and Yuri Uesaka describe training programs they have developed to cultivate pre-service and in-service teachers' competencies in promoting their students' understanding and use of effective learning strategies.

Part 6: Program/course teaching

The three chapters included in Section 6 provide details of whole courses or programs that directly address the promotion of deeper learning, dialogic learning/communication, and/or critical thinking. In Chapter 17, Takashi Kusumi describes a school-based program that incorporates critical thinking instruction and project-based inquiry learning into high school science courses to cultivate students' critical thinking dispositions, inquiry learning skills, learning competencies, and self-efficacy. Chapter 18 by Chris Sheppard introduces the use of task-based language teaching for the development of English-as-a-second-language skills beyond grammatical knowledge, and explains how the use of appropriately designed language tasks can promote the accuracy, complexity, and fluency of students' language production. Finally, in Chapter 19, Christine M. Cunningham and Gregory J. Kelly describe important design and implementation aspects of elementary engineering school curricula that foster creativity, problem solving, and communicative competence in students.

Conclusion

Most of the chapters in each of the six sections deal with multiple facets of deeper learning, dialogic learning, and critical thinking. They provide not only descriptions of the strategies for promoting these capabilities, but also brief theoretical accounts of the issues or problems addressed by the strategies, and research evidence that indicates the efficacy and usefulness of those strategies. The intention is for this volume to be genuinely useful for teachers and researchers: for it to provide useful, practical ideas for taking the necessary steps toward implementing some of the changes necessary for the education we are providing to match the requirements of the current century. The focus here is on the classroom (in the broad sense of it) because, to implement the necessary changes, teachers need to be equipped with the "know-how" – in other words, they need to know what new or alternative methods they can use, what techniques they can incorporate into their current teaching practices, and what modifications they can make to improve those practices.

Notes

1 Dialogic learning is a key element (and one could argue, *requirement*) of effective communication, but the term itself is not very well known or understood (see, e.g., Koschmann, 1999). The majority of teachers would be better acquainted with the concept and importance of "effective communication."
2 Such evidence – either or both quantitative and qualitative – is important: especially when investing considerable amounts of time, effort, and resources into enhancing classroom practices, some indication of what outcomes can realistically be expected – based on qualified evidence – would be reassuring.
3 The ethnographic approach, in very simple terms, is one in which the researcher becomes a participant in the research he or she is conducting, being immersed in the culture and practices that he or she is investigating.

References

Ananiadou, K., & Claro, M. (2009). *21st Century skills and competences for new millennium learners in OECD countries. OECD Education Working Papers, No. 41.* Paris: OECD.

Bailin, S. (1987). Critical and creative thinking. *Informal Logic, 9,* 23–29.

Dunlosky, J. (2013, Fall). Strengthening the student toolbox: Study strategies to boost learning. *American Educator,* 12–21.

Ennis, R. H. (1985, October). A logical basis for measuring critical thinking skills. *Educational Leadership,* 44–48.

Facione, P. A. (1990). *Critical thinking: A statement of expert consensus for purposes of educational assessment and instruction: The Delphi report.* Millbrae, CA: California Academic Press.

Fisher, A., & Scriven, M. (1997). *Critical thinking: Its definition and assessment.* Norwich, UK: Centre for Research in Critical Thinking.

Glassner, A., Weinstock, M., & Neuman, Y. (2005). Pupils' evaluation and generation of evidence and explanation in argumentation. *British Journal of Educational Psychology, 75,* 105–118.

Griffin, P., McGaw, B., & Care, E. (2012). The changing role of education and schools. In P. Griffin, B. McGaw, & E. Care (Eds.), *Assessment and teaching of 21st Century skills* (pp. 1–16). Dordrecht, Germany: Springer.

Halpern, D. F. (1998). Teaching critical thinking for transfer across domains: Disposition, skills, structure training, and metacognitive monitoring. *American Psychologist, 53,* 449–455.

Holmes, T. H., & Rahe, R. H. (1967). The Social Readjustment Rating Scale. *Journal of Psychosomatic Research, 11,* 213–218.

Koschmann, T. D. (1999). Toward a dialogic theory of learning: Bakhtin's contribution to understanding learning in settings of collaboration. In C. M. Hoadley, & J. Roschelle (Eds.), *Proceedings of the Computer Support for Collaborative Learning (CSCL) 1999 Conference* (pp. 308–313). Mahwah, NJ: Lawrence Erlbaum.

Marton, F., & Säljö, R. (1976). On qualitative differences in learning: I - Outcome and process. *British Journal of Education Psychology, 46,* 4–11.

McTighe, J., & Wiggins, G. (2013). *Essential questions: Opening doors to student understanding.* Alexandria, VA: Association for Supervision and Curriculum Development.

National Research Council (2012). *Education for life and work: Developing transferable knowledge and skills in the 21st Century.* Washington, DC: National Academies Press.

OECD (2018). *The future of education and skills: Education 2030.* Paris: OECD.

Oyama, Y. (2017). Promoting learners' spontaneous use of effective questioning: Integrating research findings inside and outside of Japan. In E. Manalo, Y. Uesaka, & C. A. Chinn (Eds.), *Promoting spontaneous use of learning and reasoning strategies: Theory, research, and practice for effective transfer* (pp. 31–45). London: Routledge.

Paul, R. W., & Elder, L. (2006). *The miniature guide to critical thinking: Concepts and tools* (4th ed.). Dillon Beach, CA: Foundation for Critical Thinking.

Rabkin, J. G., & Struening, E. L. (1976). Life events, stress, and illness. *Science, 194,* 1013–1020.

Rotherham, A. J., & Willingham, D. T. (2010, Spring). "21st Century" skills: Not new, but a worthy challenge. *American Educator,* 17–20.

Schleicher, A. (2018). *World class: How to build a 21st-century school system.* Paris: OECD.

Thomm, E., & Bromme, R. (2011). It should at least seem scientific! Textual features of scientificness and their impact on lay assessments of online information. *Science Education, 96,* 187–211.

Wegerif, R. (2007). *Dialogic education and technology: Expanding the space of learning.* New York: Springer-Verlag.

Wegerif, R. (2017, August 8). Defining 'dialogic education' [Web log post]. Retrieved from http://www.rupertwegerif.name/blog/defining-dialogic-education

PART 1
Structuring dialogue

1

THE PLAYGROUND OF IDEAS

Developing a structured approach to the Community of Inquiry for young children

Laura Kerslake

Summary

The Community of Inquiry is a pedagogy which allows children to participate in collaborative discussion, and has been a key practice of Philosophy with Children since its inception. This chapter presents research findings which support the claim of the educational benefits of this approach, and also considers barriers to participation by all children, especially those who have not developed early communicative competency. I therefore present the Playground of Ideas, which provides a structured discussion framework approach in order to support children's critical thinking skills and dispositions through collaborative dialogue. Two case studies with children aged 6 and 7 and their teachers indicate that the Playground of Ideas contributes to the development of a classroom culture of dialogue and collaborative thinking.

Background

In 2014, I started a Primary Post Graduate Certificate of Education (PGCE) course with a school-based provider in England. The instruction included a number of weeks' observations of different teachers in a school, followed by the start of our own practice. This was interspersed with days of center-based training, which was primarily carried out by an educational consultancy company.

It soon became apparent that there was a considerable disparity between the information given to us on training days about what would and should happen in the classroom, and the reality of what occurred in classroom practice.

A particular example of this was on the maths instruction days. The sequence of events, according to our trainers, was similar to the following:

1. Put children into small groups (pairs or groups of three);
2. Provide visual and tactile materials to represent number concepts (number lines, Cuisenaire rods, Numicon, etc.);
3. The children will talk together and in doing so come to a greater understanding of mathematical concepts. Higher-ability children will increase their understanding by explaining the concepts that they have already grasped to lower-ability children; lower-ability children will increase their understanding by collaborating with higher-ability children.

The discrepancy arose in that children did not talk in the way that had been indicated. In the practical context, children's talk was not always productive: some children argued, others understood problems quickly but did not communicate their understanding to others, some children were not confident to speak – or, in other words, children exhibited all of the usual behavior one might expect from a group of children in a classroom.

Reflecting on this, there seemed to be a gap between steps 2 and 3 in the list above. Providing small groupwork activities for children seemed to be giving them the *opportunity* to talk, but it did not follow that children had the *skills* to do so in a way which was productive for the lesson.

This was not wholly unexpected. The work on mathematical collaboration in primary schools was carried out by Askew (2012), popularizing the work of Boaler (1999) for a UK practitioner readership. Further reading of Askew determined that he does not tend to undertake one-off sessions in schools because children need training in order to be able to carry out productive discussions. Indeed, Askew writes that teachers tend to adopt a "See, I told you these kids couldn't do that" attitude.

What was missing from the sequence above, and from my PGCE training, was a way of teaching the children how to engage in productive talk in the classroom. This lack of guidance is also reflected in the new National Curriculum document for Speaking and Listening (Department for Education, 2013), which contains a single page of speaking and listening guidelines to cover all of primary school instruction. There are no specific guidelines as to how teachers should teach speaking and listening skills.

This is a concern also highlighted by Ofsted, the body which is responsible for school inspections in the UK. A review of school inspection documents for Devon schools in the last three years highlights a number of comments that reveal concerns about the spoken communication abilities of children at school-entry age. A school which was identified as "requires improvement" received the following comment: "a significant number have low speaking and listening skills" with "not enough focus on learning and acquiring the basic [talking] skills" (Ofsted, 2014, p. 4). This is compared to an outstanding school in which children are "routinely challenged with probing questions which make pupils think deeply" (Ofsted, 2015, p. 6). This comment also makes explicit the connection between talking and thinking.

One reason for the disparity in children's speaking and listening skills could be the socioeconomic status of the child. In the UK, the National Literacy Trust (NLT, 2016) State of Nation Report 2015/16 reports that children who receive free school meals (used as a measure of disadvantage as receipt is primarily dependent on low income or being in care) are less likely to have achieved required standards for communication in Early Years Foundation Stage (EYFS). The EYFS presents the educational expectations for children up to the age of 5 in the areas of Listening and Attention, Understanding, and Speaking, and 77%, 76% and 75%, respectively, of such children attained the expected level in these areas in 2015. The data for children who do not receive free school meals shows attainment of 87%, 86%, and 86%, respectively, in the assessed areas (NLT, 2016, p. 4).

That is already a sizable gap at the age of 5, and this does not diminish in the early years of schooling, as Key Stage 1 data from the NLT report show that teacher assessment in Speaking and Listening criteria sees 82% and 92% of children receiving free school meals and *not* receiving such free meals, respectively, attaining the expected level (NLT, 2016, p. 10). This pattern is repeated across other areas of the literacy curriculum.

It is therefore possible to trace a path between EYFS communication deficit and lower attainment in assessments and national testing right up to the end of formal schooling. This culminates in figures for UK national exams taken at age 16, which show that in the 2014/15 academic year, 33.1% of children receiving free school meals achieved five passing grades (including English and maths), compared to 60.9% of other children (NLT, 2016, p. 20). This is a considerable gap, and while it would of course be a presumption to attribute this entirely to children's ability to participate successfully in productive classroom talk situations, a number of educationalists and researchers connect productive talk with children's ability to access curriculum content (Alexander, 2004; Askew, 2012; Boaler, 1999; Mercer, 2008).

Critical thinking and classroom discussion

The previous section introduced the importance of classroom talk to educational practice, drawing connections between classroom talk and critical thinking skills. This section clarifies the meaning of those terms and further establishes the connections between them.

Attempts at defining critical thinking tend to be lengthy, highlighting Schwarz and Baker's (2018, p. 96) recent complaint that it is a term which is "not well delineated." As early as 1963, Ennis identified ten criteria which comprise critical thinking: deduction, assumption-finding, definition, explanation, reliability of evidence and authorities, generalization, hypothesis testing, evaluating theories, detecting ambiguities, and detecting over-vague and over-specific claims (p. 18). A key claim of Ennis' is that a thinker who becomes competent in only one or two of these criteria should not be considered a competent critical thinker, highlighting the interplay between the range of skills noted above.

In 1990, 46 panelists with philosophy, psychology, education, and social science backgrounds produced the Delphi Report (Facione, 1990). The statement is of considerable length, but some key points, which expand on Ennis' are

- Critical thinking is "essential as a tool of inquiry";
- The ideal critical thinker is "habitually inquisitive," "willing to reconsider," "open-minded," and "flexible";
- Educating critical thinkers involves "nurturing those dispositions which consistently yield useful insights."

(p. 18)

This definition of critical thinking indicates that being a good critical thinker involves dispositional elements and that critical thinking is a collaborative endeavor for the sharing and refining of knowledge.

This conception of critical thinking is highly commensurate with the pragmatist origins of the Community of Inquiry, which was initially conceived of by Peirce (see Kerslake, 2018b). A central tenet of pragmatism is a denial of the Cartesian duality of knowing for certain or relinquishing all claims to knowledge. Instead, doubt is perceived as "simply a necessary fact of being in the world" (Ellerton, 2016, p. 112). In an inquiry, beliefs are held cautiously, to be doubted, questioned, and reformulated as further beliefs to be held tentatively. Dewey (1933) summed this up as: "there is no belief so settled as to not be exposed to further enquiry" (pp. 8–9).

As inquiry takes place in the form of discussion within a community, the connection between the development of critical thinking skills and classroom discussion is clear. It can also be seen clearly from the description of the spoken language requirement for pupils across all ages of UK formal schooling (age 5–16):

> Pupils should be taught to speak clearly and convey ideas confidently using Standard English. They should learn *to justify ideas with reasons; ask questions* to check understanding; develop vocabulary and build knowledge; negotiate; *evaluate and build on the ideas of others*; and select the appropriate register for effective communication. They should be taught to give *well-structured descriptions and explanations* and develop their understanding through *speculating, hypothesising and exploring ideas*. This will enable them to *clarify their thinking* as well as organise their ideas for writing.
> (Department for Education, 2013, section 3.1)

The italics are my own, and highlight the ways in which spoken language teaching is a mechanism for the development of critical thinking skills which have been posited by Ennis and the Delphi Report.

The Playground of Ideas

The previous section expounds on the connection between classroom discussion and critical thinking skills. However, I have also highlighted the difficulties which are posed by the reality of the classroom environment in holding productive discussions. This could be due to the different levels of communicative competence that children develop before attending school. Michaels, O'Connor, and Resnick (2008) also identify a barrier to effective classroom talk, giving the example of a boy who is, in technical terms, highly competent at discursive practice: "questioning premises, making claims, bringing counter-examples" (p. 294). However, what is also clear from the boy's speech is that the contributions made by the group don't matter. The authors go on to state that this is "pervasive" (p. 294) in the examples at which they have looked. Therefore there is a key dispositional element which is also necessary to develop, in which group members come to understand that shared inquiry is a collaborative experience in which discussion relies on the contributions of the entire group.

While holding a Community of Inquiry gives children opportunities to talk, without further guidance on the specific skills and dispositions that are required for critical discussion not all children may be able to do so effectively. In response to these difficulties, I developed the Playground of Ideas (Kerslake, 2018a). It takes the position that these discussion skills need to be explicitly presented to young children in order for the skills to be employed productively in the classroom from Key Stage 1 (ages 6 and 7). This section sets out the development of the Playground of Ideas as a pedagogical approach.

It aims to overcome these difficulties by acknowledging that the kind of skills which were detailed in the previous section are abstract (e.g., evaluation or reasoning) and that consideration needs to be given to the ways in which these are presented to young children. It also aims to develop critical thinking skills through discussion in a way which emphasizes the collaborative element of holding an inquiry.

From the National Curriculum document presented above I extrapolated five key areas:

1. Speculating, hypothesizing, and exploring ideas;
2. Conveying ideas confidently;
3. Building on the ideas of others;
4. Justifying ideas with reasons;
5. Evaluating.

I wanted to find a means of enabling children to develop these skills using terminology that would be familiar to them as part of their experience as children. In addition, I wanted this terminology to be familiar to all children of a similar age at school and this seemed important because of potential differences in the home environment, as described previously. Some children, with the experience of extended discussion in the home environment, would be able to hypothesize,

22 Kerslake

TABLE 1.1 Playground equipment and skills/dispositional development

Play equipment image	Corresponding skill development
Swing	Speculating, hypothesizing, and exploring ideas
Slide	Conveying ideas confidently
Climbing frame	Building on the ideas of others
	Justifying ideas with reasons
Seesaw	Evaluating
Lookout tower	Noticing what others are saying

justify, and so on, even if they did not know the terminology for what they were doing. Other children would not have had much experience in doing this, and hence the rationale for an explicit model.

It is obvious that the task to find a common terminology is a difficult one. Differences – not only in home discourse patterns but also culture, reading ability, gender, mother tongue, and other unknown and unconsidered factors – preclude many options. However, I hypothesized that images of equipment found in children's play parks – and indeed school playgrounds – could provide a means by which to anchor the abstract terms of evaluation, justification, and so on.

In addition to this, there is a neat overlap in the form and function of play equipment with those areas of development which I identified above. This led to an initial development of the Playground of Ideas, as follows:

Swing: Giving opinions. Children decide what they think about a question and are either on one side of the swing or the other. If they haven't made up their mind they are in the middle on the swing. They can physically move from one side of the classroom to the other in order to show their thinking. This means that at the beginning of the sessions, children can show their thinking rather than having to verbalize it.

Slide: Being brave with your ideas. The slide reminds children that speaking up in front of the whole class can feel intimidating, such as the feeling they might get when sitting at the top of a tall slide – but if one is brave and goes down the slide, it can feel exciting. It helps young children to identify the anxious feelings that situation might produce.

Climbing frame: Building on each other's ideas. The climbing frame is to help children to listen to each other and add more information to ideas. It uses sentence starters to help children to do this: "Following on from what Jack says, I think…"; "I agree with Emily because…"; "I disagree with Patricia because …." The climbing frame develops skills by giving children the vocabulary to continue a discussion, and it also encourages listening to one other because children must be aware of others' contributions in order to be able to use one of the sentence starters given above.

Seesaw: Giving reasons and deciding which are the best reasons. The seesaw focuses children on giving reasons for their ideas. It encourages the group to think about how valuable they think reasons are – a good reason makes the seesaw tip a lot, as it is a "heavy" reason. It also helps children to evaluate reasons. For example, there might be five reasons on one side of the seesaw, but only one on the other, but that one reason still might make the seesaw tip farther because it is so important.

Lookout tower: Listening to and noticing what others are saying. The lookout tower asks children to climb to the top and look out over the rest of the playground. Can they see anyone on the slide who is being brave? Is there anyone giving reasons on the slide? This piece of equipment is used at the ends of sessions as a plenary. First of all, the teacher models it by explaining what the lookout tower is for and saying "I noticed Lucas was on the climbing frame because he disagreed with what Marc was saying." Other children then follow this example.

The Playground of Ideas in classrooms

The image of each item of play equipment is introduced a week at a time throughout 10 weeks of sessions. I then wrote a series of session plans to accompany the images, with each week presenting a new philosophical question for children to discuss. A number of Philosophy with Children commentators comment on the suitability of philosophical questions for inquiry learning and critical thinking development (Cassidy & Christie, 2013; Daniel & Auriac, 2011) because of the conceptually laden nature of philosophical questions. I followed Worley's (2015) concept of the philosophical "grammatically closed, conceptually open" question format for the session subjects.

This structure, first of all, encourages children to answer "yes" or "no." The initial questions are in a simple "Would you rather…?" format, for example, "Would you rather be rich or clever?" The Swing allows children to move to opposite sides of the classroom depending on their answer. Each member of the class can see each other's thinking, and that some children have thoughts different to their own. This forms the basis for the discussion: children must then give reasons for why they have chosen their answer, other children may counter with their own reasons, and then children may move to a different side if they have changed their mind.

A further example of a question is "Is it better to make one person very happy or ten people a little bit happy?" This occurs in one of the first sessions, but the same concept is revisited in later sessions with the Trolley Problem (Foot, 1967). This is a well-known ethical dilemma in philosophy, in which a train with brakes that have failed is heading toward five people on the tracks, and there is no escape. The only option that one has is to pull a lever and change the direction of the train onto a different track on which there is only one person. The dilemma is: should one pull the lever?

The problem has the same issue as the first as one must consider the number of people involved when making ethical decisions. The second problem is more complex, however, but it is introduced once children have had practice with all of the pieces of play equipment. By introducing the initial division of "yes" or "no" answers, children must justify their reasoning to each other and understand the underlying concepts behind the question from their own and others' point of view.

Case studies

The following section reports on two case studies of the Playground of Ideas being used as an intervention in classrooms. The research project was carried out as an iterative, design-based process, which was chosen because Design Based Research (DBR) aims to discover not just whether a learning process has worked or not, but to discover how and why this is the case (Brown, 1992). In addition, McCandliss Kalchman and Bryant (2003) highlight that DBR is a collaborative dialogue of methods which is particularly important for a classroom-based intervention in which there are many stakeholders. This research project took the stance that the contributions of all of the participants are key to understanding how the intervention works.

Case study 1: Does the design of the Playground of Ideas work conceptually for the children? The first iteration was carried out in order to ascertain:

- If the language and imagery of the playground equipment was understood by children;
- If the philosophical questions chosen were suitable for children in Key Stage 1;
- How the classroom teacher perceived the Playground of Ideas sessions.

In addition, I wanted to clarify practical classroom matters relating to the intervention, such as the length of the sessions and the suitability of the activities chosen.

The first iteration was carried out in a Year 2 classroom in a primary school in England. I taught the sessions myself as a researcher-practitioner, with the classroom teacher observing in order to make suggestions about the material. I interviewed the teacher midway through the intervention and produced a questionnaire for the children, as well as carrying out a group interview with selected children at the end of the intervention. I also kept a researcher's reflective journal throughout in order to be able to compare my experiences of teaching the sessions with the responses from the teacher and the children. This is concordant with a DBR methodology which allows for researchers to be "research impressionists" (Kelly, 2004, p. 115), like their artistic counterparts the Impressionist painters being able to portray naturalistic, realistic images. This implies a qualitative perspective in which the research reflects the experiences of the various participant groups such as children and their teachers, as well as reflecting the researcher perspective.

Case study 1: Evidence for effectiveness

Children are able to develop abstract thinking skills through the Playground of Ideas

In the interview with the class teacher (CT), the CT made a number of comments which indicated that the playground images were understood by the children. She identified that they provided a scaffold for the children, as they "kept looking at them and trying to use them."

There was also an indication that children were using the skills that they developed in the sessions to think about issues in other curriculum subjects. In the last session, the children came in from lunch and a number of them spoke about their science lesson. They had been growing vegetables in the school garden and they were asking about what had come first – the vegetable, or the seed from which it had grown. They were actively engaged in this inquiry, and they identified it as a philosophical question. From their comments, the basis on which they did so was that they identified it as a question to which they thought there might not be one answer, and that they had different ideas with good reasons for both sides. This indicates that they were beginning to identify the philosophical basis of other curriculum subjects.

Children become more confident in sharing their ideas

Excerpt from the group interview with six children and the researcher (LK)

JANE: Yes, I like it because everybody has, they can actually, like I like the slide because sometimes I do get very nervous of talking so it kind of encourages me, um, cause I have stage fright sometimes.
LK: OK.
JANE: And it encourages me to talk.
JONATHON: Are you on the bottom slide then?
LUCY: I think she's on the top because if you're on the bottom slide then you can just go down it like – boring.
LK: (to Jane) What do you think?
LUCY: Cause the top bit's the scariest bit.
JANE: I think probably the top.

The exchange above is taken from the group interview. It indicates not only that a child (Jane) who was not confident about sharing her ideas is reassured by the slide, but also how children's understanding can be enhanced through their interaction with one another. When Jane says that she is "nervous of talking," Jonathon demonstrates misunderstanding by asking if Jane was on the "bottom slide." A number of children had this conception that the top slide was for if you were happy to talk and the smaller slides were for if you weren't feeling brave. If this were an individual interview, then as the researcher-practitioner I would have corrected Jonathon, but in this case it is Lucy who steps in and corrects Jonathon. My contribution is quite limited in this exchange, and most of the talk is between the learners.

The teacher has a better sense of her class's ability to take part in philosophical discussion

A number of the teacher's comments in interview revealed that she hadn't considered the children as able to discuss these questions; however she also made a number of comments which indicated that the sessions were a transformative experience for her in the way that she viewed her class. For example, despite her view that the "questions seem quite grown up and challenging," she also expressed the view that she was "really surprised" and the children responded "really positively and quite maturely." She also referred to the skills that the children were developing as "exactly where they need to be." Therefore her professional experience is that the sessions are developing skills which are in line with their age group but are also challenging.

In addition to this, the class teacher (CT) indicated in her interview that she was also beginning to think about the ways in which philosophical questions can apply to other curriculum subjects:

> CT: I was thinking about maybe how you could use the ones from fairy tales, you know, from books that they're reading, characters. We do Jack and the Beanstalk, I was thinking afterwards well actually there were some philosophy questions that could have come out of that. Should Jack have stolen the hen – was it OK that Jack stole the golden hen?
>
> (excerpt from interview with the class teacher)

Case study 2: Does the Playground of Ideas (PoI) work as an intervention across contexts? This iteration was carried out in order to understand if:

- The resource pack which was produced following the first iteration was able to be used by other teachers;
- Children had a comparable conceptual understanding of the PoI when it was taught by a nonspecialist teacher;
- The PoI had an impact on teaching practice.

In contrast to the previous case study, in which I took the role of researcher-practitioner, in this iteration I was specifically interested in whether or not I had produced a resource pack which could be used as a resource which stood alone from researcher input. Participants self-selected following an advertisement on social media, and resource packs were sent out to these teachers. This case study reports on the use of the resource pack in one primary school in England which was selected because it is a large urban school with a broad demographic of children. The class teacher had 26 years of teaching experience, but had not taught any philosophy with children previously.

I asked the children and the teacher to carry out a questionnaire post-intervention. The children's questionnaire was the same as for the children in the previous case study because I wanted to be able to compare the children's perceptions of the PoI across contexts.

Case study 2: Evidence for effectiveness

Children understand the concepts in the PoI when taught from the resource pack

The questions in the children's questionnaire were asked in order to clarify their conceptual understanding of specific pieces of playground equipment. Table 1.2 below presents a selection of comments from the questionnaires from both case studies, indicating comparable responses from children who participated in sessions taught by me and by the class teacher. The responses

TABLE 1.2 Levels of children's understanding of the slide and climbing frame

Level of understanding (with criteria for level)	Iteration 1 (Researcher-led) % of responses	Iteration 2 (Teacher-led) % of responses
Slide		
1. No mention of being brave or talking	4.2	12.5
2. Mention of being brave or talking but appearing to misunderstand	12.5	8.3
3. Mentions being brave OR talking	16.7	16.7
4. Mentions being brave in connection with talking	50	45.8
5. Mentions the criteria for previous levels and adds more details	16.7	21
Climbing Frame		
1. No mention of building on or adding ideas	8.3	4.1
2. Mentions adding to or building but misunderstanding	0	4.1
3. Mentions adding on or climbing up	20.9	12.5
4. Mentions adding on or climbing up in connection with sharing ideas	50	54.1
5. Mentions the criteria for previous levels with specific reference to the sentence starters	20.9	25

were coded into levels of understanding of the connection between the play equipment item and the specific skill it represents. The table above indicates the criteria for each level and the number of responses per level in the researcher- and teacher-led iterations.

In both cases, the majority of children were at level 3 or above, indicating that children are able to connect an item of play equipment with the thinking skill it represents. I interviewed the children whose responses were coded at level 1 or 2. A large number of these children were able to verbally indicate a greater understanding than they had written, indicating that the barrier was the questionnaire.

The table below gives some examples of answers to the question "Why do we go on the climbing frame?" The number in brackets is the level at which it was placed according to the criteria above.

The responses to the second question in Table 1.3 exemplified the children's responses in both sets of questionnaires. Three categories of response emerged from the questionnaires: some referenced individual pieces of play equipment that they particularly liked, while others focused on the discussion questions themselves. A third category of response was a reference to "Would you rather…?" questions, which were a warm up game played before each session. The coding of responses indicated that the children's responses in both case studies were evenly split between these three aspects of the PoI sessions.

The PoI resources have a positive impact on teachers' practice

> Yes. We teach maths mastery and part of this is children being able to confidently explain their reasons. Playground of Ideas helped with this as the children were encouraged to share their ideas and listen to each

TABLE 1.3 Selected responses from the children's questionnaire

Question	Case study 1	Case study 2
Why do we go on the climbing frame?	"Adding an idea to another idea. So we're trying to get to the top" (Emma) (4) "We can add to people's ideas (Lizzie)" (3) "To follow on from what other people say and climb up the climbing frame" (Peter) (5)	"To climb to the top and be above" (Max) (2) "To climb on top of people's ideas" (Chloe) (4) "To go on top of each other's opinions to the top" (Elsie) (4)
What did you like talking about?	"The Swing when you get to choose what side you're on" (Caleb) "I liked talking about the hamster meat and going on the swing" (Sky)	"The slide because it was being brave and I like being brave" (Chloe) "I liked talking about the people on the train track" (Oliver)

other. It helped develop their confidence as well as their listening and speaking skills. I refer to the equipment in other lessons I teach and the children speak clearly and confidently when joining in discussions. It was great to see two very shy children gain confidence and join in with the last few Playground of Ideas lessons.

(excerpt from questionnaire from the class teacher)

The above extract is taken from the teacher's questionnaire as a response to the question "Do you think it changed your teaching? In what way?" The teacher makes a clear link between the skills being developed in the PoI sessions to other curriculum subjects, specifically maths. Boaler's (1999) work has shown that a collaborative approach to maths results in higher attainment in exams taken at age 16 because children have developed the skills to "think for themselves, select relevant information from irrelevant and work together proactively" (Kerslake & Rimmington, 2017, p. 28). This is corroborated by Askew's (2012) work, which takes the approach that "talk is central to mathematics lessons" (p. 136).

This is concordant with the findings from one of the best-known recent studies into philosophy with children, a randomized control trial conducted by the Educational Endowment Fund (EEF) (2015), which looked at children's curriculum attainment following a philosophy with children intervention in which children took part in Community of Inquiry philosophy sessions in schools. Children who received the intervention in Years 4 and 5 (age 8 and 9) then went on to make additional gains of between 2 and 4 months in English and maths when taking their Standardized Attainment Tests (SATs) at the end of Year 6 (age 10 and 11).

This has been heralded by the Society for the Advancement of Philosophical Enquiry and Reflection in Education (SAPERE), who conduct a great deal of philosophy with children in-school teacher training, as a good indication that philosophy can allow children to improve in curriculum subjects with no additional input in those subjects. The EEF study found that these gains in testing were particularly the case for disadvantaged children, indicating that explicitly taught collaborative thinking and discussion skills are important to addressing inequality issues within education because the acquisition of these skills underpins so much else (Alexander, 2004; Mercer & Littleton, 2007; Michaels et al., 2008).

Concluding remarks

The responses from teachers and children indicate not only a development of skill but also a change in disposition. The teachers' comments indicate an increase in the children's confidence, and also in the way they listened to each other. The change in disposition is not limited to learner-learner interaction, but also applies to the ways in which the teachers perceive the discursive abilities of the children in their classes. A Community of Inquiry approach therefore has the potential to change teachers' practice, which has also been noted by other teachers and researchers who have undertaken such sessions in their classrooms (Roche, 2011), with Scholl (2014) recognizing that "crucial" to a Community of Inquiry approach is that teachers "genuinely view themselves as learners" (p. 90). Both teachers in these case studies also considered how to adapt other curriculum subjects to incorporate Playground of Ideas material, indicating that they were also reacting as learners and that this approach therefore has an impact on classroom culture.

These case studies indicate that a framework for collaborative inquiry based on play equipment is effective in that children are able to take part in more sophisticated discussions in terms of their talking and thinking skills. They have become more aware of their own and each other's contributions to discussion, which is commensurate with both Ennis's and Facione's definitions of critical thinkers who demonstrate a range of skills. A key element of this is that they utilize these skills to develop an inquiry as a community, where both teachers and learners exhibit the dispositions that are prerequisite for critical thinking to flourish.

The design-based approach has allowed "continuous evolution of design as it is tested in authentic practice" (Anderson & Shattuck, 2012, p. 19), meaning that the perspectives of teachers and learners have featured prominently in the design and redesign of the Playground of Ideas. Design research also, however, requires a quantitative as well as qualitative element, so the next iteration of the Playground of Ideas will be to collect measurement data on how children's collaborative skills improve as a result of taking part in Playground of Ideas sessions. This data will particularly feature the discursive abilities of disadvantaged children in order to ascertain if the skill development and change in disposition (e.g., confidence to share ideas) has an impact on this group's collaborative contributions to group tasks.

The Playground of Ideas: Thinking and talking together in Key Stage 1 has since been published as a complete teaching resource by Cambridge Thinking Press.

References

Alexander, R. (2004). *Towards dialogic teaching: Rethinking classroom talk* (4th ed.). Cambridge, England: Dialogos.

Anderson, T., & Shattuck, J. (2012). Design-based research: A decade of progress in education research? *Educational Researcher, 41*, 16–25.

Askew, M. (2012). *Transforming primary mathematics*. London, England: Routledge.

Boaler, J. (1999). Participation, knowledge and beliefs: A community perspective on mathematics learning. *Educational Studies in Mathematics, 40*(3), 259–281.

Brown, A. (1992). Design experiments: Theoretical and methodological challenges in creating complex interventions in classroom settings. *The Journal of the Learning Sciences, 2*(2), 141–178.

Cassidy, C., & Christie, D. (2013). Philosophy with children: Talking, thinking and learning together. *Early Child Development and Care, 183*(8), 1072–1083.

Daniel, M. -F., & Auriac, E. (2011). Philosophy, critical thinking and philosophy for children. *Educational Philosophy and Theory, 43*(5), 415–435.

Department for Education (2013). *English programmes of study: Key stages 1 and 2 National Curriculum in England*. Retrieved from https://www.gov.uk/government/uploads/system/uploads/attachment_data/file/335186/PRIMARY_national_curriulum_-_English_220714.pdf

Dewey, J. (1933). *How we think: A restatement of the relation of reflective thinking to the educative process*. Boston, MA: Heath.

Education Endowment Foundation (2015). *Philosophy for children: Evaluation report and executive summary*. Retrieved from https://educationendowmentfoundation.org.uk/uploads/pdf/Philosophy_for_Children.pdf

Ellerton, P. (2016). Pragmatist epistemology, inquiry values and education for thinking. In M. Gregory, J. Haynes & K. Murris (Eds.), *The Routledge international handbook of philosophy for children* (pp. 111–118) London, England: Routledge.

Ennis, R. H. (1963). Needed: Research in critical thinking. *Educational Leadership, 21*(1), 17–39.

Facione, P. (1990). *The Delphi report*. Millbrae, CA: California Academic Press.

Foot, P. (1967). The problem of abortion and the doctrine of double effect. *Oxford Review, 5*, 5–15.

Kelly, A. (2004). Design research in education: Yes, but is it methodological? *The Journal of the Learning Sciences, 13*(1), 115–128.

Kerslake, L. (2018a). *Playground of ideas. Thinking and talking together in key stage 1*. Exeter, England: Cambridge Thinking Press.

Kerslake, L. (2018b). From pragmatism to posthumanism: Thinking through the community of philosophical inquiry. In L. Kerslake & R. Wegerif (Eds.), *The theory of teaching thinking* (pp. 57–72). London, England: Routledge.

Kerslake, L., & Rimmington, S. (2017). Sharing talk, sharing cognition: Philosophy with children as the basis for productive classroom interaction. *Issues in Early Education, 1*(36), 21–32.

McCandliss, B. Kalchman, M., & Bryant, P. (2003). Design experiments and laboratory approaches to learning: Steps toward collaborative exchange. *Educational Researcher, 32*(1), 14–16.

Mercer, N. (2008). Talk and the development of reasoning and understanding. *Human Development, 5*, 90–100.

Mercer, N., & Littleton, K. (2007). *Dialogue and the development of children's thinking. A sociocultural approach*. London, England: Routledge.

Michaels, S., O'Connor, C., & Resnick, L. (2008). Deliberative discourse idealized and realized: Accountable talk in the classroom and in civic life. *Studies in the Philosophy of Education, 27*, 283–297.

National Literacy Trust (2016). *State of the nation and impact report 2015/16.* Retrieved from http://www.literacytrust.org.uk/assets/0003/6318/Impact_report_2015-16_spreads_FINAL.pdf

Ofsted (2014). *School inspection report kings ash academy.* Retrieved from https://reports.ofsted.gov.uk/inspection-reports/find-inspection-report/provider/ELS/138773

Ofsted (2015). *School inspection report marine academy primary.* Retrieved from https://reports.ofsted.gov.uk/inspection-reports/find-inspection-report/provider/ELS/139604

Roche, M. (2011). Creating a dialogical and critical classroom: Reflection and action to improve practice. *Educational Action Research, 19*(3), 327–343.

Scholl, R. (2014). Inside-out pedagogy: Theorising pedagogical transformation through teaching philosophy. *Australian Journal of Teacher Education, 39*(6), 89–106.

Schwarz, B., & Baker, M. (2018). *Dialogue, argumentation and education: History, theory and practice.* Cambridge, England: Cambridge University Press.

Worley, P. (2015). Open thinking, closed questioning: Two kinds of open and closed question. *Journal of Philosophy in Schools, 2*(2), 17–29.

2

THE *THINKING TOGETHER* APPROACH TO DIALOGIC TEACHING

Neil Phillipson and Rupert Wegerif

Summary

Dialogic teaching approaches involve teaching through dialogue and teaching for quality dialogue. Engaging in dialogue can promote deeper conceptual understanding as participants explore ideas from different perspectives in a caring, collaborative, critical, and creative manner. Reflective practice supported by "ground rules" that help to define and develop good quality dialogue enhances efficacy and promotes personal development. The *Thinking Together* approach, developed by Dawes, Mercer, and Wegerif in the 1990s, has been shown to be effective through evaluations in the UK, Mexico, South Africa, and China. We outline the main principles for teaching *Thinking Together* and summarize the research evidence.

Introduction

What is dialogue?

Thinking Together is one of a number of dialogic teaching strategies that have been shown to have a positive impact on learning and attainment in schools. One thing these approaches have in common is, perhaps unsurprisingly, that they encourage teaching *through* dialogue. They also involve teaching students how to get better at dialogue – teaching *for* dialogue. It seems to follow that any success with the application of dialogic approaches in the classroom will probably need to be founded on an understanding of the nature of dialogue.

The word *dialogue* does not, as some people seem to think, refer only to an interaction between two people. The Greek roots of the term are *dia*, which can be translated as "through" or "across," and *logos*, which is a resonant term often translated as "discourse," "speech" or "reason." We might then ask, what is it that people are speaking or reasoning across or through? One answer to this question is that they are reasoning across the difference between perspectives, often the difference between their personal and most immediate perspective and another perspective experienced as being other to them or outside them (whether it be the perspective of one or more other people with whom they are speaking, or the perspective of the author of a text they are reading, or a perspective that has been at the back of their mind since they heard it or read it some time ago).

The important point here is that to engage in dialogue is to acknowledge and respond to other perspectives; to seek to understand them, to be sensitive to the differences between them and one's own understandings; and to use these differences as a resource to generate new perspectives and to achieve richer understandings of ideas and of other people. To enter into dialogue is not to endeavor to impose one's own view or to uncritically accept the view of a more authoritative other, but rather to engage in a shared search for understanding and meaning; it is to enter into a relationship based on mutual respect. Indeed, engaging in a dialogue could be defined as an act of 'thinking together,' the name of the approach to dialogic teaching explored in this chapter.

A great deal of theory surrounds the nature of dialogue, and some understanding of the central ideas can deepen teachers' thinking about the subject and indeed influence their practice. A thorough introduction to this theory is beyond the scope of the present chapter; Wegerif (2019) offers a useful review of the literature.

The Jewish thinker Martin Buber encourages us to think about dialogue in terms of the way in which we relate to others. He distinguishes between what he calls just experiencing others and entering into relation with them. When we experience others we see them as objects external to ourselves; we seek to learn about them, but always from our own external perspective: "The man who experiences has no part in the world. For it is 'in him' and not between him and the world that the experience arises. [The world] does nothing to the experience, and the experience does nothing to it." (Buber, 1958, p. 13). Buber referred to this as an "I-It" attitude which, although necessary for day-to-day life, does not allow one to enter into genuine dialogue but rather to engage in instrumental transactions. In the "I-Thou" attitude, by contrast, we encounter the other as a whole being; rather than gaining experience of each other in our individual minds, we encounter each other in a space that Buber referred to as the "in-between" – our minds enter into relation with each other. "Relation is mutual. My thou affects me as I affect it." (Buber, 1958, p. 20). For Buber, entering into dialogue involves entering into an "I-Thou" relationship with the other.

Mikhail Bakhtin, the Russian philosopher and literary theorist, provides us with a commonly referenced definition of dialogue as interaction in which every answer gives rise to another question; this leads us to think of dialogue as an unending process or quest for truth, not a short exchange in which "correct" answers are accepted uncritically (Bakhtin, 1986, p. 168). Bakhtin also makes an important distinction between the "authoritative word" and the "persuasive word." The authoritative word instructs or transmits but does not call us into dialogue. Consider a sign that reads "No smoking": we can accept or reject the instruction, but we are not invited to seek further understanding of it. The persuasive word in contrast is framed with us in mind – it might take on our own vocabulary or concerns, for example. It "enters into us" and stimulates our own answering words, calling us to think and make meaning. Bakhtin might argue that the dialogic persuasive voice is essential for deeper learning because to truly understand something we need to be able to express it ourselves with our own words.

So, from a more practical point of view, how might we recognize exchanges in the classroom that are more "dialogic?" Robin Alexander (2017a), whose work on dialogic teaching has been central to its development in the UK, offers a set of principles which might usefully guide us. He states that dialogic teaching should be:

- Collective (the classroom is a site of joint learning and enquiry);
- Reciprocal (participants **listen to each other**, **share ideas** and **consider alternative viewpoints**);
- Supportive (participants feel able to **express ideas freely**, without risk of embarrassment over "wrong" answers, and they **help each other to reach common understandings**);
- Cumulative (participants **build on their own and each other's contributions and chain them into coherent lines of thinking and understanding**);
- Purposeful (classroom talk, though open and dialogic, is structured with specific learning goals in view).

The bolded text provides us with some useful indicators of what classroom dialogue might involve. The section on "ground rules" later in this chapter is also concerned with developing a shared understanding of what dialogue might "look like" in the classroom.

Why is dialogue educationally valuable?

Much of schooling is concerned with helping students see the world in new ways by introducing them to disciplines such as mathematics, science, and history. This means introducing them to ideas that are removed from everyday experience, sometimes by providing them with new language and new concepts with which to think, and sometimes by bringing new meaning to existing concepts. For example, students will have plenty of everyday experience of the concept of love, but will probably not be familiar with the way that the term is used in Christian theology or in other faith traditions.

The Russian psychologist Lev Vygotsky referred to the kind of concepts encountered in academic disciplines as "scientific concepts" and suggested that they are formed through systematic instruction which introduces them in relation to a range of other concepts. "Everyday concepts," in contrast, are learned in a more unconscious, less systematic way through interactions with the world in the course of normal living. The set of everyday concepts that a person acquires will depend on their experiences, and everybody's experiences are unique (Wells, 1999).

This presents a challenge to the teacher trying to introduce a student to scientific concepts. We make meaning of all new ideas by relating them to our existing understandings of the world, including our everyday concepts. If we all have a unique set of everyday concepts, it seems inevitable that we will come to understand new ideas in different ways. This means that teaching about scientific concepts requires more than the transmission of linguistic definitions from teacher to student. The student is actively involved in constructing his or her own knowledge, and the knowledge constructed by different students is different.

Vygotsky believed that the development of higher mental functions, including the development of conceptual understanding, is a social process:

> Any function in the child's cultural development appears twice or on two planes. First it appears on the social plane and then on the psychological plane. First it appears between people as an inter-psychological category, and then within the child as an intra-psychological category. Social relations... genetically underlie all higher functions and their relationships. (Vygotsky, 2012, p. 163)

Dialogue (between teacher and student or between students) provides the social plane on which conceptual understanding can be developed. It offers students the opportunity to construct and reconstruct knowledge through a shared process of questioning, answering, explaining, exemplifying, comparing, connecting, applying, evaluating, and so on. It enables students to become sensitive to the differences between their understandings and those of their peers or teachers and to use these differences to stimulate further meaning making. Ultimately, coming to understand a discipline or school subject involves making a switch from one's own everyday perspective to the perspective of the discipline; the ability to switch perspectives in this way is precisely what is learned in dialogues.

Two more points should briefly be made about the educational value of dialogue, although a deep exploration of them is beyond the scope of this chapter. First, there is growing evidence that dialogic education is an effective way to teach general and transferable thinking skills and dispositions (Sutherland, 2006; Wegerif, 2018). This is based on the view that thinking can be described as an attribute of dialogue. In dialogues we learn to engage with other points of view in caring, collaborative, creative, and critical ways. These dispositions can be internalized; they can become part of the way we think and can complement rigorous disciplinary knowledge.

Second, and perhaps most important of all, there is a moral obligation to teach dialogue. The philosopher Dmitri Nikulin (2010) tells us, "Dialogue is a therapy

– perhaps *the* therapy – against the misrecognition of one person by another." In a world in which so much suffering is caused by the failure of one person to recognize the humanity of another, we would argue that not teaching dialogue is an abdication of our moral responsibility as educators.

To what extent do we find dialogue in the classroom?

The brief descriptions of dialogue given above might be sufficient to make us question how much of the oral interaction seen in classrooms is dialogic. Observational studies have tended to "not much" (Littleton & Mercer, 2013).

Most teachers will be able to identify with research suggesting that a routine known as Initiation-Response-Evaluation (IRE) is ubiquitous in schools (see Vrikki et al., 2019, and references therein). In this model of interaction teachers initiate discourse with questions that are often intended to check recall and require only brief responses from students; they then evaluate these responses with regard to their "correctness" (Sinclair & Coulthard, 1975). The aim of such exchanges seems to be to ensure that correct answers have been memorized and can be recalled; students are being encouraged to uncritically accept the authoritative word rather than being called to think and make meaning on the social plane by the persuasive word, and teachers are only engaging with students' perspectives in a limited manner – the relationship is very much one of "I-It."

Other studies have found that students are much more likely to be involved in "disputational talk" (characterized by individuals trying to impose their views on others in an egocentric way) or "cumulative talk" (characterized by individuals uncritically agreeing with each other in order to maintain group harmony) than they are in productive dialogue (Wegerif & Scrimshaw, 1998).

Perhaps it should be stressed at this point that forms of classroom talk other than dialogue are useful. Robin John Alexander (2017b) is keen to point out the value of the teacher using a repertoire of talk types (which includes exposition, recitation, and rote). And Mortimer and Scott (2003) suggest that teachers need to match their "communicative approach" to their teaching purpose; there are times when an authoritative approach (including the use of IRE) is needed.

However, if we are to support students in bridging the gap between their everyday perspectives and the perspectives of their teachers and ultimately of the disciplines they are being introduced to, then we need to create more opportunities to engage them in dialogue.

So far, we have introduced the idea that teaching for dialogue should have a central role in teaching for deeper understanding and for general intellectual as well as ethical dispositions and competencies. The next section provides a description of one dialogic approach that has had a proven impact in developing conceptual understanding and thinking skills in the classroom: *Thinking Together*.

The *Thinking Together* approach

Overview

The *Thinking Together* approach was originally developed by Lyn Dawes, Neil Mercer, and Rupert Wegerif in the 1990s (Dawes, Mercer & Wegerif, 2000). The approach offers a way of teaching through and for dialogue that fits easily into the teaching of subjects within a normal school curriculum, offering an alternative to potentially more time-consuming approaches such as Philosophy for Children. The teacher develops the capacity for dialogue in the classroom by working with students to establish shared "ground rules for talk." The co-construction of an accessible set of ground rules involves the children in the process of improving the quality of dialogue, creating better opportunities for reflection and metacognition than those created by some dialogic teaching approaches, and perhaps increasing the likelihood of students recognizing and moving away from unproductive and often implicit social norms. The ground rules are applied to create an environment in which "Exploratory Talk" can flourish, both in whole-group activities and in small-group activities (the latter being the main focus of the original approach). Exploratory Talk is dialogic talk with a focus on shared inquiry, asking questions, explaining, exploring alternatives, and generally seeking to understand the other participants' perspectives and the topic at hand.

The use of ground rules to support the development of classroom dialogue was a response to research (discussed above) suggesting that talk that might be described as dialogic occurs relatively rarely in schools and that classroom talk is more likely to be "disputational" or "cumulative," rendering much classroom talk unproductive (Wegerif & Scrimshaw, 1998). It could be argued that the implicit ground rules students bring with them to the classroom are responsible for these types of talk. If a student has an implicit belief (or ground rule) such as "You have to win an argument to be strong," then they are likely to become involved in disputational talk. An implicit belief such as "Argument is a bad thing" might give rise to cumulative talk. Through shared reflection on classroom talk, these ground rules can be made explicit and alternatives can be proposed which might become a shared resource with which students and teachers can create an environment for dialogue. If students internalize these ground rules for talk, then they will be more likely to use dialogic talk in contexts beyond the classroom; the way they "think together" with others may be fundamentally changed (as indeed may their habits of thinking as an individual).

The use of ground rules

A teacher looking to use the *Thinking Together* approach in the classroom might begin by explicitly teaching children about the value of talk for communicating and learning together. It might be acknowledged that there are different "kinds" of talk (including cumulative and disputational) that may be useful in different situations, and that not all classroom talk is productive. Students can be encouraged to reflect on the quality of talk that is productive – when they are trying to solve problems together, for example. The way language can be used as a tool for *Thinking Together* might be explored: the value of terms like "I think…," "because…," and "why…?" for sharing and justifying thinking and reasoning together can be discussed. In this way, we begin to give the students the tools they will need to develop "higher mental functions" and co-construct meaning on the social plane. Students can then consider together what "ground rules" might guide them to produce the desired quality of talk.

The authors of *Thinking Together* intended that the ground rules used would emerge from students' developing awareness of what worked and what did not work for them; ground rules would be somewhat different in each context and would evolve during a period of reflective practice. Nevertheless, some common features that might be expected include commitments to:

- Sharing relevant knowledge;
- Listening to everyone's ideas attentively and treating them respectfully;
- Accepting that claims should be challenged and that the reasons underpinning claims and challenges should be shared and explored;
- Actively seeking and considering alternatives before any decisions are taken;
- Taking shared responsibility for decisions;
- Reaching agreement whenever possible.

The need to encourage students to reach agreement could be questioned in the light of the foregoing discussion about the nature of dialogue, but Littleton and Mercer (2013), citing evidence from a number of authors, suggest that the effort to reach consensus (perhaps more importantly than the realization of this goal) encourages students to engage more deeply with the views of others and to give more consideration to their own ideas and the reasons underpinning them.

A practical guide for teachers introducing *Thinking Together* into the classroom has been provided by Dawes et al. (2000) and includes lesson plans for developing and applying a set of ground rules. Materials and references are available on the website https://thinkingtogether.educ.cam.ac.uk.

An alternative approach to Thinking Together *ground rules*

In our 2017 book *Dialogic Education: Mastering core concepts through thinking together*, we suggest that the *Thinking Together* approach might be enhanced by the application of the "4Cs Framework" used to develop the quality of dialogue in Philosophy for Children (P4C) (Phillipson & Wegerif, 2017).

The American educator Matthew Lipman developed P4C in the 1960s and '70s; he considered good thinking (which might include good *Thinking Together*, or dialogue) to be multidimensional (Lipman, 2003). His three proposed modes of thinking – critical, caring, and creative – were later augmented with a fourth

Thinking Together **39**

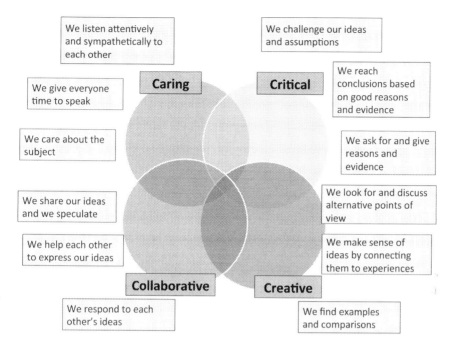

FIGURE 2.1 Ground rules for critical, caring, collaborative, and creative thinking.

mode – collaborative – by UK educator Roger Sutcliffe. The four modes of thought are very much interrelated.

The 4Cs can be defined to some extent through the development of related "ground rules" as illustrated in Figure 2.1.

While such ground rules certainly do not provide a comprehensive delineation of the 4Cs and will need to be reviewed and developed over time, they provide an overview of what good *Thinking Together* entails and can be used to support students on their journey toward it.

These ground rules are a template to guide teachers. They are not simply imposed. Each class is asked to suggest ground rules after an experience of group work. Teacher reformulations of suggested rules in discussion with the class lead to the generation of a class set of ground rules for talk in the students' own words and do so in a way that students can feel ownership over them. These ground rules can then be revisited and developed as awareness of talk and sophistication in dialogue increases.

The importance of reflection

Whatever ground rules are established, deliberate and reflective practice is essential if they are to have the desired impact on the quality of talk. The value of metacognition and self-regulation to effective learning has become well-recognized (you can find a useful summary of the evidence at https://educationendowmentfoundation.org.uk/evidence-summaries/teaching-learning-toolkit).

Metacognition involves developing a conscious awareness of the strategies used to tackle a problem, as well as developing the capacity to evaluate the effectiveness of those strategies and adapt them accordingly. Ground rules represent an explicit statement of the strategies used to make *Thinking Together* effective. Teachers can guide students to identify when specific ground rules are being followed and to reflect on the impact they have on the dialogue and on progress toward tackling the problem at hand. Littleton and Mercer (2013) follow Vygotsky in suggesting that the responsibility for regulating Exploratory Talk passes from the teacher (external regulation) to the group (co-regulation) and to the individual student (self-regulation).

Reflection on the ground rules and their application may prompt some revision of the rules, and it also will allow the group to identify the skills and dispositions they need to focus on. These skills can be made the focus of subsequent sessions; lesson objectives may refer to both subject knowledge and the quality of talk. The value of skills such as "finding real examples to make your idea clearer" can be openly discussed, and the skill itself (including the features of language that might be indicative of its use) can be modelled. In addition to reviewing learning content at the end of a session, the progress made with the focus skills and dispositions can also be reviewed and fresh targets can be set.

If groups feel they are having difficulty enacting certain ground rules, then devices can be put in place to support them. For example, if members of a group feel that they are finding it difficult to give sufficient time for people to articulate complex ideas before being interrupted, then it might be suggested that an object is introduced, to be held by the speaker; speakers are not finished until they choose to pass the object to a person from whom they would like a response. If a group finds that some voices are becoming dominant and others are being excluded, the number of contributions that any one speaker can make might be limited (by issuing counters to be relinquished each time a contribution is made, e.g.). Once the device is deemed to have served its purpose it can be removed, and another skill can be focused on.

The use of ground rules to develop metacognition and self-regulation and to support groups to identify "next steps" in their development of dialogic talk is important. It allows groups to make progress with the quality of their dialogue and avoid "plateauing" at a relatively superficial level where ideas are politely exchanged but no real "thinking together" is done. This is the deliberate "teaching for dialogue" that characterizes all successful dialogic teaching approaches.

Lesson structure/grouping

The way the *Thinking Together* approach is used is, of course, flexible and will be informed by the teacher's professional judgment. Both whole-group and small-group activities are likely to be used, and the first thing to consider might be the classroom layout.

For whole-group sessions, a circle or horseshoe layout (with or without desks) can have real advantages because it allows all participants to see each other and so facilitates deeper listening and responding. It also allows the teacher to take a position within the circle; this might signal that in this particular mode the teacher is not seeking to introduce authoritative knowledge but rather to facilitate students' thinking about the knowledge they have already engaged with (in the language of Mortimer and Scott (2003), we might say that the teacher is signaling a conscious decision to change the communicative approach to one that is both interactive and dialogic). Even in small-group sessions of three or more a circular (or, in the case of threes, triangular) seating arrangement will be useful.

A typical *Thinking Together* session might involve three main sections. In the first section, the teacher might introduce the session's purpose to the whole class. Relevant prior learning might be reviewed, and the objective of the current session, in terms of the subject knowledge being developed, might be explored. A learning objective relating to the quality of the students' talk may then be identified (it may indeed have been identified following a review of the previous session), possibly with reference to the class's ground rules. The skills and language involved in meeting this objective can be discussed and modelled; the group might play a short game to focus themselves on the skills being developed (e.g., a game involving listening, responding, or reasoning).

In the second section, the class might be given the opportunity to engage in small-group dialogue around a question or problem. The composition of these groups is worthy of consideration. Groups of three work well because they introduce a plurality of perspectives without allowing too many voices to be heard. Other factors to consider include gender and level of prior attainment; the task's literacy demands might also be taken into account.

In the final section, the whole group might come back together to share ideas and questions emerging from the group work. During this session, the teacher might focus on the need to ensure that any differences between the students' ideas and the "correct" ideas the teacher wishes the children to learn are noted and addressed. It is important that this doesn't become a session in which misconceptions are shared and exacerbated, but is rather one in which the students and the teacher work together to reveal flaws and inconsistencies in reasoning and discrepancies between the students' understandings and the accepted view. This can be seen as an important point in bridging the gap between everyday concepts and scientific concepts, as discussed in the introduction. In sum, assessment is an important part of the process; dialogue is a useful way of making students' learning "visible," and joining the dialogue enables the teacher to respond effectively to his or her students.

Facilitation of dialogue

There is more to the facilitation of dialogue than might be anticipated. We have already pointed out the important differences between talk that might be described as dialogic and the Initiation-Response-Evaluation-style exchanges seen in many classrooms. Perhaps the first decision to be made by the teacher-facilitator is whether to be present at all. In the presence of the teacher, students can be less willing to engage in active meaning-making (often characterized by a willingness to make tentative suggestions and hypotheses) and more likely to present closed assertions that can be judged by the teacher (Barnes, 1976). This could be used to justify the decision to allow students the opportunity to work with small groups of peers in the absence of the teacher; it seems likely that students will be more actively involved in making meaning of their learning.

When teachers decide to join the dialogue, they need to be conscious of the potential impact of their presence; it might be useful to be explicit with the students that in this session the "rules of the game" are changed and that the teacher is interested in the students' ideas and understandings. In a sense, teachers are positioning themselves as part of a process of enquiry and as learners. For a good portion of the time the teachers might choose to be absent in the sense that he or she does not seek to influence the content of the dialogue. Instead, any questioning might be designed to encourage students to elaborate and to respond to each other's ideas. Here the 4Cs framework suggested above can be a useful guide – how can the facilitator encourage caring, collaborative, critical, and creative thinking without inhibiting the students' sharing of ideas? At this stage, a Socratic questioning style is often useful; examples of Socratic questions include: "Can you tell us more about that?," "What are the reasons/what is the evidence supporting that?," "Can you give an example of that?," "Would somebody like to respond to that?," "Are the points made by X and Y the same or are they different?," "Is there an alternative point of view?," "Can we think of an example where that wouldn't work?," "Who can summarize what's been said – have we reached any conclusions?" Such questions will support students to think harder and to engage in a richer dialogue without influencing their thinking.

The teacher/facilitator may also use questioning to support students to make meaning by connecting abstract ideas to lived experiences. For example, if students are grappling with an abstract idea such as "force," asking for examples of forces experienced in the classroom and in everyday life may be useful. In this way, students can use examples to identify common features of forces and construct a provisional definition of force, and they can check the validity of that definition by applying it to various real examples (the facilitator of dialogue is building bridges between everyday experiences and disciplinary knowledge, and between Vygotsky's everyday concepts and scientific concepts). In one such discussion in the first author's classroom, the suggestion that a force "makes things move" was challenged through reflection on the students' experiments with and everyday experiences of air resistance and friction, leading them to adopt the idea that a force "changes the way things move." It is certainly worth noting here that the success of this strategy is predicated on the students having rich experiences on which to reflect.

In all of this, the teacher as facilitator is seeking to deepen the collective thinking of the group and at the same time is modelling the use of questioning to deepen thinking and open up dialogue. At some point, however, the teacher's view of the knowledge in question needs to re-enter the dialogue.

One of the principles of the successful dialogic teaching approach "Accountable Talk" is accountability to knowledge (Resnick & Schantz, 2015). In their explanation of this idea, Michaels, O'Connor, and Resnick (2007, p. 289) state that, "A knowledgeable and skilled teacher is required to provide authoritative knowledge when necessary and to guide conversation toward academically correct concepts" (they also stress the synergistic relationship between the effective acquisition of knowledge and good discourse). Alexander (2017a, p. 6) also acknowledges the tension between a "Bakhtinian commitment to dialogue as unending" and the need to pass on accurate knowledge as it is currently understood. This might involve the teacher asking substantive questions that reveal the inadequacies of some of the ideas that have been offered and the superiority of other ideas. The first author, Neil Phillipson, facilitated one discussion in which 9-year-old pupils were divided as to whether lava cooling and forming rock was an example of freezing, the main objection being that freezing happened "at or below 0°C." The facilitator asked questions such as "Do you think the liquid gold we saw earlier freezes at or below 0°C?," "Does chocolate need to be below 0°C before it becomes a solid?," and "Is water the only substance that freezes?" to challenge the misconception that had emerged. Teachers will find it useful to consider likely misconceptions such as the one described above and to plan their substantive questions in advance of the session.

The teacher may decide at the end of a dialogue to return to an exposition of the accepted version of the knowledge under discussion, perhaps stepping out of the circle to indicate the change of "mode" of teaching or communicative approach. In this case, it may still be useful to respond to the ideas shared by the students rather than giving an authoritative explanation that makes no reference to their ideas and perhaps thereby devalues them and disenfranchises them from the process of active meaning making. The talk would become less interactive, but it would remain dialogic in the sense that the students' views are represented and valued by the teacher.

Some argue that as soon as a predetermined endpoint is introduced, the talk ceases to be recognizably dialogic. One response to this might be to return to the "bigger picture" of education as dialogue. The teacher might openly acknowledge that any conclusions reached in the discussion are provisional and will develop as the students' experience (and indeed the experience of the relevant discipline and of humanity) grows. This might encourage students to maintain a curious and questioning disposition toward the subject and to remain open to fresh perspectives. As long as the overall endpoint of the education remains the achievement of fuller participation in dialogue – the dialogue of scientific enquiry, for example – then this process of guided scaffolding can be understood as part of dialogic education.

Evidence for the effectiveness of *Thinking Together*

There have been several experimental implementations and evaluations of the *Thinking Together* approach in the UK and other countries, including Mexico and South Africa. These evaluations show that significant improvements can be achieved in curriculum areas and also in reasoning test results. When *Thinking Together* was applied to science teaching for 1 year in upper primary to about 200 students, it produced statistically significant gains in relation to a control group on both a standardized science knowledge test and a standardized nonverbal reasoning test (Mercer, Dawes, Wegerif, & Sams, 2004). A separate intervention study at upper primary level with 64 students (ages 9 and 10), compared the effects of teaching *Thinking Together* in an experimental class with the same measurements in a matched control group. The study, which lasted over three months with a single, 1-hour *Thinking Together* lesson taught each week, led to average increases of 10% in scores on nonverbal reasoning both for groups and for individuals (Wegerif, Mercer, & Dawes, 1999). Similar results were reproduced in Mexico (Wegerif, Linares, Rojas-Drummond, Mercer, & Velez, 2005), South Africa (Webb, Whitlow, & Venter, 2017), and Belgium (T'Sas, 2018). The recent study in Belgium was particularly interesting because it was an accurate reproduction study of the original work in the UK. It achieved very similar results, suggesting that the positive impact of *Thinking Together* on reasoning and also on learning in science is a robust finding. As with most classroom-based intervention research, criticisms could be raised about the rigour of each of these studies. The extra attention paid to students in the target condition might have led to a Hawthorne effect, which is a positive increase in motivation due to the interest of teachers and researchers. Some critics have suggested that the increased scores in nonverbal reasoning for individuals might have been influenced by group nonverbal reasoning tests done before the individual tests.

However, this quantitative evidence has been matched with qualitative research exploring how and why groups learn to think better together through engaging in Exploratory Talk promoted by the *Thinking Together* approach. Often this evidence is stronger than any statistical evidence because it is sometimes possible to show clearly how groups solve problems by talking together using the ground rules of *Thinking Together* that they could not solve before the intervention (Wegerif et al., 1999).

Why does *Thinking Together* work?

It appears that *Thinking Together* and other dialogic teaching approaches have an effect not only on the quality of classroom dialogue and groups' ability to effectively think together but also on the quality of individual thinking as measured by tests and achievement in specific curriculum areas. Thus we need to think about the mechanism of these impacts.

Mercer (2016) offers three explanations. The first of these is that, when engaged in Exploratory Talk (dialogic talk as defined above), students can *appropriate* and apply the problem-solving strategies articulated by others; strategies are transmitted from one person to another through the use of language as a tool for *thinking together*. The second explanation relies on the idea that Exploratory Talk enables students to pool alternative strategies for solving a problem (or perhaps alternative perspectives on a concept), and hold them in creative tension together and *co-construct* new and better approaches (or understandings) which individuals learn and apply to other problems. Mercer points out that this explanation "locates the genesis of effective cognitive strategies in collective reasoning," thus linking individual learning and development to social activity and *Thinking Together* in accordance with Vygotsky's theory.

Mercer's third explanation points at the *transformation* of the individual through engagement in dialogic talk. Reflection on the quality of such talk, perhaps with reference to ground rules such as those discussed earlier in this chapter, allows a student to develop a metacognitive awareness of the effective strategies being used. Having experienced the value of searching for examples and counter-examples, searching for other points of view and so on in a dialogue, the student ultimately develops the disposition to do these things individually: their intramental thinking is transformed through intermental activity. The culturally based, social use of language leads to psychological development, again in accord with Vygotsky's ideas (Mercer, 2016).

It may also be that students become more comfortable with inhabiting a space in which multiple possibilities are held in tension together until a creative solution emerges (Wegerif, 2012). It may be that they begin to identify less with themselves and the need for their view to be validated (a disposition that leads one to become involved in disputational talk as described previously) and less with the group and their perceived position within it (a sense of identity that might lead one into cumulative talk) and more with the open-ended process of dialogue itself.

Developing students' ability to switch perspectives during dialogue may be fundamental to the impact of dialogic approaches. It is tempting to think that if a group of students have all sat through the same lecture – about justice, for example – then they will all have acquired the same "objective" understanding of the concept. But, as discussed earlier in the chapter, the sense we make of new ideas is dependent on our previous experiences. To make meaning of another's understanding of a concept like justice – to inhabit that perspective for a time without losing sight of our own perspective – is an effortful process and one that requires practice.

Perhaps it is this ability to genuinely inhabit other perspectives and encounter others in an "I-Thou relationship" that makes the words of others harder to dismiss and enables them to "enter into us" – to call us to think and make new meaning – in order for us to learn more deeply (see our earlier discussion of Buber and Bakhtin).

Conclusion

In this article, we have presented a case for the centrality of dialogue in education for deeper understanding. To that end, we have illustrated this case with one approach to dialogic education, which is education that teaches an improved quality of dialogue. There is good research evidence that this approach, *Thinking Together*, not only improves thinking in groups but also thinking for individuals. It does this through addressing communicative competence and promoting dialogic dispositions, including dispositions such as listening carefully so as to be able to understand the perspectives of others.

References

Alexander, R. (2017a). *Developing dialogue: Process, trial, outcomes.* Paper presented as part of the symposium on professional development in dialogic teaching: Commonalities and constraints, 17th Biennial EARLI conference, Tampere, Finland. Retrieved from http://www.robinalexander.org.uk/wp-content/uploads/2017/08/EARLI-2017-paper-170825.pdf

Alexander, R. J. (2017b). *Towards dialogic teaching: Rethinking classroom talk* (5th ed.). Osgoodby, Yorkshire: Dialogos UK Ltd.

Bakhtin, M. M. (1986). *Speech genres and other late essays.* Austin, TX: University of Texas Press.

Barnes, D. (1976). *From communication to curriculum.* London, England: Penguin.

Buber, M. (1958). *I and Thou* [R. G. Smith, Trans.]. Edinburgh, Scotland: T & T Clark. (Original work published 1923).

Dawes, L., Mercer, N. & Wegerif, R. (2000). *Thinking Together: A programme of activities for developing speaking, listening and thinking skills in children aged 8-11.* Birmingham, England: Imaginative Minds.

Lipman, M., (2003). *Thinking in education* (2nd ed.). Cambridge, UK: Cambridge University Press.

Littleton, K. & Mercer, M., (2013). *Interthinking: Putting talk to work.* Abingdon and New York: Routledge.

Mercer, N. (2016). Education and the social brain: Linking language, thinking, teaching and learning. *Éducation & Didactique, 10*(2), 9–23.

Mercer, N., Dawes, L., Wegerif, R., & Sams, C. (2004). Reasoning as a scientist: Ways of helping children to use language to learn science. *British Educational Research Journal, 30*(3), 359–377.

Michaels, S., O'Connor, C. & Resnick, L. B. (2007) Deliberative discourse idealized and realized: Accountable talk in the classroom and civic life. *Studies in Philosophy and Education, 27*(4), 283–297.

Mortimer, E., & Scott, P. (2003). *Meaning making in secondary science classrooms.* Berkshire, UK: McGraw-Hill Education.

Nikulin, D. (2010). *Dialectic and dialogue.* Stanford, CA: Stanford University Press.

Phillipson, N. & Wegerif, R. (2016). *Dialogic education: Mastering core concepts through thinking together.* Abingdon and New York: Routledge.

Resnick, L. B., & Schantz, F. (2015). Talking to learn: The promise and challenge of dialogic teaching. In L. B. Resnick, C. S. C. Asterhan, & S. N. Clarke (Eds.), *Socializing intelligence through academic talk and dialogue* (pp. 441–450). Washington, DC: American Educational Research Association.

Sinclair, J. M., & Coulthard, M. (1975). *Towards an analysis of discourse: The English used by teachers and pupils.* Oxford, UK: Oxford University Press.

Sutherland, J. (2006). Promoting group talk and higher-order thinking in pupils by 'coaching' secondary English trainee teachers. *Literacy, 40*(2), 106–114.

T'Sas, J. (2018). *Learning outcomes of exploratory talk in collaborative activities* (Unpublished doctoral thesis). University of Antwerp, Belgium.

Vrikki, M., Kershner, R., Calcagni, E., Hennessy, S., Lee, L., Hernández, F., ... Ahmed, F. (2019). The teacher scheme for educational dialogue analysis (T-SEDA): Developing a research-based observation tool for supporting teacher inquiry into pupils' participation in classroom dialogue. *International Journal of Research & Method in Education, 42*(2), 185–203.

Vygotsky, L. S. (2012). *The collected works of L .S. Vygotsky: Scientific legacy.* New York: Springer Science & Business Media.

Webb, P., Whitlow, J. W., & Venter, D. (2017). From exploratory talk to abstract reasoning: A case for far transfer? *Educational Psychology Review, 29*(3), 565–581.

Wegerif, R. (2012). Learning to think as becoming dialogue: An ontologic-dialogic account of learning and teaching thinking in primary classrooms. In B. Ligorio & M. Cesar (Eds.), *Interplays between dialogical learning and dialogical self* (pp. 27–45). Charlotte, NC: IAP – Information Age Publishing.

Wegerif, R. (2018) A dialogic theory of teaching thinking. In L. Kerslake & R. Wegerif (Eds.), *Theory of Teaching Thinking: International perspectives* (pp. 89–105). Oxon and New York: Routledge.

Wegerif, R. (2019) Dialogic education. *Oxford research encyclopedia of education.* Oxford, UK: Oxford University Press.

Wegerif, R., & Scrimshaw, P. (Eds.). (1998). *Computers and talk in the primary classroom.* Bristol: Multilingual Matters.

Wegerif, R., Linares, J. P., Rojas-Drummond, S., Mercer, N., & Velez, M. (2005). Thinking together in the UK and Mexico: Transfer of an educational innovation. *Journal of Classroom Interaction, 40*(1) 40–48.

Wegerif, R., Mercer, N., & Dawes, L. (1999). From social interaction to individual reasoning: An empirical investigation of a possible socio-cultural model of cognitive development. *Learning and Instruction, 9*(6), 493–516.

Wegerif, R., & Scrimshaw, P. (Eds.). (1998). *Computers and talk in the primary classroom.* Bristol: Multilingual Matters.

Wells, G. (1999). *Dialogic inquiry: Towards a sociocultural practice and theory of education.* Cambridge and New York: Cambridge University Press.

3

COMPARE AND DISCUSS TO PROMOTE DEEPER LEARNING

*Bethany Rittle-Johnson, Jon R. Star,
Kelley Durkin, and Abbey Loehr*

Summary

Compare and Discuss is an instructional method to promote deeper learning and communicative competence. In the compare phase, students compare two examples, making sense of each and identifying their similarities and differences. In the discuss connections phase, students reflect on key points about the comparison, communicating their ideas with a partner and with the whole class. Evidence-based guidelines for effectively supporting a Compare and Discuss instructional method in the classroom are provided. A supplemental algebra curriculum that incorporates these guidelines for helping students compare and discuss multiple strategies is reviewed to illustrate implementation of the method. Finally, evidence for the effectiveness of the Compare and Discuss instructional method for promoting student maths learning is reviewed.

Compare and Discuss to promote deep learning

We often learn through comparison. For example, we compare different brands and models of products, we compare one health treatment option to another, and we compare new words, objects and ideas to ones we already know. These comparisons help us recognize what features are important and merit more attention, which can lead to deeper understanding (Gentner, 1983). Indeed, research indicates that comparison promotes learning across a range of topics, including maths, science, and language (Alfieri, Nokes-Malach, & Schunn, 2013). In this chapter, we focus on using comparison to support mathematics learning. In addition, we briefly consider using comparison to teach other academic subjects.

In mathematics education, comparison of multiple solution strategies is a recommended instructional method in countries throughout the world (Australian Education Ministers, 2006; Kultusministerkonferenz, 2004; National Council of Teachers of Mathematics, 2014; Singapore Ministry of Education, 2012). Teachers are encouraged to have students share, compare, and discuss multiple strategies for solving a particular problem (e.g., discuss the similarities and differences in the strategies). This recommendation is based on observations that expert teachers in countries such as the United States and Japan sometimes have students compare and discuss multiple strategies for solving problems during mathematics instruction, which is thought to promote their understanding and flexibility (Ball, 1993; Lampert, 1990; Shimizu, 1999).

In contrast, students too often memorize ideas without understanding the ideas or being able to flexibly apply them to new contexts. This is true in many school subjects, including maths, science, and reading. For example, only 13% of 15-year-olds from around the world could work strategically using broad, well-developed thinking and reasoning skills to solve maths problems. Even in a high-performing country such as Japan, only 24% of students engaged in this type of thinking and reasoning (OECD, 2016). To improve students' understanding and flexibility, teachers can support comparison of multiple strategies.

Use of comparison in maths textbooks and classrooms

Textbook analyzes and classroom observations suggest that comparison should be used more often and be better supported in mathematics. First, textbooks provide some opportunities for comparing strategies, but opportunities vary by textbook and are often limited. We examined a variety of textbooks in the United States and Japan and coded how frequently the worked examples (a problem plus a step-by-step strategy for solving it) included more than one strategy for solving the same problem, which is a building block for comparing the strategies. Using textbooks from the United States, we coded the unit on equation solving in ten Algebra 1 textbooks. Multiple strategies were presented for an average of 20% of worked examples in the unit, with a range from 0% to 34% of worked examples. We also coded the nine units on algebra in the 7th to 9th-grade textbooks that are mostly commonly used in Japan (Tokyo Shoseki and Gakko Tosho). In both textbooks, only 2% to 3% of worked examples included multiple strategies for solving the same problem, with no instances in the 9th-grade texts. Japanese mathematics education researchers note that comparing multiple strategies is common in elementary school maths instruction (Shimizu, 1999), so we examined Japanese elementary school textbooks by the same publishers. Presenting multiple strategies for a problem was more common in these textbooks. For example, in the first half of the 5th-grade textbooks, 12% to 18% of examples involved presentation of multiple strategies, with one to two instances per unit. Although we did not systematically code for whether comparison was explicitly prompted in the texts, we only noticed prompts for comparison in a few instances.

Second, observations in maths classrooms suggest that teachers, at least in the United States, are limited in the frequency and effectiveness with which they use comparison. In one study in the United States, students were exposed to multiple strategies in 38% of observed algebra lessons, but teachers or students explicitly compared the strategies in only 9% of lessons (Star et al., 2015c). In another study in the United States, when asked to design a lesson around a correct and an incorrect strategy for solving an algebra problem, a majority of teachers in training did not plan to explicitly compare the strategies (Schenke & Richland, 2017). Further, when US teachers do use comparison, the teachers usually do most of the intellectual work, only asking students to assist in elaborating ideas or performing calculations (Richland, Holyoak, & Stigler, 2004). As a result, it is unclear if students are understanding or learning from the comparisons. In Japan, 8th-grade teachers provide more support for comparison, such as having both examples visible during the comparison and using spatial cues or gestures to help students make comparisons (Richland, Zur, & Holyoak, 2007).

Description of a Compare and Discuss instructional method

To help teachers use comparison more frequently and effectively in their instruction, we have developed a Compare and Discuss instructional method. We include discussion because it helps students articulate and reflect on what they have learned and supports learning from comparison (Lampert, 1990; Stein, Engle, Smith, & Hughes, 2008; Webb et al., 2014). We have developed the method for helping students learn maths, but others have shown that a similar method can be effective for a range of academic subjects, especially science (Alfieri et al., 2013; Gadgil, Nokes-Malach, & Chi, 2012; Kurtz, Miao, & Gentner, 2001; Schwartz, Chase, Chin, & Oppezzo, 2011).

First, students compare two examples, making sense of each and identifying their similarities and differences. In maths, the examples are often two different strategies for solving the same problem. In science, the examples could be two strategies for solving a problem, two real-world examples of the same concept, or a naïve and expert perspective. In reading, the examples could be two different stories, with a focus on comparing the characters or story lines. In history, the examples could be two historical events or people. In all of these domains, the first phase of instruction should focus on students comparing the two examples, identifying similarities and differences. Subsequently, students discuss key points about the comparison, such as when one is better than the other or what the similarities in the examples reveal about a general idea. At the end of the activity, the teacher summarizes the main points of the comparison

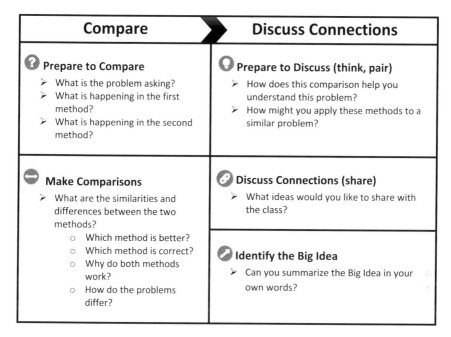

FIGURE 3.1 Overview of a Compare and Discuss instructional method for maths.

and discussion. An overview of a Compare and Discuss instructional method for maths is shown in Figure 3.1.

In maths instruction, this instructional method is useful for various instructional goals, including learning multiple strategies and why and when to use them and for revising incorrect strategies and misconceptions. Other instructional goals, such as consolidating a newly learned strategy, are better met by using other instructional methods, such as problem-solving practice.

Guidelines

We recommend two phases to instruction: a compare phase and a discuss connections phase. We have developed evidence-based guidelines for each phase (see Table 3.1). In Figures 3.2 and 3.3, we provide examples of materials for the compare phase, and in Figure 3.4, we provide an example of materials for the discuss connections phase, along with a sample student response.

In the Compare Phase, it is important for teachers to:

1. *Select two examples that have important similarities and/or differences* (Markman & Gentner, 1993). When examples are too similar or too different, students focus on obvious, unimportant features of the examples, which leads to unproductive discussions. The two examples can be prepared in advance

TABLE 3.1 Guidelines for effectively supporting Compare and Discuss

Compare phase

1. Select two examples that have important similarities and/or differences.
2. Make the examples visible and clear.
3. Use a variety of comparison types, matched to your instructional goals, such as *Which is correct? Which is better?* and *Why does it work?*
4. Present both examples simultaneously, not one at a time.
5. Present examples side by side and use gestures, common language, and other cues to guide attention to important similarities and differences.
6. Prompt students to explain, preferably to a peer.
7. Provide additional support if both examples are unfamiliar to students.

Discuss connections phase

8. Prompt students to reflect on a key point about the comparison (e.g., *discuss connections prompts*).
9. Use a Think-Pair-Share instructional routine (think on own, pair with another student, discuss with whole class).
10. Summarize the main points of the comparison and discussion.

or created by students. More than two examples can be used, but it may overwhelm students to compare them without considerable support.

2. *Make the examples clear and visible.* In maths and some science topics, *worked examples* (a problem and step-by-step strategy for solving it) are very effective examples to help novices learn new procedures and related concepts (Atkinson, Derry, Renkl, & Wortham, 2000; Sweller & Cooper, 1985). They clearly lay out solution steps and are commonly included in textbooks, so they are familiar to students. They also provide a visual record of the solution steps. Without visual aids, verbal descriptions of multi-step processes or complex ideas can be difficult for students to process because they have to both remember and make sense of the examples (Richland et al., 2007).

3. *Use a variety of comparison types, matched to your instructional goals.* We primarily use three types to support maths learning.

    - *Which is better?* Examples are two correct strategies for solving the same problem, with the goal of learning when and why one strategy is more efficient or easier than another strategy for a given problem type (see Figure 3.2 for an example). This type of comparison promotes procedural knowledge and flexibility – knowledge of multiple strategies and when to use them (Rittle-Johnson & Star, 2007).
    - *Which is correct?* Examples are one correct and one incorrect example, with the goal of understanding and avoiding common incorrect ways of thinking (see Figure 3.3 for an example). The examples can be a correct and an incorrect strategy or a naïve and expert perspective. Comparing correct and incorrect strategies supports gains

Compare and Discuss **53**

Which is better? Topic 2.6

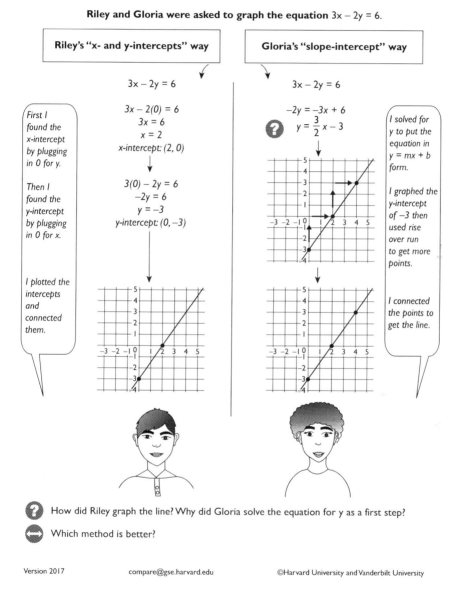

FIGURE 3.2 Sample Worked Example Pair (WEP) for a *Which is better?* comparison.

in procedural knowledge, retention of conceptual knowledge, and a reduction in misconceptions (Durkin & Rittle-Johnson, 2012).
- *Why does it work?* Examples are also two correct strategies for solving the same problem, but with the goal of illuminating the conceptual rationale in one strategy that is less apparent in the other strategy.

54 Rittle-Johnson, Star, Durkin, and Loehr

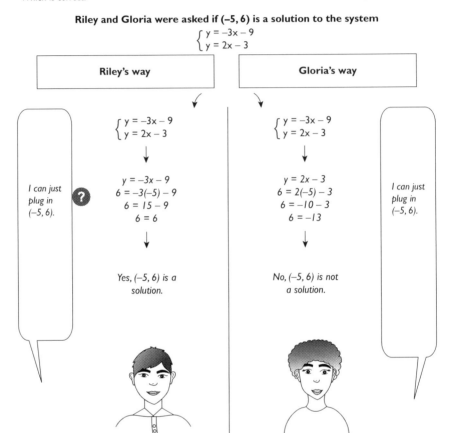

FIGURE 3.3 Sample Worked Example Pair (WEP) for a *Which is correct?* comparison.

This is in contrast to the *Which is better?* comparisons, where the goal is to learn when and why one strategy is better for solving particular types of problems. More frequent use of *Why does it work?* comparisons in the classroom is related to greater conceptual and procedural knowledge (Star et al., 2015c).

4. *When engaging in comparison, present both examples simultaneously*, not one at a time. Students will make better comparisons because they do not have to

Compare and Discuss **55**

Which is correct? Ch 5.1

Discuss Connections

Can both Riley and Gloria be correct? Can a point be both a solution and not a solution?

 Think, Pair. First, think about the question(s) above independently. Then, get with a partner and discuss your answers. After talking with your partner, what is your answer?

Riley and Gloria are both correct. This is because (−5, 6) was only a solution for the equation y = −3x − 9. A point can be a solution and not a solution because one point might only be on one line.

 Share. After reviewing the worksheet as a class, summarize the answer(s) your class agrees on. Was this different from your original response?

→ Solution = 2 lines meet
→ Can't be no solution + solution at the same time
→ Solution to equation only (Riley)
→ Gloria is correct

 Big Idea. When your teacher tells you to do so, write what you think is the big idea of this example, in your own words:

The big idea is to show that if the solution isn't an intersection point, it isn't a solution to the system of equations.

FIGURE 3.4 Sample worksheet for Discuss Connections Phase of WEP in Figure 3.3 Sample. student responses included. Typed student explanations in notes.

rely on their memory of one example while comparing (Begolli & Richland, 2015; Gentner, 1983).

5. *Present examples side-by-side and use gestures, common language (e.g., terms such as equivalent, factors, etc.) and other cues (e.g., highlight key parts in the same color) to guide attention to important similarities and differences in the examples.* For example, students were more likely to notice that the altitude of a triangle must pass through a vertex if they studied two examples next to each other, one an example of a triangle with an added red line that passed through a vertex and the other an example of the same triangle with an added red line that did not pass through the vertex (Guo & Pang, 2011). Without supports like these, students may fail to notice important features of the examples that are similar or different, such as whether the proposed line of altitude passes through the vertex (Marton & Pang, 2006; Namy & Gentner, 2002; Richland et al., 2007).

6. *Prompt students to explain, preferably to a peer.* First, prompt students to explain each example individually to be sure they understand each one. Then, prompt students to compare the two, using both general prompts (e.g., "What are some similarities and differences between the two examples?") and prompts focused on specific aspects of the examples to compare (e.g., "How is their first solution step different?"). Students can do this independently or with a peer, but we recommend students talking with a peer. Generating explanations improves students' comprehension and transfer (Chi, 2000; McEldoon, Durkin, & Rittle-Johnson, 2013), and talking with peers improves learning and communicative competence (Johnson & Johnson, 1994; Webb, 1991).
7. *Provide additional support if both examples are unfamiliar to students.* It is easier to compare an unfamiliar example to a familiar example, such as comparing a new strategy to a strategy students have already learned (Rittle-Johnson, Star, & Durkin, 2009). Students can learn from comparing two unfamiliar examples, but it requires additional support, such as providing more time for the compare phase and providing carefully crafted explanation prompts that guide students' attention toward key ideas (Rittle-Johnson, Star, & Durkin, 2012).

In the Discuss Connections Phase, it is important for teachers to:

8. *Prompt students to reflect on key points about the comparison (i.e., discuss connections prompts),* such as when one strategy is better than the other or what the similarities in the examples reveal about a general idea. Example prompts are: "On a timed test, would you rather use Alex's way or Morgan's way? Why?" and "Even though Alex and Morgan did different first steps, why did they both get the same answer?" Prompts to discuss connections encourage students to think critically about the examples and improve learning from comparison more than they would if they used generic prompts to compare (Catrambone & Holyoak, 1989; Gentner, Loewenstein, & Thompson, 2003). In addition, when teachers use more open-ended questions that prompt students to verbalize the main ideas of the lesson, students learn more (Star et al., 2015b).
9. *Use a Think-Pair-Share instructional routine to support high-quality discussion, communicative competence, and critical thinking.* First, students *think* on their own for a minute about the discuss connections prompt. Next, each student *pairs* with another student to discuss the prompt, summarizing their ideas in writing. Students who collaborate with a partner tend to learn more than those who work alone (Johnson & Johnson, 1994; Webb, 1991). Then, students *share* their ideas in a whole class discussion. Teachers should call on multiple students to answer the same question and ask students to build on each other's ideas (e.g., "What do you think about Abbey's idea?"). Such classroom discussions promote critical thinking and improve student learning and communicative competence (Lampert, 1990; Stein et al., 2008; Webb et al., 2014).
10. *Summarize the main points of the Compare and Discuss connections phases.* Direct instruction on the key points supplements learners' comparisons

and improves learning from comparison (Gick & Holyoak, 1983; Schwartz & Bransford, 1998; VanderStoep & Seifert, 1993). We recommend students to then write a summary of the main points in their own words to be sure they understood and so they can practice communicating their ideas in writing.

Sample curriculum materials: *Comparison and Explanation of Multiple Strategies (CEMS)*

For a Compare and Discuss instructional method to deepen student learning, many of the ten guidelines above need to be in place. Given the high demands on teachers to effectively support the Compare and Discuss method, we have created a set of instructional materials using the method that incorporate all of these guidelines. Our project is called *Comparison and Explanation of Multiple Strategies (CEMS)*, and we have developed materials for algebra instruction in the 8th and 9th grades. At the core of the curriculum are *worked-example pairs (WEPs)* to compare. Each WEP shows the mathematical work and dialogue of two hypothetical students solving an algebra problem. We use the three types of comparison outlined above: *Which is correct? Which is better?* and *Why does it work?* As shown in Figures 3.2 and 3.3, two worked examples are presented side by side. To facilitate processing of the examples, we include spatial cues and common language to help students identify similarities and differences. We provide specific explanation prompts to guide student attention to important information. With each WEP, we include a worksheet for students to use during the Discuss phase, a statement of the main takeaway of the WEP to display at the end of the lesson, and a teacher guide with additional explanation prompts, expected student explanations and the main point of the WEP. Our materials cover major algebra topics such as linear equations, functions, systems of linear equations, polynomials and factoring, and quadratic equations. We also designed a 1-week, 35-hour professional development institute to familiarize teachers with the materials and approach. Teachers review and discuss the materials and view videotaped exemplars of other teachers using the materials. In addition, teachers work in groups to plan and teach sample lessons to their peers using the materials, which were implemented and then debriefed by the group. See Newton and Star (2013) for more information on the professional development.

Evidence of effectiveness

We have conducted extensive research to evaluate the effectiveness of using a comprehensive Compare and Discuss method to deepen algebra knowledge, which includes our CEMS project, overviewed here and reported in detail elsewhere (see also Durkin, Star, & Rittle-Johnson, 2017; Rittle-Johnson, Star, & Durkin, 2017; Star, Rittle-Johnson, & Durkin, 2016). We only report results that were statistically significant.

Short-term, researcher-led studies

In our initial research, we redesigned two to three maths lessons on a particular topic. Researchers implemented these lessons during students' mathematics classes (e.g., Rittle-Johnson & Star, 2007, 2011; Star et al., 2016). In most studies, students in the experimental condition compared two correct strategies, focusing on when each strategy was most appropriate to use (*Which is better?* comparisons). Other students were randomly assigned (e.g., using the flip of a coin) to the control condition, and they studied the same content sequentially and one at a time, without comparing strategies. This allowed us to isolate the effectiveness of comparison because all students studied multiple strategies. In addition, all students worked with a partner and discussed their ideas. Most studies were with middle-school students learning about equation solving, and one study was with 5th-grade students learning about computational estimation (e.g., estimating the answer to 34×69).

For example, in Rittle-Johnson and Star's (2007) study, US 7th-grade students ($N = 70$) in pre-algebra classes learned about solving multistep linear equations during three class periods. Students completed a packet of worked examples with their partners, explaining the procedures and answering explanation prompts. Before and after participating in the intervention, students completed an assessment of our three outcome measures. The procedural knowledge measure involved solving algebra equations and the conceptual knowledge measure involved recognizing or explaining algebra concepts, such as like terms indexed. Procedural flexibility was measured in two ways. The first was *use* of more efficient solution methods when solving equations; the second was *knowledge* of multiple ways to solve equations, including acceptance of nonstandard ways to solve equations. As predicted, those who compared methods gained greater procedural flexibility. They also acquired greater procedural knowledge. The two groups did not differ in conceptual knowledge in this study.

Across five studies, with hundreds of students, those who compared strategies gained greater procedural flexibility, often gained greater procedural knowledge, and sometimes gained greater conceptual knowledge (for study details, see Rittle-Johnson & Star, 2007, 2009; Rittle-Johnson et al., 2009, 2012; Star & Rittle-Johnson, 2009). In one study, comparing strategies was more effective for students who were familiar with one of the strategies than students who were not (Rittle-Johnson et al., 2009). To address this potential limitation of asking students with limited prior knowledge to compare strategies, we gave students more time to learn a smaller amount of material. With these added means of support, comparing strategies immediately supported greater procedural flexibility than delaying exposure to multiple strategies, with or without comparison of the strategies, for all students (Rittle-Johnson et al., 2012). In large part because of our research, Educator's Practice Guides from the US Department of Education identified comparing multiple solution strategies as one of five recommendations for improving mathematical problem solving (Woodward et al., 2012) and teaching students to intentionally choose from alternative algebraic strategies when solving problems for improving algebra knowledge (Star et al., 2015a).

Year-long, teacher-led studies

Given the promise of the Compare and Discuss method to promote maths learning, we created the *Comparison and Explanation of Multiple Strategies (CEMS) for Algebra* materials and the professional development described in the previous section. We have been refining and evaluating this method in two large studies with teachers.

In the first study, we conducted an initial evaluation of teachers' effective use of our CEMS method (see Star et al., 2015c). Sixty-eight algebra teachers in the United States and their students ($n = 1367$) volunteered to participate and were randomly assigned to implement our CEMS curriculum as a supplement to their regular curriculum (*CEMS teachers*) or to continue using their existing curriculum and methods ("*business as usual*" control condition). CEMS teachers were asked to use our materials a few times a week (with about 36 weeks in a school year), deciding which materials to use and when. We supported the compare phase using all six guidelines in Table 3.1, but we provided less support for the discuss connections phase in this initial study (e.g., support for Guideline 8, but not 9 or 10, was provided). Teachers completed a log each time they used the materials and submitted a videotape of instruction once a month. CEMS teachers used our materials much less often than requested (i.e., an average of 20 times, for about 4% of their maths instructional time, with 30% of teachers using the materials five times or fewer). Coding of the videotapes indicated that teachers implemented the compare phase as intended, but they often did not support sustained class discussion. At the end of the school year, students' algebra knowledge was not higher in classrooms in which our materials were available (based on over 1,600 students). Greater use of our comparison materials was associated with greater student learning, suggesting the approach has promise when used sufficiently often. These results indicated that teachers needed more support in their implementation of our CEMS instructional method.

In a second study, which is ongoing, we are working to better support algebra teachers in their frequent and effective use of CEMS. Figure 3.1 has an overview of the revised method. First, we focus on a smaller number of topics and help teachers plan when they should use all of our materials in conjunction with their existing curriculum. Our guidance includes whether the material is best used at the beginning, middle or end of a lesson on the topic. Second, we provide the Think-Pair-Share instructional routine (Guideline 9) to better promote discussion, critical thinking, and communicative competence. This includes a worksheet for students to record their ideas during each phase (see Figure 3.4). The worksheet promotes use of the routine and provides opportunities for students to communicate ideas in writing. We also provide teachers with additional support for the lesson summary, using ideas in Guideline 10 (e.g., see the Big Idea prompt on the bottom of the worksheet in Figure 3.4 asking students to summarize the big idea of the example). Finally, we provide ongoing professional development to the teachers during the school year, providing feedback on lessons they have implemented and how to improve their support for a Compare and Discuss method.

In 2017–2018, nine Algebra I teachers (one 8th grade teacher and eight 9th grade teachers) and their students used our materials. To explore the effectiveness of our teacher professional development for using CEMS, we are coding videos of lessons and comparing the quality of teachers' instruction when teachers were using our materials to when the same teachers were using other curricular materials. Although coding and analysis is ongoing, coding of 33 videos thus far suggests teachers provide higher-quality instruction when using our materials. First, teachers were more likely to support procedural flexibility, such as when one strategy might be more efficient than another, while using our materials. Second, teachers were much more likely to ask "why" and open-ended questions when using our materials than when using other curriculum materials, asking questions such as "Can you generate another problem where Riley's strategy could not be used?" rather than simple questions such as "What is the answer?" Third, students were generating higher-level responses, focused on understanding, such as explaining why an answer was correct or why a particular strategy might have been a good choice. Fourth, discussion among students was more common. Although preliminary, this suggests that using CEMS is improving the quality of their instruction. At the same time, the nine teachers varied substantially in the quality of their instruction with and without our materials. Evaluation of whether using a CEMS approach improves students' maths performance more than typical classroom instruction is in progress.

Discussion

Compare and Discuss is an effective instructional method to promote deeper learning and communicative competence. In the compare phase, students compare two examples, making sense of each and identifying their similarities and differences. In the discuss connections phase, students reflect on key points about the comparison, such as when one is better than the other or what the similarities in the examples reveal about a general idea. Students communicate these ideas aloud with a partner, with the whole class, and in writing. Ten evidence-based guidelines improve the effectiveness of a Compare and Discuss instructional method, as outlined in Table 3.1.

Theory and evidence for how people learn helps explain why a Compare and Discuss method is effective. Novices have difficulty knowing what features of examples are important, often focusing on surface features (e.g., what letter is used to represent a variable) and because of this, they learn shallow information that they cannot apply to new examples or new contexts (Sweller, van

Merrienboer, & Paas, 1998). Comparing examples helps us notice important features of the examples and go beyond surface similarities to more important structural features that can be generalized to new examples and contexts (Gentner, 1983). For example, comparing examples helps students learn that you can add or subtract a variety of quantities from both sides of an equation and maintain equivalence. These strategies for maintaining equivalence can then be used more flexibly in more situations. Further, learning multiple strategies helps us respond appropriately to different situations and can spur invention of additional strategies (Siegler, 1996). To enhance sense-making, generating explanations during learning helps us make inferences, identify errors and integrate ideas (Chi, 2000). Finally, humans are social creatures, and discussing our ideas with others is a critical source of new ideas and helps us refine our own thinking (Tomasello, Carpenter, Call, Behne, & Moll, 2005).

Discussions help students make their ideas more explicit and better integrated with their prior knowledge, especially when teachers and peers support this process (Lampert, 1990; Stein et al., 2008; Webb et al., 2014). Too often, these core learning processes are not harnessed to support academic learning in schools. A Compare and Discuss method integrates all of these core learning processes to promote academic learning. At the same time, Compare and Discuss requires substantial mental effort of students, who can become overwhelmed by it without adequate support.

Future research needs to continue the development and evaluation of curriculum materials and techniques that can be realistically implemented by teachers to effectively incorporate comparison into their classrooms. This includes identifying and evaluating variations of a Compare and Discuss approach used in different countries, at different grade levels, and for different subjects. For example, Japanese elementary school teachers ask students to share and compare their own solution strategies, not hypothetical students' solution strategies (Shimizu, 1999). The advantages and disadvantages of using students' own strategies need to be identified (e.g., the added demands on teachers to select which strategies to have students present and how to support comparison of them).

We must also identify approaches to professional development and curriculum design that adequately support teachers in infusing Compare and Discuss in their instruction. Our initial effort to provide secondary maths teachers in the United States with materials to promote Compare and Discuss, along with some professional development was not sufficient to improve student learning (Star et al., 2015c). Some teachers struggled to find time to include the materials in their instruction, using the approach very infrequently. Some teachers were not comfortable leading discussions, providing little time for students to generate explanations in response to open-ended questions and to build on each other's ideas (Star et al., 2015b). Our current efforts to provide more support for integrating our comparison materials into the existing curriculum and for leading productive discussions is promising, but additional approaches are needed.

In conclusion, comparing examples and discussing connections between them can be a powerful instructional method. We need to continue exploring and evaluating ways to most effectively use the method to deepen student learning.

References

Alfieri, L., Nokes-Malach, T. J., & Schunn, C. D. (2013). Learning through case comparison: A meta-analytic review. *Educational Psychologist, 48,* 87–113.

Atkinson, R. K., Derry, S. J., Renkl, A., & Wortham, D. (2000). Learning from examples: Instructional principles from the worked examples research. *Review of Educational Research, 70,* 181–214.

Australian Education Ministers. (2006). Statements of learning for mathematics.

Ball, D. L. (1993). With an eye on the mathematical horizon: Dilemmas of teaching elementary school mathematics. *The Elementary School Journal, 93,* 373–397.

Begolli, K. N., & Richland, L. E. (2015). Teaching mathematics by comparison: Analog visibility as a double-edged sword. *Journal of Educational Psychology, 108,* 194–213.

Catrambone, R., & Holyoak, K. J. (1989). Overcoming contextual limitations on problem-solving transfer. *Journal of Experimental Psychology: Learning, Memory, and Cognition, 15,* 1147–1156.

Chi, M. T. H. (2000). Self-explaining: The dual processes of generating inference and repairing mental models. In R. Glaser (Ed.), *Advances in instructional psychology: Educational design and cognitive science* (Vol. 5, pp. 161–238). Mahwah, NJ: Lawrence Erlbaum.

Durkin, K., & Rittle-Johnson, B. (2012). The effectiveness of using incorrect examples to support learning about decimal magnitude. *Learning and Instruction, 22,* 206–214.

Durkin, K., Star, J. R., & Rittle-Johnson, B. (2017). Using comparison of multiple strategies in the mathematics classroom: Lessons learned and next steps. *ZDM: The International Journal on Mathematics Education, 49,* 585–597.

Gadgil, S., Nokes-Malach, T. J., & Chi, M. T. H. (2012). Effectiveness of holistic mental model confrontation in driving conceptual change. *Learning and Instruction, 22,* 47–61.

Gentner, D. (1983). Structure-mapping: A theoretical framework for analogy. *Cognitive Science: A Multidisciplinary Journal, 7,* 155–170.

Gentner, D., Loewenstein, J., & Thompson, L. (2003). Learning and transfer: A general role for analogical encoding. *Journal of Educational Psychology, 95,* 393–405.

Gick, M. L., & Holyoak, K. J. (1983). Schema induction and analogical transfer. *Cognitive Psychology, 15,* 1–38.

Guo, J.-p., & Pang, M. F. (2011). Learning a mathematical concept from comparing examples: The importance of variation and prior knowledge. *European Journal of Psychology of Education, 26,* 495–525.

Johnson, D. W., & Johnson, R. T. (1994). *Learning together and alone: Cooperative, competitive and individualistic learning* (4th ed.). Boston, MA: Allyn and Bacon.

Kultusministerkonferenz. (2004). *Bildungsstandards im fach mathematik für den primarbereich [Educational standards in mathematics for primary schools].* Munich, Germany: Luchterhand.

Kurtz, K. J., Miao, C. H., & Gentner, D. (2001). Learning by analogical bootstrapping. *Journal of the Learning Sciences, 10,* 417–446.

Lampert, M. (1990). When the problem is not the question and the solution is not the answer: Mathematical knowing and teaching. *American Educational Research Journal, 27,* 29–63.

Markman, A. B., & Gentner, D. (1993). Splitting the differences: A structural alignment view of similarity. *Journal of Memory and Language, 32,* 517–535.

Marton, F., & Pang, M. F. (2006). On some necessary conditions of learning. *Journal of the Learning Sciences*, 15, 193–220.

McEldoon, K. L., Durkin, K. L., & Rittle-Johnson, B. (2013). Is self-explanation worth the time? A comparison to additional practice. *British Journal of Educational Psychology*, 83, 615–632.

Namy, L. L., & Gentner, D. (2002). Making a silk purse out of two sow's ears: Young children's use of comparison in category learning. *Journal of Experimental Psychology: General*, 131, 5–15.

National Council of Teachers of Mathematics. (2014). *Principles to actions: Ensuring mathematical success for all*. Reston, VA: National Council of Teachers of Mathematics, Inc.

Newton, K. J., & Star, J. R. (2013). Exploring the nature and impact of model teaching with worked example pairs. *Mathematics Teacher Educator*, 2, 86–102.

OECD. (2016). *Pisa 2015 results (volume 1): Excellence and equity in education*. Paris: OECD Publishing.

Richland, L. E., Holyoak, K. J., & Stigler, J. W. (2004). Analogy use in eighth-grade mathematics classrooms. *Cognition and Instruction*, 22, 37–60.

Richland, L. E., Zur, O., & Holyoak, K. J. (2007). Cognitive supports for analogies in the mathematics classroom. *Science*, 316, 1128–1129.

Rittle-Johnson, B., & Star, J. R. (2007). Does comparing solution methods facilitate conceptual and procedural knowledge? An experimental study on learning to solve equations. *Journal of Educational Psychology*, 99, 561–574.

Rittle-Johnson, B., & Star, J. R. (2009). Compared to what? The effects of different comparisons on conceptual knowledge and procedural flexibility for equation solving. *Journal of Educational Psychology*, 101, 529–544.

Rittle-Johnson, B., Star, J. R., & Durkin, K. (2009). The importance of prior knowledge when comparing examples: Influences on conceptual and procedural knowledge of equation solving. *Journal of Educational Psychology*, 101, 836–852.

Rittle-Johnson, B., & Star, J. R. (2011). The power of comparison in learning and instruction: Learning outcomes supported by different types of comparisons. In J. P. Mestre & B. H. Ross (Eds.), *Psychology of learning and motivation: Cognition in education* (Vol. 55, pp. 199–222). Waltham, MA: Elsevier.

Rittle-Johnson, B., Star, J. R., & Durkin, K. (2012). Developing procedural flexibility: Are novices prepared to learn from comparing procedures? *British Journal of Educational Psychology*, 82, 436–455.

Rittle-Johnson, B., Star, J. R., & Durkin, K. (2017). The power of comparison in mathematics instruction: Experimental evidence from classrooms. In D. C. Geary, D. B. Berch, & K. M. Koepke (Eds.), *Mathematical cognition and learning* (Vol. 3, pp. 273–296). Waltham, MA: Elsevier.

Schenke, K., & Richland, L. E. (2017). Preservice teachers' use of contrasting cases in mathematics instruction. *Instructional Science*, 45, 311–329.

Schwartz, D. L., & Bransford, J. D. (1998). A time for telling. *Cognition and Instruction*, 16, 475–522.

Schwartz, D. L., Chase, C. C., Chin, D. B., & Oppezzo, M. (2011). Practicing versus inventing with contrasting cases: The effects of telling first on learning and transfer. *Journal of Educational Psychology*, 103, 759–775.

Shimizu, Y. (1999). Aspects of mathematics teacher education in Japan: Focusing on teachers' roles. *Journal of Mathematics Teacher Education*, 2, 107–116.

Siegler, R. S. (1996). *Emerging minds: The process of change in children's thinking*. New York: Oxford University Press.

Singapore Ministry of Education. (2012). Secondary mathematics syllabuses.

Star, J. R., & Rittle-Johnson, B. (2009). It pays to compare: An experimental study on computational estimation. *Journal of Experimental Child Psychology*, 101, 408–426.

Star, J. R., Caronongan, P., Foegen, A., Furgeson, J., Keating, B., Larson, M. R., ... Zbiek, R. M. (2015a). *Teaching strategies for improving algebra knowledge in middle and high school students (NCEE 2014-4333)*. Washington, DC: National Center for Education Evaluation and Regional Assistance (NCEE), Institute of Education Sciences, U.S. Department of Education.

Star, J. R., Newton, K., Pollack, C., Kokka, K., Rittle-Johnson, B., & Durkin, K. (2015b). Student, teacher, and instructional characteristics related to students' gains in flexibility. *Contemporary Educational Psychology, 41*, 198–208.

Star, J. R., Pollack, C., Durkin, K., Rittle-Johnson, B., Lynch, K., Newton, K., & Gogolen, C. (2015c). Learning from comparison in algebra. *Contemporary Educational Psychology, 40*, 41–54.

Star, J. R., Rittle-Johnson, B., & Durkin, K. (2016). Comparison and explanation of multiple strategies. *Policy Insights from the Behavioral and Brain Sciences, 3*, 151–159.

Stein, M. K., Engle, R. A., Smith, M. S., & Hughes, E. K. (2008). Orchestrating productive mathematical discussions: Five practices for helping teachers move beyond show and tell. *Mathematical Thinking and Learning, 10*, 313–340.

Sweller, J., & Cooper, G. A. (1985). The use of worked examples as a substitute for problem solving in learning algebra. *Cognition and Instruction, 2*, 59–89.

Sweller, J., van Merrienboer, J. J. G., & Paas, F. G. W. C. (1998). Cognitive architecture and instructional design. *Educational Psychology Review, 10*, 251–296.

Tomasello, M., Carpenter, M., Call, J., Behne, T., & Moll, H. (2005). Understanding and sharing intentions: The origins of cultural cognition. *Behavioral and Brain Sciences, 28*, 675–735.

VanderStoep, S. W., & Seifert, C. M. (1993). Learning "how" versus learning "when": Improving transfer of problem-solving principles. *Journal of the Learning Sciences, 3*, 93–111.

Webb, N. M. (1991). Task-related verbal interaction and mathematics learning in small groups. *Journal for Research in Mathematics Education, 22*, 366–389.

Webb, N. M., Franke, M. L., Ing, M., Wong, J., Fernandez, C. H., Shin, N., & Turrou, A. C. (2014). Engaging with others' mathematical ideas: Interrelationships among student participation, teachers' instructional practices, and learning. *International Journal of Educational Research, 63*, 79–93.

Woodward, J., Beckmann, S., Driscoll, M., Franke, M. L., Herzig, P., Jitendra, A. K., ... Ogbuehi, P. (2012). *Improving mathematical problem solving in grades 4 to 8: A practice guide*. Washington, D.C.: National Center for Education Evaluation and Regional Assistance, Institute of Education Sciences.

PART 2
Facilitating meaning construction

4

REFINING STUDENT THINKING THROUGH SCIENTIFIC THEORY BUILDING

Hillary Swanson

Summary

Theory building is a central activity of science. I argue that children can engage in an intellectually honest version of scientific theory building in the classroom. I present a method for helping students build theories of patterns (such as threshold and equilibration) exemplified by phenomena across domains. Through iterative cycles involving both creative and critical thinking, the approach helps students refine their theories in terms of *alignment with scientific conceptions*, *deeper structure*, *explanatory power*, and *abstraction*. Empirical findings suggest the approach helps students construct scientific understanding while also developing communicative competence and qualities of a theoretical turn-of-mind.

Introduction

According to Albert Einstein (1936, p. 349), "The whole of science is nothing more than a refinement of everyday thinking." This observation conveys the constructivist perspective on learning, where a learner builds formal knowledge by reorganizing and refining their informal knowledge (diSessa, 1993). In this chapter, I describe a theory-building course designed to help students refine their thinking through theory invention, test, and revision.

The course focused students on building theories of patterns in system behaviors (including threshold and equilibration) that can be seen in examples across domains, from physical to psychosocial. Threshold, for example, can be seen in the tipping point of a tower of blocks, and in the limit of a person's patience. Both phenomena exemplify a pattern of *pre-phase, limit, reaction*, where a parameter is varied during a *pre-phase* until a *limit* is exceeded and the system *reacts* by making an irreversible transition to a new state. Equilibration can be seen in a glass of cold milk warming to room temperature, and in the calming of a person's emotions. Both phenomena exemplify a pattern of *difference drives rate,* where a system tends toward equilibrium quickly at first, and then more slowly as it approaches that state. Patterns like threshold and equilibration are concerned with the behavior that underlies phenomena, or their *deeper structure.* They often capture causal relationships between events and therefore have *explanatory power.* They are exemplified by many phenomena and are therefore best articulated in general terms, as *abstract* constructs.

These qualities make patterns a good target for theory building in the science classroom. Scientific theories are meant to convey the deeper structure underlying a class of phenomena (Hempel, 1974; Toulmin, 1958), to explain those phenomena (Hempel & Oppenheim, 1948), and to apply to a broad range of phenomena (Atkins, 2010). Identifying deeper structure and abstraction, however, are commonly considered beyond the capacity of young learners (Chi, Feltovich, & Glaser, 1981; Larkin, 1983).

Because patterns are essentially the abstract deeper structure underlying multiple examples, they can be thought of as the *relational structure* (Gentner, 1983) or *schema* (Gick & Holyoak, 1983) instantiated by analogs (examples that are similar by analogy). Findings from research on analogical reasoning can therefore be leveraged to support students' abstraction and articulation of patterns. As well, patterns can be explored through many different phenomena, so students can generate their own examples and construct their theories in contexts where they have some expertise. Students' pattern theories vary in the degree to which they achieve deeper structure, explanatory power, and abstractness. All students can succeed, however, at generating an initial theory, and all students can improve their theories by thinking about their own and their peers' ideas more carefully (Swanson & Collins, 2018).

Description of the method

In this section, I introduce the key components of my theory-building approach. First, I will provide a sketch of the theory-building course that I developed and researched. The goal of the course was to engage students in an "intellectually honest" (Bruner, 1977) version of scientific theory-building, so that they might cultivate elements of a "theoretical turn-of-mind" (diSessa, 1991). I also expected students might refine their pattern theories to more closely align with scientific conceptions of the patterns they investigated.

The course was implemented over an entire school year and met during a 40-minute elective period on Monday, Tuesday, and Thursday mornings, for a total of 52 hours of instruction. It was offered at a public middle school located in an economically depressed neighborhood of a large city in the United States. I taught the course, having been a high school science teacher for 6 years before transitioning to research. I arranged to teach the course with the intention of cultivating a classroom culture that supported students in sharing, making sense of, and refining their everyday thinking. Twenty-one 8th-grade students (ages 13–14; 11 girls and 10 boys), participated in the course. Eighteen of the students had immigrated with their families to the United States from Mexico and Central America. Two students identified as African American and one as Bosnian American. The majority of students attending the school were low-income and designated as "English-language learners."

Students created theories for patterns of threshold, equilibration, exponential growth, and oscillation; however, I will only report on threshold and equilibration here. Pattern units were interspersed with smaller units and single lessons focused on the nature of patterns and how building pattern theories related to theory building in science. In order to make the task of building a pattern theory more accessible, I separated it into smaller components and staged their introduction over the course. These included 1) describing a behavior underlying a single phenomenon (i.e., articulating a phenomenon's *deeper structure*), 2) explaining the cause of the behavior (i.e., giving the theory *explanatory power*), and 3) generalizing the description by articulating the elements of the behavior that could be found in multiple phenomena (i.e., making the theory *abstract*).

For each unit, students constructed theories through an iterative cycle that involved steps of example exploration and theory generation, test, and refinement. For each pattern, they individually produced three theory drafts. They produced the first draft after considering two example phenomena. They tested their theory on a third example and refined their ideas, producing a second draft. They generated a list of examples that followed the pattern and tested how well their theories fit their examples. They refined their ideas and produced a third and final draft of their theory. Table 4.1 outlines this cycle for the first three units of the theory-building course.

Students wrote their theories on their own; however, they were encouraged to share their ideas with their classmates. The 21 students were distributed across six tables, with four groups of four, one group of three, and one group of two

TABLE 4.1 Cycle of example exploration and theory generation, test, and refinement for the first three pattern units

Unit	Example exploration	Theory generation	Theory testing	Theory refinement	Theory testing	Theory refinement
Introductory Unit	Chocolate chip cookie, oatmeal cookie	Draft 1	Graham cracker, Oreo	Draft 2	Student-generated examples	Draft 3
Threshold	Spaghetti bridge, drops-on-a-coin	Draft 1	Salt-water and floating egg	Draft 2	Student-generated examples	Draft 3
Equilibration	Cold milk warming, hot tea cooling	Draft 1	Beans-in-a-box	Draft 2	Student-generated examples	Draft 3

students.[1] I randomly assigned their seats at the beginning of each month. When students investigated examples, they worked in pairs (with one of their tablemates). When they created group artifacts such as posters, they worked with the other students at their table.

The key components of the approach are: 1) introducing new concepts and processes through example and experience, 2) moving back and forth between empirical and theoretical activities, 3) providing a range of familiar examples, 4) eliciting and refining student ideas, 5) moving back and forth between individual and group thinking, and 6) reflecting on products and processes.

Introducing new concepts and processes through example and experience

It can be helpful to introduce students to new ideas, such as abstraction, by giving them concrete examples, and it can be helpful to introduce them to a new process by walking them through it in a familiar context. I introduced my students to ideas related to abstraction at the beginning of the course through two activities. The first activity introduced the ideas *general* and *specific*. I opened class by projecting the results of a Google image search for the word *vampire* and asking students what they saw. Some students named vampire characters while other students replied "vampires." I pointed out that each of the characters was a *specific* example of a *general* category called vampires. I continued with image searches for zombies, birds, and reptiles, asking students to explain what was general and what was specific in each case. I asked students how they would define general and specific and recorded their ideas on the board. For *general*, they shared "simple" and "huge category." For *specific*, they shared "not random," and "focuses on a small topic."

The second activity gave students practice characterizing a general category and introduced them to the iterative cycle of example exploration and theory generation, test, and refinement. I began the activity by giving each table a chocolate chip cookie and an oatmeal raisin cookie. I asked them to think of a name for the general category to which the two belonged and to brainstorm a list of characteristics they had in common. The students did this individually and then shared their ideas with their tablemates. They created a poster showcasing their category's name and characteristics, which they presented to their classmates. I then gave them two new objects with which to "test" their "theory": an Oreo and a graham cracker. Some groups expanded their categories to include the graham cracker (e.g., renaming the category from "cookies" to "snacks"). Some groups narrowed their categories to exclude the graham cracker (e.g., making a circular shape a distinguishing feature of a cookie). They then brainstormed examples that fit into their categories and tested their category names and characteristics against these. They refined their ideas and produced a final draft description of their category. All along, I asked students to identify examples of *general* and *specific* in their work. Understanding how to create a general description is critical for creating an abstract, broadly applicable theory.

Moving back and forth between empirical and theoretical activities

Teachers can engage students in a theory-building process that loosely mirrors that of scientists by having them generate theories and then test them against empirical observations. In the theory-building course, students refined their theories through an iterative process that moved back and forth between empirical and theoretical activities. During the empirical activities, students investigated pattern exemplars to seed their initial theory or to guide their refinement of an existing theory. During the theoretical activities, students articulated and revised their theories in response to the examples they had investigated.

Students were introduced to the task of describing a *deeper structure* behavior in the threshold unit. They began by investigating two phenomena that exemplified the threshold pattern. First, they added coins to a cup hanging from a spaghetti bridge. With the addition of coins, the bridge collapsed and crashed to the floor. In the second example, they added drops of water to the surface of a coin until the water flowed onto the table. For both investigations, they took notes on the behavior that they observed. Following the investigations, they wrote initial theories for the pattern (i.e., the behavior the two examples had in common). When students named their patterns, some focused on the *pre-phase* ("Getting More"), some on the *limit* ("Maximum Capacity"), and some on the *reaction* ("The Break"). Students' theories ranged in focus from common surface features ("Both used pennies and had to have a special technique") to common deeper structure ("Both had to carry something until it couldn't hold more").

The students tested their theories on a third example, adding salt to a glass of water until a submerged egg floated to the surface. The students then wrote about how this example was similar to, and different from, the previous examples. I presented PowerPoint slides featuring a representative sample of students' initial pattern theories (which I left anonymous). I then facilitated a brief group reflection on students' initial pattern theories, during which an aesthetic for generality emerged. One student raised his hand and noted that calling the pattern "The Break" was problematic, because: "Actually, not everything [had to do with] something breaking. Because you know the one where we squirted the drop of water onto the pennies? It didn't break, it spilled..." I used this student's comment as an opportunity to highlight the appropriate level of abstraction and acknowledged that "break" might be too *specific* a word, and that students might want to choose a more *general* word.

Following the discussion, students wrote second drafts of their theories. They then generated their own examples that exhibited the pattern. They worked with others at their table to create posters to showcase their examples and then conducted a gallery walk (Kolodner et al., 2003), sticking notes on each other's posters to indicate where they agreed or disagreed with examples. I used two contentious examples ("bothering someone until they burst" and "getting your hair cut") as the basis of a whole-class debate. Following the debate, I reviewed students' earlier theories and invited them to revise their drafts a final time. Most students characterized the pattern as either *pre-phase, limit, reaction* ("We added something till something happened"), or *pre-phase, limit* ("We put something until it couldn't hold it anymore").

Students were introduced to the task of explaining a pattern's *cause* in the next unit on equilibration. They began by investigating two phenomena that exemplified the equilibration pattern. For the first example, they used computer software to collect data for temperature over time as ice water (simulating cold milk) warmed to room temperature. Following the investigation, students interpreted the data (shown in both graph and table), arriving at a description of the general pattern they found in the rate of temperature change over time as "fast and then slow."

They individually generated explanations for this pattern, which served as the basis of a whole-class theory-building discussion. Students began the discussion with idiosyncratic ideas about the temperature of the milk "slowing to a stop" like a runner slowing to avoid crashing into a wall, and the temperature increasing quickly at the start because it was far away from the wall and therefore safe to go fast. Gradually, through guided discussion, the students refined their ideas into a *difference drives rate* explanation reflective of Newton's law of heating (Swanson & Collins, 2018).

For the second example, they used the software to collect temperature data as boiled water (simulating hot tea) cooled to room temperature. They engaged in another theory-building discussion to create a causal explanation for why the tea cooled fast and then slow. Following these investigations, students wrote down their initial pattern theories. They named their patterns versions of "fast and then slow" and described the pattern similarly.

The students tested their theories on a third example, particle diffusion, which they simulated with a partitioned box filled on one side with two tablespoons of dried beans. They shook the box back and forth, and beans moved in both directions through a small gap in the middle of the partition. The students recorded the number of beans on the initially empty side of the box every ten shakes and then graphed the total number of beans on that side over 100 shakes. Their resulting graphs, which they drew on the front board to analyze, showed a similar shape (here representing number of beans over total shakes) as the warming and cooling investigations. In this example, the *difference* between the number of beans on either side of the box could be inferred as *driving the rate* of the redistribution of beans on either side of the box.

The students engaged in a theory-building discussion to collaboratively create a causal explanation for why the beans diffused fast and then slow. They wrote about how this example was similar to and different from the previous examples. I presented a sample of students' initial pattern theories and their thoughts about how the third example compared to the first two. Students then wrote second drafts of their theories. About 40% of the students included the idea of *difference drives rate* in their pattern theories, though most of these students also included the nonnormative idea that the final state also drove the rate (e.g., "Slows down to reach equilibrium, goes fast in the beginning because it has more room to cover").

Students then generated their own examples that exhibited the pattern. As in the threshold unit, they worked with the others at their table to create posters to showcase their examples and participated in a gallery walk to view and comment on each other's examples. Again, I used contentious examples (e.g., emotions calming down) as the basis of a whole-class debate. I then reviewed students' earlier theories and invited them to revise their drafts a final time. By the final draft, over half the theories were solely *difference drives rate* (e.g., "Fast because there is more space to cover and it slows down because every time less space is available and with less space it can slow down").

Providing a range of familiar examples

Teachers can help students find deeper structure and create abstract theories by giving them a range of examples. Research on analogical reasoning has shown that it is quite difficult for people to identify an abstract deeper structure with just one example, but given two examples, it is possible (Gick & Holyoak, 1983). Research has further shown that it is easier for people to find a deeper structure in two examples that are similar on the surface (Loewenstein & Gentner, 2001). It is therefore helpful to provide students with examples that are closely related. Once they have identified a common deeper structure, they can see it in more distant examples. Giving them examples that are distantly related is also beneficial, as it helps them generalize their theory so that it is more broadly applicable. In the theory-building course, students began their exploration of the threshold pattern by investigating two similar examples: the spaghetti bridge and drops-on-a-coin. In both cases, a discrete amount of something is "added" to an object that "holds" it (e.g., a stick of spaghetti, a bead of water) until it reaches capacity and "breaks" (the spaghetti breaks, the bead of water bursts). These examples helped students notice a deeper pattern in behavior where "we had to keep on putting something until it broke." The third example that they explored was more distantly related, as it did not show something breaking. Instead, it showed that after they had added enough salt to a cup of water, a submerged egg floated to the surface. This example helped students further generalize their language, by replacing "break" with a more general reaction as in: "Adding something to something until it changes."

For the equilibration unit, students worked in a similar way with closely related (heating and cooling of liquids) and then more distantly related (particle diffusion) examples. The closely related thermal examples helped students find a common pattern in behavior, for example, "Both go fast then slow. Goes slow to reach maximum room temperature." The more distantly related diffusion example helped students generalize their language, for example, "Fast because there is more space to cover and it slows down because every time less space is available and with less space it can slow down."

It is also important to give students familiar examples. All examples students considered were either from their investigations or generated by the students. Generating their own examples allowed students to think carefully about the pattern in a context in which they had some expertise. In this way, students created their own on-ramps to engaging in the complex task of theory building in a rich and meaningful way.

Eliciting and refining student ideas

At the heart of theory building lies the refinement of everyday thinking. Students can refine their thinking by articulating and making sense of their ideas. The teacher can facilitate this process by eliciting, showcasing, and engaging students in making sense of their own and their classmates' ideas. Eliciting and showcasing student ideas created the raw material for the class to refine through collaborative sense-making. When engaging students in making sense of ideas, it is important to get students to think critically about their own and their peers' ideas. It is through careful consideration of these ideas that students will refine their own thinking.

Throughout the theory-building course, I employed strategies to elicit, showcase, and engage students in making sense of ideas. I elicited students' ideas by asking them to share their pattern theories (e.g., for threshold or equilibration), or their theory for a particular phenomenon (e.g., why cold milk warmed fast and then slow). I showcased students' ideas by presenting screenshots of their pattern theories to the whole class via PowerPoint and displaying posters of their pattern exemplars. I revoiced and wrote student contributions on the board during class discussions. I engaged students in collaborative sense-making during whole-class theory-building discussions and pattern-example debates.

One activity structure that facilitated students' articulation and refinement of ideas was the theory-building discussion, where students worked to build a causal explanation for an everyday phenomenon. A teacher can facilitate a theory-building discussion by using moves that elicit, showcase, and engage students in making sense of ideas. I illustrate this with a discussion where students developed an explanation for why a glass of cold milk warmed fast at first and then slowed as it approached room temperature (for more details see Swanson & Collins, 2018).

Moves that elicit student ideas

These moves draw out students' knowledge by asking them to articulate their ideas and unpack their reasoning. Such eliciting moves spark creative thinking and guide students to generate the raw material they will refine into more formal knowledge. Specific moves that elicit students' ideas include: 1) asking students to explain a phenomenon, 2) asking students to restate their contribution, 3) asking students to elaborate their contribution, and 4) checking with a student to clarify their contribution.

To begin the discussion, I read aloud students' (anonymous) explanations for why cold milk warmed fast and then slow, then asked for additional explanations. When students' responses were hard to hear or follow, I asked them to repeat their contribution. When students gave minimal explanations, I asked them to elaborate, and when I wasn't sure I had understood, I checked with them to clarify. These moves had the effect of eliciting *more* student ideas. Even when a student restated their contribution, they tended to add new ideas, because they tried to justify it for others.

Moves that showcase student ideas

These moves create shared artifacts on which the community can reflect and refine their explanation. Some of the moves create momentary artifacts (e.g., verbal restatements) while others create more permanent artifacts (e.g., writing ideas on the board). Specific moves that showcase students' ideas include: 1) repeating a contribution, 2) restating a contribution, 3) characterizing the nature of a contribution, 4) recording a contribution on the board, 5) distinguishing contributions, and 6) connecting contributions.

During the theory-building discussion, I either repeated or restated virtually every contribution made by a student (both spoken and written), in part, to give them a chance to correct me if I had misheard them, and in part, to amplify each student's thinking for the class to hear. When students contributed explanations that were clearly distinct from those that were previously given, I showcased their ideas by writing them on the board for later consideration. Sometimes when I showcased students' explanations, I characterized them as belonging to a more general category (e.g., as an explanation focused on stopping at room temperature). Other times, I explicitly distinguished or connected their ideas with those given by other students. All of these moves had the effect of bringing attention to particular ideas and reifying those ideas for the duration of the period. Often, I brought their attention to a particular idea as an object of inquiry, to see if they understood it and, if so, whether the logic made sense.

Moves that engage students in making sense of ideas

These moves help students consider their classmates' ideas more carefully. They sometimes lead to the production of new ideas, but their main function is the modification of existing ideas by facilitating critical thinking. Specific moves that engage students in making sense of ideas include: 1) asking students to evaluate another's contribution, 2) asking students to restate another's contribution, 3) asking students to justify another's contribution, and 4) mediating students' interactions. I often fell into a pattern with students, asking them to take a position on an idea that I had just showcased, and if they agreed with it, asking them to restate it in their own words and explain why they thought it made sense. In some cases, students argued among themselves and critiqued each other's ideas.

Occasionally their critiques were unproductive and I intervened to mediate their interactions to help them understand their classmate's idea, instead of just dismissing it.

Moving back and forth between individual and group thinking

In facilitating students' articulation and refinement of ideas, it is important to give them time to think on their own and together. This gives them space to access intuitive knowledge that may be difficult to articulate quickly or under pressure (diSessa & Minstrell, 1998). It also supports their critical thinking by working collaboratively with their peers to make sense of ideas. The elicit-showcase-sense-make sequence naturally structures the integration of individual thinking with group sense-making. In the theory-building course, pattern units began by eliciting students' individual thoughts in response to example phenomena. Students then shared their ideas with their classmates through presentations and poster gallery walks and engaged in collaboratively making sense of their ideas through whole-class discussions and debates. In the theory-building discussions, students first wrote their own explanations for phenomena (e.g., why the cold milk warmed fast and then slow), and then engaged in collaboratively making sense of their ideas.

Reflecting on products and processes

The teacher can help students improve the products and processes of their theory building by facilitating reflection and peer-critique activities. Throughout the theory-building course, students shared the products of their work with each other, and engaged in reflecting on their products and how they could be improved. These reflections occurred in the context of PowerPoint presentations of student work, poster gallery walks, and whole-class discussions. This gave the students a sense for the ideals toward which they should strive. Finally, I led the students in several reflections on how their activities (in particular, example exploration and theory invention, test, and refinement) related to the activities of professional scientists.

Evidence of effectiveness

I argue that the theory-building approach to science instruction promotes deeper learning, competence with elements of communication that are essential to science, and thinking skills that belong to a theoretical turn-of-mind. As evidence, I summarize results from my analysis of student work. The analysis is based on a qualitative coding of students' three theory drafts with respect to four aspects of scientific thinking. Another researcher and I independently coded the theories and then met to compare results and reach consensus. Through a social moderation process (Frederiksen, Sipusic, Sherin, & Wolfe, 1998), we reached 100% agreement for all codes for all drafts.

Deeper learning occurs when students construct new knowledge on the basis of their prior knowledge (Smith, diSessa, & Roschelle, 1994). In the case of the theory-building course, students refined their ideas into pattern theories that aligned with scientific conceptualizations.

Alignment with scientific conceptualizations

Students wrote three drafts of their theories over each pattern unit. I developed coding schemes to determine the structure of students' pattern theories according to the elements of the canonical scientific conceptualization that they had included. For the threshold unit, a comparison of pattern structures across drafts (shown in Figure 4.1) suggests students refined their theories over time to include more elements (i.e., *pre-phase, limit, reaction*) of a scientific threshold structure. Many students began with theories that were either focused on surface features (e.g., "Both used pennies") or included only one of the elements of the scientific threshold structure (e.g., "Both had something that had been broken, destroyed in the process"). By the end of the unit, half of the class had constructed theories that included all three elements (e.g., "Adding something to something until it changes"). A third of the class constructed theories that approached the scientific conceptualization, missing only the *reaction* (e.g., "Adding or taking something away till it reaches the maximum").

Rank scores (ranging from 0–3) were assigned to the theories based on the number of elements they included. Students' rank scores for first and final drafts

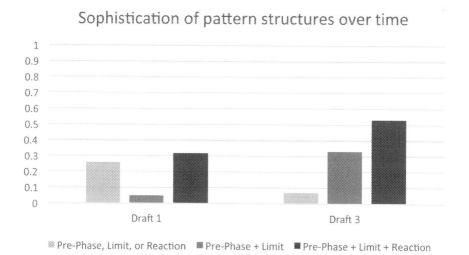

FIGURE 4.1 Proportion of theories featuring one, two or three elements of the scientific conception of the threshold pattern.

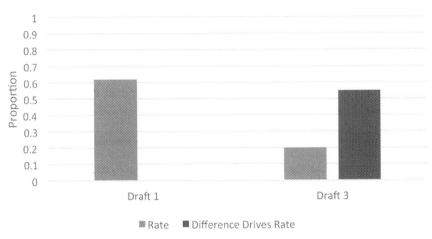

FIGURE 4.2 Proportion of theories featuring one or two elements of the scientific conception of the equilibration pattern.

were compared using the Wilcoxon signed-rank test with continuity corrections. Results showed that improvements in students' theories were statistically significant ($p = .02$).

The same method was used to analyze students' work from the equilibration unit. Comparison of pattern structures across drafts (shown in Figure 4.2) suggests students developed their theories over time to include more elements of the scientific equilibration structure (i.e., *rate* and *difference*). The class trajectory moved from theories that merely described a change in *rate* (e.g., "Starts off fast then it starts to slow down"), to ones that explained the change in *rate* as driven by a *difference* (e.g., "In large distance it goes fast, then when the space gets smaller it goes slow, then when there's no more space it stops"). By the end of the unit, 55% of the class constructed *difference drives rate* theories of the equilibration pattern. Students' rank scores for first and final drafts were compared using the Wilcoxon signed-rank test with continuity corrections. Results showed that improvements in students' theories were statistically significant ($p = .003$).

In science, it is important to communicate ideas through theories that attend to deeper structure (Hempel, 1974; Toulmin, 1958), possess explanatory power (Hempel & Oppenheim, 1948), and are abstract (Atkins, 2010). I analyzed students' theory drafts for both threshold and equilibration units using coding schemes designed to evaluate them along each of these dimensions.

Deeper structure

I operationalized this as articulating a *behavior* exemplified by multiple phenomena, rather than *surface feature* matches between their objects. Students showed a statistically significant ($p < .002$) decrease in their inclusion of surface features (e.g., "Both involved household items"), and a statistically significant ($p = .03$) increase in attention to deeper structure (e.g., "The space is greater at first which makes it go fast"). This suggests that the course helped students shift attention from surface features to deeper-structure patterns in behavior.

Explanatory power

I operationalized this as going beyond *describing* a behavior to *providing a potential cause* for it. For equilibration, all students merely described the pattern for their first drafts (e.g., "They both start out fast and then slow down") while over half offered a cause conceptually similar to Newton's law of heating for their third drafts (e.g., "The space is greater at first which makes it go fast, then it slows down as the amount of space decreases"). The increase in the number of students explaining the equilibration behavior was statistically significant ($p < .0001$). The theory-building discussion, which was introduced for the first time in this unit, may have played an important role in this shift.

Abstraction

I operationalized this as using general language to describe the pattern in behavior, rather than describing it in a specific example. Over the course of both units, students improved their theories by decreasing their use of specific examples and increasing their use of general language. The decrease in specific examples was statistically significant ($p = .03$), meaning that fewer students described the pattern in the context of a particular phenomenon (e.g., "We used pennies, we put the pennies in a container, we counted, we did it again"). The increase in general language was statistically significant ($p = .02$), meaning that by the equilibration unit, students described the pattern without referencing particular phenomena (e.g., "In large distance it goes fast, then when the space gets smaller it goes slow. Then when there's no more space stops."). These changes suggest that the course helped students learn to craft more abstract theories.

Discussion

The results of the study suggest that given appropriate instructional support, young learners are capable of engaging in, and developing skills for, activities that are commonly considered beyond their developmental capacity. In particular, the course supported their refinement of theories in terms of *alignment with scientific conceptualizations, deeper structure, explanatory power,* and *abstraction*. Below, I speculate on the features of the theory-building course that may have promoted refinement along each of these dimensions.

Alignment with scientific conceptualizations

Eliciting and refining student ideas

Students constructed pattern theories that aligned with scientific conceptualizations by refining their everyday thinking. The features of the instructional approach that supported this were the activities and teacher moves that elicited students' ideas and engaged them in collaboratively making sense of those ideas. This approach is based on a theory of learning called Knowledge in Pieces (KiP; diSessa, 1993). On the KiP view, knowledge is seen as a complex system of elements. People draw on their knowledge elements to explain the events they experience. Sometimes they use one element, sometimes many. Professional scientists have been trained to draw on elements that work well together to explain their observations. Their knowledge consists of a network of elements that are reliably connected together. Nonscientists have a knowledge network that is less stable than that of the expert. From a KiP perspective, scientific thinking develops through the reorganization and refinement of the learner's existing knowledge network. A nonscientist's prior knowledge is viewed as a resource for the construction of more expert understanding. KiP instruction is therefore designed to elicit and refine student thinking.

Deeper structure

Providing examples that are closely related

For both threshold and equilibration units, students began by exploring two examples that were quite similar. They identified the pattern based on the first two examples and then tested their theory on a third example, which was more distantly related. It is possible that looking at the similar examples helped students identify the pattern, and that knowing the pattern helped them see it in the third example and the later ones they invented. In her research on analogy, Gentner found that giving novices two near-analogy examples (examples that matched both in terms of relational structure *and* surface features) helped them identify relational structure in those examples. Novices were then more likely to notice the relational structure in a more distant example (Loewenstein & Gentner, 2001). She gave the name *progressive alignment* to the process of helping students find relational structure in more distant analogies by having them first identify the relational structure in near examples.

Explanatory power

Attending to causal relationships

In the theory-building course, students were first introduced to the task of articulating a causal explanation in the context of the equilibration unit. The activity that supported this was the theory-building discussion, during which students worked collaboratively to build a causal explanation for a particular pattern phenomenon. Their first discussion focused on a glass of cold milk that warmed to room temperature "fast and then slow." They engaged in similar discussions for the second (hot tea cooling) and third (beans diffusing) examples, as well. The theory-building discussion brought students' attention to the *causal* elements of the underlying relational structure of each example. According to Gentner and Colhoun (2010), looking for causal relationships (or *higher-order* relational structures) is a natural thing for people to do. The theory-building discussion therefore supports students' natural tendency to look for causal relationships and build explanations.

Abstraction

Introducing new concepts and processes through example and experience

The students were first introduced to abstraction through an activity on vampires. In a second activity, they characterized a general category that included chocolate chip and oatmeal cookies, and possibly graham crackers and Oreos. Through this activity, they practiced writing abstract definitions of their category by using general language. Practice, when given proper guidance and feedback, leads to learning because it affords opportunities to gain a felt-sense for how to do something the appropriate way, through a process that is both guided and exploratory (Trninic, 2018).

Providing more than one example

The students were always asked to find the pattern exemplified by more than one phenomenon. Gick and Holyoak (1983) called the process of abstracting a common "core idea" from multiple analogs "schema induction." They conjectured that schema induction involved "deleting the differences between the analogs while preserving their commonalities" (Gick & Holyoak, 1983, p. 8). In their research, they found that subjects struggled to derive schemas given a single analog, but given two, they succeeded.

Providing examples that are more distantly related

Presenting students with examples that were analogically distant helped students create theories that were abstract. As their theory had to be expanded to include more and more distant examples, elements of surface-features common to earlier, more similar examples had to be removed. This can be seen in threshold, where one student's initial pattern theory (that was general to the spaghetti bridge and drops-on-a-coin example) had to be revised from featuring a *reaction* of "breaks" to one of "changed," in order to include the third example, where the egg is not destroyed but rather floats.

Conclusion

The theory-building approach fosters deeper learning, communicative competence, and thinking skills. By engaging students in articulating, making sense of, and refining their ideas, theory building facilitates a knowledge-construction process that yields deep understanding of scientific patterns. By guiding students to refine their theories along dimensions that are germane to the expression of scientific knowledge, it develops their competence with scientific communication practices. By focusing on these particular dimensions, it develops thinking skills that reflect a theoretical turn-of-mind, including: 1) articulating consequential and empirically valid aspects of phenomena, 2) articulating deeper structure, 3) articulating causal relationships, and 4) abstraction.

The development of deeper learning, communicative competence, and thinking skills is interconnected. As students make sense of and refine their thinking, they get a clearer picture of a pattern's deeper structure and its possible cause. They begin to understand what aspects of the pattern are general to multiple phenomena. Their improved clarity in thinking allows them to articulate their theories more precisely along these dimensions, thereby enhancing their communicative competence. The increased precision of their theories, in turn, allows them to consider their ideas more carefully, and further refine them.

In this way, deeper learning and communicative competence are mutually supportive – the development of each leads to the development of the other. Focusing on the development of both deeper learning and communicative competence by engaging in knowledge refinement, in turn fosters the development of thinking skills that reflect a theoretical turn-of-mind. The development of these skills, in turn, supports students' construction of pattern theories that align with canonical scientific conceptualizations and are more theoretically sophisticated in their articulation. In this way, the development of thinking skills is synergistic with deeper learning and communicative competence.

Note

1 I chose this grouping to facilitate students' movement between pair work and small group work. Had there been an even number of students in the class, I would have used groups of four (with one group of two, if necessary).

References

Atkins, P. (2010). *The laws of thermodynamics: A very short introduction*. Oxford, England: Oxford University Press.

Bruner, J. S. (1977). *The process of education*. Cambridge, MA: Harvard University Press.

Chi, M. T., Feltovich, P. J., & Glaser, R. (1981). Categorization and representation of physics problems by experts and novices. *Cognitive Science, 5*(2), 121–152.

diSessa, A. A. (1991). If we want to get ahead, we should get some theories. In R. G. Underhill (Ed.), *Proceedings of the Thirteenth Annual Meeting of the North American Chapter of the International Group for the Psychology of Mathematics Education. (Plenary Lecture and Reaction.) Vol. 1* (pp. 220–239). Blacksburg, VA: Virginia Tech.

diSessa, A. A. (1993). Toward an epistemology of physics. *Cognition and Instruction, 10*(2-3), 105–225.

diSessa, A. A. & Minstrell, J. (1998). Cultivating conceptual change with benchmark lessons. In J. Greeno & S. Goldman (Eds.) *Thinking practices in mathematics and science learning* (pp. 155–188). Mahwah, NJ: Lawrence Erlbaum.

Einstein, A. (1936). Physics and reality. *Journal of the Franklin Institute, 221*(3), 349–382.

Frederiksen, J. R., Sipusic, M., Sherin, M., & Wolfe, E. W. (1998). Video portfolio assessment: Creating a framework for viewing the functions of teaching. *Educational Assessment, 5*(4), 225–297.

Gentner, D. (1983). Structure-mapping: A theoretical framework for analogy. *Cognitive Science, 7*(2), 155–170.

Gentner, D., & Colhoun, J. (2010). Analogical processes in human thinking and learning. In A. von Muller & E. Poppel (Series Eds.), & B. Glatzeder, V. Goel & A. von Muller (Vol. Eds.), *On thinking: Vol. 2. Towards a theory of thinking* (pp. 35–48). Berlin, Germany: Springer-Verlag.

Gick, M. L., & Holyoak, K. J. (1983). Schema induction and analogical transfer. *Cognitive Psychology, 15*(1), 1–38.

Hempel, C. (1974). Formulation and formalization of scientific theories: A summary-abstract. In T. S. Kuhn, & F. Suppe (Eds.), *The structure of scientific theories* (pp. 244–254). Chicago, IL: University of Illinois Press.

Hempel, C. G., & Oppenheim, P. (1948). Studies in the logic of explanation. *Philosophy of Science, 15*(2), 135–175.

Kolodner, J. L., Camp, P. J., Crismond, D., Fasse, B., Gray, J., Holbrook, J.,... Ryan, M. (2003) Problem-based learning meets case-based reasoning in the middle-school classroom: Putting learning by design into practice. *Journal of the Learning Sciences, 12*(4), 495–547.

Larkin, J. H. (1983). The role of problem representation in physics. In D. Gentner & A. L. Stevens (Eds.), *Mental models* (pp. 75–98). Hillsdale, NJ: Lawrence Erlbaum.

Loewenstein, J., & Gentner, D. (2001). Spatial mapping in preschoolers: Close comparisons facilitate far mappings. *Journal of Cognition and Development, 2*(2), 189–219.

Smith, J. P. III, diSessa, A. A., & Roschelle, J. (1994). Misconceptions reconceived: A constructivist analysis of knowledge in transition. *The Journal of the Learning Sciences, 3*(2), 115–163.

Swanson, H., & Collins, A. (2018). How failure is productive in the creative process: Refining student explanations through theory-building discussion. *Thinking Skills and Creativity, 30,* 54–63.

Toulmin, S. E. (1958). *The philosophy of science* (Vol. 14). Guildford, England: Genesis.

Trninic, D. (2018). Instruction, repetition, discovery: Restoring the historical educational role of practice. *Instructional Science, 46*(1), 133–153.

5

EXTENDING STUDENTS' COMMUNICATIVE REPERTOIRES

A culture of inquiry perspective for reflexive learning

Beth V. Yeager, Maria Lucia Castanheira, and Judith Green

Summary

In this chapter, we make visible how Beth (first author), a bilingual elementary grade teacher, developed a *culture of inquiry* with her linguistically, culturally, socially, and academically diverse students (10- to 11-year-olds). We share four principles of practice that guided the teacher in engaging students in being co-ethnographers with her and the external research team. We describe ways in which she supported her students in extending their communicative repertoires (spoken and written), and in deepening their understandings of inquiry processes and practices as they learned how to think and inquire as mathematicians, social scientists, artists, authors, and community members. By sharing these guiding principles, we hope to support teachers interested in "deeper learning" in developing a culture of inquiry with students.

Introduction

At the end of each year in a 5th-grade bilingual elementary classroom on the California coast, students wrote essays about what they thought it meant to be a member of their particular class community. Lizbeth, for example, wrote the following (excerpted from a longer text):

> "As an ethnographer[1], I want to tell you what it means to be a member of the Tower[2] community. What I have done as an ethnographer to help me learn these things about my community is take notes and observe kids...
>
> ... The only thing that counts in the Tower is that you can work hard as an ethnographer, historian, anthropologist, mathematician, reader or scientist..."

Every day, teachers walk into public school classrooms where they face new challenges, such as how to navigate standards while providing students with opportunities for engaging in complex, "deeper" learning often in the context of teaching multiple disciplines. They also wonder how they and their students can make this kind of learning visible to others. Those challenges are often exacerbated by deficit-based language around what linguistically, culturally, academically, and socially diverse students, in particular, cannot do, based on things such as standardized test scores. Knowing that students like Lizbeth (a native Spanish speaker) were among these thousands of nameless children who were being labeled in public discourse (e.g., in public meetings, in newspaper articles) as "at risk" and even as "failing" because of this deficit perspective, served as a driving force for Beth, their teacher and the coauthor of this chapter. Like many teachers, Beth could see these same diverse students in her classroom reading complex texts, talking about difficult ideas, and writing to communicate those ideas. It was this clash between how students like hers were being perceived and talked about in public discourse (a "rhetoric of failure" [Yeager, 2006]) and what she could see happening in her classroom that drove her (teacher-as-ethnographer) and her external interactional ethnographic (IE) research partners, Judith and Maria Lucia, coauthors (and other team members across years), to examine over time what was happening in her classroom and find a way with students to make that visible, as well as to find a language to talk about what students *could* do, rather than what they could *not* do.

When Lizbeth and other students like her in Beth's classes wrote about their classroom community at the end of each year with some authority (i.e., as "experts" on the community), they made visible ways of being students that were part of everyday life in these classes. They identified inquiry-based processes and practices that were valued and important in their class(es), such as being an "ethnographer," "take(ing) notes," "observing," and "working as" members of disciplines, all of which were part of a larger instructional design approach that Beth drew on in her efforts to address the same kinds of challenges teachers are facing today. Beth describes this approach as taking up a *stance* as inquirers (Cochran-Smith & Lytle, 2009) – teachers and students together. In other words, ordinary parts of everyday life in her classroom included co-constructing a *culture of inquiry* in which students and teacher actively engaged in understanding, talking, and writing about their own class community and what was available to be learned, their own work in that context, as well as the inquiry-based processes and practices of disciplinary work, and in acting on what they learned and communicating it to others.

In this chapter, we make visible what co-constructing a *culture of inquiry* that supports students in developing disciplinary processes and practices, as well as ways of looking at and communicating about their own learning drawing on those practices, looked and sounded like in Beth's 5th- and 6th-grade classes. We share how this work supported diverse students in extending their spoken and written *communicative repertoires* (i.e., their resources for communicating) to include ways of engaging in collaborative inquiry processes and practices with class members within and across different disciplines. We make visible how Beth developed ways of engaging her linguistically, culturally, academically, and socially diverse students in becoming social scientists, mathematicians, scientists, artists, readers, and authors, as well as in engaging in a *reflexive process* as part of the culture of inquiry (reflectively and reflexively looking at their own work in order to responsively take new action).

In the following sections, we present four guiding principles for Beth's logic of design and instruction. In the first section, we share how what we call an ethnographic perspective (Castanheira, Crawford, Dixon & Green, 2001; Green & Bloome, 1997) as a way of looking became an integral part of the theory/practice relationship and logic-of-design in Beth's classes – for her *and* for her students – and had particular kinds of consequences for what became available as opportunities for learning (Tuyay, Jennings, & Dixon, 1995) to students like Lizbeth.

Guiding Principle 1: Developing a conceptual foundation for design and decision making

In this section, we share how having a conceptual vision for students, from an inquiry stance, and a conceptual/theoretical rationale for her approach to teaching and learning were critical to Beth's design and instructional decisions, enabling her to learn to *step back* from the challenges of the teaching moment, to breathe a little, in order to take *informed action* (Freire, 2000, original 1970) in developing a culture of inquiry with her students.

Surfacing and articulating goals: Origins of a culture of inquiry approach

Like many teachers, Beth and her students took many things about everyday life in her classroom for granted, simply because they were "ordinary." In other words, some of what may have been guiding decisions leading to whatever was "ordinary, everyday practice," including the development of a culture of inquiry, actually became invisible. Beginning in 1991, Beth became a founding teacher member of a university/school research partnership and community, the Santa Barbara Classroom Discourse Group, a research community that was meant to be a short-term research process, but that turned into a 10-year collaborative ethnography in Beth's classes that both informed and became, over time, an integral part of the evolving culture of inquiry and an ongoing collaboration with Beth that continues today.

Although Beth had, in 1991, been teaching for 21 years and had also been a teacher researcher, this new partnership offered new eyes (through external research partners, in her classroom, like Judith and Ana in 1991, and Maria Lucia in 1996-97, with video cameras) and, particularly, new ways of looking and conceptualizing that made sense in the context of what was actually happening in practice, in everyday life. In other words, theory and practice came together in ways that made sense in the context of Beth's goals for students-as-learners in her classes and that offered new ways of talking about those goals. Before explaining those conceptual ways of looking and theorizing that made sense to Beth, we first share her goals for developing students as inquirers in Table 5.1 below, based on what she surfaced in 1991-92 by taking time to step back and purposefully look at what was happening in her classroom (Yeager, Floriani & Green, 1998).

In this statement, Beth is making visible her approach to student learning, one that reflects her background as a teacher across different levels of schooling (pre-K through grades 5 and 6). Just like students, teachers bring a history to each new school year that informs the lens through which they see students and design instruction, which is why understanding her/his own roots and how she/he conceptualizes a vision and goals for students (beyond meeting "grade level expectations") is so critical for a teacher. In her statement, Beth also makes visible her conceptual understanding of the learning-teaching relationships that shape what she *made present* (Kelly, 2006; Yeager, 2003) to her diverse group of students.

Finally, Beth also foregrounds her goals for reflexivity (not simply reflecting "back on," but thinking reflexively in the moment as part of the learning process) and how she developed ways of engaging students in this process. This goal is visible in her description of how she engaged students in contrasting their actions

TABLE 5.1 Beth's goals for developing students as inquirers

Beth
My goal is to help students develop strategies for learning that they can use both in and out of school. From my first year as a preschool teacher (1970), I have wanted all students to be able to inquire into their thinking, to examine their procedures and processes for learning, and to be able to understand the ways in which the class community was being constructed through the ways they interacted with others.
As I have moved across grade levels, I have become concerned with helping my students acquire discipline-based knowledge. I want my students to understand how discipline knowledge is the product of actions of people and how they can "take up" the actions associated with particular disciplines. I want them to be able to "envision" themselves as anthropologists, artists, readers, historians, writers, scientists, and mathematicians.
To put my goals into practice, I create opportunities to explore how people in each discipline go about their work. We explore the ways artists work by entering their lives through their words and creations. For example, we enter the life of Faith Ringgold by reading Tar Beach ([book]1990) and talking about her story quilts. We use what we learn about her as an artist to explore our own writing and painting. As we work as artists, we look back on her process and see how our process is similar to and different from hers. We record our observations and ideas in our writer's notebooks (Calkins, 1990) and our learning logs.
The processes of inquiry and our ways of exploring the work of people within the disciplines for ourselves enable us to create a common language for learning. It also makes visible the processes and practices of those disciplines so that students can take up these practices and can see relationships across disciplines. I also try to communicate this approach to parents so that we, the parents and I, can build a support for student inquiry and exploration. This is especially important since some of the projects involve parents.

with those of Faith Ringgold, author and artist. In this chain of actions, she framed ways in which students were afforded the opportunity to learn through contrastive analysis, not about the content itself, but about ways of knowing and doing the work of authors and artists. In framing her goals in this way, she made transparent that her instructional processes were designed to go beyond the reproduction of disciplinary knowledge (content) and outcomes that are assessed in formal tests external to classroom opportunities for learning.

In engaging in this process of surfacing and articulating her underlying vision and goals by stepping back and asking questions about what she was seeing in the "ordinary" life of her classroom, Beth, herself, was engaging in a reflexive process. It was a process grounded in a conceptual/theoretical, inquiry-based, way of looking and thinking about everyday life that was consistent with what she knew as a teacher, like many other teachers.

Taking an ethnographic perspective as part of a conceptual foundation

Why did the Interactional Ethnographic (IE) perspective brought by her new external research partners make sense to Beth, as a teacher, for herself and later for her students? Teachers know that everyday life in their classrooms is complex. It is not something that can be seen and understood in the moment (teachers understand that especially when visitors make snap judgments about what is happening or not happening after only brief observations). However, although teachers "know" what is happening, they may not have a common language for making visible what they know (Yeager, 2003, 2006). Knowing that there was a conceptual base for what was happening in her classroom was critical to Beth in finding a language to talk about what she and her students were doing together to develop a culture of inquiry.

In the following excerpt from an essay written in 2006 (Table 5.2), Beth explained the relationship between what she and other teachers know and some key concepts underlying an ethnographic perspective (Yeager, 2006).

In her statement, Beth makes visible the dynamic nature of classroom life in which members (students, teachers, others) co-construct ways of being, knowing and doing through their actions and interactions; in other words, through what they do, say, write, and graphically create together. As teachers know, this, like learning, does not happen in one moment (or one week at the beginning of the year). For this reason, we talk about classrooms as cultures-in-the-making or, in Beth's classes, as cultures-of-inquiry-in-the-making. She also makes visible that, as they do this, the class constructs a *language of the classroom* (Lin, 1993), or ways of talking and writing about what is happening that everyone in that group understands – what Agar (1994) would call a *languaculture*. Beth explains that the *processes* that become *practices*, or patterned ways of doing/acting, talking, writing, become part of students' *repertoires of actions*. When we talk in this chapter about the ways Beth supported students in extending their *communicative repertoires* for

Extending students' communicative repertoires **89**

TABLE 5.2 Beth's connections between what she knew as a teacher and key concepts underlying an ethnographic perspective

---

A central concept for our work [as a university/school research community using an Interactional Ethnographic perspective] was a view, from an anthropological perspective, of **classrooms as cultures** or dynamic **cultures-in-the-making**, in which members (teachers, students, families, others) construct together patterned ways of being, knowing, and doing through their actions and interactions. The concept of classrooms as cultures and the situated, local nature of classroom life (Dixon, Green & Frank, 1999) made sense to me. As a teacher, like many teachers, I had often noted that "this group" of students was not like "last year's group." I also knew that, even when we planned similar activities or instructional approaches as a grade-level team, my classroom would not look or sound exactly like the teacher's classroom next door…

I also knew that not only did I bring a history and ways of doing and teaching to the classroom, but that each student brought his or her own history from multiple school, family and community experiences. And I knew that we **constructed** a new collective history each year, drawing on all that we brought and on what we did together. No year or group was ever "exactly the same." It is not only teachers who understand this. Students understand it as well…

… I also later came to understand that, in and through our interactions together, shaping and re-shaping what we all brought to the community, we constructed **repertoires of actions** (such as the practices we talked about in our own **language of the classroom** and used for writing essays and doing investigations). These repertoires became potential resources for students to draw on to make sense of what was available to them in the classroom and to produce multiple kinds of texts (e.g., oral, written, visual) (Yeager, 2003). This again made sense to me since, as a teacher, I had come to recognize that lessons weren't isolated activities. What we did in one context, I hoped, drew on [and connected to] what we'd already done and what we already brought (and drew on as resource) and was connected to what we might do in the future [or **intertextual and intercontextual links within and across actions/events over time, with consequences for future actions/events**]

(Putney, Green, Dixon, Durán, & Yeager, 2000; Dixon, Green, & Brandts, 2005).

---

inquiry, we mean the ways particular inquiry-based ways of talking and writing (communicating) were constructed over time. They were constructed through what the teacher proposed, and what students and teacher did, talked about, and wrote about over time by drawing on these resources (as part of their evolving culture-of-inquiry-in-the-making).

In making these connections between what she knew as a teacher and key concepts from Interactional Ethnography, Beth was then able to take up particular ways of looking at her classroom and engage her students in doing the same. If, for example, as teachers know, learning cannot necessarily be seen in the moment (Bakhtin, 1986), then it makes sense *to look over time* (a key component of taking up an ethnographic perspective).

If a culture of inquiry is co-constructed in and through the actions and interactions of people (what they do, say, and write), then it makes sense to observe/look at what students and teachers (and other members of the class) do, say, or write (looking at what happens, at students' work, at what members construct together or individually, etc.). As Lizbeth said, she spent time "observing kids" in order to understand her own classroom community.

Beth began to call her own process of *stepping back* from what was known (Green, Skukauskaite & Baker, 2012; Heath, 1982), in order to examine how she was engaging students in developing a culture of inquiry within and across disciplines, a process of *zooming in and zooming out* (Yeager, 2003); that is, being in the moment of teaching and stepping back or zooming out to ask questions of what she was seeing, then zooming in again to take action on what she was learning. This reflexive process, grounded in ethnographic theory, also led to what she developed with students to support their own reflexive actions for exploring their own community, for exploring *self-as-learner* across time and disciplines, as well as what supported them in exploring inquiry processes within and across disciplines.

Guiding principle 2: Developing inquiry processes and practices with intention from day one

First days count. In order to develop a culture of inquiry that defined ordinary, everyday life in her classes, Beth was guided by this notion. First days of school are when teachers begin to frame, with students, intentionally or unintentionally, what kind of class culture will develop. Because she had explicit goals for students-as-learners and inquirers, an explicit view of teaching-learning relationships, and a conceptual foundation that grounded her logic-of-design, Beth wanted to *intentionally* and *purposefully* co-construct with students a particular kind of class culture. For this reason, she began developing cultural and reflexive processes that would potentially support a culture-of-inquiry-in-the-making from the first day of school.

We begin by sharing, briefly, one cycle of activity that Beth introduced on the first day of the school year(s), the Watermelon Problem, in which students recorded their thinking and shared it (in Spanish and/or English) with others in their linguistically diverse class(es) (across multiple years) (Castanheira, 2000; Yeager 2003). Figure 5.1 presents a graphic (re)presentation of the investigation as it happened on the first day of school in 1996, in which students tackled a common task (determine a final estimate of the cost of the individual watermelons given to their particular table group).

For this investigation, students were afforded opportunities to work in different configurations (as the whole class, within small table groups, as individuals, and as table groups reporting to the whole class) in and through which Beth introduced them to ways of thinking, acting, and communicating as mathematicians. These ways of working in different configurations shifted across the investigation, offering students opportunities to engage in reflexive processes of estimating, reporting, questioning, revising, and (re)reporting, while documenting their individual processes for arriving at their personal and group estimates. Her use of the watermelon, as a basis for the exploration of mathematical problem solving, created a process that made the walls of the classroom *permeable* ("insider" term), to support students in seeing mathematics as a resource beyond

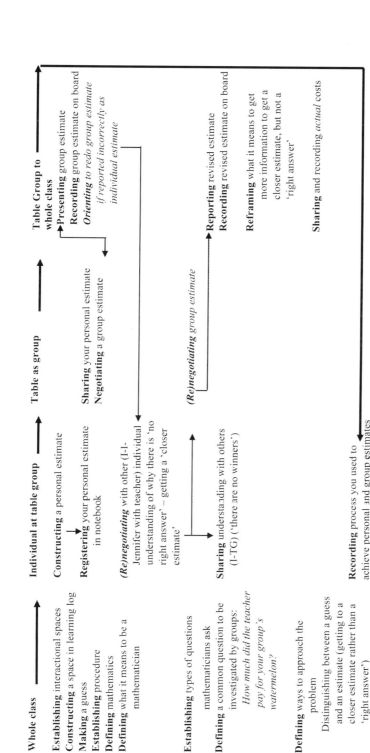

FIGURE 5.1 Watermelon problem across multiple individual/group configurations (1996).

the walls of the classroom. This process was one she used to design tasks across the school year across disciplines.

As part of this process, Beth used a kind of explicit *metadiscourse*[3], or talk *about* practice, throughout the investigation in order, for example, to provide a "big picture" rationale for engaging in particular processes or to support students in envisioning their work *as* mathematicians. At the conclusion of this first day's investigation, she used this metadiscourse to shift students' angle of vision from the actions they did as the actions of "students" to the actions of "mathematicians," saying, here shown in English (excerpt):

> *There are all kinds of ways that mathematicians get information…*
> *so you did a fantastic job for your very first day of school*
> *and your very first investigation as mathematicians…* (Yeager, 2003)

First days count, but in order for a culture of inquiry to develop, processes that are introduced once do not necessarily become ongoing practices unless they are repeated over time or are reformulated. The same practice is reformulated when it is used for a different purpose and/or in a different context (e.g., observing watermelons and later observing the actions of people as ethnographers or observing in order to paint self-portraits as artists). When the process is repeated over time, it becomes a *pattern of practice* and reflects the culture-of-inquiry-in-the-making that is being developed by the teacher *with* students. In Beth's class, the Watermelon Problem continued as a cycle of activity for 5 more days (including, among other pieces, graphing results), during which, evidence shows, processes were repeated over time, demonstrating a pattern of practice (Green, Castanheira, & Yeager, 2011). Those practices, as shown in Table 5.3, became part of what counted as the culture of inquiry in Beth's classes within and across multiple disciplines.

Equally important, these practices make visible how oral, written, and graphic texts were interrelated in this developing culture and, therefore, how they served as potential resources on which students could draw as part of their communicative repertoires, *if* they were aware of them – if what resources were available to be drawn on, when, where, under what conditions, and so on were made *present* for them as they used what we call their *ethnographic eyes* (Frank, 1999).

Guiding principle 3: Making inquiry practices, communicative resources *present*

Sometimes we assume that when students have been introduced to an action or practice, they will automatically know that this is the time and place to draw on a particular practice (inquiry or communicative) *as a resource*. Many teachers know that this is not necessarily the case. Sometimes students don't make the

Extending students' communicative repertoires 93

TABLE 5.3 Watermelon cycle of activity: Reformulating practices across days

Practice by day	1	2	3	4	5	6
Structuring practices						
Working in different interactional spaces	X	X	X	X	X	X
Using different languages	X	X	X	X	X	X
Literate practices						
Labeling, dating log and data entries	X	X	X	X	X	
Recording notes	X	X		X		
Talking to share information and ideas, reach consensus	X	X	X	X	X	X
Drawing on others as resource (e.g., peers)	X	X		X	X	X
Writing to learn (e.g., explaining a process)			X			
Reading data (e.g., reading a graph)	X			X	X	X
Reporting data in public space	X		X	X		X
Inquiry practices						
Observing for different purposes	X	X				
Gathering information from multiple sources	X	X				
Recording data	X	X	X			
Supporting with evidence	X	X		X		X
Determining a problem/question	X					
Investigating a problem	X		X	X	X	X
Estimating/predicting	X					
Interpreting data	X	X	X	X	X	X
Re-presenting data in different ways for different purposes (e.g., graphing, charting)		X	X	X	X	
Understanding different points of view	X	X	X	X	X	X

connection independently that something they learned in one context is now available to be used in this new context.

A third and critical principle guiding Beth in developing a culture of inquiry with her students is the notion of *making something present* (Kelly, 2006; Yeager, 2003) for students; bringing it forward, supporting students in making the connections between one context and another (*intercontextual* links [Floriani, 1993]). For Beth, this is another way in which *metadiscourse* about practice is critical in supporting students in becoming aware of when a resource is a resource, for what purposes, under what conditions, in what ways. Using metadiscourse to *make present* what resources are potentially needed and/or available at a particular time or in a particular context is essential in extending students' capacity for engaging in discipline-based processes and practices and their communicative repertoires for sharing understandings. It is sometimes as simple as saying, for example, "Remember when we did *x*? Well, now we're going to use that practice again, but in order to do *y*."

The following short transcript excerpt is from a cycle of activity (e.g., project, linked activities; Green & Meyer, 1991) as historians that built on practices initiated during the earlier Watermelon Investigation. Beth wanted to introduce named roles (leader, reporter, etc.) for a particular brainstorming activity. Students had taken up practices associated with these roles in other contexts, but they were now being *reformulated*, or framed to be used in new ways, in this new context, through the teacher's metadiscourse:

TEACHER

(Speaking Spanish) *(English translation)*

Desde el principio del año uds. han Since the beginning of the year you have
tomados unas acciones cuando taken some actions when
estén trabajando en grupos. you're working in groups.
Yo he visto personas escribiendo, I've seen people writing,
personas platicando, personas people talking, people
reportando, personas que son reporting, people who are
líderes o otras que no son líderes. leaders or others who aren't leaders.

(Teacher switches to English)

… today we're going to take up those
actions ahead of time and know what
everybody's going to do

As shown, students were accustomed to engaging in different kinds of actions (practices) as members of a group. While teacher and students discussed these various actions as practices (e.g., talking with each other, listening, reporting, working to include everyone), they were not, to this point, formally named and assigned in advance of group work – with everyone knowing "ahead of time" what "everybody's going to do." In this excerpt, the teacher makes present (makes visible and connects) many of these practices as they have been used in previous contexts. She then explicitly lets students know that "today" will be different and that students will take up those same practices in new ways. Making links in order to *make present* resources available to be drawn on (for talking, doing, writing) was integral to the ways in which Beth supported students in making connections over time and in drawing on their repertoires of action and communication.

Guiding principle 4: Constructing reflexive processes – Engaging students as ethnographers of their own community and of themselves-as-learners

With each of these guiding principles for constructing a culture of inquiry, Beth herself engaged in a reflexive process as she examined her teaching in the context of learning and then taught from that learning. At multiple points, she stepped back to purposefully interrogate her practice in the context of her conceptual understandings and of what she saw happening with students (orally, in writing, graphically, in action) and then reflexively and responsively made intentional decisions for action. At the same time, she supported students in developing these same reflexive processes and practices to examine their own community in the context of learning (to understand what was *available* to be learned – what counted, what was everyday practice, etc.) and then to examine self-as-learner in the context of what was available to be learned (not what was prescribed from outside, but what was actually available).

Beth's reflexive process is unfolded in Figure 5.2 and makes visible the interrelationships among the inquiry and reflexive processes and practices introduced on the first day and the reflexive process as it developed across the year both for individual students (self-as-learner) and for the community as a whole.

As previously discussed, the inter-relationships among oral, written, and graphic texts were also integral to the reflexive process as they were to understanding and taking up the work of different disciplines, and the developing culture of inquiry as a whole. It is also important to point out that family members were also part of this reflexive process across the year (e.g., student-led student/family/teacher conferences).

Process

As further indicated in Figure 5.2, as part of this reflexive process, students were given opportunities across the school year to actively examine their own class community and what was available to be learned (e.g., mapping the classroom spaces). They also had the opportunity to *inscribe*[4] their perspectives on themselves as learners to their parents as well as their teacher during conferences and/or presentations—completing strengths and stretches (described in column 2 of Figure 5.2) and individual and community reflexive essays (columns 4 and 5, Figure 5.2).

We share two essays from two different school years in which students, Arturo and Erica, inscribe themselves (Ivanic, 1994) and their communities in particular ways (Table 5.4) in their end-of-the-year Community Essays, making visible that this was an ongoing practice that Beth used to engage students. Each essay inscribes their particular set of community processes, making visible that the practice was situated within a particular developing languaculture in each year.

As inscribed in each essay, students drew on what they had learned as both a group (discussion) and as individuals in writing their end-of-year essays. While the essay content differed, each had a common goal, to identify what a new member might need to know on entering their particular class community (culture of inquiry) in their particular year. This essay further confirms the practices framed by Lizbeth in her essay that was selected for the introduction to this chapter. As indicated in Figure 5.2, this process involved Beth in discussing with students, before writing began, what they had previously uncovered about the community, as part of her process of creating a basis for making present available intertextual and intercontextual resources in each year. The students then made choices about what they wrote as individuals, including what language they would write in (English or Spanish). As indicated in Lizbeth's, as well as Arturo's, and Erica's essays shown in Table 5.4 below, what was inscribed reflected the different languacultural processes and practices constructed across years.

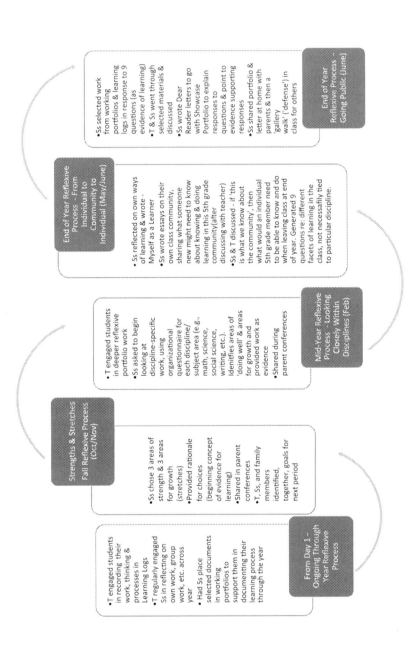

FIGURE 5.2 Students as ethnographers of their class community and self-as-learner: Reflexive process.

TABLE 5.4 Students-as-ethnographers inscribing what counts as being a community member

Arturo (1994–1995)	Lirica (1996–1997)
In our Tower community, we have our own language as well as the languages we bring from outside (like Spanish and English) which helped us make our own language. So, for example, someone that is not from our classroom community would not understand what insider, outsider, think twice, notetaking/notemaking, literature log and learning log mean. If Ms. Yeager says we are going to "make a sandwich," the people from another class or room would think that we were going to make a sandwich to eat. Of course, we aren't, but that is part of our common language. To be an insider, which means a person from the class, you also need to know our Bill of Rights and Responsibilities which was made by the members of the Tower community. And if Ms. Yeager said, "Leave your H.R.L. on your desk," people would not understand unless someone from the Tower community told him/her and even if we told him/her that H.R.L. stands for "Home Reading Log," they still would not understand what it is and what you write in it. If we told a new student, "It's time for SSL and ESL," he would not understand. These words are all part of the common Tower community language and if someone new were to come in, we would have to explain how we got them and what they mean. We also would tell them that we got this language by reports, information, investigations, and what we do and learn in our Tower community.	I'm an ethnographer in the Tower. An ethnographer means that you have a folder where it says Notetaking/Notemaking. In notetaking, you write what the class is doing and how we are behaving. Then on the right side, the notemaking side, you write what you think your notes mean. That is how you are an ethnographer in the Tower. You might be an ethnographer to know how everybody's doing their work. Ethnography helps me to know about the class. That is how I know how the class works. What I think about the Tower is that we are all ethnographers, because each week different groups meet with Ms. Yeager and she explains to us how we have to do it. We all work in groups. I think it's good to have table groups as ethnographers, because that's how we know and remember that day. It's really fun to be an ethnographer, because you sometimes get to use a camera. You get a folder for one week. We divided the pictures evenly so that we all could take the same amount of pictures. I took pictures of just for fun things, like when we were doing math with pattern blocks. We also take notes on what we are doing in the class. I think it's so fun to be an ethnographer. You get to do all the fun things. In the Tower we work in groups and we have to have evidence for whatever we write, because people would ask you, "What is your evidence?" We also work sometimes in pairs, like on the Island History Project. Sometimes we work with different people or alone. This year I learned that ethnographers have evidence for what they say, for their point of view. If there were a new student in the Tower, he/she would have to know that we are ethnographers. We try, we all do our jobs. That's what we all have to do, what we are supposed to do, be students. When we are big, we could come to Ms. Yeager and ask her if she still has the ethnographer book and we can still remember what happened. Our children or grandchildren could be ethnographers like we were in the 5th grade. So that's what I have to tell you about how we are ethnographers in the Tower. Believe me, we have fun. Sometimes we do not have fun, because we talk a lot, but most of the time it is fun. We do many different things in the class. That's what an ethnographer is and how our Class of 1997 is. I will use all I have learned this year in the Tower. To be in the Tower community means that you participate in everything, put effort into what you do, and have fun by learning in the Tower.

Furthermore, as Arturo and Erica show, the metadiscourse constructed by the teacher with students reflected a common set of practices, ones that focused them on understanding, as well as communicating to others, ways of being a student in this *culture of inquiry*. In addition, Erica inscribed herself in a particular way, taking up, like Lizbeth, an academic identity as an ethnographer. Both Arturo and Erica share what outsiders need to know, understand, and do to participate as students in the class. Both also frame the concept of community that was a central part of their communicative repertoires constructed over time in the class.

Evidence of learning: The Dear Reader Letter

As shown in the Reflexive Process (Figure 5.2), the Community Essay examining the community and what was available to be taken up by the group, was one of three reflexive texts that students wrote at the end of the year. The other two were a Myself as a Learner piece, asking students to think about themselves holistically as a learner. The third was the Dear Reader Letter that would accompany a Showcase Portfolio of work selected by students. This letter makes visible how Beth engaged students in articulating and communicating with readers where they would find evidence of particular forms of learning. In their Dear Reader Letter, students were required to provide a rationale for their selection of a particular activity, process or text that they identified as evidence of learning. The questions that they addressed, as indicated in Figure 5.2 (column 4), were co-generated by students with Beth, prior to their reflexively revisiting their *Working Portfolios* and *Learning Logs* to make selections that responded to the questions.

The process leading to the generation of nine questions was based on an *if... then...* logic. This logic engaged students in the following way of thinking about their essays: *if*, based on the community essays you wrote, a member needs to know, understand and do x, y, and/or z to be a member of our community, *then* what can you personally, as a 5th-grader, know as you leave the 5th grade? This process led students to seek, and then present, sources of evidence in their Dear Reader letters, of what they were able to do as they were leaving the 5th grade. As students completed their selection process and began to draft their letters, they conferenced individually with Beth to discuss their selections and their rationales for choosing them as evidence for their responses to the nine questions, to support them in writing the letters, given that readers would include family members and others. Thus, in this end-of-year process, they had other opportunities to talk with the teacher and colleagues during the writing process as well in order to articulate their thoughts both orally and in writing in a recursive fashion to different audiences.

Table 5.5 provides an example of how Erica took up this process, in her Dear Reader Letter. We selected her introduction and her responses to three of the nine questions from her letter to provide illustrative evidence of how Erica inscribed sources of evidence about where she demonstrated her developing capacity to engage in inquiry and communicative processes and practices across disciplines in this class.

TABLE 5.5 Erica's end-of-year Dear Reader Letter for Showcase Portfolio (excerpt – 3/9 responses)

Dear Reader,
My name is Erica U. I'm going to tell you about my Showcase Portfolio. Our class in the Tower did nine questions about what we should be able to do in fifth grade. We had to look for good work and explain why we chose that and why it is our evidence. Where we had to look was in our portfolio where we have part of our work that we have done this year in the Tower community and in our logs. The most work we have in our portfolios are mostly projects like the colony, Spaghetti dinner and other projects that we have done. When we do our projects, we sometimes work in groups of 2 or 5 or sometimes alone, but we work more in groups of 4 or 5, with our table groups. So now I'm going to talk with you about my Showcase Portfolio.

Can I conduct an investigation?
Yes, I can. I chose the Spaghetti Dinner Investigation, because I did not know how to do a budget before, but now I do know how to do them. In this investigation, some girls and boys went to stores to see how much things cost. With my group, I found out which store had the cheapest spaghetti, salad, garlic, and other things. I had to find out the income, the prices, the profit and other things. We worked in table groups. We had to find out how many people were coming and how much food we should get. Now I know how to make a budget and how to work to get everything ready. That is why I chose my Spaghetti Dinner for an investigation.

Can I analyze a process and understand my own thinking and way of learning?
Yes, I can. I chose my problem of the week called "Four Times as Big," because I had to figure out from a little group of four squares how to make it four times bigger than it was, like $4 \times 4 = 16$. In that I had to use tables and drawings to figure it out. Then on Friday, after recess, we shared our ways of doing the problem and we all got different answers and different ways of doing it and we all had to analyze all of the class' work. I also had to write and explain how I solved this problem. That is what I chose for analyzing a process.

Can I write clearly, effectively and thoughtfully to communicate an idea?
I chose my Tolerance essay, because I explained my ideas and wrote what I thought about my ideas clearly. I really thought about it. We read them to a partner.
When we went to the Museum of Tolerance, we had to listen carefully. I had ideas of how it looked, how they (the children in a camp, information added) felt back then in that time. I made my ideas and thought about how I was going to write them in order. That is what I chose for writing clearly.

Although this excerpt does not reflect all nine questions, these three excerpts and the introduction to her Dear Reader letter, make visible that Erica had developed a deep understanding of how to communicate what she learned, when, how and in what ways with whom. Thus, in these three questions, Erica demonstrates her capacity for constructing a detailed rationale for choosing a particular project (cycle of activity) to support her response to a particular question. Although not the full scope of her Dear Reader letter, these excerpts make visible her capacity to identify processes/practices associated with particular disciplinary actions and to communicate, clearly and in depth, what she learned through being a member of this 5th-grade class. These excerpts from Erica's letter further confirm her awareness of the processes and practices that she articulated in her Community Essay.

Evidence of learning: Beyond Erica, Lizbeth, and Arturo

Erica was not alone in responding to the Dear Reader questions constructed by students and teacher each year in the ways she did (and in selecting pieces of evidence to support her responses) or in the ways in which she, like Arturo and Lizbeth, wrote her Community Essay. Each year, Beth examined students' written work both formally (e.g., Yeager, 1999; Yeager, 2001; Yeager, 2003) and informally. Between 1994–95 and 1999–2000, for example, Beth found that, while specific content and choices in Dear Reader letters differed, most students made nine selections of appropriate work samples, and explained their selections (provided a rationale), supporting their responses with evidence (in Spanish or English). While the level of sophistication of language and capacity for conceptualizing their rationales varied across a continuum, all students, whether school-defined (systemically defined) as "learning challenged," as "at risk," or with other systemic characterizations, or those characterized as "achieving" by systemic measures, engaged in the reflexive process and took up the same practices as Erica did in constructing their Dear Reader letters. The same is true of Community Essays written across multiple years.

Members of our research community have written both nationally and internationally from a strength-based perspective about (and documented success for) students in Beth's classes drawing on Community essays, Dear Reader letters, and Beth's approach to constructing a culture-of-inquiry. They have also written about this approach in relation to school-defined "special needs" students and inclusive practices (e.g., Castanheira, Green, & Yeager, 2009) and linguistically diverse students (e.g., Yeager & Green, 2008), as well as in relation to disciplinary work and academic identities (e.g., Brilliant-Mills, 1993; Castanheira, Green, Dixon & Yeager, 2007; Floriani, 1993; Heras, 1993; Hill-Bonnet, Green, Yeager, & Reid, 2012), students as ethnographers (Yeager et al., 1998), and teaching for social justice (e.g., Yeager, Pattenaude, Fránquiz, & Jennings, 1999).

From our perspective, it is not that Beth's approach – for example, taking up an ethnographic perspective with students as resource, co-constructing a practice-based culture-of-inquiry over time, supporting students in engaging in a responsive/reflexive process – is particularly focused on diverse students. It is that this approach enabled Beth, students, and external researchers to ask "who can say or do what, where, when, how, for what purposes, under what conditions, with what potential consequences and outcomes" (Santa Barbara Classroom Discourse Group, 1992), a set of questions that make visible issues of equity of access to deeper learning opportunities for diverse students. What we have found is that students in Beth's classes across school-defined academic "achievement" and linguistic levels took up particular kinds of academic identities as ethnographers, historians, anthropologists, and students, from particular angles of vision (e.g., Yeager, 2003). They wrote and talked in complex ways about complex issues (e.g., supporting with evidence, defending evidence, using the language of historical and anthropological inquiry) *as* members of academic disciplines and experts on their data or topic. This suggests that what students were accomplishing challenged the competence/incompetence model for assessing and talking about what it means to be a "successful" student in the context of the work that is accomplished in the complexity of everyday classroom life.

An interesting postscript to what has been discussed in this chapter is that Beth and colleagues (e.g., Córdova, 2008; Córdova & Balcerzak, 2015; Hirsch-Dubin & Puglisi, 2011; Yeager & Córdova, 2009; Yeager, Córdova, Puglisi, & Hirsch-Dubin, 2018) currently use principles guiding the construction of a culture of inquiry and an ethnographic perspective in work with administrators and classroom teachers exploring their instructional design and practices with their own linguistically, academically, culturally, and socially diverse students. One 2nd-grade teacher in a dual language program has reported, "I have gained more confidence in leading students through their own educational inquiries and this has helped me take on more of a role of a facilitator. This has allowed my students to obtain a bigger sense of ownership and become more active participants in their own learning…Through our partnership, my students have developed interdisciplinary actions which have allowed them to make connections and develop their identities not only as learners, but as authors, artists, creators, mathematicians, scientists, and investigators."[5]

A closing and an opening

In this chapter, we shared four principles that guided Beth, the teacher-ethnographer of 5th- and 6th-grade bilingual classes, in developing a culture of inquiry with her linguistically, culturally, socially and academically diverse students:

- Developing a conceptual foundation for design and decision making;
- Developing inquiry processes and practices from day one;
- Making inquiry processes and practices and communicative resources *present*;
- Constructing reflexive processes – engaging students as ethnographers of their own community and of themselves-as-learners.

As part of these principles, we made visible the ways in which teachers can use a metadiscourse *about* practice, about everyday classroom life and a developing culture-of-inquiry-in-the-making. In sharing what these four principles looked and sounded like in action, we made visible what was made present to students through opportunities for learning processes/practices within and across disciplines in this culture of inquiry model constructed by Beth.

We made visible, in particular, the potential for teachers in Pre-K-12 facing a variety of challenges, including working within and across multiple disciplines, of finding a lens for both themselves and their students through which they can intentionally engage in reflexive practices from within a culture of inquiry. In doing this themselves, along with administrators, and supporting their students in doing the same, they can develop a common language (Edwards & Mercer, 1987) for talking from evidence about what students, particularly diverse students, *can* do. In presenting classroom life from participants' points of view and by unfolding guiding principles of practice, we sought to lay a foundation for readers to explore ways of understanding classroom life, from within a culture of inquiry, as well as ways of providing evidence of what counts as learning, and what learnings count in such communities (Heap, 1991,1995).

Notes

1 "Ethnographer" as it's used here is based on a particular way of looking taken up in these classes, to be further explained in subsequent sections of this chapter.
2 "Tower" was the name given to a large second floor classroom space, without a room number, beneath a bell tower in this school.
3 Metadiscourse is language used to talk *about* practice (i.e., talk about actions and language use). This idea supports a view of teacher *discourse* (ways of talking), rather than instances of teacher "talk", as central to making historical connections, linking texts, making available what it is students need to bring and use to make sense of the evolving text of classroom life. Teachers make discursive choices *with* students, to contextualize practices, while making the connections necessary for students to make sense of disciplinary work and reflexive processes (Yeager & Córdova, 2009).
4 Inscribe as it's used here draws on Ivanic (1994) and on our own work to mean the ways in which writers *write themselves, their lived experience, identities, and worlds into their texts*. We argue that students inscribe worlds, *their* worlds, based on their lived and/or observed experiences and understandings (they inscribe based on what's been available to them to be understood and learned). Therefore, written texts, as products, become potential sources of evidence about what students have experienced or what was made available to them over time.
5 This excerpt was taken from a teacher's letter to Beth Yeager, received in April 2016.

References

Agar, M. (1994). *Language shock: Understanding the culture of conversation*. New York: William Morrow.
Bakhtin, M. M. (1986). The problem of speech genres. In C. Emerson & M. Holmquist (Eds.), *Speech genres and other late essays* (pp. 60–102). Austin, TX: University of Texas Press.
Brilliant-Mills, H. (1993). Becoming a mathematician: Building a situated definition of mathematics. *Linguistics and Education 5*(3–4), 301–334.
Calkins, L. (1990). *Living between the lines*. Portsmouth, NH: Heinemann.
Castanheira, M. (2000). *Situating learning within collective possibilities: Examining the discursive construction of opportunities for learning in the classroom* (Unpublished doctoral dissertation). University of California, Santa Barbara.
Castanheira, M., Crawford, T., Dixon, C., & Green, J. (2001). Interactional ethnography: An approach to studying the social construction of literate practices. *Linguistics and Education, 11*(4), 353–400.
Castanheira, M. L., Green, J., Dixon, C., & Yeager, B. (2007). (Re)Formulating identities in the face of fluid modernity: An Interactional Ethnographic approach. *International Journal of Education Research, 46*(3–4), 172–189.
Castanheira, M. L., Green, J.L., & Yeager, E. (2009). Investigating inclusive practices: An interactional ethnographic approach. In K. Kumpulainen & M. César (Eds.), *Investigating classrooms: Methodologies in action* (pp. 235–268). Rotterdam, The Netherlands: Sense Publishers.

Cochran-Smith, M., & Lytle, S. L. (2009). *Inquiry as stance: Practitioner research for the next generation.* New York: Teachers College Press.

Córdova, R. A. (2008). Writing and painting our lives into being: School, home, and the larger community as transformative spaces for learning. *Language Arts, 86*(1), 18–27.

Córdova, R. A. & Balcerzak, P. (2015). Co-constructing cultural landscapes for disciplinary learning in and out of school: The next generation science standards and learning progressions in action. *Cultural Studies of Science Education, 4*(10). Retrieved from https://www.academia.edu/19928287/Co-constructing_cultural_landscapes_for_disciplinary_learning_in_and_out_of_school_the_next_generation_science_standards_and_learning_progressions_in_action on 2/17/19.

Dixon, C., Green, J., & Brandts, L. (2005). Studying the discursive construction of texts in classrooms through Interactional Ethnography. In R. Beach, J. Green, M. Kamil, & T. Shanahan (Eds.), *Multidisciplinary perspectives on literacy research* (pp. 349–390). Cresskill, NJ: Hampton Press/National Conference for Research in Language and Literacy.

Dixon, C., Green, J., & Frank, C. (1999). Classrooms as cultures: Understanding the constructed nature of life in classrooms. *Primary Voices K-6, 7*(3), 4–8.

Edwards, D. & Mercer, N. (1987). *Common knowledge.* New York: Methuen.

Floriani, A. (1993). Negotiating what counts: Roles and relationships, texts and contexts, content and meaning. *Linguistics and Education 5*(3–4), 241–274.

Frank, C. (1999). *Ethnographic eyes: A teacher's guide to classroom observations.* Portsmouth, NH: Heinemann.

Freire, P. (2000). *Pedagogy of the oppressed.* 30th Anniversary Edition. New York: Bloomsbury Academic. (Original work published in English 1970)

Green, J. & Bloome, D. (1997). Ethnography and ethnographers of and in education: A situated perspective. In J. Flood, S. B. Heath, & D. Lapp (Eds.), *Handbook for literacy educators: Research in the communicative and visual arts* (pp. 181–202). New York: Macmillan.

Green, J., Castanheira, M. L., & Yeager, B. (2011). Researching the opportunities for learning for students with learning difficulties in classrooms: An ethnographic perspective. In C. Wyatt-Smith, J. Elkins, & S. Gunn (Eds.), *Multiple perspectives on difficulties in learning literacy and numeracy* (pp. 49–90). Dordrecht, The Netherlands: Springer.

Green, J. & Meyer, L. (1991). The embeddedness of reading in classroom life: Reading as a situated process. In C. Baker & A. Luke (Eds.), *Towards a critical sociology of reading pedagogy* (pp. 141–160). Philadelphia, PA: John Benjamins.

Green, J., Skukauskaite, A., & Baker, W. D. (2012). Ethnography as epistemology. In J. Arthur, M. I. Waring, R. Coe & L. V. Hedges (Eds.), *Research methods and methodologies in education* (pp. 309–321). London: Sage Publishers.

Heap, J. L. (1991). A situated perspective on what counts as reading. In C. Baker & A. Luke (Eds.), *Towards a critical sociology of reading pedagogy* (pp. 103–139). Philadelphia, PA: John Benjamins.

Heap, J. L. (1995). The status of claims in "qualitative" educational research. *Curriculum Inquiry, 25*(3), 271–292.

Heath, S. B. (1982). Ethnography in education: Defining the essentials. In P. Gillmore & A. A. Glatthorn (Eds.), *Children in and out of school: Ethnography and education* (pp. 35–55). Washington, DC: Center for Applied Linguistics.

Heras, A. (1993). The construction of understanding in a sixth-grade bilingual classroom. *Linguistics and Education 5*(3–4), 275–300.

Hill-Bonnet, L., Green, J. L., Yeager, B. & Reid, J. (2012). Exploring dialogic opportunities for learning and (re)negotiating selves: An ethnographic telling case of learning to be social scientists. In M. B. Ligorio & M. César (Eds.), *Interplays between dialogical learning and dialogical self* (pp. 319–360). Charlotte, NC: Information Age Publishing.

Hirsch-Dubin, F. & Puglisi, J. (2011, April). *Ethnomathematics at a K-8 public school: Making mathematics accessible to diverse populations*. Paper presentation to the Annual Meeting of the American Educational Research Association (AERA), New Orleans, LA.

Ivanic, R. (1994). I is for interpersonal: Discoursal construction of writers identities and the teaching of writing. *Linguistics & Education, 6*, 3–15.

Kelly, G. J. (2006). Epistemology and educational research. In J. Green, G. Camilli, & P. Elmore (Eds.), *Handbook of complementary methods in education research* (pp. 33–55). Mahwah, NJ: Lawrence Erlbaum.

Lin, L. (1993). Language of and in the classroom: Constructing the patterns of social life. *Linguistics and Education 5*(3 & 4), 367–409.

Putney, L., Green, J., Dixon, C., Durán, R., & Yeager, B. (2000). Consequential progressions: Exploring collective-individual development in a bilingual classroom. In C. Lee & P. Smagorinsky (Eds.), *Vygotskian perspectives on literacy research* (pp. 86–126). Cambridge, UK: Cambridge University Press.

Santa Barbara Classroom Discourse Group (1992). Do you see what we see? The referential and intertextual nature of classroom life. *Journal of Classroom Interaction, 27*(2), 29–36.

Tuyay, S., Jennings, L., & Dixon, C. (1995). Classroom discourse and opportunities to learn: An ethnographic study of knowledge construction in a bilingual third grade classroom. *Discourse Processes, 19*(1), 75–110.

Yeager, B. (1999). Constructing a community of inquirers. *Primary Voices, 7*(3), 37–52.

Yeager, B. (2001, December). *Talking and writing about complex ideas in a linguistically diverse setting: Inscribing academic identities – what is possible?* Report of research submitted on completion of requirements for the National Council of Teachers of English (NCTE) Teacher Researcher Grant. Champaign-Urbana, Illinois.

Yeager, B. (2006). Teacher as researcher/Researcher as teacher: Multiple angles of vision for studying learning in the context of teaching. *Language Arts Journal of Michigan, 22*(1), 26–33.

Yeager, E. (2003). *"I am a Historian": Examining the discursive construction of locally situated academic identities in linguistically diverse settings* (Unpublished doctoral dissertation). University of California, Santa Barbara.

Yeager, E. & Córdova, R.A. (2009). How knowledge counts: Talking family knowledge and lived experience into being as resource for academic action. In M. L. Dantas & P. Manyak (Eds.), *Home-School connections in a multicultural society: Learning from and with culturally and linguistically diverse families* (pp. 218–236). New York: Taylor and Francis.

Yeager, B., Córdova, R.A., Puglisi, J. & Hirsch-Dubin, F. (2018, April). *Discursively entering teachers into a new STEAM school design process*. Paper presentation to the Annual Meeting of the American Educational Research Association (AERA), New York.

Yeager, B., Floriani, A., & Green, J. (1998). Learning to see learning in the classroom: Developing an ethnographic perspective. In A. Egan-Robertson & D. Bloome (Eds.), *Students as researchers of culture and language in their own communities* (pp. 115–139). Cresskill, NJ: Hampton Press.

Yeager, B. & Green, J. (2008). We have our own language as well as the languages we bring: Constructing opportunities for learning through a language *of* the classroom. In J. Scott, D. Straker, & L. Katz (Eds.), *Affirming students' right to their own language: Bridging language policies and pedagogical practices* (pp. 153–175). New York: Routledge with National Council of Teachers of English.

Yeager, B., Pattenaude, I., Fránquiz, M., & Jennings, L. (1999). Rights, respect and responsibility: Toward a theory of action in two bilingual classrooms. In J. Robertson (Ed.), *Teaching for a tolerant world* (pp. 196–218). Champaign-Urbana, IL: National Council of Teachers of English.

6
TRANSFORMING CLASSROOM DISCOURSE AS A RESOURCE FOR LEARNING

Adapting interactional ethnography for teaching and learning

W. Douglas Baker

Summary

This chapter shows how an interdisciplinary team of instructors (a professor of literature and a professor of English education) transformed classroom talk from a graduate class into a resource for constructing interpretive principles and practices of literary texts and generated deeper learning opportunities for the students, most of them practicing classroom teachers. By integrating an Interactional Ethnographic perspective, the instructors examined selected classroom discourse and engaged students in reflexive processes to explore classroom interactions and recognize how the experiences may lead them to (re)think and expand repertoires for interpreting and teaching literature.

Introduction

For instructors teaching higher education or secondary school students how to interpret literary texts, one of the challenges is making visible to students interpretative principles and practices through discursive strategies (i.e., "the spoken words that…teachers [use] during classroom conversations to explore critical issues related to teaching (Rex & Schiller, 2009)," cited in Vetter, Schieble, & Meacham, 2018, p. 256). By "practices" and discursive strategies I refer to actions situated within particular sociocultural contexts that become norms for a group (e.g., students and teachers in classrooms) and shape and are shaped by the group's discourse (Bloome, Carter, Christian, Otto, & Shuart-Faris, 2005; Gee & Green, 1998; Street, 2016). Teachers of literature have no agreed upon set of interpretative principles or practices, yet they construct with students over time what *counts* as interpretation and learning (cf. Olsen, 2018). For example, some instructors who focus on training teachers of literature as preparation for language arts instruction incorporate the metaphor of "lenses," ostensibly reflecting literary theories intended to encourage students to recognize particular interpretative assumptions and practices (e.g., a "feminist lens") (Appleman, 2009; Wilson, 2014).

Teachers' disciplinary understandings, experiences and pedagogical knowledge shape classroom practices and learning opportunities (Carney & Indrisano, 2013), especially because teachers often teach how they were taught (Marshall & Smith, 1997). Therefore, teachers' experiences with literary texts, including classroom discourse, inform how students learn to interpret literature and how they recognize and acknowledge interpretative norms. For example, during my undergraduate literature courses, professors drew on New Criticism, an interpretative tradition focused explicitly on the text, not situated within cultural, political, or authorial contexts (cf. Francis, 2008). Consequently, as a high school teacher, I focused on New Critic principles and introduced students to other theories only as I experienced them later.

Elisabeth Däumer, a colleague and a professor of literature, and I, a professor of English education, began to explore through interdisciplinary conversations how teachers learn to interpret texts and the apparent consequences of their experiences for their students, and how teachers might learn to build on experiences to deepen their knowledge and repertoires. Although we are situated within the Department of English Language and Literature and we prepare teachers, we do so in courses centered on our disciplines. Elisabeth provides opportunities for students to read literary texts and explore interpretive traditions; I guide students to design literature curricula for students. In part because of disciplinary backgrounds, we discovered limits to how certain we could be about selected phenomena of each other's area of expertise, especially when concepts appeared similar (Baker & Green, 2007). For example, based on our disciplinary traditions we defined "theory" and "critical theory" differently; we debated the use of "lenses" as a metaphorical, interpretative tool; and what constituted research for each of us differed. For Elisabeth, closely reading literary texts, constructing, and representing arguments supported by interpretative principles and cultural perspectives reflected her inquiry approach; for me, adapting an ethnographic perspective and analyzing classroom discourse were features of my research – and integral to my teaching. However, we learned our disciplinary differences could become resources for learning, for us and for our students (Baker & Däumer, 2015a).

Our conversations led us to create an interdisciplinary, team-taught graduate course to examine literary texts with practicing teachers (who were seeking a graduate degree) and to explore how the experiences influenced their knowledge of interpretative principles and practices and, consequently, how they communicate principles and practices to their students. The logic of our inquiry, and increasing reflexivity of the process, had consequences for how we (re)designed the course and for deeper learning opportunities we afforded the teachers, including how they enhanced their communicative competence of describing interpretative approaches to literary texts. By adapting an ethnographic perspective

(Green & Bloome, 1997) of classroom discourse and discursive strategies, we observed how we constructed interpretative principles and practices with students and how the interactions between us modeled interdisciplinary conversations as resources for students' deeper learning.

Focus of the chapter

For teachers of literature, classroom interactions ostensibly lead to interpretations of texts; however, the conversations typically rely on participants' memory of texts read before class, or of previous discussions and interpretative approaches. Since we planned to work with graduate students, I suggested we record classroom talk, transcribe, examine and archive interactions throughout the semester; therefore, we would not rely on memory. As I will show, the records of classroom talk led us to better understand what we were collectively accomplishing. I recorded classroom talk and transcribed it into written text, which provided a record of the interactions and allowed me to map events of a class meeting. An *event* is conceptually linked with social practices, emphasizing what is accomplished through discursive interactions (Bloome et al., 2005; Green & Meyer, 1991). In other words, transcripts provided physical texts as a resource to Elisabeth and me for deepening our understanding of selected classroom interactions and for students to observe, acknowledge, and recognize significance connections among texts, or intertextual links (Bloome et al., 2005), and for what they were learning (cf. McCann, 2014).

As I will show, transforming selected classroom discourse into written texts allowed us to observe how we were constructing discipline-based principles of interpreting literary texts with the students. Further, I describe how, by adapting an Interactional Ethnographic perspective (Castanheira, Crawford, Dixon, & Green, 2001), we created a metadiscourse for us to develop ways of talking or negotiating interdisciplinary discussions and understandings (Baker & Däumer, 2015b). An Interactional Ethnographic perspective uses principles of ethnography to examine discursive interactions (e.g., seeking an "insider's" point of view, triangulating evidence to support claims, and engaging in abductive thinking); therefore, for example, we strived to understand students' perspectives through analysis of their discourse. By metadiscourse, I refer to "how we use language out of consideration for our readers or hearers based on our estimation of how best we can help them process and comprehend what we are saying" (Hyland, 2017, p. 17; cf. Tang, 2017). Elisabeth and I sought to make visible links among our disciplinary discourses, personal experiences, and shared classroom practices; the language and principles of Interactional Ethnography (IE) assisted us in our efforts.

Our goals for the course included guiding students to enhance their communicative competence as teachers of literary texts. That is, we provided students with learning opportunities to reflect on past literary practices, examine classroom interpretative events, and become more reflexive as readers and as teachers of literary texts. In the process, as I will show, students deepened their understanding of how literary principles and practices are constructed through discursive strategies and engaged others (i.e., their peers and students) in demonstrating linguistic and discursive knowledge (Gumperz, 1997; Hymes, 1972), especially in terms of interpreting literature (Blau, 2014).

In particular, I address the following questions:

- How might observing, analyzing, and tracing discursive interactions guide teachers to engage with students as inquirers in order to provide opportunities for deeper learning and to enhance teachers' and students' capacity to develop communicative competence as interpreters of literary texts?
- How might interdisciplinary conversations between teachers, especially ones based on analysis of classroom discourse, lead to deeper understanding of classroom interactions and disciplinary perspectives for teachers and their students?

The course: An interdisciplinary approach to shaping opportunities for learning

As an interdisciplinary team, Elisabeth and I designed the graduate course, "Reading, Interpreting, and Responding to Literary Texts," for practicing teachers interested in teaching literature and earning a Master's degree. The 15-week class met once a week for 3 hours, and most of the 13 students (nine of them) were secondary school teachers (grades 6–12). Since we would be interacting across grade levels and disciplines, we recognized the need to develop a shared language, a metadiscourse, particularly because classroom language shapes and is shaped by teacher and students' interactions over time; in turn, the interactions expand "the concept of meaning in context to explore how within and across the face-to-face and moment-by-moment interactions, teachers and students construct a language of the classroom" (Rex & Green, 2008, p. 575).

The metadiscourse would serve as a language to help us observe disciplinary perspectives and differences and to infer theoretical assumptions when interpreting literary texts (e.g., raising a series of questions, such as, what counts as an interpretation to a particular group or person?). Central to this perspective is our understanding of disciplines, as well as classrooms, as *languacultures* (Agar, 1994; Baker & Däumer, 2015a), which refers to how members of a group interweave cultural assumptions or norms and language in particular contexts, or "language-in-use." Languaculture, coined by anthropologist Michael Agar (1994), implies that a language and culture cannot be separated; language is imbued with culture, a conceptual system constantly being constructed. From this perspective, members of a social group interact and generate local norms through discursive strategies, particularly for recognizing what *counts* to the group as knowledge. Thus, through social and literate practices over time, participants negotiate what phenomena are important, how knowledge of objects or concepts or intertextual links are constructed, defined, recognized, acknowledged, and interactionally accomplished as significant to members (Bloome et al., 2005, pp. 40–41).

Of course, between groups there will be moments of misunderstanding or confusion. Here, Agar (1994) provides another useful concept, "rich points," or "moments when something happens [between people of different cultures] and participants suddenly 'don't know what's going on' between them," or are confused (p. 106). So, if disciplines and classrooms can be viewed as languacultures, members of different disciplines or classrooms may be confused at times during interactional moments, generating potential "rich points," which may be ignored or examined. However, even within a classroom, teachers and students may observe rich points, particularly since teachers and students may, of course, have very different understandings of phenomena, and the rich points may become resources for participants to acknowledge and discuss and build deeper understandings of a phenomenon.

For example, during the first 2 weeks of the course one of the students, Denise, described in a reflective essay contextual factors she required when she was younger to become engaged as a reader: freedom to choose texts on topics of interest, adult readers as models, and authentic experiences for reading. However, during the first class meetings, she admonished her secondary school students for their lack of motivation as readers, their occasional attendance, and apparent disrespect for her. Elisabeth and I, after analyzing her written assignment and classroom talk, observed a "rich point" between Denise and her students: Denise acknowledged her needs as a younger reader for particular contexts; yet, she had not offered her students similar opportunities. That apparent disconnect would prove worth exploring, as I describe later.

Recording and transforming verbal text to a transcript, proved vital to recognizing potential rich points, particularly since classroom conversations occur moment-by-moment in "real" time and may be difficult to recall in detail. Therefore, our decision to analyze classroom discourse provided the students and us with opportunities to (re)examine interactions, (re)design curricula, and enhance our collective reflexivity (cf. Rex & Schiller, 2009). More specifically, recording, transcribing, and analyzing discursive interactions in the classroom provided resources to deepen students' learning, and ours, often reshaping what we thought we understood. Interactional Ethnography (IE) became integral to our instruction and how we observed referential links, developed evidence for analytic claims, and (re)designed curricula based on new information or patterns uncovered.

Adapting an interactional ethnographic perspective

Ethnography can be viewed as epistemology, a way of coming to understand phenomena (Anderson-Levitt, 2006), guiding a (teacher) researcher to develop a "logic-in-use," one reliant on particular principles of operation (Green, Skukauskaite, & Baker, 2012). IE recognizes classroom discourse as a basis for discursive interactions and for understanding what counts to members of a classroom as local, social, and literate practices and disciplinary knowledge (Kelly, Luke, & Green, 2008). Adapting an Interactional Ethnographic perspective for observing and analyzing classroom interactions led us to engage in principled actions similar to those of ethnographers of education, who are often external to classrooms and other educational settings (Bloome, Castanheira, Leung, & Rowsell, 2018): describing what we observed; avoiding evaluation in the moment – a challenge because teachers are always assessing students' responses; raising questions to clarify what we think we observed or heard; and gathering multiple perspectives or iterations of observations to support claims we made.

Through my earlier research in an intergenerational (grades 9–12) studio art class (Baker, 2001; Baker, Green, & Skukauskaite, 2008), I recognized the potential of using principles and language of ethnography to observe and listen to a teacher and students, as I strived to get close to an "insider's" perspective of the class, particularly for understanding what constituted being an artist in the class. Therefore, I described in fieldnotes what I observed, video recorded class sessions, transcribed selected days, and analyzed sequences. This approach helped me demonstrate my intentions to the teacher and students, particularly dissuading me from evaluating or making assumptions about the class or studio art without triangulating evidence, and revealing limitations to what I could claim (Baker & Green, 2007). The Interactional Ethnographic perspective, which draws on theories of communicative competence, sociolinguistics, and anthropology (Castanheira et al., 2001), therefore, guided and led me to similarly record interactions for the graduate course.

Because of my experience with IE, I acted as "cultural guide" for Elisabeth, describing methodological assumptions and principles and showing how discourse of ethnography provided a common language, or a metadiscourse, for observing classroom interactions and constructing shared or common knowledge for the class (cf. Edwards & Mercer, 1987). Furthermore, our agreement provided space to dialogically explore discourse from each other's discipline; that is, we inquired and sought to understand more from the other person's perspective, not impose our assumptions about what we thought we observed or heard. Moreover, we avoided monologic or authoritative perspectives (Hunt, 2018), including our privileged positions as instructors. Instead, we questioned authoritative perspectives of our fields to build shared expertise with each other and with the students. Although these agreements aligned well with our plans for the course, they proved challenging.

Analytical sequence: Recording and transcribing classroom discourse

With permission of the students, I audio recorded each class session and wrote fieldnotes (when I was not leading discussion). Each class period began with a printed agenda, including a list of assigned readings (students were to have read). Class meetings typically included a guest speaker for the first 60 minutes (many of them were colleagues from the literature or English education programs, or alumni who were secondary school teachers). Next, a student would lead us through a "reading event," comprised of the student selecting and reading a text, providing context for its selection, and initiating a discussion about it. Generally, the third hour was devoted to students' projects and discussion of assigned readings.

After each meeting, I transcribed most of the classroom talk before the next class session, creating a "running record" of the discourse and interactions, and this process represented a first layer of analysis. Next, from the running record, I generated an "event map," a list of the actual, sequenced activities, bounded and named according to topic; and I listed clock and recorded time. Finally, I added relevant information from fieldnotes (or "headnotes"). These three analytical practices provided an initial transcript and map of classroom events, creating opportunities for microanalysis of selected interactions. In the next section, I describe how an interpretative principle was constructed through engaging in classroom conversations, analyzing selected sequences of discourse, and acknowledging thematic connections of the discourse across multiple classroom events and meetings.

Classroom participants as inquirers: Using transcripts to trace the construction of interpretative principles and practices

One course goal, stated in the syllabus, was to *"construct, engage in, and reflect on research-based practices over the semester."* We expected students to engage in recursive processes: read assigned texts, examine suggested research-based practices of various scholars, and explore and develop interpretative principles and practices. But we avoided simply providing students with answers; rather, we encouraged students to become inquirers and seek answers. Tracing connected events requires teachers or researchers to observe how participants of a class recognize and acknowledge an event or concept as significant. Next, I describe two examples of tracing concepts tied by discourse and different classroom events.

Example 1

On January 30 (third class meeting), Elisabeth and I initiated a series of classroom activities and discussions about how readers draw on experiences to interpret texts. We began with Mellor, Patterson, and O'Neill (2000), who suggest readers fill "gaps" of literary texts based on readers' cultural norms and experiences (e.g., gender). During the next class (February 6) we read a poem and another short text to further discuss how readers fill gaps based on tone, diction, and context. Then, on February 13, we discussed *Prince Cinders* by Babette Cole, a children's picture book that reverses the gender of the traditional story of Cinderella. Prior to reading *Prince Cinders,* I suggested to the class to adapt a "feminist" approach

112 Baker

TABLE 6.1 Classroom interaction on using literary lenses (February 13)

Speaker	Line	Discourse	Notes
Elisabeth	101	You know this idea Doug	i.e., literary "lens"
	102	"knowing a lens" is a little *artificial* actually	
	103	you know	
	104	It's really just something to teach theory	literary theory
	105	It's not *really*	
	106	how individual theorists necessarily	
	107	interact with texts	
	108	Most people use like a kaleidoscope	different metaphor
	109	You know do different things at the same time	i.e., bring theories together
	110	I always use psychoanalysis and gender	Example
	111	and sometimes the texts themselves seem to invite particular approaches more than others	
	112	Still a very useful way to start	i.e., "lenses"
Maya	113	It seems kind of like what um	i.e., lenses
	114	Dr. Blau was saying about	earlier in the class
	115	[pause]	
	116	directing the meaning they take from a text	critiques lenses
Elisabeth	117	yeah	
Maya	118	You know Doug said	
	119	in however he introduced that book	*Prince Cinders*
	120	I was listening to it from a feminist perspective	while reading
Elisabeth	121	yes	
Maya	122	Maybe because it's like you said "Cinderella"	
	123	But it kind of ruins the story	the particular lens
	124	you know	
	125	[pause]	
	126	But I would like to have what you call	voice lowers
	127	the tools and the language	of literary theory
	128	you know	
Doug	129	what do you mean it ruins the story?	seeking clarification
Maya	130	well the whole time I'm thinking	while listening
	131	like	
	132	I'm trying to figure out	
	133	from a feminist perspective	
	134	what I should be offended by	
All	135	[laugh]	

to interpreting the story (that is, examine our cultural norms on gender and how the writer appears to challenge them), and I implicitly raised a question about "literary lenses" as a metaphor for literary theories. After generating a "running record" of the class, I created a transcript of the interaction (presented in Table 6.1), which allowed Elisabeth and me to examine what occurred and design links for the next class meeting (February 20).

Elisabeth described the metaphor of lenses as a "heuristic device" and as "a little artificial" (Line 102), because it does not adequately portray how literary scholars apply theories; at this point in the developing interaction, she offers an alternative metaphor, "a kaleidoscope" (Line 108). One of the students, Maya,

TABLE 6.2 Sequence of intertextually linked events: How readers fill "gaps" of literary texts

January 30	February 6	February 13	February 20
Discussed Mellor, Davies, and O'Neill (2000): readers fill gaps using assumptions from cultural experiences.	Discussed a poem and how readers fill gaps based on tone, background experiences, etc.	Discussed literary theory and metaphor of literary "lenses"; example: "feminist" reading of *Prince Cinders*.	Discussed interactional sequence from Feb. 13: Elisabeth's and Maya's perspectives of lenses.

pointed to a statement made earlier in the class by guest speaker, Dr. Sheridan Blau: teachers should not make students dependent on teachers for interpretations. Maya followed Elisabeth's critique by implying the suggestion of using a particular "lens" directs students to a specific type of interpretation (Line 116). She recalled how I, moments before the reading of *Prince Cinders*, suggested interpreting the text from a feminist perspective. She implied my proposal diluted her interest in the story. Instead of preparing to experience the story, which she said children would enjoy on its own merit – regardless of their knowledge of Cinderella or gender norms, Maya said, "I'm trying to figure out/from a feminist perspective/what I should be offended by" (lines 132–134).

My analysis of the interaction, and subsequent conversations with Elisabeth, led us to show the transcript to students during the February 20 class session to reflect on Maya's position and assumptions, and what both revealed about her perspective of a feminist reading and her – and Elisabeth's – critique of "lens" as a metaphor. By constructing and (re)presenting transcripts, we demonstrated to students how classroom discourse offered opportunities for discussion and how the analysis influenced the design of the next class session and deepened our understandings of the role and limitations of a concept ("lens"). Furthermore, the analysis was part of a larger sequence of how readers fill gaps in literary texts based on their knowledge and experiences (see Table 6.2). In the next section, I describe a second example of how intertextually tied events led to the construction of a particular interpretative principle, shifting back to February 13.

Constructing principles of literary interpretation for teaching

Example 2

On February 13, guest speaker Sheridan Blau opened the class meeting with perspectives on teaching literary texts, including a critique of prereading activities. Denise, returning to her dilemma with her "unmotivated" students, asked him how to engage students in difficult texts (her example, *Things Fall Apart* by Chinua Achebe), particularly questioning him about the value of "prereading" activities to generate students' interest. Sheridan stated he eschews "prereading" activities; rather, he chooses texts for students to "interrogate," particularly so students can explore relevant topics, characters, or themes and become interested through the process (cf. Blau, 2003). Sheridan stated his main concern with "pre-reading" activities is teachers may prepare students in ways construed as "kind of fake" (that is, providing activities that do not engage students in ways *experienced* readers become engaged). For example, asking students to read about euthanasia before reading John Steinbeck's *Of Mice and Men* suggests an interpretation before students have had a chance to "interrogate" the text. Experienced readers would not typically read about euthanasia before entering the text, although the text may lead readers to inquire about the concept. Implicitly, therefore, Sheridan suggested teachers make visible to students practices of experienced readers.

On February 20, two significant, related interactions occurred. First, based on a comment during Sheridan's discussion, Elisabeth and I selected "The Story of an Hour" by Kate Chopin for students to read. Following the public reading, I raised a question about the value of literary discussions in classrooms, especially observing the many interpretations offered and the conundrum for teachers about what to do with them. As we describe in more detail in another study (Baker & Däumer, 2015a), Elisabeth argued, the value is not in offering interpretations; rather, students must develop a "stake" in their interpretation. In the next event, one of the students, Annalise, led the class through a "reading event," selecting the poem "Shirts" by Robert Pinsky. She followed the pattern of previous reading events: read the text aloud, encourage responses, and lead a discussion of the text. However, she also provided students with history behind the allusions in the poem; therefore, according to Sheridan's principle, she made us dependent on her for interpretation. Upon analysis of the "running record," Elisabeth and I viewed this moment as a "rich point" for all of us, because Annalise's approach to the text, the class norm to that point, reflected what Sheridan cautioned against.

These two events and principles (encourage students to have a stake in their argument and create opportunities for students to become independent readers) led us to (re)design the next class meeting (March 5 – the class did not meet on February 27). However, most importantly, observations of these two events that led to the design of March 5 became obvious only *after* we examined transcripts and agreed on implications of what we had observed.

After analyzing transcripts of the two class meetings (February 13 and 20), and microanalyzing selected sequences, Elisabeth and I designed a two-poem activity for March 5. We agreed to each choose a poem and provide students with opportunities to read and interrogate the texts. We further agreed the discussion of each poem would include concepts discussed in recent class meetings: students developing a stake in their textual argument (Elisabeth's focus), teachers providing students with opportunities to engage as experienced readers, and readers consulting relevant material to guide interpretation as necessary (my focus).

On March 5, I briefly described to the class relevant events from the previous two class meetings, providing students with a handout showing conceptual links.

Next, Elisabeth introduced the poem "St. Roach" by Muriel Rukeyser, and, as had been the pattern, she asked two students to each read the poem aloud, permitting time for all to peruse and interrogate the text. Elisabeth raised questions about what students needed as readers to develop a *stake* in their argument and support it with textual evidence. For the second poem, "In Jerusalem" by Mahmoud Darwish, I invited students to read the poem silently; then a student read it aloud, and I initiated a conversation about the text, including what aspects proved challenging and worthy of exploration, potentially through other texts (e.g., the poet's background experiences, allusions to place, etc.). I supplied a few texts students could choose to read.

An important outcome of the two events was a discussion about the potential value of teachers exploring texts as inquirers with students, instead of arriving to class as an expert on the text, one who prompts students toward predetermined answers or acceptable interpretations. Elisabeth briefly described the value of teachers and students becoming "inquirers and searchers" of textual interpretations and how teachers should avoid signaling to students that teachers have the answers. The intonation of her voice indicated an example teacher proposing to students to "become *inquirers*," suggesting teachers avoid expecting students to already know aspects of texts; rather, teachers should approach students as fellow inquirers: "Let's find out/and let's begin searching" for answers to our questions about a text.

Next, I responded by adopting the role of a teacher whose actions might annoy students, using a mocking tone of voice: "I know the text really well/and I know the answer to every question I ask/and I'm waiting to see if you've *got* it [the answer]." Elisabeth responded from a student perspective: "Why should I make the effort if you already know?" I concluded by linking Sheridan's perspective on the value of student-generated inquiry. The sequence, therefore, modeled the inquiry approach we encouraged, beginning with our analysis of classroom interactions and questions and modeling how we were in the process of constructing interpretative principles.

Figure 6.1 charts the described sequence to demonstrate intertextual links across class periods and represents the construction of an interpretative principle (guiding students to become independent readers). Beginning on February 13, Sheridan introduced the principle and Maya echoed it. Although the focus of class during February 20 was the potential value of literary theories, which was one reason we read and discussed "The Story of an Hour," Elisabeth's suggestion of a "stake" in an interpretation and Annalise's "rich point" led us to explore the sequence and link it to the principle of guiding students to become more independent as interpreters of texts.

Discussion

I have explored the value of incorporating an Interactional Ethnographic perspective to examining classroom interactions for purposes of teachers and students developing deeper understandings of literary interpretation by what is getting

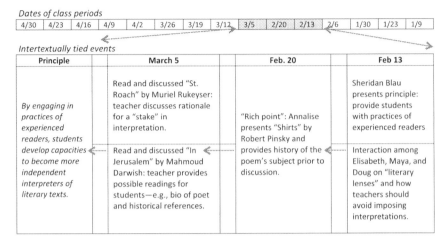

FIGURE 6.1 Constructing an interpretative principle.

accomplished through discursive actions. I unfolded how an inquiry approach and exploration of classroom discourse became a model for students, particularly as Elisabeth and I demonstrated links among (inter)disciplinary perspectives and conversations, students' experiences as readers and teachers of literary texts, and principles and practices constructed over time in the course. By adapting an Interactional Ethnographic perspective, we generated a metadiscourse and initiated multiple layers of analysis (e.g., "running records" and event maps) that led us to (re)design curriculum; and analysis of selected sequences led students and us to deeper understandings of selected phenomena.

By analyzing discursive interactions, we were able to better understand the interactions, which we may have missed during real-time exchanges. Although teachers cannot transcribe each session of a course, they may elect to record and transcribe selected sequences and use transcripts as a practice of the class, as we did. We used transcripts, for example, to show interactional sequences and how (re)examination of an event may lead to deeper understandings; I gave transcripts to individual students to observe how they described their research, or how others responded; and I demonstrated to students how to use transcripts to trace ideas and their developing understandings of particular phenomena.

For example, initially Denise described a conflict she faced as an instructor: her students appeared unmotivated, particularly displaying a lack of interest in reading the novel *Things Fall Apart*; yet, she described a list of needs that had led her to become a reader, needs she had not supplied to her students. On March 12 (following the sequenced described above, February 13–March 5), Denise described to the class her recent discoveries about her students and instructional approach, including shifting away from a deficit model perspective. Table 6.3 is a partial transcript of Denise demonstrating her deepening understanding of her students and of her role as the more experienced other. First, she recounted the students'

TABLE 6.3 Denise reflects on the need for negotiation with students

Line	Discourse	Notes
201	When you're inviting [students] to talk about something	
202	you have to give them something they want to talk about	
203	and usually it's about "why I don't like reading this book"	
204	which essentially amounts to a lot of fear.	
205	A lot of what they say is	As an example is…
206	"I'm afraid"	
207	"I'm afraid I don't know"	
208	"I'm afraid I will sound stupid"	
209	So this there's the curriculum negotiation	
210	there's the negotiation between the student and the teacher	
211	that says "I'm not going to do this	
212	until you tell me why	
213	and I know that you're going to help me"	

apparent lack of respect for authority and of her as an instructor; however, she said she had begun to realize she was expecting students to read a difficult text but was ignoring their needs as readers and as students. She recognized students needed her to address concerns, such as, "why I don't like reading this book" (line 203), and alleviate their fears, which she inferred from their questions and comments (cf. lines 206–213), and, most importantly, state how she would help them read difficult texts.

To further encourage Denise's (re)examination of her dilemma, I gave her the transcript of the 5-minute discussion, which became a resource for her final project, an essay describing her progress on encouraging students to read challenging texts. Denise had recognized the initial "rich point" and addressed it in the conclusion of the essay, including the need for her to select a different text for her students. (She also used transcripts from her class to exemplify observations.) The following excerpt demonstrates how she had enhanced her capacity to communicate the complexities of the apparent disconnect and how she planned to resolve it, including selecting a different text.

> First, I expected students to engage in discussions at the beginning of the year before students knew or trusted me, or their peers. Classroom community was not formed yet,… Furthermore, I did not give explicit instruction about how to engage in authentic discussion or the value of doing so. My expectations were not clear …. I also learned from the students that they need a book with characters their age and facing similar, age-appropriate conflicts. The exposure to world literature requires that students can easily see themselves in the characters, which was not so with *Things Fall Apart*.

Furthermore, Denise, as Elisabeth and I had encouraged students to recognize, implies she had learned when exploring teacher/student interactions in classrooms, that interactions are "a continuing, cumulative experience for the participants,… [who] draw on their shared history all the time when they communicate," and we must examine interactions over time if we want to "do justice to what teachers and learners achieve, or fail to achieve, every working day" (Mercer, 2010, p. 10).

References

Agar, M. (1994). *Language shock: Understanding the culture of conversation.* New York: William Morrow.

Anderson-Levitt, K. M. (2006). Ethnography. In G. Camilli, P. Elmore, & J. Green, (Eds.) *Handbook of complementary methods in education research* (3rd ed., pp. 279–295). Washington, DC: American Educational Research Association.

Appleman, D. (2009). *Critical encounters in high school English: Teaching literary theory to adolescents.* Urbana, IL: NCTE.

Baker, W. D. (2001). *Artists in the making: An ethnographic investigation of discourse and literate practices as disciplinary processes in a high school advanced placement studio art classroom* (Unpublished doctoral dissertation). University of California, Santa Barbara.

Baker, W. D., & Däumer, E. (2015a). Designing interdisciplinary instruction: Exploring disciplinary and conceptual differences as a resource. *Pedagogies: An International Journal, 10*(1), 38–53.

Baker, W. D., & Däumer, E. (2015b). Understanding *understanding*: Implications of interdisciplinary articulation for instruction and assessment. *Language Arts Journal of Michigan, 31*(1), 28–38.

Baker, W. D., & Green, J. L. (2007). Limits to certainty in interpreting video data: Interactional ethnography and disciplinary knowledge. *Pedagogies: An International Journal, 2*(3), 191–204.

Baker, W. D., Green, J. L., & Skukauskaite, A. (2008). Video-enabled ethnographic research: A mircroethnographic perspective. In G. Walford (Ed.), *How to do educational ethnography* (pp. 77–114). London, England: Tufnell.

Blau, S. (2003). *The literature workshop.* Portsmouth, NH: Heinemann.

Blau, S. (2014). Literary competence and the experience of literature. *Style, 48*(1), 42–47.

Bloome, D., Carter, S. C., Christian, B. M., Otto, S., & Shuart-Faris, N. (2005). *Discourse analysis and the study of classroom language and literacy events.* New York: Routledge.

Bloome, D., Castanheira, M. L., Leung, C., & Rowsell, J. (2018). *Re-theorizing literacy practices: Complex social and cultural contexts.* New York: Routledge.

Carney, M., & Indrisano, R. (2013). Disciplinary literacy and pedagogical content knowledge. *The Journal of Education, 193*(3), 39–49.

Castanheira, M. L., Crawford, T., Dixon, C. N., & Green, J. L. (2001). Interactional ethnography: An approach to studying the social construction of literate practices. *Linguistics and Education, 11*(4), 353–400.

Edwards, D., & Mercer, N. (1987). *Common knowledge: The development of understanding in the classroom.* London, England: Methuen.

Francis, J. (2008). Aesthetic confusion: The legacy of new criticism. *Language Arts Journal of Michigan, 24*(1), 28–33.

Gee, J. P., & Green, J. L. (1998). Discourse analysis, learning, and social practice: A methodological study. *Review of Research in Education, 23*, 119–169.

Green, J. L., & Bloome, D. (1997). Ethnography and ethnographers of and in education: A situated perspective. In S. B. Heath, J. Flood, & D. Lapp (Eds.), *Handbook for research in the communicative and visual arts* (pp. 181–202). New York: Macmillan.

Green, J., & Meyer, L. (1991). The embeddedness of reading in classroom life: Reading as a situated process. In C. D. Baker & A. Luke (Eds.), *Towards a critical sociology of reading pedagogy* (pp. 141–160). Philadelphia, PA: John Benjamins.

Green, J. L., Skukauskaite, A., & Baker, W. D. (2012). Ethnography as epistemology: An introduction to educational ethnography. In J. Arthur, M. Waring, R. Coe, & L. V. Hedges (Eds.), *Research methodologies and methods in education* (pp. 309–321). London, England: SAGE.

Gumperz J. J. (1997). Communicative competence. In N. Coupland & A. Jaworski (Eds.), *Sociolinguistics* (pp. 39–48). London, England: Palgrave.

Hunt, C. S. (2018). Toward dialogic professional learning: Negotiating authoritative discourses within literacy coaching interaction. *Research in the Teaching of English, 52*(3), 262–287.

Hyland, K. (2017). Metadiscourse: What is it and where is it going. *Journal of Pragmatics, 113*, 16–29.

Hymes, D. H. (1972). On communicative competence. In J. B. Pride, & J. Holmes (Eds.), *Sociolinguistics* (pp. 269–293). Baltimore, MD: Penguin.

Kelly, G. J., Luke, A., & Green, J. (2008). What counts as knowledge in educational settings: Disciplinary knowledge, assessment, and curriculum. *Review of Research in Education, 32*, vii–x.

Marshall, J., & Smith, J. (1997). Teaching as we're taught: The university's role in the education of English teachers. *English Education, 29*(4), 246–268.

McCann, T. M. (2014). *Transforming talk into text: Argument writing, inquiry, and discussion, Grades 6-12*. New York: Teachers College Press.

Mellor, B., Patterson, A., & O'Neill, M. (2000). *Reading fictions: Applying literary theory to short stories*. Urbana, IL: NCTE.

Mercer, N. (2010). The analysis of classroom talk: Methods and methodologies. *British Journal of Educational Psychology, 80*, 1–14.

Olsen, A. W. (2018). How language defines 'learning': A classroom view. *Acta Paedagogica Vilnensia, 41*, 58–71.

Rex, L., & Green, J. (2008). Classroom discourse and interaction: Reading across the traditions. In B. Spolsky, & F. M. Hult (Eds.), *The handbook of educational linguistics* (pp. 571–584). Hoboken, NJ: Blackwell.

Rex, L. A., & Schiller, L. (2009). *Using discourse analysis to improve classroom interaction*. New York: Routledge.

Street, B. (2016). Learning to read from a social practice view: Ethnography, schooling and adult learning. *Prospects, 46*, 335–344.

Tang, K-S. (2017). Analyzing teachers' use of metadiscourse: The missing element in classroom discourse analysis. *Science Education, 101*(4), 548–583.

Vetter, A., Schieble, M., & Meacham, M. (2018). Critical conversations in English education: Discursive strategies for examining how teacher and student identities shape classroom discourse. *English Education, 50*(3), 255–282.

Wilson, B. (2014). Teach the how: Critical lenses and critical theory. *English Journal, 103*(4), 68–75.

PART 3
Cultivating questioning

7

QUESTION BASED INSTRUCTION (QBI) PROMOTES LEARNERS' ABILITIES TO ASK MORE QUESTIONS AND EXPRESS OPINIONS DURING GROUP DISCUSSIONS

Yoshinori Oyama and Tomoko Yagihashi

Summary

Generating questions is a fundamental skill for critical thinkers. This chapter describes Question Based Instruction (QBI), a teaching method in which classroom lessons are based on learner-generated questions; subsequently, learners discuss the questions they have generated. This method was used in an elementary school class, and measurements were taken to assess students' abilities to ask questions and express opinions. The results of the data analysis indicate that QBI promoted increases in students' utterances and questions during group discussions. This chapter also explains the teaching steps required to carry out QBI and discusses reasons for its effectiveness and its potential applications.

Benefits of developing learners' questioning skills

The generation of questions is an essential skill for learners on the path toward becoming lifelong learners. As Oyama (2017) explained, if learners can generate their own questions, they will seek answers; thus, a continuation of inquiry-based learning will likely be facilitated. For example, when learners read some study material and come up with questions, and an instructor asks those learners to share and discuss the questions with each other, their understanding of the material can deepen. Additionally, through the inquiry process, new questions arise and inquiry-based learning can continue to deepen knowledge. Based on their questions, learners communicate with each other to tackle issues in a cooperative manner and, through that process, their commutation skills can improve. Moreover, to generate questions, learners must see things critically; therefore, their critical thinking skills can also be developed.

Teaching questioning skills

In the late 1980s and early 1990s, King (1989, 1991, 1992) led research on question generation and lecture comprehension. For instance, King (1989) trained college students to generate questions on lecture content. Comparing the questioning strategy with a review of lecture content, she reported that use of the questioning strategy resulted in better lecture comprehension.

To better understand the most important points that questioning studies have revealed, Rosenshine, Meister, and Chapman (1996) conducted a meta-analysis of 26 studies on question generation. They reported that one effective training activity is the use of "questioning stems" (e.g., fill in the blanks, as in: "What is the main idea of _____?," "How is _____ related to _____?"), which are designed to prompt the generation of useful questions. They also noted that it is effective to use "signal words" (e.g., provide learners with the initial key words of questions, such as "who," "what," "where," "when," "why," and "how").

Concerning intervention studies to promote question generation, Ikuta and Maruno (2005) assisted elementary school pupils to generate questions according to a "three-step instruction" method they developed. For the first step, an instructor helped pupils recognize gaps between what they knew and what was in the study material or what other classmates said. In the second step, the instructor assisted pupils in generating appropriate questions by providing a format, such as "What are the advantages and disadvantages?" In the third step, the instructor assisted pupils in stating their questions. If the wording of questions was unclear, the instructor helped the pupils to modify the expressions used in the questions. After the three-step instruction, pupils' motivation to "want to know more" was found to be higher than at their pre-training stage.

Yuzawa (2009) categorized junior high school students' questions as follows: confirmation of learning content (e.g., "What is GDP [Gross Domestic Product]?"), the structure of learning content (e.g., "Why did European countries form the EU?"), and the application of learning content (e.g., "Why did countries A and B sign the Free Trade Agreement?"). Then, he asked students to generate questions on the subject material, and to categorize their questions according to the above. Yuzawa reported that most of the students' questions were of the "confirmation of learning content" type. Only a few students generated questions about "application of learning content." Regarding this point, Yuzawa (2009) intervened by showing students model questions. For example, when an instructor wants students to generate questions for the application of learning content, the instructor shows a model question – such as, "How can we apply this to the real world?" Then, students are asked to generate similar questions. Yuzawa also reported that training in questioning has a "trans-subject" effect. For example, in a literature class, students were trained to take other people's perspectives and generate questions, such as "What would Alice from *Alice in Wonderland* say if she visited our society?" In a history class, the same students were later observed to ask questions such as "What would the Roman emperor, Caesar, say if he observed the modern political system?"

Under what conditions do learners generate questions?

Instructors need to understand the cognitive processes inherent in learners' generation of questions and provide training tips to promote learners' questioning skills. Therefore, this section examines the processes for generating questions from the perspective of cognitive psychology.

From the researcher's perspective: Cognitive models of generating questions

Regarding this topic, Otero (2009) provided an insightful review of cognitive models that have been proposed for question generation. Three hypotheses relating to such models have been proposed: "knowledge deficit," "knowledge clash," and "obstacle + goal."

Knowledge deficit hypothesis

According to the knowledge deficit hypothesis, "a question is conceived as driven by a lack of knowledge" (Otero, 2009, p. 48).

However, the knowledge deficit hypothesis (Otero & Graesser, 2001) cannot be regarded as automatic. Sometimes, people cannot detect their knowledge deficit on their own. However, if others ask them questions, they notice gaps. For example, when tourists come to a country and ask locals, "What's the population of your capital?," most people do not know the answer and recognize their knowledge deficit.

Another way to raise consciousness of the knowledge deficit is to employ questioning stems. As mentioned previously, questioning stems comprise a list of questioning formats, usually with blanks or missing parts. The blanks are to be completed with words from students' reading materials (e.g., "What is a new example of _____?"). King (1992) used questioning stems to stimulate learners to generate questions, and their comprehension improved, in contrast with learners who did not generate questions.

Knowledge clash hypothesis

However, the knowledge deficit hypothesis is not the only explanation for question generation. In Miyake and Norman's (1979) study, learners were asked to say aloud all the questions and thoughts that occurred to them while they were learning. They reported that with the easier material, novice learners (who possessed less knowledge) asked more questions than trained learners; however, with the harder material, trained learners (who possessed more knowledge) asked more questions than novice learners. This result suggested that "knowledge gaps" alone cannot explain question generation.

Based on Miyake and Norman's (1979) finding, Otero and Graesser (2001) proposed the "knowledge clash" hypothesis. According to Otero and Graesser, people generate questions when they detect an incongruency between their background knowledge and the information they encounter. They hypothesized that readers with more knowledge will ask more questions after reading more difficult materials because there would be a greater probability of inconsistencies occurring between their internal knowledge and the external information that is provided in the difficult material. In contrast, readers with less knowledge would ask fewer questions after reading the difficult material because they would be less likely to detect inconsistencies between that material and the limited knowledge they possess (i.e., if they do not know much about it, there would be a low likelihood of inconsistencies occurring).

Obstacle + goal hypothesis

Otero (2009) suggested that there was a third hypothesis that explained question generation – that is, the "obstacle + goal hypothesis." Otero claimed that question generation is driven by recognition of obstacles when attempting to attain a particular goal. For example, when individuals read materials to understand it, the goal is "understanding the material." When readers encounter new vocabulary and do not know the meanings of some of those words, they encounter obstacles, and questions such as "What does _____ mean?" are generated. Therefore, it is important for teachers to design their instruction so that learners would encounter certain obstacles toward reaching their goal: that way, they would generate questions that are authentically meaningful to them.

Regarding this point, the Japanese researcher Hosoya (1977) proposed "operation provoking questions" in which an instructor ask learners "How can you/we [do or achieve something] as [quality or level of achievement] as possible" type of questions. For example, in an elementary school science lesson on electromagnets, an ordinary instruction is "make your own electromagnet." However, when using "operation provoking questions," the teacher asks, "How can you make an electromagnet as strong a magnet as possible?" This kind of question ignites learners' intellectual curiosity as they try to overcome obstacles by asking additional questions (e.g., "How can we make the electromagnet strong?" and "What makes the electromagnet strong?") to achieve the goal. Therefore, from Otero's viewpoint, "operation provoking questions" establish a goal for learners, and by generating further questions, they try to overcome obstacles to achieve the goal.

Question generation requires an understanding of the material and cognitive gaps

Students generate questions based on the three hypotheses of Otero (2009) – knowledge deficit, knowledge clash, and obstacle + goal. However, developing questioning skills requires learners to have an adequate background knowledge of the subject. For example, according to Otero's knowledge deficit hypothesis, it is crucial for learners to have an adequate amount of background knowledge to be able to detect the deficit. Likewise, such background knowledge is necessary for learners to notice the gaps between what they have learned and what they are about to learn. Therefore, for Question Based Instruction (QBI) to fully function, it is necessary to ensure that learners possess basic knowledge first before asking them to generate questions.

Some instructors rush in asking learners to generate questions. In extreme cases, at the beginning of the lesson, instructors already ask learners to, "Make questions; we are going to discuss and answer them later on." However, it is most often the case that learners cannot generate quality questions worth discussing or even answering. Based on the knowledge clash hypothesis by Otero and Graesser (2001), for learners to generate questions they must comprehend materials presented in the lesson. On this point, Graesser and Olde (2003) examined how participants in their study experienced cognitive disequilibrium, triggered by contradictions, anomalies, obstacles, salient contrasts, and uncertainty, and how their level of understanding of the subject matter might influence the quantity and quality of the questions they produced. The results showed that participants with deep comprehension did not ask more questions; however, they generated a higher proportion of good questions. Thus, the researchers concluded that participants' levels of comprehension affected the quality of the questions they generated.

Therefore, instructors should initially ensure that learners in their classes comprehend the material for which questions will be generated. Otherwise, there would be no discrepancy or incongruency between learners' prior knowledge and information presented in the lesson, and the learners could only create factual questions or ones that require definition of technical terms (e.g., "What is A?"). In contrast, learners would be able to generate more thought-provoking questions (e.g., "Considering Britain's situation in the 1940s, what kind of diplomatic strategies would you have taken if you were in Churchill's position?") if they are first required to obtain background knowledge about the topic under consideration (e.g., World War II and the situations in England and other countries at that time).

Problems with previous question generation practices

Based on descriptions in previous sections regarding the cognitive processes involved in question generation and the instructional practices often used for facilitating such generation in learners, this section considers two of the main problems or limitations of those practices.

Learners' understanding of the material is not always guaranteed

Some practices have as an underlying assumption that learners already have sufficient knowledge or fully understand the material they are dealing with. However, this assumption is not always correct. Learners with little knowledge or those who have only a superficial understanding of the material can only generate surface-level questions. According to findings of Otero (2009) mentioned in the previous section, in order for learners to experience cognitive gaps, it is crucial that they have enough knowledge about the material on which questions are to be based. Only under these conditions can learners contrast their understanding of the material with their background knowledge; if they detect gaps between the two, they generate questions. Therefore, it is crucial for the instructor to take concrete steps that would ensure learners fully understand the material for which they are expected to generate questions.

Learners' generated questions are not effectively used

Almost all practices that have been developed in Japan and in other parts of the world are focused on the generation of learners' questions. However, how they use the questions in teaching is not always clear. Learners become demotivated if their questions are not used and they may think question generation is useless. Teaching practices for generating questions should put more emphasis on the application of learners' questions in a lesson. Thus, learners will understand why they need to create questions. Possible ways to use learners' questions are group discussions about the questions, the formation of pairs for answering questions, and inquiry-based learning.

Question Based Instruction (QBI)

This section presents a possible solution to those problems and limitations: QBI. This method emphasizes that learners understand the material in the first part of the lesson (**steps 1–3**). In addition, by contrasting their preexisting knowledge and new information provided in the lesson, learners experience cognitive gaps and therefore generate questions. In the second part of the lesson (**steps 4–8**), an instructor leads a classroom activity based on the questions learners generated so that they can experience the efficacy of the questions in deepening their understanding of the material. Details of QBI are shown below.

First part of the lesson

1. The instructor explains the study material to learners.
2. The instructor ensures that the learners understand the material by the instructor asking questions and writing a summary on the board. In some cases, the instructor has learners explain the material in pairs to check their comprehension.
3. The instructor asks learners to generate questions about the material.

Second part of the lesson

4. The instructor forms groups based on the questions learners generated.

5. The instructor asks learners to discuss the questions they generated.
6. The instructor collects opinions from each group and shares them with the class.
7. The instructor asks the main question he/she prepared for the entire class (as what learners want to discuss and what the instructor wants the learners to discuss sometimes differ, so this part enables the instructor to draw learners' attention to what he/she considers important).
8. The instructor summarizes key points from the lesson.

One important feature of the instruction outlined above is learners forming groups based on similar questions; their questions are therefore "shared" in the group and discussed with others who have related concerns. Sharing a learner's own question in the group may have a positive effect on the learner's motivation to engage in the lesson and communicate with other learners effectively. This activity may also give learners the impression that the lesson is enjoyable or exciting. Additionally, learners speak out more during group discussions when the topic is shared and relevant to their questions. However, only a few studies have examined the effects of sharing questions and having a group discussion based on learners' questions. Therefore, Study 1 (described below) explored the effect of generating questions and using those as essential components of the group discussion topic.

Study 1

The objective of Study 1 was to examine the effect of QBI on the amount and quality of utterances during a discussion and the way it motivates learners to engage in the lesson.

Method

Participants

Ninety-one 3rd-graders (elementary school pupils, 45 males and 46 females), participated in this study. Participants were from three classes (class 1 = 31 pupils, class 2 = 29 pupils, class 3 = 31 pupils). Each class received different instructions (randomly assigned).

Materials

The Japanese folktale, "Naita Akaoni" ("The Red Ogre Who Cried"), written by Hirosuke Hamada, was chosen for its simple storyline; thus, it was anticipated that pupils could easily comprehend the content. Moreover, it includes numerous points that pupils may wish to discuss.

The story is about a red ogre who wants human friends. A blue ogre proposes a plan to the red one. According to the plan, the blue ogre, assuming the role of a human enemy, vandalizes the village where humans live, and the red ogre beats up the blue one to win humans' trust and friendship. However, one day, the red ogre receives a letter from the blue one that says, "Dear Red Ogre, I hope you have been having wonderful days with the humans. If you meet with me again, the humans would doubt your sincerity, so I won't meet you again ever. Take care of yourself and have a great life. Your friend forever, Blue Ogre." The red ogre cries and cries after reading this letter.

Instructions

In this study, the three classes received different instructions to examine the effect of variations in those instructions on learners' engagement in the group discussion and their impressions of the lesson.

For pupils in a "generate questions" group (class 1), in the first period of the lesson (45 minutes), the instructor explains the "Naita Akaoni" story to pupils, and the instructor asks pupils to generate questions about the material. The instructor collected the questions pupils generated at the end of the first period. Between the first and the second periods of the lesson, the instructor grouped similar questions together. As a result, four question categories were formed, revolving around each of these questions: 1. Why does the red ogre want human friends?, 2. Why does the blue ogre sacrifice himself to help the red ogre?, 3. Why does the gentle red ogre get angry?, and 4. Why does the blue ogre leave the village? In the second period of the lesson (45 minutes), the instructor forms pupil groups, based on the similarities of the questions they generated, to ensure that pupils discuss the same or similar issues as the question they generated.

For pupils in a "choose a question" group (class 2), in the first period of the lesson, the instructor explains the "Naita Akaoni" story to the pupils but did not ask them to generate questions about the material. In the second period of the lesson, the instructor showed the four question categories based on what the pupils in class 1 generated, and the pupils chose the question they wanted to discuss from those options. The instructor formed discussion groups based on the questions that pupils chose.

For pupils in a "teacher decides" group (class 3), in the first period of the lesson, the instructor explains the "Naita Akaoni" story to pupils but did not ask pupils to generate questions about the material. In the second period of the lesson, the instructor formed groups of pupils and assign one of the four question categories (i.e., same as the categories generated by pupils in class 1) to each group.

Based on the above procedure, the following items were measured:

1. The number of questions during the discussion (to measure pupils' critical thinking skills; cf. Kruger, 1992; Kuramori, 1999);
2. The number of opinions expressed during the discussion (to measure pupils' communicative skills; cf. Kruger, 1992; Kuramori, 1999);
3. Pupils' impressions of the lesson (to measure how engaging the lesson was).

Results

Among the four questions categories, one-third of the pupils in the "generate questions" group (class 1) made questions that fell into either the "Why does the red ogre want human friends?," or the "Why does the blue ogre sacrifice himself to help the red ogre?" categories. Therefore, this study compared the utterances of pupils who were in groups that discussed those two question categories (class 1: n = 21, class 2: n = 7, class 3: n = 14).

With pupils' number of utterances (turn-takes in speaking) in discussing these two questions as the dependent variable, and the instruction/group and the time duration as the independent variables, a two-way repeated measures ANOVA was performed. The results showed that the main effect of the instruction/group was statistically significant ($F(2, 39) = 3.40$, $p < .05$); the post-hoc analysis revealed that pupils in the "generate questions" group (class 1) talked more than pupils in the "choose a question" group (class 2) ($p < .05$) (see Figure 7.1). However, the main effect of the time duration was not statistically significant ($F(7, 273) = .73$, ns). The interaction effect was statistically significant ($F(14, 273) = 2.01$, $p < .05$), and the post-hoc analysis revealed that at 1:00~, pupils in the "generate questions" group (class 1) talked more than pupils in the "choose a question" group (class 2) and the "teacher decides" group (class 3) ($p < .05$). Also, at 2:00~, pupils in the "generate questions" group (class 1) talked more than pupils in the "choose a question" group (class 2) ($p < .05$) (see Figure 7.1).

Quality of utterances

This study focused especially on the number of questions and opinions that the pupils produced during the group discussion. Based on a method employed by Kuramori (1999), two raters worked together to categorize pupils' utterances

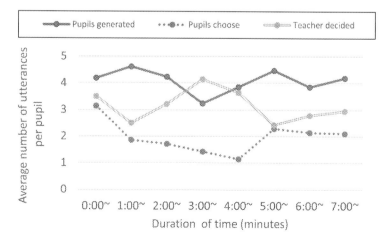

FIGURE 7.1 Average number of utterances per pupil during a discussion (in minutes).

TABLE 7.1 Mean number of utterances per pupil for opinions and questions, according to instruction groups

	Pupils generate (N = 21)	*Pupils choose (N = 7)*	*Teacher decides (N = 14)*
Opinions	10.76 (3.65)	5.14 (0.38)	9.36 (2.40)
Questions	2.16 (0.47)	0.53 (0.20)	1.63 (0.43)

Note: Numbers in the parentheses are standard deviations.

into "opinions," "questions," and "other." When they had disagreements or differences in the categorizations, the raters continued their discussion until they could agree on one of the categories.

A one-way ANOVA was performed for the number of opinions and questions expressed during the discussion (see Table 7.1). The results showed that the number of opinions ($F(2, 39) = 9.46, p < .01$) and number of questions ($F(2, 39) = 4.75, p < .01$) were statistically significant, and the post-hoc analysis revealed that the pupils in the class that generated their own questions (class 1) expressed more opinions ($p < .05$) and asked more questions ($p < .05$) than pupils in the class that chose one of the questions from the teacher (class 2). The results suggest that pupils in the class generating questions were more engaged in discussions; they thought more critically (as suggested by the number of questions they asked) and communicated better (as suggested by the number of opinions they expressed) than pupils who simply chose their question from the options provided by the teacher (see Figure 7.2).

Pupils' engagement with the lesson

A hypothesis put forth in this study was that if learners discussed questions that they themselves generated during the lesson, they would be more motivated to engage with that lesson. Therefore, this section includes an analysis of the way

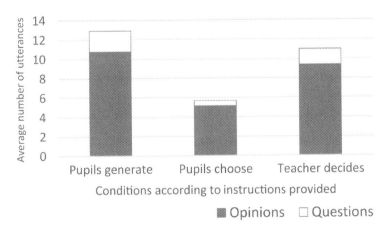

FIGURE 7.2 Average number of utterances for opinions and questions (based on instructions).

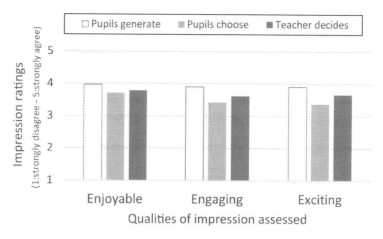

FIGURE 7.3 Pupils' impressions of the lesson (based on instructions).

QBI influenced pupils' engagement with their lesson. After the lesson, pupils rated it according to three items: "How enjoyable was the lesson?," "How engaging was the lesson?," and "How exciting was the lesson?"

The results showed that pupils in class 1 who generated their own questions had the highest ratings of all classes for the "Enjoyable," "Engaging," and "Exciting" items (see Figure 7.3). ANOVA revealed that the difference among the classes was not statistically significant for "Enjoyable" ($F(2, 88) = 2.14$, ns), but differences were statistically significant for "Engaging" ($F(2, 88) = 5.54$, $p < .01$) and "Exciting" ($F(2, 87) = 4.32$, $p < .05$). The result of post-hoc comparisons showed that the pupils in the "generate questions" group (class 1) had higher ratings for the "Engaging" and "Exciting" items than the pupils in the "choose a question" group (class 2).

Discussion of Study 1 findings

Study 1 compared three conditions in terms of group discussion questions. The results showed that pupils in the "generate a question" group (class 1) had more utterances than pupils in the "choose a question" group (class 2) during group discussions. Class 1 pupils also asked more questions and expressed more opinions during their discussions than pupils in class 2. In addition, pupils in class 1 perceived the lesson as more engaging and more exciting than pupils in class 2. In this study, measurements of quality and quantity relating to the discussions were compared between groups of pupils that discussed the same questions. However, only 7 out of 29 pupils in the "choose a question" group (class 2) selected the two questions that we analyzed responses to. Therefore, some caution is necessary in interpreting the 'less favorable' performance of pupils in that class.

Regarding pupils' utterances, "gaps between friends' opinions" – was manifested in the class session using "Naita Akaoni." One pupil had an opinion about the question, "Why does the red ogre want human friends?," and said, "The red ogre lived near the human village and wanted to invite humans to his home and entertain them." However, another pupil said, "The red ogre might have thought that if he could become friends with a human, ogres and humans could become friends." Another thought that the red ogre had a broader vision, wanting the entire ogre tribe and the human village to become friends. When there was a discrepancy among pupils, they tried to persuade classmates or reach a mutual conclusion; thus, their understanding of the material deepened and their communication skills improved.

However, the problem with QBI was that some learners generated questions unrelated to the purpose of the teaching material. For example, some pupils asked questions such as "Why were the ogres red and blue, not yellow and purple?" This kind of question is of course sometimes worth discussing. However, in most cases, it leads to endless, fruitless discussions. To ensure that learners generate appropriate debatable questions for deeper comprehension of the material and quality discussions, an instructor needs to teach learners how to refine their questions.

The main reason learners ask such questions is that they do not have a clear image regarding what the appropriate questions might be. "Appropriate" in this context means the questions that have the potential to deepen learners' understanding of the material and theme. Additionally, learners cannot generate appropriate questions when they have not been shown a sufficient number of appropriate model questions. Therefore, in the next study, the effects of showing "appropriate and inappropriate questions" to learners and explaining "why some questions are appropriate and some are not" were examined.

Study 2

The objective of Study 2 was to develop a method for training learners to generate quality questions, to promote a deeper understanding of the material and to stimulate discussion among peers.

Question generation requires "model questions" and explanations

The approach employed here was based on Wong's (1985) review, which noted that showing model examples of questions to learners is key for successful training in generating useful questions. Therefore, the hypothesis put forth in this study was that showing models of "good questions" to learners would help them imagine appropriate questions and, as a consequence, they would be able to generate content-related questions. However, an additional assumption in this study was that just showing learners good questions was not enough. It is also essential for learners to understand the nature of "good questions" through becoming aware of and understanding the reasons that make them "good questions." Therefore, the instructor should show them model questions and explain

TABLE 7.2 Summary of the contents of the instructions provided, according to the instruction groups

	Good model	Bad model	Explanation
1. Good question models only	O	—	—
2. Good question models with explanation	O	—	O
3. Good and bad question models with explanation	O	O	O

explicitly why they are good ones. It was also hypothesized in this study that it would be better to show learners both good and bad examples for contrast and explain why they are "good" and "bad."

Three instruction methods were compared: "showing good questions only," "showing good questions and providing an explanation," and "showing both good and bad questions and providing explanations." Table 7.2 summarizes the instructional design. It was hypothesized in this study that showing good and bad examples and providing explanations would be the most effective method for training learners to generate content-related questions.

Method

Participants

A total of 83 1st-grade elementary school pupils (males = 44, females = 39) participated in this study. The pupils came from three different classrooms.

Instructions

Instructions encompassed three lesson periods. In the first period, pupils read material about ethics geared toward elementary school students. "Ponta and Kanta" (illustrated as two raccoons) is a "dilemma story" about friends who argue whether they should play on a dangerous playground or stop their friends who are playing there. In this study, after ensuring that pupils fully understood the material, the teacher asked them to write down as many questions as possible on a worksheet provided to them (i.e., this was the pre-questions generation test).

In the second period, three different instructions (showing good questions only, showing good questions and providing an explanation, and showing good and bad questions and providing explanations) were randomly assigned to each of the three classes. After receiving instructions, pupils practiced generating questions on new material they were provided (i.e., this was the post questions generation test). Details of the instructions are provided below.

Good question models only (class n = 29)

The instructor only showed learners good questions; no explanation was provided. Therefore, learners most likely did not acquire the characteristics of good questions. An example of a good question related to "Ponta and Kanta" is, "What is true friendship?"

Good question models with explanation (class n = 30)

The instructor showed learners good questions and explicitly explained the reasons for why they were "good." Therefore, learners most likely grasped the characteristics of good questions. An example of a good question is the same as above, but learners also received an explanation such as, "This is a good question because it is related to the point of the story we've read, and we can discuss it to deepen our understanding."

Good and bad question models with explanation (class n = 24)

The instructor showed good and bad questions and explained why those questions were considered as either "good" or "bad." An example of a good question is the same as above, and an example of a bad question is, "Why is Ponta a raccoon and not a fox?" The instructor's explanation for the assessment of this question as "bad" was: "It is a bad question because it is unrelated to the point of the story we've read, and we cannot reach any conclusion even if we discuss it."

Quality of questions generated by pupils

In the third period, the instructor asked pupils to write down as many questions as possible on another worksheet they were given. Two raters worked together to assess the quality of the questions and their relevance to the theme of the material as "related" or "unrelated." If there was incongruency between the raters, they discussed their differences until they reached consensus.

Results

The purpose of Study 2 was to develop a method for training learners to generate quality questions. Therefore, this section focuses on the number of questions generated by the pupils that were related and unrelated to the content of the material studied (see Figure 7.4).

First, a two-way mixed-design ANOVA was conducted, with the number of content related questions pupils generated at the pre- and post-test as the repeated variable and the set of instructions as the between-subjects variable. The results showed that the main effect of the test was statistically significant ($F(1, 80) = 15.28$, $p < .01$), the main effect of the instruction was not statistically significant ($F(2, 80) = 2.29$, ns), and the interaction was statistically significant ($F(2, 80) = 3.03$, $p < .05$). The post-hoc analysis showed that "the good question models only" resulted in a decrease in the number of content related questions that the learners produced.

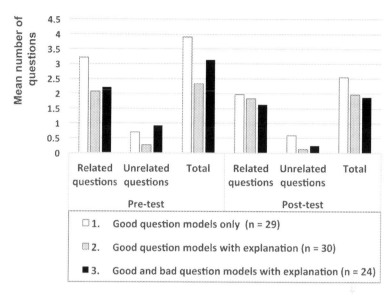

FIGURE 7.4 Mean number of content-related, unrelated, and total questions that pupils generated before and after training, according to the instruction groups.

Second, a two-way mixed-design ANOVA was conducted, with the number of content related questions pupils generated at the pre- and post-test as the repeated variable and the set of instructions as the between-subjects variable. The results showed that the main effect of the test was statistically significant ($F(1, 80) = 7.32$, $p < .01$), the main effect of the instruction was statistically significant ($F(2, 80) = 3.89$, $p < .05$), and the interaction was statistically significant ($F(2, 80) = 2.52$, $p < .05$). The post-hoc analysis showed that only "the model with good and bad questions and explanations" resulted in a decrease in the number of unrelated questions.

Finally, a two-way mixed-design ANOVA was conducted, with the total number (sum of related and unrelated questions) of questions pupils generated at the pre- and post-test as the repeated variable and the set of instructions as the between-subjects variable. The results showed that the main effect of the test was statistically significant ($F(1, 80) = 26.26$, $p < .01$), the main effect of the instruction was statistically significant ($F(2, 80) = 3.32$, $p < .05$), and the interaction was statistically significant ($F(2, 80) = 2.77$, $p < .10$). The post-hoc analysis showed that two instructions – "the good question models only" and "the model with good and bad questions and explanations" – resulted in a decrease in the total number of questions learners generated.

Discussion of Study 2 findings

The total number of questions that learners generated were found to decrease in both "the good question models only" and "the model with good and bad questions and explanations" conditions. However, in the "good question models only" condition, both content related questions and the total number of questions decreased. In contrast, in the "good and bad question models with explanation" condition, the content *unrelated* questions decreased, although the total number of questions also decreased. Therefore, results of Study 2 suggest that "the good question models only" was not effective in either promoting the generation of content related questions or decreasing content unrelated questions. Also, the "good question models with explanation" condition neither promoted generation of content related questions nor decreased content unrelated questions. Only the "good and bad question models with explanation" condition was found to be effective for decreasing the number of content *unrelated* questions that learners produce. However, further research is necessary to examine more carefully the influence of the material for which learners have to generate questions, and to reduce the possibility of instructions having a negative effect of inhibiting learners in generating questions (e.g., through concern about not generating "good enough" questions).

Conclusion

The results of Study 1 suggested that generating questions motivated pupils to find out the answers; they asked more questions in the group discussion activity and expressed more opinions. However, some pupils did not have sufficient skills to generate content-related, appropriate questions. Therefore, in Study 2, the effect of question generation training activities was examined. The result of this investigation suggested that showing pupils both good and bad examples of questions and providing explanations for those helped pupils avoid generating content unrelated questions.

The potential value of this chapter is in showing the effectiveness of QBI, which promotes pupils' positive emotions (i.e., engaging, and exciting) and pupils' positive behaviors, such as asking questions or expressing opinions during discussions.

Combining the results of Studies 1 and 2, QBI needs to include presenting good and bad question models and explanations to learners to improve their ability in generating appropriate content-related questions. Therefore, the revised QBI strategy should be as follows:

1. Ensure that learners understand the material.
2. Present good and bad question models – and explanations for those – to learners.
3. Instruct learners to generate questions.
4. Plan activities using learners' questions (e.g., discussions in a group, asking questions in a pair).

Concerning the use of learners' questions, this chapter described the use of group discussions, but other approaches – such as learners asking each other questions in pairs or fostering inquiry based learning based on learners' questions – are also possible for helping learners realize the importance of generating questions and promoting a deeper understanding of the materials they are studying.

Today, the lecture-style class, in which a teacher simply explains the lesson content, remains as the most frequently used instructional method at all levels of education. Teachers and learners assume that a teacher is the main agent for conveying knowledge and asking questions. This chapter emphasizes the importance of learner-generated questions in the classroom, showing how we can take advantage of such questions in the lesson so that learners become active contributors to their knowledge development.

In the 21st century, knowing a vast amount of information is less important, but how to use information is increasingly proving to be of greater value. However, this does not mean that basic knowledge or information is unnecessary. As this chapter has pointed out in QBI procedures, for learners to generate high-quality questions, it is essential that instructors take steps to ensure that learners acquire/develop adequate background information. Only by contrasting their prior knowledge with new information can learners generate appropriate questions. As we learn to appreciate more the value of question generation in education, an essential part of an instructor's role will be educating learners to ask questions and training them to learn from their questions. Therefore, QBI is one instructional approach that could be of genuine value to educational practitioners.

References

Graesser, A. C., & Olde, B. A. (2003). How does one know whether a person understands a device? The quality of the questions the person asks when the device breaks down. *Journal of Educational Psychology*, 95(3), 524–536.

Hosoya, J. (1977). Dai shizen no chiteki tanken ni okeru "Kimari" no yakuwari [The role of laws in intellectual discovery in the great nature]. *Kyoka Kenkyu Shougakkou Rika [Subject Study: Elementary School Science]*, 59, 1–5.

Ikuta, J., & Maruno, S. (2005). Sitsumon dukuri wo chushin ni shita shidou ni yoru jido no jyugyo shu no sitsumon seisei katudo no henka [Change of children questioning in elementary school class through question generation centered instruction]. *Japanese Society for Educational Technology*, 29, 577–586.

King, A. (1989). Effects of self-questioning training on college-students comprehension of lectures. *Contemporary Educational Psychology*, 14(4), 366–381.

King, A. (1991). Effects of training in strategic questioning on children's problem-solving performance. *Journal of Educational Psychology*, 83(3), 307–317.

King, A. (1992). Comparison of self-questioning, summarizing, and notetaking-review as strategies for learning from lectures. *American Educational Research Journal*, 29(2), 303–323.

Kuramori, M. (1999). Analysis of the negotiation process: Influence of elementary school children's attitudes on the negotiation process and their performance in discussion. *Japanese Journal of Educational Psychology*, 47, 121–130.

Kruger, A. C. (1992). The effect of peer and adult-child transactive discussions on moral reasoning. *Merrill-Palmer Quarterly*, 38, 191–211.

Miyake, N., & Norman, D. A. (1979). To ask a question, one must know enough to know what is not known. *Journal of Verbal Learning and Verbal Behavior, 18*(3), 357–364.

Otero, J., & Graesser, A. C. (2001). PREG: Elements of a model of question asking. *Cognition and Instruction, 19*(2), 143–175.

Otero, J. (2009). Question generation and anomaly detection in texts. In D. J. Hacker, J. Dunlosky, & A. C. Graesser (Eds.), *Handbook of metacognition in education* (pp. 47–59). New York: Routledge

Oyama, Y. (2017). Promoting learners' spontaneous use of effective questioning Integrating research findings inside and outside of Japan. In E. Manalo, Y. Uesaka, & C. Chinn (Eds.), *Promoting spontaneous use of learning and reasoning strategies: Theory, research, and practice for effective transfer.* London, England: Routledge.

Rosenshine, B., Meister, C., & Chapman, S. (1996). Teaching students to generate questions: A review of the intervention studies. *Review of Educational Research, 66*(2), 181–221.

Wong, B. Y. L. (1985). Self-questioning instructional-research: A review. *Review of Educational Research, 55*(2), 227–268.

Yuzawa, M. (2009). Jiko sitsumon seisei ni yorukastuyou ryoku no koujyo [Improvement of application skill thorough self-question generation]. In H. Yoshida, & E. De Corte (Eds.), *Application of children' logic into classroom practice: Educational practical psychology in designing class.* Kyoto, Japan: Kitaouji Shobou.

8

AUGMENTEDWORLD

A location-based question-generating platform as a means of promoting 21st-century skills

Shadi Asakle and Miri Barak

Summary

This chapter introduces a new web-based platform named *AugmentedWorld* that was designed to allow science teachers and students to generate location-based multimedia-rich questions. A study among 98 pre-service science teachers indicated that deep learning of science concepts can be promoted by generating and solving interactive questions connected to a specific location and real-world applications. The use of *AugmentedWorld* may foster ICT literacy, critical thinking, contextualization, and creativity – four essential skills required for 21st-century education. Our study shows that the method is most effective when using a taxonomy for question generation.

Introduction

Science educators worldwide have devoted effort to promote dramatic changes in the design and use of new pedagogy (e.g., Barak, 2017a; Barak, 2018; Bell, Maeng, & Binns, 2013). These changes, in turn, require dramatic changes in the way teachers and students use educational technologies (Barak, 2017b). Web-based platforms have evolved, allowing learners worldwide to interact and collaborate with each other as creators of content in online environments. In the field of science education, web-based platforms facilitate learning through virtual field trips, scientific inquiry, simulations, and the formation of learning communities (e.g., Barak & Rafaeli, 2004; Crippen, Ellis, Dunckel, Hendy, & MacFadden, 2016; Ketelhut, Nelson, Schifter, & Kim, 2013). Such platforms have become a prominent component of science education practices in schools and universities, introducing a wide range of instructional approaches (Barak, 2014; 2018; Barak & Ziv, 2013; Crippen et al., 2016). Web-based technologies provide new learning environments that support the generation of high-level questions (Barak & Asakle, 2018; Barak & Ziv, 2013). These environments allow users to add multimedia components such as pictures, animations, videos, and interactive simulations to text-based questions. However, they still lack location-based features that allow the connection to authentic locations and events. In addition, location-based platforms, based on global positioning systems (GPS), facilitate authentic and collaborative learning (Barak & Asakle, 2018; Barak & Ziv, 2013); yet, they have not reached their full potential in the science classroom.

Web-based technologies in science education

Advanced web-based technologies facilitate science education through modeling, simulations, data analysis, and the generation of learning communities (Barak, 2017b; Barak & Ziv, 2013; Ketelhut et al., 2013). Web-based technologies in the form of virtual environments and social applications show promising possibilities for shifting from traditional teaching of scientific facts to active and interactive construction of knowledge (Barak, 2017a; Bell, et al., 2013; Crippen et al., 2016). As science education curricula and instructional materials are adapted to meet the new challenges of the 21st century, new questions arise, such as: What assessment methods are most appropriate for the new vision of K-12 science education? And how can science learning in rich and complex environments be measured? These important questions are at the center of several recent studies on web-based learning and assessment (Barak & Asakle, 2018; Crippen et al., 2016).

International programs for science education assessment have integrated computer-based assignments as part of students' testing practices. For example, since 2015, the Programme for International Student Assessment (PISA) included web-based assessments of the mathematics, science, and collaborative problem-solving skills of students (OECD, 2016). Namely, the PISA Computer-Based Assessment of Science (CBAS) was designed specifically to replace paper-and-pencil methods of assessment. Paper-and-pencil assessment, including exams, portfolios, and lab reports, is well grounded in science education curricula. In order to change the nature of assessment in the science classroom, teachers and students must have as many opportunities as possible to practice web-based assessment. In response to this idea, *AugmentedWorld* was designed as an open and adaptive system to enable teachers and students to generate their own multimedia and inquiry questions, and answer and assess questions generated by others (Barak & Asakle, 2018). The importance of generating questions has been recognized by educators in the past three decades (e.g., Brown & Walter, 2005; Dori & Herscovitz, 1999). Question generation was identified as a meaningful strategy for improving understanding and comprehension of mathematics topics (Brown & Walter, 2005), improving motivation to learn science (Chin, Brown, & Bruce, 2002); enhancing problem-solving abilities in chemistry (Dori & Herscovitz, 1999); encouraging independent learning in biology (Marbach-Ad & Sokolove, 2000); and providing an alternative assessment method as an authentic way for examining students' scientific understanding (Hardy et al., 2014; Herscovitz, Kaberman, Saar, & Dori, 2012).

Generating questions

Science education emphasizes inquiry-based learning and higher-order thinking. Therefore, posing high-level questions should be an integral part of the learning process (Barak & Rafaeli, 2004; Dori & Herscovitz, 1999; Hofstein, Navon, Kipnis, & Mamlok-Naaman, 2005; Marbach-Ad & Sokolove, 2000). Generating questions is an important skill for both teachers and students; yet, questions are usually thought of as fact-demanding queries that assessment experts pose, rather than as an authentic, thought-provoking assignment (Barak & Rafaeli, 2004). The literature distinguishes between *question-asking* activities and *question-generating* activities. Question-asking activities stimulate questions posed at the end of a learning session, when reading an article, or while conducting a lab experiment, when the learner does not know the answer or what to expect. On the other hand, question-generating activities encourage learners to create high-level, open- or closed-ended questions that are similar to those generated by educational experts. Question-generating activities are conducted as a means of reinforcing students' understanding of the subject matter (Barak & Rafaeli, 2004; Hardy et al., 2014) and of scaffolding cognitive growth (Barak & Asakle, 2018; Dori & Herscovitz, 1999; Marbach-Ad & Sokolove, 2000).

Question-generating assignments can be used as an alternative assessment method of students' learning (Barak & Rafaeli, 2004; Sanchez-Elez et al., 2014; Yu & Chen, 2013). Such assignments are an authentic way of revealing students' understanding (or lack thereof) of the study materials (Barak & Rafaeli, 2004; Dori & Herscovitz, 1999). Rather than assigning grades based on learners' ability to answer questions (e.g., tests and examinations), they are given according to the quality of the questions that the learners generate (Hardy et al., 2014; Marbach-Ad & Sokolove, 2000).

With the evolution of graphical user interfaces and web-based systems, sophisticated question-generating platforms have been created, allowing users (instructors and learners) to add pictures, animations, videos, and interactive simulations to text-based questions (e.g., Barak & Rafaeli, 2004; Sanchez-Elez et al., 2014; Yu & Chen, 2013). Web 2.0 question-generating platforms include social elements such as forums and recommendation systems (Barak & Rafaeli, 2004; Hardy et al., 2014). However, they lack applications such as location-based systems that allow the connection of questions to authentic locations and events. Location-based applications that use GPS and digital maps have the potential to generate new learning environments by adding new meaning to the term *learning in context*. The learning in context approach is a learning process in which students are able to connect scientific concepts to location-based events and construct meaning based on their own experiences (Barak & Asakle, 2018). In terms of technology, the learning in context approach emphasizes the contribution of advanced technologies to context awareness in education (Barak & Asakle, 2018; Bell et al., 2013). Hence, in this study we introduce *AugmentedWorld*, a web-based platform that uses location-based services to facilitate the generation of multimedia-rich scientific questions while connecting scientific topics to relevant locations and real-world events.

The *AugmentedWorld* platform

AugmentedWorld is an open, collaborative, and interactive location-based platform, designed to provide an easy to use tool for science teachers and students to generate multimedia-rich questions. It is based on the notion that questions are the source of all knowledge and that students should be skilled in generating questions and not only in answering them. *AugmentedWorld* was purposefully developed to offer educational solutions that other applications do not offer, or offer only partially. It allows science teachers and students to provide layers of information in a collaborative and accumulative way, hence the name "Augmented World" – having been made greater in size and value.

AugmentedWorld can be accessed using any internet-connected device (e.g., desktop computer, laptop, tablet, smartphone) and any HTTP-compliant browser. It is unique in that it is free, open, and democratic. All users, be they teachers or students, or even the general population, may create questions, collect and analyze data, and share results and ideas. The platform allows the formation of interactive assignments by clustering several related questions into a single learning task. *AugmentedWorld* is designed to foster science education through four pedagogical pillars: question generation (as the center of the learning process), collaborative learning, feedback and research, and information management. The four pedagogical pillars are presented below.

1. *Question Generation* is the central pedagogical pillar of *AugmentedWorld*. When users click on the "Sign In" button, the homepage wizard opens automatically with a textbox and content editor that allows users to formulate a question (Figure 8.1). *AugmentedWorld* facilitates two main types of questions: multimedia questions (multiple choice or numerical) and inquiry questions. The multimedia questions, are closed-ended multiple-choice or numerical questions that include multimedia features such as short videos, animations, and/or simulations. The inquiry questions are open-ended queries that are based on the citizen science approach; they encourage public participation in a scientific research (Price & Lee, 2013).

Based on a Google application, each question in *AugmentedWorld* includes a digital interactive map. On this interactive map, question generators (students, teachers, and researchers) can connect the scientific topics to authentic locations by adding virtual markers as location-based information points.

Figure 8.2 is an example of a multimedia question created by a pre-service science teacher who connected the topic of ocean acidification and jellyfish abundance to beaches in Israel. The question begins with a brief explanation of the

FIGURE 8.1 The *AugmentedWorld* content editor for writing questions.

phenomenon, supported by graphs that show the rising levels of carbon dioxide (CO_2) in the atmosphere, rising CO_2 levels in the ocean, and decreasing pH in the water. It includes a short video on how the phenomenon affects fish. Following this introduction, users are prompted to answer the following question:

How can ocean acidification impact jellyfish population?

- Jellyfish cannot survive in acidic ocean areas.
- Jellyfish proliferation is encouraged by high amount of CO_2 in ocean water.
- Fish population is decreased in acidic water and jellyfish fill the ecological niche.
- Vertebrate animals, which provide food to jellyfish, are abundant in acidic water.

Figure 8.3 is an example of an inquiry question that is based on the World Water Monitoring Challenge for raising public awareness and involvement in protecting water resources around the world. The inquiry question was: "What is the quality of local water bodies around the world, and how does it relate to its location?" Participants from the United States and Israel were prompted to use a

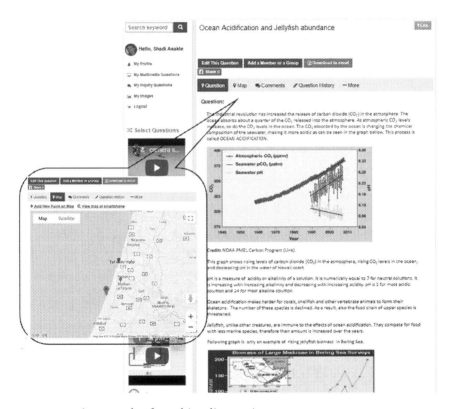

FIGURE 8.2 An example of a multimedia question.

water-testing kit to examine acidity, turbidity, temperature, and dissolved oxygen. They uploaded findings via text, pictures, and/or videos on the interactive map, according to the relevant location in which data was collected.

2. Collaborative learning, the second pedagogical pillar includes three components: question sharing, location-based information points, and peer assessment. Question sharing, the first collaborative component, refers to *AugmentedWorld*'s default "Public" mode. Accordingly, the questions that users generate are open online to the public, even to nonregistered users. Location-based information points, the second collaborative component, refer to virtual markers on an interactive digital map, which are linked to a specific question. Learners can become members of a scientific community in which they can share authentic events connected to scientific topics, engage in research, discuss new ideas, and reach consensus. Hence, by clicking on "Add a New Point on the Map" for the multimedia questions or on "Add Data" for the inquiry questions, students worldwide can add supplementary information that connects the scientific topics to authentic locations (e.g., nature reserves, mineral mines, museums, industrial factories), real-world applications (e.g., volcano eruption, earthquakes), and even everyday life situations (e.g., kitchen-based chemistry, domestic geometrical shapes). Peer

FIGURE 8.3 An example of collecting data for an inquiry question.

assessment, the third collaborative component, is an open forum that allows students to provide comments and constructive feedback. Comments can relate to the question's clarity and level of difficulty, as well as the quality of the multimedia and visualization features.

3. *Feedback and research,* the third pedagogical pillar, includes two types of responses: immediate feedback, which addresses multimedia (closed-ended) questions, and data collection and analysis, which relate to inquiry questions. Immediate feedback refers to the response learners receive when they try to solve multiple-choice or numerical questions: a wrong answer immediately results in the appearance of a red X, while a correct answer elicits a green check mark. In addition to the automated feedback, specific explanations and scaffolding may be provided for each distractor (i.e., a wrong answer within the multiple choices given). Data collection and analysis refers to the response learners are requested to provide to the inquiry questions. Following the citizen science approach, students are asked to collect data by conducting observations or performing short experiments. They are prompted to report the data (numbers, text, pictures, and/or video) by generating an information point on the digital map, at the location at which the experiment was conducted. The data, which is collected from multiple participants, can be downloaded to an electronic sheet, analyzed by the inquiry question generator, and presented to other users.

4. *Information management,* the fourth pedagogical pillar, comprises six components that together present the contents that each student generates. This includes building a personal profile, tagging and retrieving information, uploading and managing images and other visualization features, handling shared questions, and managing the generated multimedia and inquiry questions. The platform promotes ICT practice and literacy by encouraging students to use http protocols, and to upload, edit, or delete contents and multimedia features.

Overall, *AugmentedWorld* serves as an interactive learning platform for both question generators and question solvers (Figure 8.4). Question generators can create and share multimedia questions, write explanations for immediate feedback, and connect scientific topics to authentic locations on a digital interactive map. They can also generate and share inquiry questions, analyze data collected by others, and publish their results and conclusions. Question solvers can answer multimedia questions, provide peer assessment to help improve the questions, receive immediate feedback, and provide additional information upon the digital map. They can also participate in inquiry projects, based on citizen science, collect data, and upload it to the online platform.

Evidence for effectiveness

In the previous section, we described the *AugmentedWorld* platform and its pedagogical pillars. In this section, we report on the implementation of the platform among pre-service science teachers, prior to its implementation in schools. An exploratory study was conducted to provide insights into the way

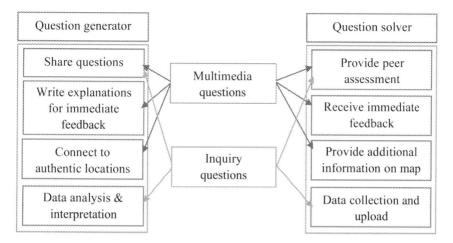

FIGURE 8.4 Activities of question generators and question solvers using *AugmentedWorld*.

pre-service science teachers generate location-based online questions. The study examined views on *AugmentedWorld*'s pedagogical attributes and on the impact a question-generating taxonomy has on the quality of the learning outcomes.

This goal raised the following research questions:

1. What are the views of pre-service science teachers about the *AugmentedWorld* platform?
2. What is the quality of location-based questions generated by pre-service science teachers?
3. What is the quality of peer-assessment performed by pre-service science teachers?

Participants and settings

The study included 98 pre-service science teachers, of which 64% were females and 36% were males. The teachers ranged in age between 20 and 31 years ($M = 24$, $SD = 3.7$). They were introduced to the *AugmentedWorld* platform in the framework of a science teaching methods course. They received explanations on how to generate multimedia questions and were exposed to examples from the PISA assessment tool (OECD, 2016). Their learning assignment included the generation of a multimedia-rich multiple-choice question on any topic from the science and technology curriculum, adding information points on a digital map, and providing peer assessment.

All the teacher participants worked on the same question-generating assignment via *AugmentedWorld*, which included four 2-hour classroom sessions and about 6 additional hours of online and outdoor activities. In order to make comparisons, the participants were randomly divided into two groups: those who were introduced to the question-generating taxonomy ($N = 58$) and those who were not ($N = 40$). The question-generating taxonomy is presented in the next section.

Question-generating taxonomy

A question-generating taxonomy, adapted from Barak and Rafaeli (2004), was used to evaluate and grade the participants' learning outcomes based on four components: authentic situation, multimedia, cognitive level, and relevant location (Table 8.1). Each component was graded on a 3-point scale with a maximum score of 12, which was weighted to 100 points.

Methodology, data collection, and analysis

The study employed the convergent parallel mixed methods approach (Creswell, 2014), merging quantitative and qualitative data to provide a comprehensive examination. Data were collected through semi-structured interviews and analysis of digital documents, consistent with the case study method in educational research (Stake, 1980). The semi-structured interviews took place in a computer classroom as informal conversations between the researchers and the pre-service science teachers, as the latter were generating multimedia-rich questions using the *AugmentedWorld* platform. The researchers examined the

TABLE 8.1 Components and learning outcomes of the question-generating taxonomy

Component	Learning outcome (on a 3-point scale)
Authentic situation	• Weak or no connection between the question and an authentic event (e.g., chemical energy and car accident) • Strong connection with no explanations (e.g., chemical energy and photosynthesis in plants) • Strong connection with elaborated explanations (e.g., chemical energy and an explanation of the photosynthesis process)
Multimedia	• Non-original videos, animations, or pictures, uploaded from web-based sources (e.g., Google apps) • Simulations from web-based sources (e.g., YouTube, Phet) • Original videos, animations, or simulations, created by the learner (self-production using digital cameras or smart phones, and graphical apps)
Cognitive level	• Memorization of scientific concepts (content knowledge) • Comprehension of scientific processes (procedural knowledge) • Application of scientific principles and constructs (epistemic knowledge)
Relevant location	• General location (e.g., ocean, desert, forest) • Specific location, remote from student environment (e.g., a certain museum, a certain pond) • Specific location, close to student environment (e.g., home, neighborhood)

participants' views by asking general questions, such as: "What are your views about the question-generating assignment?," "Can it contribute to science teaching and learning, and how?," "What science learning competencies can it develop among learners?"

The participants' answers were documented in researcher logs and analyzed using the inductive analysis method, which is an open-coding approach that enables themes to emerge from raw data (Hsieh & Shannon, 2005). The qualitative analysis included three main steps. First, we marked relevant text segments that (explicitly or implicitly) revealed the participants' views on the question-generating assignment. Second, the marked text segments were rearranged in new paragraphs according to four emerging themes. Third, an inter-rater reliability test was conducted, yielding Cohen's kappa of 0.81.

The digital documents included multimedia-rich questions and peer assessments. The multimedia-rich questions were examined by applying a deductive content analysis process that examined whether the question taxonomy contributed to the quality of questions, and how. The deductive analysis was based on the four components of the question-generating taxonomy: authentic situation, multimedia, cognitive level, and relevant location. For statistical purposes, the taxonomy's 3-point scale, with a maximum of 12 points, was weighted to 100 points, and averages for each component were calculated.

The peer assessment comments were analyzed according to four coding categories: Reinforcement, Statement, Verification, and Elaboration (Usher & Barak, 2018). *Reinforcement* refers to comments that provide a general praise or criticism that is not specifically directed at the project contents, and has little, if any, contribution to its improvement. *Statement* refers to comments that include factors that are present or missing in the assessed work, with little explanation. *Verification* refers to comments that determine whether the work complies with the assignment requirements, and *Elaboration* refers to comments that identify scientific gaps in the assessed work and include suggestions for revision and improvement.

The Reinforcement and Statement categories both require some cognitive effort on the part of the assessor and provide peers with little means for improving their work. They are, therefore, considered to be lower-order thinking skills. Verification requires analytical capacity and, therefore, represents a medium-high level of thinking, whereas Elaboration requires synthesis and evaluation capabilities, indicating higher cognitive abilities. Three science education experts conducted analyses based on the above-mentioned categories. A series of inter-rater reliability tests, which included Cohen's kappa measurement, indicated a high agreement rate of 0.84.

We used IBM SPSS software, version 23, to analyze the quantitative data. Descriptive statistics (e.g., means and frequencies) were summarized, and inferential tests were performed. Statistically significant tests (e.g., independent *t*-tests and chi-square) were conducted to examine the differences between the two research groups.

Findings

Views of pre-service science teachers on AugmentedWorld

Interview transcripts indicated four main competencies that the *AugmentedWorld* assignment may promote: contextualization, creativity, critical thinking, and ICT literacy. The following paragraphs present detailed descriptions of each competency and selected excerpts from participant interviews.

Contextualization, the first competency, refers to the ability to understand science by making connections between scientific concepts and personal experience (Giamellaro, 2014; Lave & Wenger, 1991). According to the interviewees, this ability was advanced by generating questions that refer to real-world applications and relevant locations. Contextualization was not easy for the participants because they were not skilled in connecting scientific topics to authentic events or daily life. For example, H.A., a pre-service biology teacher, said: "We are constantly advised to teach while connecting scientific topics to authentic events. We are provided with examples from international tests such as PISA, but we do not practice creating questions. The AugmentedWorld assignment allowed us to apply theory in practice." D.L., a physics student who is studying for a teaching certificate, said: "Although I was aware to the fact that 'science is all around us', it was difficult for me to generate an interesting multimedia question on the Coriolis Effect and connect it to a relevant location on a map."

Creativity, the second competency, refers to the ability to think outside the box, to generate original ideas, and create new things (Osborne, et al., 2003). According to the participants, this ability was encouraged by creating and uploading multimedia features (videos, animations, simulations), since the creation of original multimedia features requires intuitive and associative cognitive operations on the part of the participants. For example, L.K., a pre-service science teacher, said: "I generated a question on the impact of changes in species diversity on dissolved oxygen in water. I added a graph that shows the change in global temperature and carbon dioxide concentration over a period of 120 years. I also added a video about the effect of global warming on the diversity of coral; all these features were connected in a creative way to form a high-level multiple-choice question." T.D., a pre-service chemistry teacher, was surprised by her ability to produce a creative question: "I am usually very creative in many areas, but to generate a scientific question in a creative way is a new challenge for me."

Critical thinking, the third competency, refers to the ability to think in a clear, rational, and informed way to form a knowledgeable judgement (Barak, Ben-Chaim, & Zoller, 2007). According to the participants, this ability was encouraged by the need to provide feedback and assess questions generated by their peers. For example, H.A., a pre-service biology teacher, stated: "In order to provide good feedback, I had to read each question and information point carefully and critically, see if all the requirements were met, examine whether the work complies with the scientific facts, and provide explanations about why the question is good or bad." J.O., a pre-service chemistry teacher, said: "During the peer assessment task, we were asked to provide comments to help our classmates improve their questions… one question, about air pollution, was poorly written as it included mistakes. The information point on the digital map was not contributing to the understanding of the scientific topic, but rather included general information. Instead, I offered other ideas related to local factories that installed a device to reduce the emission of carbon dioxide."

Information and communication technology (ICT) literacy, the fourth competency, refers to the ability to use online applications and digital devices to generate, evaluate, manage, and communicate information (Barak, 2017a; Barak & Asakle, 2018). Participants indicated the importance of practicing the use of location-based social technologies in order to promote scientific understanding as well as ICT literacy. For example, D.S., a pre-service biology teacher, stated: "The AugmentedWorld assignment is a good way to promote science education among school students, as they are already connected to smart phones and laptop computers… They can build their personal profile, tag and retrieve information, create and manage multimedia features… It was an educative experience for me and I am sure it will be a great experience for school students." G.K., a pre-service physics teacher stated: "I am not a technology expert so I approached this assignment with many concerns; I was afraid I would not be able to operate the platform or that it would take me too long. I was surprised to see how easy it was to generate a question, to upload and manage images, and to create and embed videos… I was exposed to new and exciting ways of conveying information. I think it is important to expose school students to the same experience."

Quality of questions generated by pre-service science teachers

A deductive analysis of the online multiple-choice questions indicated that creating high-level multimedia-rich questions is challenging and difficult, even for pre-service science teachers. The majority of participants (62%) generated medium- or low-level cognitive questions that require memorization of scientific concepts with an emphasis on content knowledge. Less than one-third (28%) of questions generated required the comprehension of scientific processes, emphasizing procedural knowledge. Only 10% required the application of scientific principles. Our analysis showed that participants were moderately successful in generating questions that present authentic situations, such as in the case of the agricultural researcher, presented above. Most questions were situated in remote and general locations (e.g., ocean, desert, forest) and only 13% represented authentic situations from everyday life (e.g., home, neighborhood).

Overall, the difference between the pre-service science teachers who were introduced to the question-generating taxonomy and their counterparts, was statistically significant ($t(96) = 4.79$, $p < .001$). Compared to their counterparts, the question Taxonomy group received significantly higher scores for cognitive level of questions, connection of scientific topic to authentic situation, and indication of relevant location ($t(96) = 4.46$, $p < .001$; $t(96) = 2.60$, $p = .011$; $t(96) = 2.93$, $p = .004$, respectively). However, no significant difference was found for multimedia application (Table 8.2).

154 Asakle and Barak

TABLE 8.2 Means, SD, and t-tests of outcomes, by research groups

Question-generating components	Question taxonomy (N = 58)		Counterparts (N = 40)			
	Mean	SD	Mean	SD	t	p
Cognitive level	75.29	23.00	55.00	20.74	4.46	.000
Authentic situation	62.64	24.24	50.00	22.64	2.60	.011
Relevant location	60.34	22.04	46.67	23.63	2.93	.004
Multimedia application	51.15	17.90	47.50	19.81	0.95	.345

Table 8.2 indicates that the participants' weakest area was the use of multimedia. Overall, we analyzed 264 multimedia elements (i.e., pictures, videos, animations, and simulations) and while most multimedia elements were static images (65.0%), a third were videos (31.0%), and only a few were animations (2.7%) or simulations (1.3%). Only 19 participants created original pictures, and only two created original videos. One original video focused on kinetic and potential energy, showing playground swings and the other video showed a kitchen-based demonstration related to the effect of pressure on the boiling point of water. Original images appeared in 30% of questions generated by the Taxonomy group and in only 7% of the counterparts' questions [$\chi^2(2, N = 98) = 16.57, p = .020$].

Quality of peer-assessment performed by pre-service science teachers

A deductive content analysis of participants' peer feedback identified 253 comment segments written by the pre-service science teachers who were introduced to the question-generating taxonomy ($M = 4.36, SD = 1.30$) and 137 comment segments written by their counterparts ($M = 3.43, SD = 1.01$). A relatively low percentage of comments, from both groups, were classified as *Reinforcement*, providing general praise or criticism. For example, N.M., a pre-service chemistry teacher, said: "I really liked this topic and it was really fun to read about. I think you did a really great job. Well done!" Since Reinforcement comments are general statements that do not specifically refer to scientific contents, they require lower order-thinking on the part of the assessor. They contribute little or nothing to improving the question.

Participants from both groups exhibited similar percentages of Statement and Verification comments (about 30% and 24%, respectively). The Statement comments refer to factors that were present in or absent from the assessed question. For example, B.L., a pre-service engineering teacher, said: "The information that you added on the map is very useful and interesting, and relates to the main [scientific] topic of the question, but it doesn't really help solve the question … And the video, although it presents an authentic situation, doesn't add new information, it just presents the formula [of the chemical compound] in a different way."

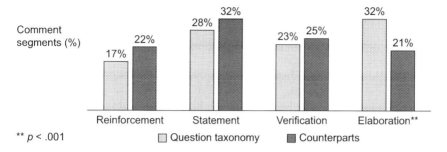

FIGURE 8.5 Distribution of the comment segments, by research group and feedback categories.

Verification comments refer to whether or not the question complies with the assignment requirements. For example, A.L., a pre-service physics teacher said: "After a lot of research and looking deeply into the [scientific] topic, I think this is an easy question, at least for me; it doesn't require higher-order thinking skills, and the right answer is quite obvious."

The Taxonomy group exhibited a high percentage of Elaboration comments, which identify deficiencies in the assessed work and include suggestions for improvement. For example, L.H., a pre-service physics teacher, stated: "I suggest adding two pictures of the same lake, one with the cyanobacteria in bloom and the other after the lake was treated, suppressing the proliferation of cyanobacteria. I also suggest that you replace the video with another one that explains how cyanobacteria bloom and how the dye restricts their proliferation... I think you should explain the term photosynthesis, because not all students are familiar with this term."

Figure 8.5 presents the distribution of the comment segments, by research group and feedback categories. The Elaboration-type comments, the highest level of feedback, were significantly more common among the Taxonomy group $[\chi^2(2, N = 98) = 23.83, p < .001]$.

Conclusions and future studies

Question generation is the central pedagogical pillar of *AugmentedWorld*, facilitating two main types of questions: multimedia questions and inquiry questions. In recent decades, advanced technologies have facilitated question-generating activities (Barak & Rafaeli, 2004; Hardy et al., 2014), yet most online platforms are designed for the use of instructors and educational experts (e.g., Pundak, Shacham, & Herscovitz, 2013). Only a few encourage learners to take an active role as creators of content (e.g., Barak & Rafaeli, 2004; Hardy et al., 2014; Sanchez-Elez et al., 2014), and most lack features that support contextual learning using GPS. *AugmentedWorld* is unique in that it enables all users—students, teachers, and experts—to generate scientific questions and connect them to everyday life using interactive maps. It is also unique in that it enables users to collaborate (from remote locations), share their questions online, and provide peers with constructive assessment. Our study show that *AugmentedWorld* provides an innovative learning environment for the promotion of scientific thinking and the development of 21st-century skills. Our findings indicated that the question-generating assignment advances four competencies: contextualization, creativity, critical thinking, and ICT literacy.

The analysis of the cognitive level of the questions generated by the pre-service teachers showed that creating high-level multimedia-rich questions is a challenging and difficult task (even for pre-service science teachers). The majority of participants generated medium-level questions that required memorization of scientific facts. Only a small number of questions required the comprehension of scientific processes or the application of epistemic knowledge. Similar results were reported by Barak and Rafaeli (2004), who found that an online question-generating assignment can serve as both learning and assessment tools, but indicated that the level of the generated questions was less than expected.

Studies have indicated that generating a question that requires higher-order thinking is not a simple task (Hardy et al., 2014; Marbach-Ad & Sokolove, 2000). This can be explained by the fact that the generation of questions requires information processing and the activation of mental schemes that depend on a deep understanding of the topics at hand. To generate a high-level question, a learner must execute several cognitive and metacognitive operations, such as the identification of the core topic and the recognition of what information is required, and what one knows or needs to know (Barak & Asakle, 2018; Barak & Rafaeli, 2004). This study demonstrated that a possible way to raise the cognitive level of questions is by applying a question-generating taxonomy. The taxonomy presented in this study helped participants both produce better questions in terms of their cognitive level and connect the scientific concepts to everyday life situations. Our analysis showed that using the taxonomy, participants were relatively successful both in generating questions that present authentic situations and in connecting them to relevant locations on appropriate digital maps.

Regarding peer-assessment, the findings revealed that the pre-service science teachers applied critical thinking in providing helpful comments. The taxonomy group provided high-level comments that included constructive feedback and detailed suggestions for improvement. This reinforces the importance of providing participants with an elaborated question-generating taxonomy, as it assisted in the generation of meaningful feedback. Similar results were reported by Sanchez-Elez and colleagues (2014), who found that critical analysis skills can be enhanced by finding and solving possible mistakes in questions generated by fellow students. Based on our results and those obtained in previous studies (e.g., Barak et al., 2007; Sanchez-Elez et al., 2014), we can conclude that once required to provide a thorough assessment, learners are inclined to study the scientific topic more carefully and are more thoughtful in analyzing their peers' work.

Overall, the current study underlines the value of *AugmentedWorld* toward the cultivation of question generation and thinking skills. The use of *AugmentedWorld* provides teachers and students with the opportunity to generate multimedia-rich questions, following new trends in assessment (e.g., Barak & Asakle, 2018; OECD, 2016). However, providing a tool like *AugmentedWorld* might be insufficient on its own because we need to develop teachers' and students' cognitive and metacognitive operations necessary for high-level question generation and assessment skills. Such cultivation is possible and can be relatively simple with the provision of the question taxonomy, as demonstrated in this study. It may also be helpful to extend training to include additional practice that will put more emphasis on higher-order thinking skills and the creation and effective use of multimedia features.

Research on the generation of location-based multimedia-rich questions as a teaching strategy is still in its infancy (Barak & Rafaeli, 2004; Hardy et al., 2014; Sanchez-Elez et al., 2014). Given its importance to scientific thinking and to 21st-century skills, further research should examine cognitive and metacognitive processes of the creation of questions. Possible questions are: "How can student-generated questions be best implemented in various STEM fields and for various age ranges?," "Should the generated questions be used for practice and/or be incorporated into exams?," "Can such questions promote students' motivation to learn science by helping them connect the material to authentic locations and real-world events?"

References

Barak, M. (2014). Closing the gap between attitudes and perceptions about ICT-enhanced learning among pre-service STEM teachers. *Journal of Science Education and Technology*, *23*(1), 1–14.

Barak, M. (2017a). Science teacher education in the twenty-first century: A pedagogical framework for technology-integrated social constructivism. *Research in Science Education*, *47*(2), 283–303.

Barak, M. (2017b). Cloud pedagogy: Utilizing web-based technologies for the promotion of social constructivist learning in science teacher preparation courses. *Journal of Science Education and Technology*, *26*(5), 459–469.

Barak, M. (2018). Are digital natives open to change? Examining flexible thinking and resistance to change. *Computers & Education*, *121*, 115–123.

Barak, M., & Asakle S. (2018). *AugmentedWorld:* Facilitating the creation of location-based questions. Accepted pending modifications. *Computers & Education*, *121*, 89–99.

Barak, M., & Rafaeli, S. (2004). On-line question-posing and peer-assessment as means for web-based knowledge sharing in learning. *International Journal of Human-Computer Studies*, *61*(1), 84–103.

Barak, M., Ben-Chaim, D., & Zoller, U. (2007). Purposely teaching for the promotion of higher-order thinking skills: A case of critical thinking. *Research in Science Education*, *37*(4), 353–369.

Barak, M., & Ziv, S. (2013). Wandering: A web-based platform for the creation of location-based interactive learning objects. *Computers & Education*, *62*, 159–170.

Bell, R. L., Maeng, J. L., & Binns, I. C. (2013). Learning in context: Technology integration in a teacher preparation program informed by situated learning theory. *Journal of Research in Science Teaching*, *50*(3), 348–379.

Brown, S. I., & Walter, M. I. (2005). *The art of problem posing* (3rd ed.). Hillsdale, NJ: Lawrence Erlbaum.

Chin, C., Brown, D. E., & Bruce, B. C. (2002). Student-generated questions: A meaningful aspect of learning in science. *International Journal of Science Education, 24*(5), 521–549.

Creswell, J. W. (2014). *Research design: Qualitative, quantitative, and mixed methods approaches* (4th ed.). Thousand Oaks, CA: SAGE.

Crippen, K. J., Ellis, S., Dunckel, B. A., Hendy, A. J. W., & MacFadden, B. J. (2016). Seeking shared practice: A juxtaposition of the attributes and activities of organized fossil groups with those of professional paleontology. *Journal of Science Education and Technology, 25*(5), 731–746.

Dori, Y. J., & Herscovitz, O. (1999). Question-posing capability as an alternative evaluation method: Analysis of an environmental case study. *Journal of Research in Science Teaching, 36*, 411–430.

Giamellaro, M. (2014). Primary contextualization of science learning through immersion in content-rich settings. *International Journal of Science Education, 36*(17), 2848–2871.

Hardy, J., Bates, S. P., Casey, M. M., Galloway, K. W., Galloway, R. K., Kay, A. E., ... McQueen, H. A. (2014). Student-generated content: Enhancing learning through sharing multiple-choice questions. *International Journal of Science Education, 36*(13), 2180–2194.

Herscovitz, O., Kaberman, Z., Saar, L., & Dori, Y. J. (2012). The relationship between metacognition and the ability to pose questions in chemical education. In A. Zohar & Y. J. Dori (Eds.), *Metacognition in science education: Trends in current research* (pp. 165–195). Dordrecht, The Netherlands: Springer-Verlag.

Hofstein, A., Navon, O., Kipnis, M., & Mamlok-Naaman, R. (2005). Developing students' ability to ask more and better questions resulting from inquiry-type chemistry laboratories. *Journal of Research in Science Teaching, 42*, 791–806.

Hsieh, H.-F., & Shannon, S. E. (2005). Three approaches to qualitative content analysis. *Qualitative Health Research, 15*(9), 1277–1288.

Ketelhut, D. J., Nelson, B., Schifter, C., & Kim, Y. (2013). Improving science assessments by situating them in a virtual environment. *Education Sciences, 3*(2), 172–192.

Lave, J., & Wenger, E. (1991). *Situated learning: Legitimate peripheral participation*. New York: Cambridge University Press.

Marbach-Ad, G., & Sokolove, P. G. (2000). Can undergraduate biology students learn to ask higher questions? *Journal of Research in Science Teaching, 37*, 854–870.

OECD (2016). Socio-economic status, student performance and students' attitudes towards science. In *PISA 2015 results (Vol. I): Excellence and equity in education*. Paris: OECD.

Osborne, J., Collins, S., Ratcliffe, M., Millar, R., & Duschl, R. (2003). What "ideas-about-science" should be taught in school? A Delphi study of the expert community. *Journal of Research in Science Teaching, 40*, 692–720.

Price, C. A., & Lee, H-S (2013). Changes in participants' scientific attitudes and epistemological beliefs during an astronomical citizen science project. *Journal of Research in Science Teaching, 50*(7), 773–801.

Pundak, D., Shacham, M., & Herscovitz, O. (2013). Integrating online assignments checking in introductory courses. *Journal of Information Technology Education: Research, 12*, 191–202.

Sanchez-Elez, M., Pardines, I., Garcia, P., Miñana, G., Roman, S., Sanchez, M., & Risco, J. (2014). Enhancing students' learning process through self-generated tests. *Journal of Science Education and Technology, 23*(1), 15–25.

Stake, R. (1980). The case study method in social inquiry. In H. Simons (Ed.), *Towards a science of the singular: Essays about case study in educational research and evaluation* (pp. 62–73). Norwich, England: Centre for Applied Research in Education, University of East Anglia.

Usher, M., & Barak, M. (2018). Peer assessment in a project-based engineering course: Comparing between on-campus and online learning environments. *Assessment and Evaluation in Higher Education*, *43*(5), 745–759.

Yu, F-Y., & Chen, Y-J. (2013). Effects of student-generated questions as the source of online drill-and-practice activities on learning. *British Journal of Educational Technology*, *45*(2), 316–329.

9
EFFECTIVE WAYS TO PREPARE FOR DEEPER LEARNING OF HISTORY

Keita Shinogaya

Summary

Deeper learning of history, such as understanding causal relationships between relevant events, was promoted in junior high school students by assigning them a task to undertake preparatory learning for the following classroom lesson. In two experimental studies, it was revealed that interventions, such as asking students to read their textbook to generate questions about the causes of historical events and to find answers to those questions during preparation, enhanced scores in a subsequent test that directly asked about the causes of each historical event. This chapter describes how effective preparation to promote deeper learning can be facilitated in school students.

Brief introduction: Importance of preparation for the next classroom lesson

When we study school subjects, it is necessary to memorize each important fact and to deeply understand and construct a higher-order knowledge network. To achieve this kind of deeper learning in the classroom, homework plays an important role. Previous studies have shown that students' homework completion positively relates to their achievement (Cooper, 1989, 2001). However, researchers have pointed out that the effect of giving homework to students is not consistent (e.g. Flunger, Trautwein, Nagengast, Lüdtke, Niggli, & Schnyder, 2015; Núñez, Suárez, Rosário, Vallejo, Cerezo, & Valle, 2015), which means that we need to consider more carefully the kinds of, and ways of, administering homework in determining its effectiveness. According to Lee and Pruitt (1979), there are several types of homework depending on its purpose: practice (practicing the material that students have learned in class), preparation (preparing for the next lesson), extension (transferring prior knowledge to new situations), and creative (integrating several competencies in a research project). In regards to these types of homework, this chapter focuses on preparation, which is to learn the contents of an upcoming class beforehand, and is arguably necessary for deeper learning in class.

Assigning students the task of undertaking preparatory learning is also important for cultivating self-regulated learners. Learning skills to undertake preparation and deepen one's own learning is necessary in social and everyday life even after school. For example, self-regulated learners who are already in the workforce read handouts beforehand, generate questions, and maximize the effects of learning when they partake in seminars within the company. It is difficult to acquire learning skills like these without training. Schunk and Zimmerman (1997) proposed that the basis of academic skills shifts from social sources to the self through four stages: 1) observational, 2) imitative, 3) self-controlled, and 4) self-regulated. As part of this process, especially from the imitative stage to the self-controlled stage, students must have the opportunity to practice studying by themselves. Therefore, preparing for the next class can be effective for enhancing students' self-regulated learning skills and deepening their understanding of classroom lessons.

Despite its importance, however, preparation has not been examined adequately in learning research (Bang, 2012; Epstein & Van Voorhis, 2001). In regards to this point, theories about meaningful learning are suggestive about the effect of preparation (Ausubel, 1968; Novak, 2002). In these theories, it is said that we can understand new information deeply when we connect it to our prior knowledge. In other words, to have prior knowledge for upcoming information is necessary for deeper learning. Research studies about advanced organizers have shown that reading a brief text about the learning materials beforehand could enhance retention of the contents (Ausubel, 1960). After Ausubel's research, many studies about advanced organizers were conducted in the 1980s. These studies revealed that if students gained knowledge about the contents of upcoming material beforehand, deeper learning, such as an understanding of the relationships between each fact or other piece of information, could be achieved (e.g., Bromage & Mayer, 1986; Mayer, 1983; Mayer & Bromage, 1980).

These findings provide useful suggestions when we consider the effect of preparatory learning for an upcoming class in which teachers use direct instruction. Of course they can be applied to learning various school subjects, but this chapter focuses especially on history learning because the effects of preparation can be considered most apt for the educational goals of this subject. In history learning at school, each historical fact (e.g., "Soon after World War I started, Japan decided to join in it") is stated, but its possible causes (e.g., "why Japan joined in it") are not usually explained in textbooks. And understanding causal relationships among facts is set as a goal of this subject. Thus, history teachers might explain "why a historical event happened," "why a person (or a country) behaved in a particular way," and so on, during classroom instruction. With this condition, deeper learning, such as understanding causal relationships among historical facts, can be achieved more efficaciously if students have already read the textbook beforehand.

Individual differences in the effect of preparation

Individual differences have to be considered with regard to the effect of preparation if school teachers are to ask their students to prepare for the next class. As mentioned above, findings of previous research studies on advanced organizers revealed the effect of preparation, but they have not adequately examined individual differences. If there are some students who cannot benefit from preparation (for reasons such as those described below), it is potentially useless to ask them to undertake preparatory learning because they could end up spending considerable amounts of time on an activity that would have no positive effect on their learning and achievement.

In this regard, learners' beliefs about learning are considered a factor that can cause individual differences in the effect of preparation. Beliefs about learning are what learners believe to be effective learning methods (Uesaka, Seo, & Ichikawa, 2009). For example, Ueki (2002) asked Japanese high school students what they believed to be important for enhancing achievement and found three factors in beliefs about learning. The three factors were "strategy use" (e.g., students with high grades are those who use effective strategies), "amount of exercise" (e.g., there is no way other than spending a lot of time studying to enhance my grades), and "environment" (e.g., if I learn in an upper-level class, I can improve my grades).

Uesaka et al. (2009) reviewed previous studies that focused on beliefs about learning and developed a new questionnaire for assessing all kinds of learning-related beliefs. In the questionnaire, they used two main categories of factors: cognitive beliefs and non-cognitive beliefs. Cognitive beliefs are beliefs that place importance on constructing knowledge and information processing. They contain subscales, such as meaningful learning (e.g., "I try to figure out relationships among different areas of knowledge") and thinking processes (e.g., "I try to find another way to solve the problem even after finding the answer"). Non-cognitive beliefs are beliefs that do not focus on constructing knowledge networks and information processing. They include subscales, such as rote memorizing (e.g., "If I remember perfectly, I can say that I understand") and outward results (e.g., "The process does not matter to me as long as my answer is correct").

Description of the strategy

As noted above, preparatory learning can be effective for promoting deeper learning in classroom instruction. If students undertake preparation and obtain prior knowledge about each fact, they can later learn more deeply. In other words, they would be able to better understand the reasons why those facts are true (e.g., "why Japan joined in World War I") during classroom instruction. In learning history, they would be able to better understand causal relationships between historical events when they read the textbook beforehand.

However, as mentioned earlier, there might be individual differences in the effect of preparatory learning. According to previous studies, non-cognitive learners are said to learn with shallow processing (e.g., Ueki, 2002; Uesaka et al., 2009). Especially the effect of preparation might not become apparent for learners who do not place importance on meaningful learning, but rather on rote memorization in learning. One way of circumventing this potential problem would be to direct learners' attention to causal relationships among historical facts in classroom instruction to enhance the effect of preparation.

In this regard, it might be effective to assign students to generate questions that ask about causal relationships during the preparatory task. It is important for students to have questions about the reason for each fact so that they perceive that solving questions is their goal in the next classroom lesson. In more concrete terms, this means they should not only read the textbook but also (1) generate questions that ask about the causes of each fact, and (2) come up with answers to those questions. These would likely be effective strategies for deepening students' learning during class. More concrete procedures for how this can be implemented are described below.

Preparation

1. Reading a textbook: to begin with, students read a textbook and gather knowledge about the contents of an upcoming classroom lesson. If teachers will deal with the content of two pages in the textbook, students need to read those two pages ahead of the classroom lesson. Using the textbook, students can usually only read brief explanations about each fact. For example, in history, explanations about what happened there (e.g., the Austrian crown prince and his wife were killed in Sarajevo) and who carried out such actions (e.g., a young Serbian) are provided in the textbook, with very limited or no analyses of causality and relationships. Learners can get these kinds of factual knowledge in advance during preparation.
2. Making questions: the explanations provided in the textbook are usually very simple, so learners often cannot understand sufficiently why the historical events happened. In history learning, to sufficiently understand "why a person carried out such action" and "why the incident happened there" during preparation is mostly impossible for the majority of learners.

    However, if teachers ask them to generate such questions, it is difficult for leaners, especially elementary school students, to clarify the problem or point for which they require an explanation. In this case, teachers could

guide or advice students to generate questions that start with "why." In cases where students are not yet capable of generating questions about what the teacher will focus on in the next classroom lesson, the teacher could generate the necessary questions and present those to students for them *to consider during preparation*.
3. Coming up with answers to the questions and setting goals for the next class: even if teachers ask students to generate questions that start with "why" or present the questions for students to use during preparation, it does not always lead to students learning more deeply. Especially, those who do not place importance on meaningful learning might generate questions that start with "why" without thinking deeply. Similarly, the questions presented by teachers may not deal with real issues or problems that students want addressed. Therefore students do not always recognize such questions during preparation as goals for the next class. In this case, teachers need to ask students *to come up with possible answers* to the questions. This activity makes it possible for students to realize that they cannot explain something well; therefore, they can recognize those questions as the problems to be solved in the next classroom lesson. If teachers inform students that the goal in a next class session would be to provide answers to those questions, students would be more likely to focus on relevant information relating to those questions during the ensuing classroom lesson.

Furthermore, assigning students to rate their confidence about their answers is also effective. For example, students could be asked to rate their confidence about their answers on a 5-point Likert-type scale (1 = *not confident at all*, 2 = *not confident*, 3 = *difficult to decide either way*, 4 = *a little confident*, 5 = *very confident*). If teachers inform students that the goal for a next class would be to increase their confidence ratings, students would be better able to appreciate the importance of clarifying the answers during that upcoming class.

Classroom lesson

After these activities in preparation, students participate in the corresponding classroom lesson. Teachers take time to explain to students the contents of the textbook, and this includes explaining the connections between each fact and the pertinent reasons that students need to understand about the content they are learning. In history learning, for example, teachers explain "why the historical event happened" and "why the person (or the country) behaved as such," and so on, in their classroom instruction. Preparation and classroom lessons like the above make it possible for students to connect each fact in the textbook and construct higher-order knowledge networks. It does not matter if teachers explain the relationships between the facts directly or make students discuss and come up with those explanations. The important thing is that learners can connect new input information in class to prior knowledge they got during preparation.

Evidence for the effectiveness of this preparation method

The effect of preparation and individual differences: Shinogaya (2008)

In this study, a summer seminar for junior high school students was held, in which classroom instruction concerning history was provided for 86 8th-grade students. The purpose of this study was to examine the effect of preparation on deeper understanding of history in class, and to examine individual differences in the way this effect manifests in the context of educational practice. The seminar was held for 5 days at a university during summer vacation. The theme was World War I. This theme comprised new content for participants at that time (they had not studied it before). In this seminar, students were randomly assigned to one of three conditions: preparation class ($n = 29$), preparation and question-generation class ($n = 29$), and review class ($n = 29$). Students in the preparation class read the contents of the upcoming classroom lessons in the textbook for 5 minutes before the class. Students in the preparation and question-generation class were instructed not only to read the textbook before the class but also to generate questions that asked about the causes of historical events in the textbook. In this class, they were asked to generate questions that start with "why" (e.g., "Why did Britain occupy India?," "Why did Japan join World War I?"). Students in the review class were asked to read the textbook for 5 minutes after classroom instruction. (To control for variations in quantity and quality of preparation the students might undertake, they were instead asked to undertake the preparation/review tasks *in class,* rather than at home.)

The students' beliefs about learning were measured with an adapted version of the questionnaire mentioned earlier (i.e., the Uesaka et al., 2009, questionnaire). Meaningful learning belief was gauged with the use of four items (e.g., "In history, it is important to understand relationships between the facts being learned"). Students were instructed to respond to these items on a 5-point Likert-type scale (1 = *not at all true of me,* 2 = *not very true of me,* 3 = *difficult to decide either way,* 4 = *a little true of me,* 5 = *very true of me*). Their mean scores in the four items were calculated and used in the statistical analysis that was subsequently conducted.

In this study, students received classroom lessons for 4 days with variations in the preparation or review activity they engaged in depending on the condition. The contents and styles of classroom instruction were the same in the three conditions, wherein the teacher taught and explained the causes of historical events described in the textbook. In explaining, the teacher used the blackboard and a world map. After four lessons, on the fifth day of the seminar, students took two tests. One test asked students to read some sentences with blanks and to supply the appropriate words to fill the blanks. The answers to this test (names of historical events, country, and persons) were all provided in the textbook. The other test was an essay test that asked students to explain the causes of historical events and the behaviors of the countries/person(s). The causes were provided only in the classroom lessons, so the two preparation conditions were expected to achieve higher scores than the review condition in this essay test.

The result of statistical analysis of the fill-in-the-blank test data revealed that the scores of the three groups did not differ, which suggests that they learned and retained the historical facts equally well. However, students in the preparation condition and the preparation and question-generation condition achieved higher scores in the essay test (that asked for the causes of historical events) compared to those in the review condition. In addition, this study checked students' notebooks for each classroom lesson and counted their spontaneous notetaking about the causes of historical events that were explained only in classroom instruction. The result of this analysis showed that the students in the preparation condition and the preparation and question-generation condition took notes on the causes of the historical events during classroom lessons. These results suggest that getting prior knowledge about each historical event beforehand can promote students paying attention to the causes of each event during classroom lessons and deepening of their understanding of history.

Individual differences in the effect of preparation

Shinogaya (2008) additionally examined individual differences in the effect of preparation in the research described above. As shown in Figure 9.1, in the essay test score, the effect of preparation was found in students with *higher* meaningful learning belief scores. However, it was not shown in students with *lower* meaningful learning belief scores. The same trend was also found in students' note taking. In this study, the number of notes that students had spontaneously written in their notebooks about the causes of historical events was counted. The analysis result revealed that students with higher meaningful learning belief

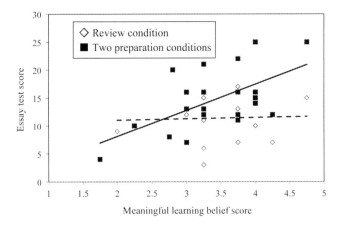

FIGURE 9.1 Effect of preparation in the essay test.

Notes. Solid line = Trend of two preparation conditions; Dotted line = Trend of review condition.

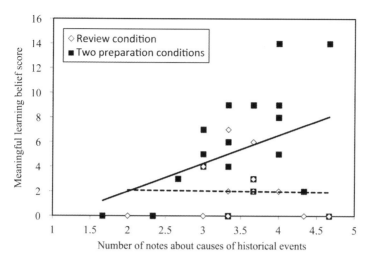

FIGURE 9.2 Effect of preparation in note taking.

Notes. Solid line = Trend of two preparation conditions; Dotted line = Trend of review condition.

scores spontaneously took more notes about the causes of historical events when they undertook preparation (Figure 9.2). In contrast, this effect of preparation was not found in students with lower meaningful learning belief scores.

Directive preparation to deepen learning in classroom lessons: Shinogaya (2011)

Shinogaya (2008) showed the effect of preparation on student achievement and how individual differences in learning beliefs can influence that effect. As a next step, the manner with which to direct students' attention to the causes of each fact being learned, and to promote deeper understanding, needed to be developed. In this regard, Shinogaya (2011) developed and evaluated a preparation strategy that may be effective for students with low scores in meaningful learning beliefs. To control for the quality and quantity of questions that students use in preparation, the teacher in this study provided the questions for students to use. For example, the textbook being used explained that Japan joined World War I because of an alliance with the UK, and thus one of the questions the teacher provided sought the reason for why Japan decided to join World War I.

In this study, a 5-day instructional seminar for students was held during the summer vacation. The 53 students who participated were randomly assigned to one of two classes. One was a "controlled preparation class" ($n = 26$) and the other was a "directive preparation class" ($n = 27$). In the controlled preparation class, students read the textbook for the upcoming class and were provided with three questions that asked about the causes of historical events in the textbook. The questions were already printed on a preparation sheet and the students were told that to find the answers to those questions was the goal of *classroom instruction*.

In the directive preparation class, the students likewise read the textbook and were provided with the same questions as the controlled preparation group. The questions and blanks for answers to them were printed on their preparation sheet. The students were asked to come up with answers to the questions *during preparation*. In addition, students were also asked to rate their confidence about each of their answers on a 5-point Likert-type scale (1 = *not confident at all*, 2 = *not confident*, 3 = *difficult to decide either way*, 4 = *a little confident*, 5 = *very confident*), and they were told that increasing their confidence ratings was the goal of classroom instruction. The time spent on preparation in both classes was the same at about 10 minutes (as in Shinogaya, 2008, the preparation activities were carried out during the class sessions in order to control for potential variations and other confounding factors).

The contents of the classroom lessons were the same as in Shinogaya (2008). Students were provided classroom instruction about World War I for four days and were administered two tests on the fifth day of the seminar. One test asked students to read some sentences with blanks in them and to fill in those blanks with appropriate words. The other test was an essay test that asked students to explain the causes of historical events and the behaviors of countries/person(s).

As shown in Figure 9.3, meaningful learning belief scores evidenced a significant positive relationship with the students' scores in the essay test in the controlled preparation class (see the dotted line). In contrast, such a significant relationship was not found in the directive preparation class (see the solid line). Although the solid line looks like a negative slope, it was not significant in the statistical analysis, which means that there were no differences in the essay test scores in the directive preparation class as a function of the students' learning

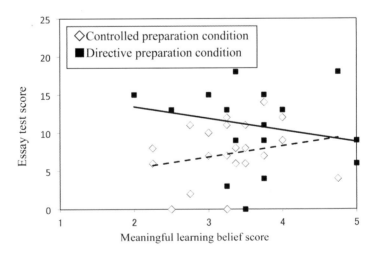

FIGURE 9.3 Effect of directive preparation and meaningful learning belief.

Notes. Solid line = Trend of directive preparation condition; dotted line = Trend of controlled preparation condition.

belief scores. This result suggests that *directive activities* in preparation can guide the attention of students with low meaningful learning beliefs to the causes of historical events in class, thus promoting deeper learning. In other words, only reading the textbook and providing questions that ask for the causes of each historical event may not be sufficient in guiding students' attention to the important information, especially those students who have low meaningful learning beliefs. With directive activities like the ones included in the directive preparation class in this study, the negative effects of low meaningful learning beliefs can be alleviated – thus making preparation equally beneficial for all students.

Discussion: What is an effective way to prepare for deeper learning?

To undertake preparation and read the textbook beforehand make it possible for students to better understand the causes of and reasons for each item of knowledge set in the textbook. However, the beneficial effect of preparation can be moderated by students' beliefs about learning. Preparation is not always effective for students with a low meaningful learning belief. In addition, simply asking students to generate questions that ask the "why" of historical events is not always effective. According to King (1992, 1994), activities like these had positive effects on deepening students' learning. However, findings from the Shinogaya (2008) study revealed that meaningful learning belief affected the extent to which students could benefit from generating questions during preparation. The process of question generation has been described as comprising (1) noticing what is not understood, (2) comparing to prior knowledge, and (3) making questions (e.g., Van der Meij, 1990). Considering this process, only generating questions that start with "Why" does not provide comparison to prior knowledge. Thus, students with low meaningful learning beliefs do not recognize the questions to be their "own" questions (i.e., not related to what they really know or not know), and they do not subsequently pay attention to information connected to those questions they generated in preparation.

In this regard, Shinogaya (2011) showed that coming up with answers to the questions and rating their confidence level about those answers are effective strategies for directing students' attention to the important information they would later encounter in class. Previous studies about text understanding have shown that coming up with answers to pre-questions deepens understanding of the textbook content (e.g., Pressley, Tanenbaum, McDaniel, & Wood, 1990; Thiede, Anderson, & Therriault, 2003). The result of the Shinogaya (2011) study is consistent with these findings. In addition, rating confidence is also effective because not "understanding deeply," but "increasing the confidence rating" is easier for students to recognize as a goal for an upcoming classroom lesson. Previous studies suggest that a clear goal increases learners' self-efficacy, then enhances their motivation for the learning activity (Schunk, 1990, 2003). In Shinogaya (2011), the students' motivation for the upcoming class was not measured; however, the findings suggest that the rating activity enhanced their motivation and then deepened their learning during the classroom instruction.

According to the SOI (Selecting, Organizing, and Integrating) model (Mayer, 1996), learners select important information, organize it, and integrate new information with prior knowledge. Directing activities, such as coming up with answers to questions and rating confidence levels during preparation, may positively affect learners' selecting process. In addition, Ito (2004) pointed out that written information functions as an "outside memory resource"; thus, if answers are written on the preparation sheet, students can compare it to new information during the classroom lesson. Even if students select important information, it is difficult to integrate new information with their own answers without having written that information (i.e., the answers). Therefore, writing down answers to the questions also improves the integration process during the classroom lesson.

The findings of the two studies described in this chapter focused on history learning, but those findings can be adapted to suit other school subjects too. Undertaking preparation and reading the textbook beforehand deepens understanding during classroom lessons, irrespective of the school subject. For example, in mathematics learning, explanations about mathematical terms (e.g., a parallelogram) and how to calculate the answers to related problems (e.g., calculating the area of a parallelogram) are provided in textbooks, but usually not the underlying logic or rationale for those. And understanding "Why this formula is correct," "Why this procedure leads to an answer," and so on is needed in classroom lessons. In this case, deeper learning might be achieved if students read the textbook and gain knowledge about each formula and solving procedure beforehand. Individual differences in the effect of preparation may be observed. Then, to guide students' attention, setting questions that ask the "why" of each knowledge set, coming up with answers to them, and rating confidence about one's answers could be effective. At first, students may not be able to generate good questions by themselves. And even if teachers instruct them to ask questions that start with "Why," students with low meaningful learning beliefs may create questions without thinking deeply. If such a problem is encountered, teachers can provide questions for students to use during preparation. Coming up with answers to the questions and rating confidence levels about the answers could then direct students' attention to important information in class and deepen their understanding. Through such experiences, it is expected that students with low meaningful learning belief would perceive the value of asking "why" in their learning.

The most important thing is to consider the relationship between the contents of preparatory learning and of classroom instruction. In the two studies described in this chapter, the students read the textbook in preparation, and the teachers explained the causes of each set of knowledge described in the textbook during the classroom lessons provided. This relationship between preparation and classroom lesson is necessary for preparation to function as an advanced organizer for the next class. If teachers do not provide deeper and more meaningful content than what is already provided in the textbook, students may perceive classroom lessons as only repeating the contents of the textbook, thus their motivation for learning during class could be decreased by the prior preparation they have undertaken (i.e., if they consider what is being taught in class as something they already know from prior preparation). Many school teachers who disagree with preparation are anxious that students would not experience novelty and instead feel classroom instruction to be boring (e.g., Ichikawa, 2004). An effective way of preparing for an upcoming class depends on the content of classroom instruction: preparation and classroom lessons cannot be designed separately. Other previous studies have suggested that what and how teachers teach in classroom lessons can affect students' spontaneous strategy use in preparation, and the effect of preparation can be affected by teachers' teaching strategies in class (Shinogaya, 2014, 2017). For example, when teachers ask students about their own opinions in class, and they provide more detailed explanations in class than what is covered in the textbook, students' spontaneous preparation increases because students can perceive the necessity and value of preparation for the upcoming class.

Limitations and directions for future research

In the two studies described in this chapter, students conducted their preparation during the experimental class sessions rather than during homework. This was because control of individual differences in preparation (e.g., length of time spent on preparation, adherence to instructions given) was necessary to examine the effects of the intervention in each study. If we administer preparation as homework, it is likely that individual difference in preparation would occur. To avoid this, teaching concrete strategies such as those described in this chapter is one effective approach.

While the two studies about preparation described in this chapter examined effective ways of preparation for understanding instruction provided by teachers in classroom lessons, it is also necessary to examine the effect of preparation on learners' interactions in class. Getting prior knowledge might also affect cognitive processing of input information during learners' interactions. As mentioned above, learners process new input information with prior knowledge. Then, learners can better understand other leaners' opinions and explanations when they have undertaken preparation. In fact, research studies about cooperative learning have shown that learners with much prior knowledge can better integrate various pieces of information during interaction and deepen their learning (Gijlers & de Jong, 2005; Schmidt, De Volder, De Grave, Moust, & Patel, 1989). So far, many research studies about cooperative and collaborative learning have examined characteristics of effective learners' interactions (e.g., Okada & Simon, 1997; Ootwijn, Boekaerts, & Vedder, 2008). However, the effect of preparation on learners' interactions has not been examined adequately. Future research studies about preparation need to investigate the effects on, and effective ways of preparation for, learning through interaction.

Recently, the importance of homework has been highlighted. However, many researchers and school teachers have largely neglected preparation as homework. Learning is not only attained with classroom instruction. Through the three learning phases of preparation, classroom lessons, and review, learning becomes deeper (cf. Shinogaya, 2012). Therefore, preparation is necessary for deeper learning in classroom lessons as learner's process new input information with their prior knowledge. In addition, to undertake preparatory learning is an important skill to keep learning effectively in everyday life. For students, it is important to connect what to learn in preparation and what to understand in classroom instruction to deepen their understanding and to develop their learning skills for the future.

References

Ausubel, D. P. (1960). The use of advance organizers in the learning and retention of meaningful verbal material. *Journal of Educational Psychology, 51,* 267–272.

Ausubel, D. P. (1968). *Educational psychology: A cognitive view.* New York: Holt, Rinehart and Winston.

Bang, H. (2012). Promising homework practices: Teachers' perspectives on making homework work for newcomer immigrant students. *The High School Journal, 95,* 3–31.

Bromage, B. K., & Mayer, R. E. (1986). Quantitative and qualitative effects of repetition on learning from technical text. *Journal of Educational Psychology, 78,* 271–278.

Cooper, H. (1989). Synthesis of research on homework. *Educational Leadership, 47,* 85–91.

Cooper, H. (2001). *The battle over homework: Common ground for administrators, teachers, and parents* (2nd ed.). Thousand Oaks, CA: Sage.

Epstein, J. L., & Van Voorhis, F. L. (2001). More than ten minutes: Teachers' roles in designing homework. *Educational Psychologist, 36,* 181–193.

Flunger, B., Trautwein, U., Nagengast, B., Lüdtke, O., Niggli, A., & Schnyder, I. (2015). The Janus-faced nature of time spent on homework: Using latent profile analyses to predict academic achievement over a school year. *Learning and Instruction, 39,* 97–106.

Gijlers, H., & de Jong, T. (2005). The relation between prior knowledge and students' collaborative discovery learning processes. *Journal of Research in Science Teaching, 42,* 264–282.

Ichikawa, S. (2004). *Manabu iyoku to sukiru wo sodateru* [Enhancing motivation and skills for learning]. Tokyo, Japan: Shogakukan.

Ito, M. (2004). *Hikkisetsumei ga kouseitekigakusyu ni ataeru eikyou* [Effect of writing explanation on constructive learning]. Tokyo, Japan: Kazama syobou.

King, A. (1992). Facilitating elaborative learning through guided student-generated questioning. *Educational Psychologist, 27,* 111–126.

King, A. (1994). Guided knowledge construction in the classroom: Effect of teacher children how to question and how to explain. *American Educational Research Journal, 31,* 338–368.

Lee, J., & Pruitt, W. (1979). Homework assignments: Classroom games or teaching tools? *The Clearing House, 53,* 31–35.

Mayer, R. E. (1983). Can you repeat that? Qualitative effects of repetition and advance organizers on learning from science prose. *Journal of Educational Psychology, 75,* 40–49.

Mayer, R. E. (1996). Learning strategies for making sense out of expository text: The SOI model for guiding three cognitive processes in knowledge construction. *Educational Psychology Review, 8,* 357–371.

Mayer, R. E., & Bromage, B. K. (1980). Difference recall protocols for technical texts due to advance organizers. *Journal of Educational Psychology, 72*, 209–225.

Novak, J. D. (2002). Meaningful learning: The essential factor for conceptual change in limited or inappropriate propositional hierarchies leading to empowerment of learners. *Science Education, 86*, 548.

Núñez, J. C., Suárez, N., Rosário, P., Vallejo, G., Cerezo, R., & Valle, A. (2015). Teachers' feedback on homework, homework-related behaviors, and academic achievement. *The Journal of Educational Research, 108*, 204–216.

Okada, T. & Simon, H. A. (1997). Collaborative discovery in a scientific domain. *Cognitive Science, 21*, 109–146.

Ootwijn, M., Boekaerts, M., & Vedder, P. (2008). The impact of teacher's role and pupils' ethnicity prior knowledge on pupils' performance and motivation to cooperate. *Instructional Science, 36*, 251–268.

Pressley, M., Tanenbaum, R., McDaniel, M. A., & Wood, E. (1990). What happens when university students try to answer prequestions that accompany textbook material? *Contemporary Educational Psychology, 15*, 27–35.

Schmidt, H. G, De Volder, M. L, De Grave, W. S, Moust, J. H. C., & Patel, V. L. (1989). Explanatory models in the processing of science text: The role of prior knowledge activation through small-group discussion. *Journal of Educational Psychology, 81*, 610–619.

Schunk, D. H. (1990). Goal setting and self-efficacy during self-regulated learning. *Educational Psychologist, 25*, 71–86.

Schunk, D. H. (2003). Self-efficacy for reading and writing: Influence of modeling, goal setting, and self-evaluation. *Reading & Writing Quarterly, 19*, 159–172.

Schunk, D. H., & Zimmerman, B. J. (1997). Social origins of self-regulatory competence. *Educational Psychologist, 32*, 195–208.

Shinogaya, K. (2008). Effects of preparation on learning: Interaction with beliefs about learning. *Japanese Journal of Educational Psychology, 56*, 256–267.

Shinogaya, K. (2011). Preparation for meaningful learning: Effects of method involving answering pre-questions and judging confidence in the answers. *Japanese Journal of Educational Psychology, 59*, 355–366.

Shinogaya, K. (2012). Learning strategies: A review from the perspective of the relation between learning phases. *Japanese Journal of Educational Psychology, 60*, 92–105.

Shinogaya, K. (2014). Students' strategies in preparation and lectures: Direct and moderating effects of teachers' teaching strategies. *Japanese Journal of Educational Psychology, 62*, 197–208.

Shinogaya, K. (2017). Motives, beliefs, and perceptions among learners affect preparatory learning strategies. *Journal of Educational Research, 111*, 612–619.

Thiede, K. W., Anderson, M. C. M., & Therriault, D. (2003). Accuracy of metacognitive monitoring affects learning of texts. *Journal of Educational Psychology, 95*, 66–73.

Ueki, R. (2002). Structure of high-school students' beliefs about learning. *Japanese Journal of Educational Psychology, 50*, 301–310.

Uesaka, Y., Seo, M., & Ichikawa, S. (2009). Students' cognitive and non-cognitive beliefs about learning as a factor in learning skills acquisition: Suggestions from cognitive counselling. In M. Sylvester (Ed.), *Transformations: Proceedings of the 2008 Annual International Conference of the Association of Tertiary Learning Advisors of Aotearoa/New Zealand*, (Vol. 4, pp. 89–100). Auckland, New Zealand: ATLAANZ.

Van der Meij, H. (1990). Question asking: To know that you do not know is not enough. *Journal of Educational Psychology, 82*, 505–512.

PART 4
Promoting engagement and reflection

10

"LAUGHTER IS THE BEST MEDICINE"

Pedagogies of humor and joy that support critical thinking and communicative competence

Jean J. Ryoo

Summary

Teachers are often told to refrain from smiling until they've achieved full "control" of their students, yet they are simultaneously expected to maintain their students' full attention while teaching challenging ideas and skills. This chapter describes a qualitative research study (following 70 students in three urban high school classrooms) in which computer science teachers' pedagogies of humor and joy were actually essential to not only engaging their students in what many initially believed to be a boring or intimidating subject but also participating in critical thinking and communication practices valued across all fields of study.

Introduction

Many of us have received the following advice before our first day of teaching: be strict and don't smile until you have firm "control" of your students. Humor, joy, laughter? Not to be expressed until later, if at all.

No wonder Ferris Bueller[1] needed that day off.

Yet ironically, many of us have also been told that our students should be fully engaged, not distracted or "off task." And what better way to convince students that learning is worth their time, if not with humor, joy, and laughter? Youth demonstrate their best achievements and are motivated to engage in learning if they actually enjoy the activities at hand (Csikszentmihalyi, Rathunde, & Whalen, 1993). So why has in-school learning come to be seen as something that should be "serious," while humor and joy are "not serious enough" for the critical thinking skills we hope to see among our students?

This is an important question to ask when considering the challenges we face in capturing and maintaining students' interests, specifically in Science, Technology, Engineering, Math (STEM), and Computer Science (CS) that, internationally, have raised concerns as segregated fields in which females and people of color are underrepresented. Research shows that students do not lack ability or interest, but rather lack access to quality learning experiences that make them feel capable and excited to pursue these fields of study (see Margolis, Estrella, Goode, Jellison-Holme, & Nao, 2008, for example, which describes how segregation in computing along race/ethnicity, gender, and socioeconomic lines is due to both institutional barriers and stereotypes about who should excel with computers). Furthermore, students have been receiving differential access to opportunities to engage with the deeper learning, critical thinking, and creative aspects of STEM and CS based on race/ethnicity, gender, and socioeconomic status, with only the elite being prepared to be the creators of new inventions while the majority are taught simply to be users of those inventions (for example, Boaler & Sengupta-Irving, 2006; Pearson, 2002; Watt, 1982). In response, efforts across the world (the United States, Africa, Europe, etc.) are now focused on broadening participation in STEM and CS for *all* our children.

This chapter illustrates why pedagogies of humor and joy are important for the success of efforts such as these, not only for increasing interest and engagement in computing specifically, but also for supporting young people's critical thinking skills and communicative competence that sit at the heart of all fields of study.

A review of research regarding pedagogies of humor and joy

Humor and joy have been shown to be effective for building the engagement *and* enjoyment we want to see in all classrooms, by: 1) supporting retention of new ideas (Derks, Gardner, & Agarwal, 1998; Hauck & Thomas, 1972; Schmidt, 1994, 2002; Schmidt & Williams, 2001; Ziv, 1988); 2) decreasing nervousness and improving test performance (Adams, 1972; Horn, 1972; Mechanic, 1962; Monson, 1968); 3) decreasing anxiety about a subject (Neuliep, 1991; Long, 1983; Smith, Ascough, Ettinger, & Nelson, 1971; Ziv, 1976); 4) improving teacher-to-student relationships by making teachers appear more accessible and responsive to students' needs (Crump, 1996; Gorham & Christophel, 1990; Wanzer & Frymier, 1999; Welker, 1977); 5) building classroom community by using humor to embrace diverse cultural practices or decrease conflict between students (Cornett, 1986; Kelly, 1983; Wallinger, 1997); 6) establishing boundaries while reinforcing positive, desired behaviors (Cornett, 1986; Kelly, 1983; Wallinger, 1997); 7) motivating students' desire to learn (Gorham & Christophel, 1992); and 8) encouraging creativity (Moran & John-Steiner, 2003; Smolucha, 1992; Vygotsky, 1978).

Furthermore, playfulness (that involves humor and inspires joy) has been described as creating a zone of proximal development for learners – the space between one's current developmental state and where one will be with maturation. As children engage in pretend-play, while "playing house" and pretending to be a mother or a father, or while "playing school" and pretending to be teachers or students, they have the opportunity to imagine different ways of thinking, acting, and reacting that supports mental growth. Vygotsky (1978) explains that, as children play, they can therefore become "a head taller" in those imaginative moments of playfulness (Vygotsky, 1978, p. 102). Relatedly, playfulness – which is "about asking what if and imagining how the ordinary can become extraordinary" (Ackermann, Guantlett, Wolbers, & Weckstrom, 2009, p. 5) – can lead to deep critical thinking practices by allowing one to look at things from different angles to derive unique and creative solutions (Ackermann, 2004; Kafai, 2006; Resnick, 2007). As Bogost (2016) notes, play can encourage people to pay closer attention to their surroundings and think outside the figurative "box" when encountering limitations in the world that are usually beyond their control, often boring, and even unpleasant.

Studying pedagogies of humor and joy – Research context and methods

Building on this body of research, this chapter describes a study conducted in three Exploring Computer Science (ECS, www.exploringcs.org) classrooms, which is an introductory high school CS course employing inquiry-based and culturally relevant teaching strategies for democratizing access to CS. Curricular activities focused on teaching youth to be the creators, not just consumers, of new technology. In many ways, the problem-solving and critical thinking skills employed in the ECS classroom are transferable to other subjects and classrooms.

Through a year-long study (following 70 students and 3 teachers; collecting 50 interviews and over 105 hours of audio/video recordings and fieldnote observation), this research illuminated how very different educators' uses of humor promoted critical thinking skills (such as considering alternative perspectives and solutions, evaluating evidence, etc.) and communicative competence (such as expressing their ideas, challenging each other's ideas, etc.). The classrooms were located in a large urban school district on the west coast of the United States, enrolling primarily Latinx and African American students in proportions representing the district's demographics. The schools were typical for the district in terms of state and national test scores, and focal teachers were chosen based on their reputations (among principals, colleagues, and students) as dynamic and dedicated teachers committed to broadening participation in computing (as articulated during CS professional developments). For these focal teachers, "broadening participation in computing" meant challenging the historical underrepresentation of people of color and women in computing by providing

CS learning experiences that could encourage underrepresented students' sense of confidence, engagement, and desire to learn CS and use CS toward their own personal, academic, and career goals.

The teachers included Ms. Mendoza, Mr. Torres, and Mr. Santos. Ms. Mendoza was a Mexican American woman in her early 30s who identified as lesbian and grew up in the local city. She came from a family of educators and was a certified social studies teacher who chose to teach CS due to her love of technology and her commitment to increasing access to CS learning for *all* students and not just those who fit the stereotype of "technology geek." Mr. Torres was a Puerto Rican American who was raised in New York City and identified as heterosexual. He was in his late 30s and newer to teaching. He began his career in the tech industry, but his desire to have a positive impact on his community through teaching resulted in a mid-life career change. Mr. Santos was a Mexican American heterosexual man in his late 40s who was a certified math teacher. He grew up in a migrant farming community in Central California. He was passionate about teaching and had been working for almost two decades at the time of this research.

Data analysis focused on examining teacher-student and student-student interactions during whole-group discussions as well as students' problem-solving processes while creating computational artifacts (e.g., websites, animations, etc.). Initial rounds of coding focused on how social interactions related to teacher practice and student engagement with CS activities, as well as the types of computational practices engaged during these interactions (e.g., *critical thinking practices* – such as analyzing the effects of computing on society, evaluating the usability of computational artifacts, using abstractions and models, engaging in algorithmic thinking to solve problems, etc. – and *communicative competence* such as explaining the meaning of results, describing the impact of technology or computational artifacts, justifying appropriateness or correctness of programming choices, etc.). These first rounds of codes surfaced themes such as "teacher practice" that involved sub-themes such as "addressing real-world issues" or "humor/joy." A second round of coding resulted in parsing down these codes into differences in kind, such as kinds of teacher assistance or types of student-to-student assistance. A third round of coding focused on outliers in the data that could help point to unique situations or new ideas about what seemed "typical" in the classrooms.

These analyses revealed the salience of humor and joy as pedagogical practices for motivating learning, encouraging critical thinking, and developing communicative competence. In what follows, teacher and student interview data describing the importance of humor and joy are shared, followed by two detailed vignettes as well as shorter descriptions from the three classrooms illuminating what pedagogies of humor and joy look like, as well as the critical thinking and communicative competencies they support. The chapter concludes with suggestions for how educators can take these ideas and put them into practice in their own classrooms.

Pedagogies of humor and joy: Research evidence of effectiveness

Teacher and student testimonies

The original intention of this study was not to examine humor in the classroom. However, when 36 of 43 students mentioned, *completely unprompted*, that they most valued having a "funny" teacher with a "nice sense of humor," and six others emphasized valuing their teachers' senses of humor when asked if their teachers made them laugh (see Figure 10.1 below), the topic became worthy of closer scrutiny.

Yet, why did pedagogies of humor and joy matter to youth in these classrooms? Across the board, students described how teachers' uses of humor made boring or intimidating material more accessible, engaging them with the learning at hand. More specifically, students described that pedagogies of humor and joy mediated their relationships to CS learning by: 1) shifting their views of CS from "boring" to "fun"; 2) increasing engagement with the learning at hand; and 3) encouraging new ways of thinking and learning by motivating interest in CS assignments.

Numerous students in all three schools described how they didn't sign up for the course, thought they would hate CS because they didn't fit the stereotypical image of "computer nerds," and even tried to change classes. However, their teachers' uses of humor convinced them to want to learn. For example, Lena[2] from Midtown High thought she would hate CS at the start of the school year, but Ms. Mendoza's "jokes, they're funny.... Which makes me want to do the work." By the end of the year, Lena successfully created complex websites and animations, and decided to study CS after high school. Julieta noted that she used to skip Mr. Torres's class at Presidential High, but she began attending regularly because of his sense of humor.

Other students described how pedagogies of humor and joy were useful for student engagement. Typical student comments described how teacher humor keeps "you more concentrated, not spacing out" (Olimpia), helps students feel that "it's not like work, just something you *like*" (Carlos), "gives [students] energy

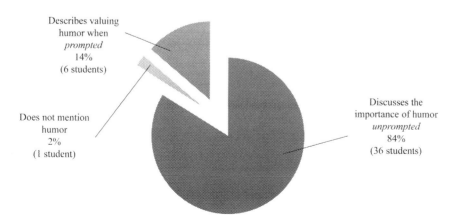

FIGURE 10.1 Students' interview responses related to humor.

to work" (Orlando), "makes me keep on going" (Enrique), "pay more attention" (Xochitl), and "makes class to be interesting" (Jesenia and Natalia) because the teacher "[makes] us smile so I feel like I should do the work" (Hyun).

Pedagogies of humor and joy also influenced students' views of CS, leading to engagement in new forms of thinking and learning. Similar to Lena above, Catalina described initially feeling insecure about coding, but "[Ms. Mendoza] show[ed] us her [programming] project and I thought it was hilarious...I was like 'Oh my gosh! I wanna do that too!'" Ms. Mendoza's website, which welcomed student laughter, included a colorful picture of a llama wearing a scarf with the statement "cooler than the other side of your pillow." Invited to engage with the critical thinking skills of CS through Ms. Mendoza's sense of humor, Catalina not only became one of Ms. Mendoza's top students by the end of the second semester, but was also observed trying to teach her classmate to think critically about data analysis the way Ms. Mendoza had taught her. Catalina pointed to her friend's pie chart and, instead of telling Annie what to think, asked: "So what can you say about this chart?" followed by a comment that, while the pie chart was colorful, it appeared that the health levels documented were all the same size.

Of course, none of the three teachers were coincidentally funny. Teacher interviews revealed the primacy of pedagogies of humor and joy in their own practice. Mr. Santos at City High intentionally kept his students laughing, comparing his pedagogy to the saying: "Luring bees is best to do with honey...Vinegar's not going to work." When Mr. Santos first started teaching, he was "told not to smile until Christmas," but he realized that this made him "miserable" while having a negative impact on the students who shirked classroom participation and struggled in the class. However, "[When I] joked around a little bit more, I was able to get more out of them than with the structured, serious teacher that I was pretending to be."

Similarly, when asked the question "What do you think makes a really good teacher?" Ms. Mendoza at Midtown High immediately replied, "Ha! A sense of humor!" More specifically, Ms. Mendoza emphasized how humor and joy helped students gain self-confidence when working with abstract ideas, allowing them to laugh at mistakes, ask questions, share answers, and figure out solutions to CS problems without feeling worried about being wrong or punished:

> [S]tudents that came in and may have been a little bit intimidated with the idea of computers and [that] this was obviously a man's thing; and to see my girls now...they're willing to say what their solution is, even if it's wrong. And I think that's where the real learning comes in.

Mr. Torres echoed this belief, adding how humor was a pedagogical tool that distinguished his classroom from others that were regimented and dull:

> They have several other classes where it's just very "okay, sit down, and get to your studies." And I try to lighten up the mood for them because...I want this to be a class that they look forward to...the teachers that I remember the most are the teachers that made me laugh!

Mr. Torres emphasized that "laughter is the best medicine" for engaging students with academic learning.

But what did it look like to teach with humor and joy? And how did such pedagogies impact students' thinking and communication practices? The following vignettes illustrate how pedagogies of humor and joy supported not only engagement with new learning but also critical thinking and communicative competence.

Supporting critical thinking

Ms. Mendoza regularly invited student participation and critical thinking with humor and joy, especially when topics were challenging to discuss. For example, in the context of a data analysis unit (the fifth of six units, taking place during the second semester of the school year), students collected their own data about the snacks they ate throughout the day[3]. The following example shows how Ms. Mendoza's use of humor encouraged critical thinking about how gender, student status, environment, and more might impact their research results.

Ms. Mendoza pulled up a graph of the health levels of the entire class's snacking data. She asked her students how the graph might be different if collected by adult men. Clara said the snacks would be unhealthy "Because men don't care what they eat." Dario quickly called out, "That's sexist!" and Ms. Mendoza smiled, asking him why. Dario explained, "Women eat unhealthy too!" **Ms. Mendoza laughed, replying: "Whoa! Whoa!" while holding a yardstick between Dario and Clara as if to prevent them from having a fist fight.** Dario laughed and Clara smiled, saying "I didn't say all guys…" Dario quipped back, "Yes, you did!" Ms. Mendoza and the class laughed, recognizing Clara's mistake. Ms. Mendoza then asked, "What if college students were doing these surveys?" Xochitl replied that healthiness "would be all over the place because some care, some don't." Jack pointed out, "It depends if there's a healthy store nearby." Ms. Mendoza added, "Or if they have a meal plan." Then she described all the different supermarkets surrounding a local university near their school, asking, "How would it be there?" Dario said, "Up and down," and Nico said, "When people are under stress, they may not have time to cook, so they'll probably eat unhealthy." Ms. Mendoza said this was a good point and asked, "So would they eat more snacks? Or would it depend on time? **Like around finals and exams time, you're all like 'aaraaraar'" and Ms. Mendoza pretended to gobble imaginary food while joking about the fact that the pizza deliveryman knew her first name, last name, and phone number during exam time.** The class erupted in laughter. Spurred on by the discussion about local options, Nico pointed out, "Doesn't it matter if we're in the city or not? In the city, there's more fast food around, but if you're in a rural area, maybe you don't have as many." Ms. Mendoza replied, "Good point! What if the university was in the middle of a rural area?" Nico thought snacks would be healthier, and Ms. Mendoza agreed this was possible, but that there were fewer options in rural areas.

Then Ms. Mendoza showed a graph of the students' snack prices and asked how these might change if they were African Americans. Students were silent and Ms. Mendoza laughed saying that it was difficult to talk about race in the classroom, but that the classroom was a safe space where people should not judge one another. Then Dario replied, "It would be cheaper because colored people are lower class." Ms. Mendoza gently corrected, "Let's say 'living in poverty.'" Then Dario clarified: "And when I say 'colored,' I mean Latino people too." The majority Latino classroom remained quiet and **Ms. Mendoza said, "Hey! We're all adults here! We can say it! Why are we so uncomfortable?" Then she joked that her eighth graders felt uncomfortable saying that President Obama was Black even though it's true.** Students laughed as she asked, "What if only White students were collecting this data?" Clara noted, "The snacks would be more expensive." Nico countered this, saying, "It depends on which state." Ms. Mendoza nodded her head and replied, "So let's say we're in our home city [a diverse, big city]." Dario reflected that not only White people were wealthy, while Jack disagreed, saying White people have more income. Ms. Mendoza asked, "What if they're white high school students living in rural Tennessee?" Jack changed his analysis, saying the snacks would be cheaper. Ms. Mendoza replied, "So you're saying that socioeconomics matter?" Jack said, "Yes, it does matter." Ms. Mendoza smiled, nodding her head in agreement.

In this discussion, students engaged in a range of critical thinking practices: 1) they interpreted graphs of their snack consumption data (health level and cost); 2) they analyzed data in relation to different contextual considerations (debating how things like gender, socioeconomic status, etc. might impact data); 3) they made inferences about various populations' behaviors and environments (thinking about the availability of resources or the intersectionalities of race and class in urban versus rural contexts); 4) they integrated different ideas across demographic and physical contexts (when considering university students' eating habits during exam time, for example); and 5) they explained their reasoning while challenging each other's thinking (questioning blanket statements about men or the wealth of White people).

To facilitate this deeper thinking, Ms. Mendoza was clearly skilled at asking students "why" (for example, when Dario challenged Clara's statement as "sexist," she neither agreed nor disagreed but gave the students an opportunity to think it through together). She built on students' ideas to push the conversation further (when Jack pointed out the importance of having a healthy store nearby, she described the local university's surroundings and asked students to consider health levels of snacks there as well). And she supported students in thinking about the language they were using to explain their thinking (such as considering the difference between saying one is "lower class" versus "living in poverty" or being able to explain that "socioeconomics matter" and not just race/ethnicity).

While these teaching practices were important for facilitating students' critical thinking and communication skills in the classroom, Ms. Mendoza's students did not begin the school year actively participating this way. In fact, most students felt forced to take the class and had little to no prior experience with CS. So what motivated their excitement to engage in the conversation and push their thinking?

Over time, the key teaching practice that consistently resulted in greater student participation in critical thinking and communicative competence was Ms. Mendoza's pedagogy of humor and joy. Ms. Mendoza always used jokes or cheerful statements to capture student attention that led to participation in the deeper thinking she wanted to see. By the time of this particular vignette, Ms. Mendoza had successfully built a community of sharing and laughter through her pedagogical approach of humor and joy. In this vignette, Ms. Mendoza demonstrated three turns of humor that served specific purposes in the classroom discussion.

The first example occurred when Dario and Clara argued about "sexism." Ms. Mendoza encouraged them to dialogue about the topic, but held up a yardstick and pretended to be fending off a fight at the same time. While this may come off as simple theatrics, Ms. Mendoza's playfulness was purposeful: she used her sense of humor to acknowledge that these kinds of discussions can be heated and personal, but that the classroom was a safe space where it was okay to disagree.

Ms. Mendoza's second use of humor and joy was visible discussing university students' snacking behaviors. Building on Nico's comment about how stress or lack of time for cooking impacted snacking, Ms. Mendoza pushed students to think critically about this, while encouraging laughter about her demonstration of frantically eating and her description of the pizza deliveryman. This laughter kept students engaged in the conversation, but her joke about the pizza deliveryman also encouraged Nico to go deeper in his thinking about context: he shared how rural areas may not have as much fast food like Ms. Mendoza's pizza place. Humor and joy not only welcomed students to remain part of the discussion but also to ask more questions regarding their various lines of reasoning.

The final example of humor occurred when Ms. Mendoza tried to encourage her majority Latinx students to reflect on the ways race/ethnicity might impact snack prices. Ms. Mendoza's joke about her younger students' hesitation to acknowledge that President Obama was Black served as a way to recognize that their discomfort was not only real and okay but also something students could overcome as "adults" in a "safe space." As a result, students engaged in thinking critically about how race might intersect differently with urban versus rural contexts or socioeconomic status.

Supporting communicative competence

In Mr. Torres's classroom, pedagogies of humor and joy were central for encouraging disengaged students with communicative competence and critical thinking. The following vignettes from the eleventh day of class mark a turning point during which Brittany and Jessica finally began participating in whole-group discussions at Presidential High. At the start of the school year, both Brittany and Jessica actively resisted both the teacher and course, proving responsible for over half of all off-task behaviors during the first ten days of class (e.g., refusing to answer Mr. Torres's questions, loudly chatting about unrelated topics, putting on makeup instead of participating in group work, etc.) during which Mr. Torres led ten extensive, whole-group discussions.

This vignette shows Brittany and Jessica's shift in participation when Mr. Torres began *consistently* integrating a sense of humor throughout the whole-group conversation in a way that he hadn't before. This particular day, he incorporated six humorous comments that solicited playful responses and generated new ideas from students. Brittany willingly contributed four ideas to the conversation, and Jessica shared her opinions on two different topics without hesitation. Both young women demonstrated a sense of pride in academic participation that was previously absent. The following vignette took place 50 minutes into a 90-minute class period that Jessica had skipped. When she arrived without an excuse, Mr. Torres did not scold her and moved seamlessly into a discussion about students' uses of communication technology:

Mr. Torres asked students how they would ask their parents' permission for something when they knew that their parents would say no: "For those of you who would say 'phone call,' why would you choose that?" Belén explained calling was best because you could hang up on your parents. **Mr. Torres widened his eyes in mock horror, explaining with a smile that he could never do that to his mother.** In response, Belén joked that you could rustle a bag of chips by the phone speaker and say that the connection was bad before hanging up. **Mr. Torres laughed, then proceeded to act out this scenario, crinkling an imaginary bag of chips next to an imaginary phone, saying: "Sorry...bad...con...ction!"** Students laughed.

Suddenly, Brittany called out, "It's better face-to-face with your parents because texting is rude." Mr. Torres asked who in the class was really persuasive and Brittany mentioned that she was persuasive and said, while batting her eyelashes and frowning, that "if you do it face-to-face, you can use a sad face and say 'Please!'" The class laughed as Veronica agreed. Mr. Torres nodded his head and asked, "Has anyone used Facebook with your parents?" Hector said that he did once and then Lissandro shared that he couldn't use Facebook anymore since his mom labeled him as her son. William joked, "You need to create a new one [account]!" Everyone laughed.

Mr. Torres asked what technologies were best for seeking homework help, and students discussed disliking Twitter because people used it to describe everything they were doing. **Mr. Torres joked about tweeting from the grocery store or about blowing his nose.** Students laughed and Jessica, again unsolicited, agreed that Twitter was "stupidness" as Hector commented Twitter users were "immature."

Mr. Torres asked students how they would mourn the loss of a loved one. Belén shared, "My aunt was pregnant and then lost her baby at birth; she posted on Facebook about it. Is that dumb?" William supportively replied, "It's not dumb. She's getting her feelings out..." Students shared what they do to grieve – showing their grief, feeling their personalities change, talking to friends on the phone – when Belén reflected, "It's bad to keep to yourself!" Jessica shook her head in disagreement, explaining, "Why talk about it? It'll make you remember that person and you'll get emotional." Mr. Torres replied, "Is it bad to get emotional?" Jessica said, "Yeah, because why cry in front of somebody? I'm not saying emotions are bad, but…" Mr. Torres nodded his head thoughtfully and asked if people agreed. Marisa noted, "It depends on the person." Emilio raised his hand and shared, "It's better to express yourself." Mr. Torres then turned back to Jessica and asked in clarification, "So Jessica, does it make you feel better to keep it inside?" Jessica responded, "I try not to think about it, try to push it out of the way." Mr. Torres replied, "Okay. There's no right or wrong, everybody deals with it differently." Then, without a pause, **Mr. Torres asked the class: "What's the saying about taxes and death…?" to which David replied, "There are only two things you can't run away from: taxes and death."** Mr. Torres and his students laughed together.

Mr. Torres used pedagogies of humor and joy to encourage participation, support students' communicative competence and critical thinking (to express what they believe and why), and even got both Jessica and Brittany actively participating despite weeks of disengagement. The on-the-spot creativity of students' ideas (e.g., pretending there was a bad phone connection, manipulating parents' decisions, etc.) and efforts to explain their reasoning (e.g., for disliking Twitter, sharing personal reactions to death, etc.) were motivated by Mr. Torres's sense of humor and his students' subsequent desire to create laughter, in kind.

Brittany and Jessica's unusual engagement – twice Jessica shared her opinions unprompted, and Brittany actively tried to make her classmates laugh while voicing her perspective – showed a willingness to share ideas, even when classmates did not agree with them. Even though the final topic of conversation – mourning – was difficult, Jessica did not hesitate to speak openly and defend her beliefs regarding the importance of suppressing one's tears and sadness. Mr. Torres validated all the students' ideas, quickly emphasizing that there were no "wrong" or "right" ways to mourn, and Jessica's engagement only grew after Mr. Torres's joke about death and taxes. Mr. Torres demonstrated how his sense of humor and willingness to share ideas could be woven together in these conversations, encouraging students to practice different forms of communicative competence: sharing, defending, and questioning ideas.

Putting pedagogies of humor and joy into practice – Concluding suggestions for teachers

But how can other teachers implement pedagogies of humor and joy in their classrooms? Below are five key ideas to reflect upon, as well as teaching practices to try for educators interested in incorporating more humor and joy in their classrooms.

First of all, lessons do not need to be perfect stand-up acts. As Mr. Torres noted, you can't "have a comedy routine every time." Teachers can begin by incorporating jokes or puns into daily practice in the simplest ways possible. As Mr. Santos exemplified, simply showing one's openness to laughter can have the important effect of capturing students' attention, which can then lead to deeper interest in learning (Gorham & Christophel, 1992). For example, as Mr. Santos went over his course syllabus, he joked that mobile phones weren't allowed because they encouraged "chismosos or chismes" (meaning "gossip" in Spanish); he called the "grades" section of his syllabus "the fun part." These weren't gut-wrenchingly funny comments, but they added a levity to daily lessons that gave students an opportunity to see that their teacher was welcoming them to be playful and joyful, while also making Spanish-speaking learners feel like they could embrace their home languages in his classroom.

Secondly, Ms. Mendoza and Mr. Torres employed senses of humor that were specific to their personalities. This is an important feature of pedagogies of humor and joy: teachers' unique selves *should* be reflected in their practice. In Mr. Santos's case, the first time he took attendance, he noted: "Sorry if I massacre your last names. My Spanish is terrible." Students laughed because Mr. Santos's first language was Spanish. Teachers building humor and joy into their classrooms need to be willing to share who they are with their students and be okay with the vulnerability of showing their students who they are.

Yet, alongside being true to oneself with one's humor, teachers must also recognize that the tone of their jokes really matter. Thus, a third key point with pedagogies of humor and joy is that there are risks to spontaneous humor in the classroom. Teachers must be careful not to unintentionally insult their students with overly sarcastic remarks or off-color comments. Even when a person has positive intentions, words can deeply harm people, and within the classroom context where teachers have more power than students, this is of particular concern when trying to engage pedagogies of humor and joy. As Mr. Santos noted in the interview, teacher humor and joy must build on a foundation of respect for all students: Teachers should "insist" on students working hard—demonstrating that teachers have high expectations about their students' abilities to do challenging work—but also incorporate humor in ways that show the teachers "still enjoy their presence." Jokes should never involve sarcasm that may be taken personally, or involve passive-aggressive comments that mask teacher criticism or judgment. To that end, the teachers in this study were very careful to never tease students; they were, in fact, quicker to laugh about themselves in front of the students instead. When incorporating pedagogies of humor and joy, teachers must clearly define boundaries for their jokes, completely avoiding jokes that demean anyone or suggest that any group is undesirable, wrong, stupid, etc. This means avoiding jokes that suggest judgment or condescension toward students, or that make individuals feel like an outcast in any way based on race/ethnicity, gender, sexual orientation, home language, religion, etc. Educators must "read their audience" to see how their humor is impacting their students and adjust accordingly. There needs to be a conscientious effort to check oneself in the moment between coming up with a spontaneous joke and actually saying it to one's students to carefully self-censor humor that might actually counteract the joy students should be experiencing.

Fourthly, as Ms. Mendoza described, pedagogies of humor can encourage underrepresented students to feel less anxious about new subjects such as CS, encouraging students to feel okay sharing ideas, even if they're not sure if they're "right." This has already been supported by research studies showing how humor encourages participation in potentially intimidating subjects (see Smith et al., 1971, for example) and being okay with sharing ideas that may not be "correct" (see Cornett, 1986, for example). Teacher pedagogies of humor and joy can also help students feel comfortable communicating their ideas, even if they conflict with other peoples' ideas (as was true in both Ms. Mendoza and Mr. Torres's classrooms above). Thus, teachers may consider creating opportunities for students to debate their ideas in ways that allow space for laughter with safety to think differently, where teachers simultaneously serve as a mediator between students, using humor to ease tension.

Fifthly, teachers should incorporate pedagogies of humor and joy as a way to think about ideas from new angles. When teachers acted out different ideas in their classrooms, for example, their theatrics inspired students to also think of new ways to express their ideas and build on class discussions. Teachers used humor to wax upon youth's perspectives, encouraging further critical thinking about the conversations at hand (such as data analysis or communication technology, for example). As Ackermann (2014) describes, the same joy at the center of humor lies at the heart of creative thinking. Playfulness encouraged through pedagogies of humor and joy can lead to ways of thinking differently and communicating those different ideas in exciting ways.

Building on these five ideas, here are some practices to try: Smiling more, laughing more, incorporating jokes or puns into daily practice, facilitating learning activities that involve play, being willing to be relaxed and playful as well, and injecting important discussions with moments of laughter as a way to break up the intimidation students may feel in communicating their ideas so that they can more freely express themselves. Teachers can try joyfully shaking their students' hands as they enter the classroom, greeting them as "computer scientists" (or whatever experts would be named in their field of study). They can begin class sharing a joke of the day or funny video related to their subject area (available online). They can give extra credit points to students who come up with school-appropriate puns or jokes related to subjects they are learning. There are a number of small ways teachers can begin demonstrating their openness to humor and joy which, in turn, can support this pedagogical practice to grow in their classrooms.

Yet teachers should also know when and how they want to draw boundaries with their students. This is because pedagogies of humor and joy will invite students to also try out their own jokes and ways to make others laugh. It is important for teachers to recognize when students' jokes are hurtful or sarcastic and to actively protect students who are potential victims of such jokes. The primary goal should always be ensuring all students feel respected so that classroom humor creates a community of learners that is positive and safe. When students try out jokes that are potentially hurtful, they should be encouraged to think about how to create laughter without also creating pain.

In conclusion, beyond motivating student engagement, the examples shared in this chapter demonstrate how pedagogies of humor and joy can encourage critical thinking and communicative competence. As humor and joy gently welcome students to engage in discussions, share and challenge different ideas, and view concepts from various angles, youth may gain new interest in subject areas they did not initially know or care about. Using such pedagogies can potentially engage more of our students in the critical thinking we value, the communicative competence we hope to develop, and the subject areas that need our diverse students' perspectives and voices, such as the segregated fields of STEM and CS.

Notes

1. Ferris Bueller – a character from the 1986 film *Ferris Bueller's Day Off* – develops an elaborate plan to get away with skipping school for a day.
2. All names of students, teachers, and schools are pseudonyms created to protect their privacy.
3. Ms. Mendoza and her students called this snack consumption data their "snacking" data.

References

Ackermann, E. (2004). Constructing knowledge and transforming the world. A learning zone of one's own: Sharing representations and flow in collaborative learning environments In M. Tokoro, & L. Steels (Eds.), *A learning zone of one's own: Sharing representations and flow in collaborative learning environments* (pp. 15–37). Amsterdam, Berlin, Oxford, Tokyo, Washington, DC: IOS Press.

Ackermann, E. (2014, August). *Amusement, delight, whimsy, and wit, the place of humor in human creativity*. Paper presented at the Constructionism International Conference, Vienna, Austria.

Ackermann, E., Gauntlett, D., Wolbers, T., & Weckstrom, C. (2009). *Defining systematic creativity in the digital realm*. Billund, Denmark: Lego Learning Institute.

Adams, R. C. (1972). Is physics a laughing matter? *Physics Teacher, 10*, 265–266.

Boaler, J. & Sengupta-Irving, T. (2006). Nature, neglect & nuance: Changing accounts of sex, gender and mathematics. In C. Skelton, B. Francis, & L. Smulyan (Eds.), *The SAGE handbook of gender and education* (pp. 207–220). London: Sage.

Bogost, I. (2016). *Play anything: The pleasure of limits, the uses of boredom, and the secret of games*. New York: Basic Books.

Cornett, C. E. (1986). *Learning through laughter: Humor in the classroom*. Bloomington, IN: Phi Delta Kappa Educational Foundation.

Crump, C. A. (1996). *Teacher immediacy: What students consider to be effective teacher behaviors*. (Research/Technical Report). (ERIC Document Reproduction Service No. ED 390 099.

Csikszentmihalyi, M., Rathunde, K., & Whalen, S. (1993). *Talented teenagers*. Cambridge, UK: Cambridge University Press.

Derks, P., Gardner, J. B., & Agarwal, R. (1998). Recall of innocent and tendentious humorous material. *Humor: International Journal of Humor Research, 11*(1), 5–19.

Gorham, J., & Christophel, D. M. (1990). The relationship of teachers' use of humor in the classroom to immediacy and student learning. *Communication Education, 39*, 46–62.

Gorham, J., & Christophel, D. M. (1992). Students' perceptions of teacher behaviors as motivating and demotivating factors in college classes. *Communication Quarterly, 40*(3), 239–252.

Hauck, W. E. & Thomas, J. W. (1972). The relationship of humor to intelligence, creativity, and intentional and incidental learning. *Journal of Experimental Education, 40*(4), 52–55.

Horn, G. (1972). Laughter...a saving grace. *Today's Education, 61,* 37–38.

Kafai, Y. (2006). Playing and making games for learning: Instructionist and constructionist perspectives for game studies. *Games and Culture,* 36–40.

Kelly, W. E. (1983, April). Everything you always wanted to know about using humor in education but were afraid to laugh. Paper presented at the Annual international Convention of the Council for Exceptional Children. Detroit, MI. (ERIC Document ED 232–381).

Long, H. B. (1983). *Adult learning: Research and practice.* New York: Cambridge University Press.

Margolis, J., Estrella, R., Goode, J., Jellison-Holme, J., & Nao, K. (2008). *Stuck in the shallow end: Education, race, and computing.* Cambridge, MA: MIT Press.

Mechanic, D. (1962). *Students under stress: A study of the social psychology of adaptation.* New York: Free Press of Glencoe.

Monson, D. (1968). Children's test responses to seven humorous stories. *Elementary School Journal, 58,* 334–339.

Moran, S. & John-Steiner, V. (2003). Creativity in the making: Vygotsky's contemporary contribution to the dialectic of development and creativity. In R. K. Sawyer, V. John-Steiner, S. Moran, R. J. Sternberg, D. H. Feldman, J. Nakamura, & M. Csikszentmihalyi (Eds.), *Creativity and development* (pp. 61–90). Oxford: Oxford University Press.

Neuliep, J. W. (1991). An examination of the content of high school teachers' humor in the classroom and the development of an inductively derived taxonomy of classroom humor. *Communication Education, 40,* 343–355.

Pearson, T. (2002). Falling behind: A technology crisis facing minority students. *TechTrends, 46*(2), 15–20.

Resnick, M. (2007, June). All I really need to know (about creative thinking) I learned (by studying how children learn) in kindergarten. Paper presented at Creativity & Cognition Conference, Washington, DC.

Schmidt, S. R. (1994). Effects of humor on sentence memory. *Journal of Experimental Psychology: Learning, Memory, & Cognition, 20*(4), 953–967.

Schmidt, S. R. (2002) The humour effect: Differential processing and privileged retrieval. *Memory, 10*(2), 127–238.

Schmidt, S. R. & Williams, A. R. (2001). Memory for humorous cartoons. *Memory & Cognition, 29*(2), 305–311.

Smith, R. E., Ascough, J. C., Ettinger, F., & Nelson, D. A. (1971). Humor, anxiety and task performance. *Journal of Personality and Social Psychology, 19,* 243–246.

Smolucha, F. (1992). A reconstruction of Vygotsky's theory of creativity. *Creativity Research Journal, 5*(1), 49–67.

Vygotsky, L. S. (1978). *Mind in society: The development of higher psychological processes.* In M. Cole, V. John-Steiner, S. Scribner, & E. Souberman (Eds.). Cambridge, MA: Harvard University Press.

Wallinger, L. M. (1997). Don't smile before Christmas: The role of humor in education. *NASSP Bulletin, 81,* 27–34.

Wanzer, M. B. & Frymier, A. B. (1999). The relationship between student perceptions of instructor humor and student's reports of learning. *Communication Education, 48*(1), 48–62.

Watt, D. (1982). Education for citizenship in a computer-based society. In R. Seidel, R. Anderson, & B. Hunter (Eds.). *Computer literacy* (pp. 53–68). New York: Academic Press.

Welker, W. A. (1977). Humor in education: A foundation for wholesome living. *College Student Journal, 11,* 252–254.

Ziv, A. (1976). Facilitating effects of humorous atmosphere on creativity. *Journal of Educational Psychology, 68,* 318–322.

Ziv, A. (1988). Teaching and learning with humor: Experiment and replication. *Journal of Experimental Education, 57*(1), 5–15.

11

IMPROVING COLLEGE STUDENTS' CRITICAL THINKING THROUGH THE USE OF A STORY TOOL FOR SELF-REGULATED LEARNING TRAINING

Pedro Rosário, José Carlos Núñez, Paula Magalhães, Sonia Fuentes, Cleidilene Magalhães, and Kyle Busing

Summary

This chapter describes the efficacy of story tools for promoting self-regulated learning (SRL) and critical thinking, through a narrative-based approach. A voluminous corpus of research shows that students who receive training in SRL strategies (e.g., goal setting, time management, help seeking) are likely to engage deeply in school tasks, display higher-order thinking skills, and show high academic achievement. We present *Letters from Gervase* as a story-tool to improve SRL for 1st year college students. The program that utilizes this story-tool is aimed at promoting competencies (e.g., SRL strategies, critical thinking skills) through narratives. We present research evidence that demonstrates its effectiveness.

Introduction

Due to the rapid evolvement of contemporary societies, institutions and citizens face ongoing challenges that impact everyday modern day life and society (e.g., dwindling natural resources, evolving technology, and ongoing changes in social life). There is a need to address these challenges and display efforts to find paths for sustainable development and life-long learning; so, not surprisingly, people worldwide grapple with the need to train students, irrespective of their grade level, to be critical thinkers, and to be able to master the use of information in their work and daily life (Moore, 2013; Phan, 2010).

Schools and universities around the world are focused on responding to this universal call; and, among other efforts, university and school administrations ask teachers to teach their students to use critical thinking skills in class.

Equipping students with critical thinking skills (e.g., analytical thinking approach, inference making, and argumentation skills) is expected to prepare them for lifelong learning and active citizenship (Hammer & Green, 2011; Moore, 2013; Phan, 2010).

Critical thinking has a complex construct and literature offers several definitions that vary in nature and scope (Yanchar, Slife, & Warne, 2008). For example, Ennis (1989, p. 4) defines critical thinking as "reasonable reflective thinking focused on deciding what to believe or do," while Bailin and colleagues understand critical thinking as "thinking aimed at forming a judgment" (Bailin, Case, Coombs, & Daniels, 1999, p. 287).

Despite the differences in the approach to the concept, in general, researchers agree that students who master critical thinking skills are likely to understand knowledge as worth pursuing, and to value knowledge as an important tool to reach robust problem-solving analysis, solid conclusions, and evidence-based decisions (Ennis 1987; Paul & Elder, 2012). However, as Johnson (2000) prudently advises, a critical thinking student is expected to be a skilled thinker, but being a skilled thinker is not enough to cope with persistent personal and societal demands. In fact, using a set of critical skills in class does not assure, by itself, that a student will meet societal expectations for professional performance.

In sum, following this line of reasoning, we may ask: is critical thinking limited to the use of a set of organized and skillful approaches to content knowledge? For example, Lau (2015), alerts educators and researchers that critical thinking requires the ability to reflect critically on the reasons for judgment and goes beyond the use of cognitive and thinking skills in class. He stresses the need to include a reflection approach that acknowledges the role of metacognition in students' training (see Flavell, 1979).

The case of self-regulated learning

Lau's (2015) assertions echo those proposed by Dewey early in the 20th century. Dewey (1933) emphasized the need to approach an idea "in light of the grounds that support it and the further conclusions to which it tends" (p. 7). Moreover, he argued that students need more than a robust corpus of knowledge to develop thinking skills. According to Dewey (1933), "reflective thinking, in distinction from other operations to which we apply the name of thought, involves (1) a state of doubt, hesitation, perplexity, mental difficulty, in which thinking originates, and (2) an act of searching, hunting, inquiring, to find material that will resolve the doubt, settle and dispose of the perplexity" (p. 12).

To master critical thinking, students are expected to develop a focused, self-disciplined (Paul, 1993), diligent and persistent approach (Facione, 1990) to acquire knowledge. In sum, students need to master self-regulation competencies, and we believe that the framework of self-regulation provides a relevant theoretical framework to the promotion of critical thinking citizens.

Brief introduction to SRL

Self-regulated learning (SRL) is an active process where students set goals that are likely to direct their learning and monitor, regulate, and control cognitions, as well as motivations and behaviors, with the purpose of achieving self-set goals (Fulano, Cunha, Núñez, Pereira, & Rosário, 2018; Rosário, Núñez, & González-Pienda, 2006; Zimmerman, 2002). Self-regulated learning occurs when students exert their efforts to focus their beliefs, thoughts and actions on their educational goals (Phan, 2010; Schunk, 1987, 2001).

Students who self-regulate their learning display cognitive and metacognitive processes to control their cognition, motivation, learning environments, and behaviors (Zimmerman & Schunk, 2011), before, during, and after learning (Rosário, Núñez, Valle, González-Pienda, & Lourenço, 2013; Zimmerman, 2000). These students are inclined to view learning as an activity to help them develop proactively rather than reactively in response to teaching (Zimmerman, 2002; Zimmerman, Greenberg, & Weinstein, 1994). Moreover, students who self-regulate their learning are likely to use learning strategies, and approach content knowledge in flexible and meaningful ways, through understanding the task, evaluating data and considering multiple perspectives to approach it (VanderStoep & Pintrich, 2003). These students typically engage in learning using a deeper learning approach; they constantly reflect on their learning behaviors and adjust them accordingly in search of meaning (Garrison & Cleveland-Innes, 2005). For example, students using deeper learning approaches are more able than their counterparts to identify potential obstacles and select strategies to attain their learning goals (Davison & Sternberg, 1998).

While learning, proficient students who use self-regulated learning strategies and deeper approaches to learning will actively seek the information needed and take necessary steps to acquire it (Paris & Oka, 1986). Their focus is on assigning meaning to content knowledge. During this process, students are aware of their thinking processes and display self-regulatory control over their cognitions (Zimmerman, 1995). These metacognitive efforts to understand and assign meaning to learning play a crucial role in the development of an individual's critical thinking (Wineburg, 1997); in fact, metacognition is one of the strongest predictors of critical thinking (Ingle, 2007).

In sum, students who master SRL focus on their agent role and assume that academic success is a byproduct of their own behaviors (Bandura, 2001). Not surprisingly, there is a voluminous corpus of data stressing the close relationships between SRL, motivation for learning and academic success (e.g., Boekaerts & Corno, 2005; Núñez et al., 2011; Rosário et al., 2010; Valle et al., 2016; Zimmerman & Martínez-Pons, 1988; Zimmerman & Schunk, 2008), as well as literature relating SRL with the individual's development of critical thinking (Brown & Campione, 1994; Zimmerman, 1990).

SRL story-tools line of research

The SRL story-tools line of research was developed in Portugal, at the University of Minho, in collaboration with researchers from the University of Oviedo in Spain. This research line addresses the promotion of SRL through stories. In recent years, investigators from Chile, Brazil, Mexico, Mozambique, Japan, and United States have been incorporated into the research team (e.g., Rosário et al., 2014). Encouraged by the need to build evidence-based intervention tools fit for students' SRL needs, school teachers, faculty, and investigators have worked together to build story-tools aimed at promoting SRL. Over the last two decades, the research team developed a set of story-tools[1] aimed at promoting SRL throughout schooling as follows: *Yellow trials and tribulations* (Rosário, Núñez, & González-Pienda, 2007) for elementary school; *Collection of Testas' (mis)adventures* (Rosário, 2002a, 2002b, 2002c; 2003; 2004a, 2004b) for 5th-through 9th-graders; and finally, *Letters from Gervase* (Rosário et al., 2006) for first-year college students.

General features of the SRL story-tools programs

SRL, from the perspective of Zimmerman (2000, 2002), is understood as an open and dynamic process that proceeds through three main phases: forethought, performance or volitional control phase, and self-reflection. These phases of the SRL process interact dynamically and follow a sequential loop (Rosário, et al., 2014; Zimmerman, 2008). Within the SRL framework, these processes are cyclic and interdependent; the forethought phase informs the volitional control phase, which influences the processes of the self-reflection phase. Each of these processes impact the following phase, shaping students learning process (Rosário et al., 2010; Zimmerman, 2000). For this reason, students are expected to understand the nature and functioning of this learning and assume agency and responsibility of their SRL process. The research literature reports that high-achieving students when compared with low achievers are more likely to use learning strategies purposefully to attain their learning goals (Zimmerman & Martínez-Pons, 1986, 1988).

Our SRL story-tools programs are designed to foster students' SRL strategies by using narratives. Narratives are the main tool for organizing our concept of time. It corresponds to the representation of an event or series of events clustered around some meaning. In this sense, stories do more than inform or instruct, they make us who we are. In one of his first books about learning and instruction, Bruner (1986) presents narrative ways of thinking as an alternative way of facing reality. He defends his narrative as a universal path used by all cultures, albeit with different matrices, to align experiences and assign meaning. Tales and stories invite people to look inside themselves, reflect about their own behaviors and subsequent consequences as long as they can identify with the story's characters and their dilemmas, choices, and narrated adventures. As noted earlier, reflection on one's own behaviors and reasons for judgment are a necessary element for effective critical thinking. (Lau, 2015).

In the above-mentioned story-tools programs, students are prompted to build their own meanings, their own understanding of the SRL narrative, to reach the target conditional learning (i.e., learn how to respond appropriately to a situation requiring self-regulatory skills), and to transfer those skills learned and discussed in class to other academic domains or own life. As Rosário (2004a) stated, "we don't learn when we are taught or when we listen, but rather when we adopt, recreate and appropriate meanings. Learning is always an author's task" (p. 11). Through a guided analysis of a narrative, children and young people may be instigated to articulate their knowledge of SRL reasoning about characters' behaviors and their own.

Students, regardless of their age, often learn vicariously by observing other people's actions directly or indirectly (e.g., in movies, on television, on the Internet, and by reading books; Zimmerman & Schunk, 2001). In this sense, the social cognitive framework – stressing that not all human learning arises from direct experience – describes how observing others' behaviors and the resulting rewards or punishments can organize and motivate the observers' behavior (Bandura, 2001). Modeling refers to the process through which observers pattern their own thoughts, beliefs, strategies, and actions after observing models (Schunk, 2001). Modeling is an important way to develop competencies, beliefs, attitudes, and behaviors. Teachers, parents, other adults, and peers become, therefore, powerful models for the learners. Behaviors, verbal utterances, and even nonverbal expressions of significant models can be considered by the observers as prompting cues for subsequent reproduction (Bandura, 1986).

Furthermore, modeling provides informative and motivational sources. Observing competent models perform actions successfully can provide individuals with useful information regarding the sequence of actions to follow, in the hope of obtaining the same results (Craig, Sullins, Witherspoon, & Gholson, 2006). However, Schunk (1987) argued that the simple observation of a model performing a task (e.g., a friend, colleague, teacher, or parent), is not enough to encourage the observer to perform it, regardless of how competent the model could have been. For this type of learning to be effective, it is important for individuals to perceive similarities between themselves and the model. In the modeling process, this is one of the most relevant motivational variables for a successful outcome. Perceived similarity with the model is a fundamental aspect of judging one's own efficacy. For example, by observing peers experiencing success, college students are likely to develop self-efficacy beliefs and become more motivated to perform the task. The opposite also holds true. When college students observe their peers being unsuccessful, they are less likely to allocate effort toward accomplishing the task. The SRL processes and strategies already mentioned (e.g., time management, organizing information, monitoring progress) could be taught by social models (Zimmerman, 2008). Students using vicarious learning can acquire not only declarative knowledge regarding the nature of the learning strategies but also procedural and conditional knowledge that can be useful tools for future independent learning.

Detailed description of SRL story-tools programs

This section is intended to briefly analyze each instructional program and their components. We describe and analyze the specific features of the learning and teaching activities to explain their rationale and purpose. We also offer specific examples from the narratives and practical tasks that will help readers understand how the story-tools projects can be run.

A main goal of the SRL training is to help students' master three types of knowledge about learning strategies: declarative, procedural, and conditional (Núñez et al., 2013; Rosário et al., 2017). Declarative knowledge of learning strategies is factual knowledge that involves information on a variety of learning strategies (e.g., know what time management is). Procedural knowledge of learning strategies is the knowledge of how to implement the learning strategies (e.g., know how to use time management tools to attain goals). Finally, conditional knowledge explains when individuals should use a learning strategy in a specific learning context (e.g., reflect on the difference between use and loss of time and act accordingly to decide when to approach a task) (Alexander, 2006).

Students engage in a hands-on approach: they are presented with a set of SRL strategies (see, Rosário et al., 2010, 2014; Weinstein, Husman & Dierking, 2000; Zimmerman & Martínez -Pons, 1986) and are asked to decide what, how, and when to use each. We believe this active methodology is likely to help students become aware of their agent role as learners, and effectively focus their attention on the contents to be learned (Rosário et al., 2007; Weinstein et al., 2000). Our ultimate goal is to develop effective thinking using SRL embedded in a story tool.

In each session of this story-tool program, and for each SRL strategy, students are asked to discuss declarative, procedural, and conditional knowledge (e.g., goal-setting, strategies for revision, strategies for organizing information). Moreover, instructors use vicarious learning to help students reflect upon declarative, procedural, and conditional knowledge of these learning strategies across diverse learning contexts (e.g., academic situations, preparing for and taking tests, and completing homework). The fostering and mediating of students' learning transfer will likely help deepen their understanding of the strategies and encourage their use in contexts other than learning (e.g., organizing their sports training sessions, organizing judgments in their interpersonal relationships).

All our story-tools follow an instructional sequence that can be summarized in three steps: reading of the chapter/letter, reflection about the narrative content, and, finally, work on practical tasks. The instructors guide discussions and explain by exemplifying how students could expand their strategy repertoire. Aiming to promote lifelong learning skills, instructors are expected to facilitate students' agency and personal control and help them reflect on and anticipate the consequences of action.

Letters from Gervase (promoting SRL in first-year college students)

The Letters from Gervase target first-year college students during their process of adapting to college life. The book is comprised of 13 texts, drafted as letters written by Gervase, a first-year university student (Pina, Rosário, & Tejada, 2010; Rosário et al., 2006; Rosário, Fuentes, Beuchat & Ramaciotti, 2016). Using a casual, friendly, and humorous style, Gervase writes about the experiences he faces as a first-year college student (e.g., reflections about the SRL processes and learning strategies, academic adaptation process, and other academic and social challenges).

This tool has a flexible nature and can be adapted to the needs of the students and the demands of the learning contexts. For example, there is no mandatory protocol, or an optimal number of sessions required. However, prior research (see Table 11.2) shows that programs should use at least six letters, one for each session. The sessions, lasting from 60 to 90 minutes, can be mediated by an instructor in class, in an extracurricular course, or even by a counselor in individual work sessions. It is also possible to use the program in e-learning settings (see, Cerezo et al., 2010; Núñez et al., 2011).

Each letter is organized around a repertoire of learning strategies set by Zimmerman and Martínez-Pons in 1986 (e.g., goal setting, organization and transformation of information, taking notes, information seeking) that correspond to the three phases of the SRL process (e.g., forethought phase, performance phase, and self-reflection phase; Zimmerman, 2002; see Table 11.1). In addition, the project manual presents a set of activities to help individuals reflect on the narrative and apply study and SRL strategies to distinct learning scenarios (Rosário et al., 2007, 2010, 2014, 2016).

This story-based tool was designed to promote students' analysis of the contents of the letters, followed by the discussion of the embedded SRL strategies with the help of an instructor. For example, during the sessions the participants discussed the contents, the presented strategies, and SRL processes through the narrative, aiming at fostering a deeper approach to learning and the development of a critical approach to thinking.

College students are invited to analyze the information in the letters, analyze and select the relevant information, and, finally, transfer this knowledge to their academic and personal lives.

In sum, working with this story-based tool provides students with the opportunity to reflect on their own learning processes, both at an individual and at a group level, with the aim of fostering their metacognition, motivation, and academic engagement.

As previously stated, the Letters from Gervase program does not provide sessions of a rigid structure, nor prescribed times to develop the suggested activities. Sessions are a vehicle to work self-regulation skills in the classroom, with a flexible nature adjustable to the speed and needs of the different readers/authors. Typically, each session is organized in four steps as described here. (1) First, and for about 15 minutes, the students read and analyze the assigned letter silently and

TABLE 11.1 Contents and SRL strategies included in a sample of Letters from Gervase story-tool

Sample of letters in the Letters from Gervase story-tool project	*Contents and self-regulating strategies addressed*
Letter 1 – What does it mean, after all, adjusting to university life?	Adaptation to university. Planning and time management.
Letter 2 – What are my goals? What really guides my actions at all levels, i.e., my studies, my university attendance, my hobbies, sports and relationship with others… and even my lassitude?	Setting goals. Rules of goal setting. Concrete Realistic Assessable (CRAss). Short-term and long-term goals. Study goals and achievement goals.
Letter 3 – How can I take better notes?	Organizing information: summaries, tables, diagrams and conceptual maps… Note-taking. Controlling distractions.
Letter 4 – Do you know how to fight procrastination, Gervase?	Time management. "To do" lists. Organizing the study environment. Procrastination. Relaxation techniques.
Letter 6 – Who rules your learning? How can one tell successful students apart?	SRL. The Cyclical model of SRL (see Zimmerman, 2008). Setting goals. Monitoring. Motivation.
Letter 12 – What is test anxiety? How can one deal with test anxiety?	Test anxiety. Aspects of anxiety (feelings and emotions). Internal and external distractors. Plagiarism and copy write. Relaxation techniques.

individually, hopefully taking notes. (2) Then, for about 45 minutes, students work in small groups to encourage the exchange of ideas, promote problem solving, and foster teamwork. Modeling, strategy learning, and reflection on the SRL strategies embedded in the letters are examples of the tools used in the sessions to transfer the new knowledge to the academic domains and daily life activities. The tasks proposed to the students are expected to be selected from a pool of activities presented in the manual of the program. For example, students discuss in the sessions that critical thinking is activated when students orchestrate a set of cognitive strategies to approach learning. To practice their critical thinking skills (e.g., Interpretation-Categorization, Clarifying Meaning; and Analysis: Examining Ideas, Identifying Arguments, Analyzing Arguments), students can be encouraged to write a draft of a newspaper advertisement aimed at selecting the most suitable candidate for a course on [a specified topic area] (cf. Rosário et al., 2006). (3) Afterwards, for about 20 minutes, each group of students shares their written drafts with the other groups and are given the opportunity to discuss ideas, ask questions, clarify information, and pose challenges to their classmates' thoughts. (4) Finally, for about 10 minutes, the instructor delivers a take home message comprising of a short summary of the major topics discussed.

Some examples of take-home messages, as well as of activities to be developed by the students during the sessions are provided in the manual of the project (Rosário et al., 2006). The activities can be selected from a recommended pool, or developed with the purpose of intervention while considering the students' goals, learning needs, their expertise on SRL, mastery of critical thinking skills, and academic proficiency.

Extant research with Letters from Gervase story tool

Examples of research studies that have used the story tool Letter from Gervase are summarized in Table 11.2. The corpus of findings gathered from this research provides grounds for the conclusion that this story-tool is efficacious for improving SRL strategies, critical thinking skills, and academic performance at college.

Conclusions

There is an open call for proactive school-based interventions aimed at promoting learning strategies and metacognitive skills. In fact, literature reviews on SRL (e.g., Boekaerts & Corno, 2005; Dignath, Buettner, & Langfeldt, 2008) suggest the need to find ways of promoting SRL in educational settings and highlighting students' proactive role (e.g., students' willingness to inquire). Therefore, faculty and college administrators could consider increasing the number of programs to improve SRL in colleges (Rosário, et al., 2014; Rosário et al., 2016). Training SRL competencies is likely to help students analyze information, ask and answer questions to clarify data, and reach a solution to a problem (see Boekaerts & Corno, 2005). This process requires development of self-judgment and reflection from students, and ultimately this will foster their critical thinking.

Following the SRL literature, we can understand critical thinking as the ability to use acquired knowledge in flexible and meaningful ways by considering multiple perspectives to approach the task or solve problems (VanderStoep & Pintrich, 2003). This perspective is consistent with the literature on critical thinking which defines critical thinkers as people who are "habitually inquisitive, well-informed, trustful of reason, open-minded, flexible, fair-minded in evaluation, honest in facing personal biases, prudent in making judgments, willing to reconsider, clear about issues, orderly in complex matters, diligent in seeking relevant information, reasonable in the selection of criteria, focused in inquiry, and persistent in seeking results" (Facione, 1990, p. 9).

Leung and Kember (2003) advocate that critical thinking is a cognitive tool that helps students further examine their learning material by using deep strategies. Moreover, Kuiper (2002) found that critical thinking skills help to facilitate the transfer of learning strategies to other learning contexts. In fact, consistent

TABLE 11.2 Summary of previous research on the story-tool Letter to Gervase

Study	Participants	Purpose	Design	Procedure/training	Variables assessed	Variables with statistically significant differences	Major highlights
Rosário, et al. (2007)	Portuguese first year college students.	Evaluate the efficacy of the "Letters to Gervase" (LtG) program.	A quasi-experimental design including an experimental group (EG) and a control group (CG), with pre and post evaluation.	The program was run in six 60-minute weekly sessions after classes. Students from the CG did not receive SRL training.	Learning strategies (LS); declarative knowledge (DK); Approaches to learning (deep and surface); SRL strategies; Perceived usefulness of SRL strategies; Structures of the observed learning outcome.	LS; DK; Surface approach to learning; Structures of the observed learning outcome.	• Participating students decreased superficial approaches but did not increase deep approaches to studying. • Participating students increased communication skills (e.g., accurate use of relevant information to support their own opinion).
Rosário et al. (2010)	First year Portuguese and Spanish college students.	LtG program was assessed in two samples (Portuguese and Spanish students).	A quasi-experimental design including an EG and a CG running in two universities from two countries. A pre-post evaluation was used.	The intervention followed the same design in both universities. Six 90-minute weekly sessions took place after classes. Students from the CG did not receive SRL training.	LS; DK; Approaches to learning (deep and surface); SRL strategies; Perceived usefulness of SRL strategies; Self-efficacy for use of SRL strategies.	LS; DK; Surface approach to learning; SRL strategies; Perceived usefulness of SRL strategies; Self-efficacy for use of SRL strategies.	• Results corroborate the efficacy of the intervention program as well as its cross-cultural validity. • Regarding SRL, students improved on self-questioning and self-validation. • Moreover, students improved on their reflection upon and justification of their own thinking process.

Núñez et al. (2011)	Spanish college students.	Assess the efficacy of LtG for promoting SRL using ICTs as support.	A quasi-experimental design including an EG and a CG with a pre-post evaluation was used.	The thirteen weekly sessions were available online for students to work with over 15 days.	SRL strategies; SRL when learning from texts; DK; Approaches to learning (deep and surface); Academic achievement.	Findings show that the program LtG was efficacious both in promoting the use of SRL strategies and in improving the motivational variables and thinking skills.
Rosário et al. (2014)	First year students from four universities at different countries (Spain, Portugal, Mozambique and Chile).	Assess the effectiveness of LtG with college students from different cultural, linguistic, and educational backgrounds.	A quasi-experimental design including an EG and a CG running in four universities from four countries. A pre-post evaluation was followed.	The four participating universities executed the program following the exact same design. The program was implemented in the first academic semester, on a weekly basis (90-minute for each of the six sessions).	Knowledge of SRL; Approaches to learning (deep and surface); SRL strategies; Perceived usefulness of SRL strategies; Structural complexity of the learning outcomes.	Participating students: - Improved their declarative knowledge; - Improved academic achievement; - Were highly satisfied with the use of a Computer Based Learning Environment (CBLE) as platform to learn SRL. - Improved their interpretation skills (e.g., articulate divergent points of view, categorize information, summarize main ideas). - Findings indicate the effectiveness of the program in enhancing a set of motivational variables and the use of SRL strategies. - Data were consistent across the different cultural and academic contexts in which the program was implemented. Students increased their deep approaches to learning (e.g., make recommendations for further inquiry; derive plausible conclusions from the given information).

with these propositions, the extant research shows that while using critical thinking to solve problems or understand new content, students need to manage prior information by excelling in the use of learning strategies (Zimmerman, 2008).

We believe that the SRL contents discussed throughout Letters to Gervase meet students' expectations, immediate academic challenges (e.g., time management, procrastination, note-taking, academic distracters, and goal setting), and their critical thinking needs (e.g., training in questioning evidence; awareness of the need to consider multiple perspectives prior to taking a position; communication strategies; awareness of what, why, how, and when people understand and display feelings about something). Note that due to space constraints we are only able to introduce the Letters to Gervase program, but – as noted earlier – there are equivalent story tools for younger students, which have also been demonstrated to be effective in several research studies (e.g., Núñez, Rosário, Vallejo, & González-Pienda, 2013; Rosário, Núñez, Rodríguez, et al., 2017; Rosário, Núñez, Vallejo, et al., 2017). The training on thinking skills and deep learning strategies provides students with valuable expertise to analyze and evaluate information and avoid misconstrued and biased information based on ad hoc opinions and common knowledge (e.g., filter, calibrate and select information on social media). This sense of usefulness and mastery of one's critical thinking may predispose students to display an agent role in their learning process. Globally, our SRL story-tools program has proven to be a positive educational tool to promote learning strategies, deeper approaches to learning, and ultimately critical thinking.

However, despite the promising results of our line of research, more investigations are needed to further examine the development of critical thinking skills through the training on SRL strategies. For example, training students to ask questions to clarify information would likely help students built a robust argument. Moreover, analyzing the efforts made by students on their time management, and discussing the consequences of using or losing time may help develop students' skills of reflection.

Note

1 The references list contains the information for the Portuguese and Spanish books for the story tools; readers can email the first author for English versions of the story-tools.

References

Alexander, P. A. (2006). *Psychology in learning and instruction.* Upper Saddle River, NJ: Pearson Merrill Prentice Hall.

Bailin, S., Case, R., Coombs, J. R., & Daniels, L. B. (1999). Conceptualizing critical thinking. *Journal of Curriculum Studies, 31*(3), 285–302.

Bandura, A. (1986). *Social foundations of thought and action: A social cognitive theory.* Englewood Cliffs, NJ: Prentice-Hall.

Bandura, A. (2001). Social cognitive theory: An agentic perspective. *American Review of Psychology, 52,* 1–26.

Boekaerts, M., & Corno, L. (2005). Self-regulation in the classroom: A perspective on assessment and intervention. *Applied Psychology: An International Review, 54*(82), 199–231.

Brown, A. L., & Campione, J. C. (1994). Guided discovery in a community of learners. In K. McGilly (Ed.), *Classroom lessons: Integrating cognitive theory and classroom practice* (pp. 229–270). Cambridge: MA: MIT Press/Bradford Book.

Bruner, J. (1986). *Actual minds, possible worlds*. Cambridge, MA: Harvard University Press.

Cerezo, R., Núñez, J. C., Rosário, P., Valle, A., Rodriguez, S., & Bernardo, A. (2010). New media for the promotion of self-regulated learning in higher education. *Psicothema, 22*(2), 306–315.

Craig, S., Sullins, J., Witherspoon, A., & Gholson, B. (2006). Deep-level reasoning questions effect: The role of dialog and deep-level reasoning questions during vicarious learning. *Cognition and Instruction, 24*(4), 565–591.

Davison, J. E., & Sternberg, R. J. (1998). Smart problem solving: How metacognition helps. In D. J. Hacker, J. Dunlosky, & A. C. Grasser (Eds.), *Metacognition in educational theory and practice* (pp. 47–68). Mahwah, NJ: Lawrence Erlbaum.

Dewey, J. (1933). *How we think: A restatement of the relation of reflective thinking to the educative process*. Boston, MA: D. C. Heath.

Dignath, C., Buettner, G., & Langfeldt, H. (2008). How can primary school students learn SRL strategies most effectively? A meta-analysis on self-regulation training programmes. *Educational Research Review, 3*, 101–129.

Ennis, R. H. (1987). A taxonomy of critical thinking dispositions and abilities. In J. B. Baron & R. J. Sternberg (Eds.), *Teaching thinking skills: Theory and practice* (pp. 9–26). New York: W. H. Freeman.

Ennis, R. H. (1989). Critical thinking and subject specificity: Clarification and needed research. *Educational Researcher, 18*(3), 4–10.

Facione, P. (1990). *The Delphi Report: Critical thinking: A statement of expert consensus for purposes of educational assessment and instruction*. Millbrae, CA: Academic Press.

Flavell, J. H. (1979). Metacognition and cognitive monitoring: A new area of cognitive–developmental inquiry. *American Psychologist, 34*(10), 906.

Fulano, C., Cunha, J., Núñez, J. C., Pereira, B., & Rosário, P. (2018). Mozambican adolescents' perspectives on the academic procrastination process. *School Psychology International, 39*, 196–213.

Garrison, D. R., & Cleveland-Innes, M. (2005). Facilitating cognitive presence in online learning: Interaction is not enough. *The American Journal of Distance Education, 19*(3), 133–148.

Hammer, S., & Green, W. (2011). Critical thinking in a first year management unit: The relationship between disciplinary learning, academic literacy and learning progression. *Higher Education Research and Development, 30*(3), 303–316.

Ingle, C. (2007). Predictors of critical thinking ability among college students. PhD dissertation, University of Kentucky, United States – Kentucky. Retrieved October 8, 2008, from Dissertations & Theses: Full Text. (Publication No. AAT 3263681).

Johnson, R. H. (2000). *Manifest rationality: A pragmatic theory of argument*. Mahwah, NJ: Erlbaum.

Kuiper, R. (2002). Enhancing metacognition through the reflective use of self-regulated learning strategies. *The Journal of Continuing Education in Nursing, 33*(2), 78–87.

Lau, J. (2015). Metacognitive education: Going beyond critical thinking, In M. Davies & R. Barnett (Eds). *The Palgrave handbook of critical thinking in higher education* (pp. 373–390). New York: Palgrave Macmillan.

Leung, D.Y.P., & Kember, D. (2003). The relationship between approaches to learning and reflection upon practice. *Educational Psychology, 23*(1), 61–71.

Moore, T. (2013). Critical thinking: Seven definitions in search of a concept. *Studies in Higher Education, 38*(4), 506–522.

Núñez, J. C., Cerezo, R., González-Pienda, J. A., Rosário, P., Valle, A., Fernández, E., & Suárez, N. (2011). Implementation of training programs in self-regulated learning strategies in Moodle format: Results of an experience in higher education. *Psicothema, 23,* 274–281.

Núñez, J. C., Rosário, P., Vallejo, G., & González-Pienda, J. A. (2013). A longitudinal assessment of the effectiveness of a school-based mentoring program in middle school. *Contemporary Educational Psychology, 38,* 11–21.

Paris, S. G., & Oka, E. (1986). Children's reading strategies, metacognition and motivation. *Developmental Review, 6,* 25–86.

Paul, R. (1993). *Critical thinking: How to prepare students for a rapidly changing world.* Santa Rosa, CA: Foundation for Critical Thinking.

Paul, R. W., & Elder, L. (2012). *Critical thinking: Tools for taking charge of your learning and your life* (3rd ed.). Boston, MA: Pearson Education.

Phan, H. (2010). Critical thinking as a self-regulatory process component in teaching and learning. *Psicothema, 22*(2), 284–292.

Pina, F., Rosário, P., & Tejada, J. (2010). Impacto de un programa de autorregulación del aprendizaje en estudiantes de Grado. *Revista de Educación, 353,* 571–588.

Rosário, P. (2002a). *007.º Ordem para estudar [007th Order to study].* Porto, Portugal: Porto Editora.

Rosário, P. (2002b). *Elementar, meu caro Testas [Elemental, my dear Sparky].* Porto, Portugal: Porto Editora.

Rosário, P. (2002c). *Testas para sempre [Sparky forever].* Porto, Portugal: Porto Editora.

Rosário, P. (2003). *O Senhor aos papéis, a irmandade do granel [Lord of trouble, the brotherhood of the caos].* Porto, Portugal: Porto Editora.

Rosário, P. (2004a). *Estudar o Estudar: As (Des)venturas do Testas [Studying study: Sparky's (mis)adventures].* Porto, Portugal: Porto Editora.

Rosário, P. (2004b). *Testas o Lusitano [Sparky the Luso].* Porto, Portugal: Porto Editora.

Rosário, P., Pereira, A., Högemann, J., Nunes, A. R., Figueiredo, M., Núñez, J. C., Fuentes, S., & Gaeta, M. (2014). Self-regulated learning: A systematic review based in scielo journals. *Universitas Psychologica, 13*(2), 781–798.

Rosário, P., Fuentes, S., Beuchat, M., & Ramaciotti, A. (2016). Self-regulated learning in a college classroom: A curriculum infusion approach. *Revista de Investigación Educativa, 1,* 31–49.

Rosário, P., González-Pienda, J. A., Pinto, R., Ferreira, P., Lourenço, A. & Paiva, O. (2010). Efficacy of the program "Testas's (mis)adventures" to promote the deep approach to learning. *Psicothema, 22*(4), 828–834.

Rosário, P., Mourão, R., Núñez, J. C., González-Pienda, J. A., Solano, P., & Valle, A. (2007). Evaluating the efficacy of a program to enhance college students' self-regulation learning processes and learning strategies. *Psicothema, 19*(3), 353–358.

Rosário, P., Núñez, J. C., Rodríguez, C., Cerezo, R., Fernández, E., Tuero, E., & Högemann, J. (2017). Analysis of instructional programs for improving self-regulated learning SRL through written text. In R. Fidalgo, K. R. Harris, & M. Braaksma (Eds.), *Design principles for teaching effective writing: Theoretical and empirical grounded principles* (pp. 201–231). Leiden, The Netherlands: Brill Editions.

Rosário, P., Núñez, J. C., Trigo, L., Guimarães, C., Fernández, E., Cerezo, R., Fuentes, S., Orellana, M., Santibáñez, A., Fulano, C., Ferreira, A., Figueiredo, M. (2014). Transcultural analysis of the effectiveness of a program to promote self-regulated learning in Mozambique, Chile, Portugal, and Spain. *Higher Education Research and Development, 34*(1), 173–187.

Rosário, P., Núñez, J. C., Valle, A., González-Pienda, J. A., & Lourenço, A. (2013). Grade level, study time, and grade retention and their effects on motivation, self-regulated learning strategies, and mathematics achievement: A structural equation model. *European Journal of Psychology of Education, 28*(4), 1311–1331.

Rosário, P., Núñez, J.C., & González-Pienda, J. A. (2006). *Cartas do gervásio ao seu umbigo. Comprometer-se com o estudar na universidade [Letters from gervase to his belly button. Committing with studying at university]*. Coimbra, Portugal: Almedina Editores.

Rosário, P., Núñez, J. C., & González-Pienda, J. A. (2007). *Sarilhos do amarelo [Yellow's trials and tribulations]*. Porto, Portugal: Porto Editora.

Rosário, P., Núñez, J. C., González-Pienda, J. A., Valle, A., Trigo, L., & Guimarães, C. (2010). Enhancing self-regulation and approaches to learning in first-year college students: A narrative-based program assessed in the Iberian Peninsula. *European Journal of Psychology of Education, 25*, 411–428.

Rosário, P., Núñez, J.C., Vallejo, G., Azevedo, R., Pereira, R., Moreira, T., Fuentes, S., & Valle, A. (2017). Promoting Gypsy children's behavioural engagement and school success: Evidence from a four-wave longitudinal study. *British Educational Research Journal, 43*(3), 554–571.

Schunk, D. (1987). Peer models and children's behavioral change. *Review of Educational Research, 57*, 149–174.

Schunk, D. (2001). Social cognitive theory and self-regulated learning. In B. Zimmerman & D. Schunk (Eds.), *Self-regulated learning and achievement: Theoretical perspectives* (2nd ed., pp. 125–151). Mahwah, NJ: Erlbaum.

Valle, A., Regueiro, B., Núñez J.C., Rodríguez, S., Piñeiro, I., & Rosário, P. (2016). Academic goals, student homework engagement, and academic achievement in elementary school. *Frontiers in Psychology, 7*, 463.

VanderStoep, S. W., & Pintrich, P. R. (2003). *Learning to learn: The skill and will of college success*. Upper Saddle River, NJ: Prentice Hall.

Weinstein, C. E., Husman, J., & Dierking, D. (2000). Self-regulation intervention with a focus on learning strategies. In M. Boekaerts, P. Pintrich, & M. Zeidner (Eds.), *Handbook of self-regulation* (pp. 727–747). New York, San Diego: Academic Press.

Wineburg, S. (1997). Reading Abraham Lincoln: An expert study in the interpretation of historical texts. *Cognitive Science, 22*(3), 319–346.

Yanchar, S. C., Slife, B. D., & Warne, R. (2008). Critical thinking as disciplinary practice. *Review of General Psychology, 12*(3), 265–281.

Zimmerman, B. (1990). Self-regulated learning and academic achievement: An overview. *Educational Psychologist, 25*(1), 3–17.

Zimmerman, B. (1995). Self-regulation involves more than metacognition: A social cognitive perspective. *Educational Psychologist, 30*(4), 217–221.

Zimmerman, B. J. (2000). Attaining self-regulation. A social cognitive perspective. In M. Boekaerts, P. Pintrich, & M. Zeidner (Eds.), *Handbook of self-regulation* (pp. 13–39). San Diego, CA: Academic Press.

Zimmerman, B. J. (2002). Becoming a self-regulated learner: An overview. *Theory into Practice, 41*(2), 64–70.

Zimmerman, B. J., & Schunk, D. H. (2001). *Self-regulated learning and academic achievement: Theoretical perspectives*. Mahwah, NJ: Lawrence Erlbaum.

Zimmerman, B. J., & Schunk, D. H. (2008). Motivation: An essential dimension of self-regulated learning. In D. H. Schunk & B. J. Zimmerman (Eds.), *Motivation and self-regulated learning: Theory, research, and applications* (pp. 1–30). Mahwah, NJ: Lawrence Erlbaum.

Zimmerman, B. J., & Schunk, D. H. (2011). Self-regulated learning and performance: An introduction and an overview. In B. J. Zimmerman & D. H. Schunk (Eds.), *Handbook of self-regulation of learning and performance* (pp. 1–15). New York: Routledge.

Zimmerman, B. J. (2008). Investigating self-regulation and motivation: Historical, background, methodological developments, and future prospects. *American Educational Research Journal, 45*, 166–183.

Zimmerman, B. J., & Martínez-Pons, M. (1986). Development of a structured interview for assessing student use of self-regulated learning strategies. *American Educational Research Journal, 23*(4), 614–628.

Zimmerman, B. J., & Martínez-Pons, M. (1988). Construct validation of a strategy model of student self-regulated learning. *Journal of Educational Psychology, 80*, 284–290.

Zimmerman, B. J., Greenberg, D., & Weinstein, C. E. (1994). Self-regulation academic study time: A strategy approach. In D. H. Schunk & B. J. Zimmerman (Eds.), *Self-regulation of learning and performance: Issues and educational applications* (pp. 181–199). Hillsdale, NJ: Lawrence Erlbaum.

12

DEBUGGING AS A CONTEXT FOR FOSTERING REFLECTION ON CRITICAL THINKING AND EMOTION

David DeLiema, Maggie Dahn, Virginia J. Flood, Ana Asuncion, Dor Abrahamson, Noel Enyedy, and Francis Steen

Summary

The process of handling breakdowns in computer programming, a practice known as debugging, provides an auspicious context for fostering teacher-student communication about critical thinking. Toward this end, this chapter explores two practical classroom designs. The first design focuses on student journaling and art making about critical thinking processes and emotional experiences that undergird debugging. The second design focuses on instructors modeling and prompting for reflection on critical thinking strategies during debugging. These teaching strategies lead to growth in students' impressions of their skills for handling failure and their confidence during failure, both vital components of environments that promote deeper learning.

Introduction

When designing classroom activities to foster communicative competence, critical thinking, and deeper learning, educators should consider a common albeit challenging event in the learning process: the moment that a course of action breaks down, ushering in "a more reflective or deliberative stance toward ongoing activity" (Koschmann, Kuutti, & Hickman, 1998, p. 26; see also Schön, 1983). Because breakdowns in learning catalyze reflection and storytelling (Heider, 1958; Herman, 2009; Weiner, 1985), they naturally elicit *communication* about the learning process (DeLiema, 2017; Heyd-Metzuyanim, 2015). In addition, the causes of failure are numerous, interconnected, and distributed across people, materials, and time (Hesslow, 1988; Suchman, 1987). Reasoning about failure thus warrants *critical thinking*: identifying facts about the breakdown, formulating alternative conjectures about possible causes, clarifying points of confusion, developing new knowledge about the problem, and presenting and weighing arguments for why an intervention might work (Facione, 1990; Greiff, Wüstenberg, Csapó, Demetriou, Hautamäki, Graesser, & Martin, 2014; Hmelo-Silver, 2004). Furthermore, moments of failure create a bedrock for *deeper content learning* when teachers provide responsive scaffolding (Kapur, 2008; Schwartz & Martin, 2004).

These observations raise a central question: How can educators take advantage of these opportunities in concert? In this chapter, we describe a pedagogical framework designed to promote deeper learning by *uniting* communication and critical thinking around moments of failure. In the proposed framework, students communicate about how they intend to address upcoming, as-yet-unknown breakdowns in learning, including by planning critical thinking strategies for moments of failure and approaches to negotiating the emotional components of failure. In turn, when breakdowns arise in learning, instructors respond to what students have communicated by modeling, prompting for, and reflecting on students' proposed strategies for handling failure. Afterwards, students reflect on past failures, evaluating the efficacy of their strategies and documenting their emotional experiences. This pedagogical approach establishes a connection between the application of critical thinking strategies *during* failure and communication about the critical thinking process *before* and *after* failure. In addition, this approach acknowledges the inextricable relationship between thinking and emotion. Beyond providing examples of how instructors engage with this approach, this chapter covers preliminary evidence that these teaching strategies lead to growth in students' impressions of their skills for handling failure and their confidence during failure, both vital components of environments that promote deeper learning.

Description of teaching strategies

Computer programming as a context for communication about critical thinking

Practice-based documentation of these teaching strategies comes from the domain of computer science. In computer science, identifying and correcting errors, known as *debugging,* is part and parcel of the pursuit. For programmers, debugging is a routine part of coding, supported by specialized tools (e.g., syntax checkers and print statements) and critical thinking strategies (Murphy-Hill, Zimmermann, Bird, & Nagappan, 2013; Perscheid, Siegmund, Taeumel, & Hirschfeld, 2017). Although programmers develop debugging skills by coding, it is challenging to learn independently (Klahr & Carver, 1988). Current techniques for supporting debugging learning include providing students with resources to make debugging more tractable or efficient (Katz & Anderson, 1987; Ko & Myers, 2009), designing game-based contexts to facilitate debugging

(Liu, Zhi, Hicks, & Barnes, 2017), and providing students with faulty artifacts to repair (Fields, Searle, & Kafai, 2016). Educational researchers have paid less attention to teaching strategies that promote and sustain student-driven communication about the critical thinking and emotional processes that surround debugging.

Planning and reflecting on critical thinking strategies for failure

Design principles

Our journaling and art making designs invited 5th- to 10th-grade students to communicate about critical thinking strategies and emotional experiences that surround debugging. To frame this work, instructors told stories about professionals' routine encounters with failure en route to progress, a practice found to normalize failure and motivate students (Lin-Siegler, Ahn, Chen, Fang, & Luna-Lucero, 2016). Students then envisioned "strategies and skills for dealing with everyday problems in school" (Oyserman, Terry, & Bybee, 2002, p. 316), specifically by planning critical thinking strategies for debugging. Students also created artwork about debugging that moved beyond conventional story archetypes about failure, examining how emotion shapes the process of building knowledge (Jaber & Hammer, 2016). Below, we outline the specifics of these instructional strategies.

Using journals for planning and reflecting

At the start of a coding session, students used personal coding journals to reflect on their past critical thinking strategies for debugging and set an intention to learn a new critical thinking strategy for debugging. Drawing on Twitter conventions, students wrote brief statements followed by hashtags: phrases that describe the topic of the message or "the tone of the message or the tweeter's emotions" (Mohammad & Kiritchenko, 2015, p. 302). Hashtags serve as "instrument(s) for creative self-expression and language play" (Heyd & Puschmann, 2017, p. 51). In our coding workshops, students wrote in personal journals responding to the following prompts:

- What debugging strategy worked well for you last time? #Hashtags
- Tweet your goal for when coding gets tough today. Choose one new debugging strategy to work on. #Hashtags

The instructors framed students' goal setting by telling a story at the beginning of class about how someone outside of a coding context insightfully responded to failure, such as how a rock climber worked through a tough section or how an artist learned to draw an object that had previously stymied her. Instructors also gave students a chance to consult a visual map of the debugging-specific critical thinking strategies students surfaced at the workshop.

212 DeLiema, Dahn, Flood, et al.

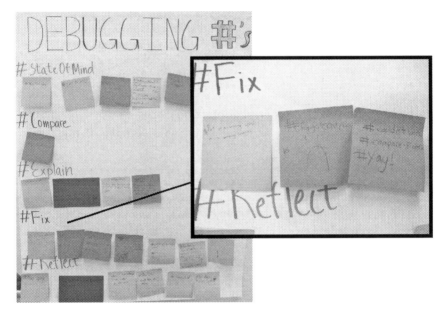

FIGURE 12.1 Students' sorted sticky note reflections; the overlaid image shows a zoomed-in portion.

At the end of class, students evaluated the efficacy of their past debugging strategies and planned their approach to the next coding session. Students wrote specifically in response to the following prompts:

- Tweet a description of a bug you encountered. #Hashtags
- How well did your debugging strategy work? #Hashtags
- How do you think the bug got into your code in the first place? #Hashtags
- How will you tackle the next bug you encounter? #Hashtags

On some days, students wrote their goals and reflections on sticky notes, placing them on a large poster board (see Figure 12.1) or next to their laptop keyboards.

Communicating about emotion and thinking processes through visual artwork

To make space for alternative forms of communication about the learning process, we capitalized on the centrality of emotion (Langer, 1953), metacognition (Goldberg, 2005), and transformation (Pelowski & Akiba, 2011) in art making. Students created abstract watercolor paintings, comic-strip-like panels, data visualizations, and code poems about coding and debugging (see examples and brief descriptions of each art project in Table 12.1). Each art class focused on an

Debugging for fostering reflection 213

TABLE 12.1 Art making activities and example projects

Description of art activity	Student example	
Abstract watercolor paintings: Students used watercolor, oil pastel, and colored pencils to create abstract depictions of emotions they experienced during moments of coding and debugging.	In this piece I wanted to show a common emotion that I felt when I solve a bug. In this case that emotion was the feeling of awareness. To me being aware feels clear, bright, colorful, curious, and experimental. I used light and (cool) bright colors to represent brightness, and contrast.	
Comic-strip-like panels: Students created a simple coding and debugging story focused on an event unfolding over time.	When I get a bug, I feel like a Rubiks Cube. Hard to solve, but looks easy. But then, an explosion becomes an answer.	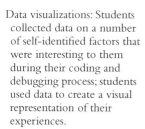
Data visualizations: Students collected data on a number of self-identified factors that were interesting to them during their coding and debugging process; students used data to create a visual representation of their experiences.	*Symbols indicate progression of how time was spent, syntax errors, # of runs until code was correct, grammatical errors, # of times me and my friends laughed, # of times me and my friends talked about code, # of times me and my friends played cards.*	
Code poems: Students printed out in-process code and then wrote free verse poems inspired by the lines in their code and memory of their experience.	This didn't look hard but it didn't look easy at all #confused I'm trying to focus but this is taking me so long #tired A syntax error, that's bad #I messed up #I have to redo it After a while I feel like my brain is going to explode #Exhausted After everything I finally completed the task #I will #Dead bug #bye bug	

essential question (e.g., "How do artists use color, shape, texture, etc., to communicate different feelings?") and began with a warm-up conversation about the topic. The warm-up invited storytelling about students' recent experiences with coding. To familiarize themselves with the art materials and the topic, students then engaged in a quick, exploratory art making activity. After considering a broad range of works of art on the topic, students then used open-ended studio time (stretching over a few days) to develop their work of art. During art making, the instructor scaffolded students' work by encouraging students to adopt flexible goals and remain open to uncertainty and surprise, allow the materials to guide exploration of the topic, ground the artwork in memories of coding experience, and embrace the challenge of producing art (Dahn, DeLiema, & Enyedy, in press). Students concluded by writing artist statements and sharing their artwork in whole class and small group settings. A central outcome of these art making activities was discovering *different ways of seeing, documenting,* and *showing experience*, in particular focused on the relationship between thinking and emotion during failure.

Engaging with critical thinking during failure

Design principles

The prior section focused on teaching strategies that encouraged students through journaling and art making to *plan before* and *reflect after* moments of failure. In this section, we describe how our instructors incorporated students' ideas about critical thinking *during* moments of failure. This teaching strategy helped form a close connection between planning, enacting, and reflecting, and ensured that students' prior communication about critical thinking strategies and emotion informed their coding practice. In particular, teachers and students focused on critical thinking strategies valuable to the process of navigating failure (Lewis, 2012), a practice programmers have long sought to support and understand (Ducassé & Emde, 1988; Freeman, 1964; Ripley & Druseikis, 1978). Below, we outline the specifics of these instructional strategies.

Modeling and prompting for critical thinking strategies during debugging

The foundation of this design is a set of critical thinking strategies for debugging that we amalgamated from research and from professional programmers' reflections on their practice (e.g., Zeller, 2009).

1. **Pre-debugging**
   a. Get in the debugging state of mind: fearlessness, curiosity, thoughtfulness.
   b. Recall student's personally selected debugging goal/strategy for the day.

2. **What is going wrong?**
    c. Describe in granular detail what the program is doing when you run it.
    d. Describe in granular detail what you want the program to do when you run it.
3. **Propose an explanation for why the program is going wrong**
    e. Propose a starting place to search for the bug.
    f. Explain what is happening in the code at that point.
    g. Explain how the code might be causing the problem when you run the program.
4. **Attempt to fix the bug**
    h. Form a plan to repair the code.
    i. Rewrite the code.
    j. Explain why this plan might work.
    k. Run the code.
    l. Return to step 2 if bug persists.
5. **Reflect on the debugging process**
    m. Reflect on the process taken during the debugging exchange.
    n. Talk about how the bug got there in the first place.
    o. Talk about goals for the next debugging exchange.

These debugging strategies correspond to recognized facets of critical thinking (Facione, 1990; Haynes, Lisic, Goltz, Stein, & Harris, 2016) by inviting students to *decode the significance* of observed outcomes of the program (c and d); *analyze the argument* or logic of their code (e and f); *evaluate* where that logic breaks down (g); *formulate alternative conjectures* about ways to fix the breakdown (h, i, and l); *justify* conjectures about the etiology and resolution for the breakdown (j and m); and *examine one's own* assumptions in iterative cycles of attempting a fix (l). In addition, the state of mind strategy aims to deliver on the goal of cultivating affective dispositions in critical thinking (Facione, 1990), such as self-confidence, open-mindedness, and alertness. Lastly, two strategies (b and o) incorporate students' *earlier* communication about critical thinking during debugging, uniting the processes of planning and enacting.

In their pedagogy, instructors participated in one-on-one and small-group debugging sessions with students. These sessions were informed by the tenets of reciprocal teaching (Palincsar & Brown, 1984). Instructors aimed to understand students' baseline debugging skills and looked for opportunities to model new and relevant critical thinking strategies, incorporating both the expert heuristics noted above and the strategies students planned in their journals. Modeling the strategy entailed carrying out the strategy and narrating what an expert might think when enacting it (Collins, Brown, & Newman, 1989). Moving forward, instructors then prompted students to use that strategy and reflect on how it works. Over the long run, instructors during debugging sessions with students aimed to listen to students articulate their strategies for debugging code.

Research evidence

This research took place in 2-week summer computer programming workshops (2 sessions; $n = 120$; 47 girls) and in 8-day weekend computer programming workshops (3 sessions; $n = 123$; 55 girls). The workshops served late elementary students, middle-school students, and early high-school students, all of whom either demonstrated financial need or attended schools with high proportions of students from low-income families. Undergraduate computer science majors at the beginning stages of developing their teaching practice worked as lead instructors. Students used four programming contexts – OpenProcessing, PixelBots, Minecraft, and Lego Robotics – to learn foundational computer science concepts in project-based environments. We documented classroom discourse during programming with multiple GoPro cameras and with screen recordings of students' coding activities, we photographed the artifacts students produced along the way (e.g., journals and artwork), and we conducted semi-structured interviews with students at the end of the workshop to gauge their thoughts about debugging. In addition, we collected survey measures of students' impressions of their own confidence and skill level with debugging.

Our analysis of artifacts and interviews involved iterative stages of looking at subsets of the data, writing memos about tentative themes emerging from the data, forming and reducing categories/constructs, sharing inferences with the research team, and returning to the data, all features of the constant comparative method (Glaser, 1965). Our analysis of classroom discourse data focused on creating multimodal transcripts of moments of debugging and considering how participants worked together to accomplish debugging. This approach followed conventions of interaction analysis research (Jordan & Henderson, 1995; Goodwin, 2018). In our transcripts below, brackets signal overlapping talk, lines with arrows connect strips of talk to co-occurring changes in the environment and/or nonverbal actions of participants, words in italics describe observable action, numbers between parentheses describe gaps in talk in seconds, and punctuation (e.g., a question mark) marks grammatical structure.

Journaling and art making about critical thinking and emotion

We found that asking students to journal about debugging generated reflection on a wide array of critical thinking strategies. Responding to the prompt to plan "one new debugging strategy" and then evaluate how well a past "debugging strategy work[ed]," students across two eight-session weekend workshops surfaced numerous strategies (see Table 12.2).

Table 12.2 documents the set of actions that *students positioned as strategies* for debugging. Many of these strategies allude to domain-general critical thinking moves (Facione, 1990; Haynes et al., 2016): examining ideas (define, prior exemplars), analyzing arguments (find the cause, stepper tool), identifying new

TABLE 12.2 Categorization of the debugging strategies students documented in their journals

Category	Strategy	Student quote
Myself	Work alone	Try to do it by myself
	Believe in myself	I want to be able to believe in myself
	Remind myself of past successes	When coding gets tough, I'm going to remind myself how far I've come
Social support	Teacher	If or when I have trouble…I would ask one of my mentors for help
	Peer	When it gets tough I will ask my peers for help
	Unspecified	When it gets tough ask someone
Emotion	Shyness	My goal is not to be shy
	Anger	Don't get mad if I fail
	Disappointment	Don't be disappointed
	Relaxation	#becalm
	Fear	When coding gets hard…don't be afraid to be wrong #Don't be Afraid
	Frustration	Don't be frustrated when it doesn't come out the way I wanted
Cognitive	Observe	My goal for when coding gets tough is to look very closely for my mistakes
	Memory	I'll try to not to forget which is left and right…
	Prior knowledge	My personal goal for the day when it gets tough is to put all of my knowledge I have learned before into one
	Think	#Think about it
Coding specific tools	Console	Joey helped me find the bug using console #thanksfam
	Stepper tool	I used the stepper to fix the problem
Miscellaneous	Effort	…I want to be able to fix it and not give up
	Novelty	Think of different ways to solve something #trydifferentstrategies
	Prior exemplars	We looked up the zene
	Experimentation	#fun experimenting (with code!)
	Play	Play with a lot then ask advice
	Focus	Consintrate on the question
	Find the cause	If coding gets tough today, I will…find whats wrong
	Make mistakes	Moreover, when we make mistakes it helps us learn
	Prepare	I will study to give me stuff that I need for the solution
	Faith	#believe
	Creativity	#be creative
	Define	Said what the x, y
	Interact	We worked with it…and got our answer
No strategy		My goal is to make it work after solving

information (console), self-examining (prior knowledge), and drawing conclusions (experimentation). Other strategies, such as play, creativity, thought, and preparation, might encompass a number of critical thinking moves without explicitly labeling them. Yet other strategies implicate resources pivotal to critical thinking: perception, memory, peers, teachers, and the students themselves. Furthermore, in line with the recognition that there are dispositional elements to critical thinking (Facione, 1990), students described a range of strategies involving emotion, such as relaxing, disposing of fear, and curtailing frustration.

Separately, three art projects (abstract emotion drawings, code poems, and three-panel stories) offered a space for students to communicate about how affect surrounds moments of critical thinking during failure. Students provided vibrant accounts of how it feels during failure, including feeling down ("when you are gloomy, you really don't see anything but nothing"), angry ("mad is a fist that you are holding up"), and alert ("the feeling of awareness"). Moreover, students documented how emotions change or layer up, such as feeling "sad because I'm getting frustrated" or "how nervousness can take over, yet can become something beautiful if you change the perspective on it." In particular, students described emotional states that arose during specific stages of the code writing process: "OH NO A BUG #MAD #feelingsmall," "The red is supposed to represent the anger when I don't get a bug," and "Bug arises. Time to fix it. #Calm #Cool." Because debugging is such a rich site for critical thinking, this artwork challenged our research-practice team to continue to grapple with how emotion, and interactions between emotions, co-occurred with and perhaps shaped how students worked through problem solving.

Importantly, students viewed making and communicating about art as capable of transforming their approach to coding. Students described a number of transformative potentials: self-understanding and awareness ("I learned how I got mad, how I got feelings"), setting expectations ("It made me understand how I feel and how I will when a bug comes"), shifting state of mind ("give me some hope and that I can fix it"), resting/relaxing/calming ("To keep you peace from overstress"), shifting emotion ("Art changed my way of feeling about coding"), and helping with confidence during problem solving ("And when I go to my other class after art, I feel like I can pass my challenge"). Similarly, students viewed their public-facing sticky note reflections as supports for thinking through and emotionally coping with debugging. Students discussed becoming aware that everyone debugs ("And when you look at other people's sticky notes you're like man I'm not the only person with this problem"), learning from the errors of their peers ("they can just go to the wall and learn from the other people's mistakes"), recalling debugging strategies ("and it helps me know what I did so that next time I make a bug I can use that same process too"), returning oneself to a calm emotional state ("I feel like it let the stress out"), recognizing the classroom's growth around debugging ("It's just fun seeing your progress with your classmates like freaking out to calm"), and communicating one's experiences ("I thought it was better to let out our feelings instead of just holding it in").

Overall, these data show that given the opportunity to communicate about failure through journaling and art making in a supportive classroom environment, students generated a wide array of critical thinking strategies and developed rich insights into how emotion surrounds thinking during failure. Moreover, students believed that these reflective experiences transformed their experience of navigating the critical thinking and affective demands of failure, such as developing self-understanding, setting new expectations, reminding themselves of effective strategies, drawing on community knowledge, or simply honoring gradual progress.

Modeling, prompting, and reflecting on critical thinking during debugging

We now turn attention to critical thinking *during* debugging. In order to support students' more autonomous resolution of bugs, instructors often attuned their questioning and referring strategies to shape students' perception of the affordances of the programming environment for debugging (Flood, DeLiema, Harrer, & Abrahamson, 2018). This enskilment process (Ingold, 2000) incorporates conversation practices such as the use of *vague references* and *contracting and expanding question agendas*. Here we describe three other teaching strategies: *modeling* a new critical thinking strategy, *prompting* for a student to apply a critical thinking strategy, and *reflecting* after the fact on the critical thinking process.

In the first excerpt, an instructor *models* a critical thinking strategy for debugging. In this exchange, a student's repeat loop is missing its final parenthesis, a bug known as a syntax error. With syntax errors, instructors can directly point them out and offer a way to remember a fix (e.g., introducing a phrase like, "every parenthesis needs a friend"). When this happens, instructors privately enact critical thinking strategies used both to find and fix the bug. In other debugging interactions with students, instructors explicitly model critical thinking strategies used to locate the bug (see Figure 12.2). In the transcript below, the instructor, Ben, models for the student, Mav, *where* to look for correct syntax and *how* to compare correct and broken syntax.

The instructor guides the student to a fix while introducing a critical thinking strategy for debugging: visually comparing correct syntax in the API with the student's broken syntax. In terms of critical thinking, this approach explicitly models how to *query* the coding environment for information, *systematically examine* competing approaches to writing code (the API syntax and the student's own syntax), *draw a conclusion* about a missing element, and ultimately *self-correct*. By publicly narrating and showing how to compare broken and accurate syntax, the instructor makes visible a set of critical thinking moves during failure that the student could independently apply to subsequent syntax errors.

220 DeLiema, Dahn, Flood, et al.

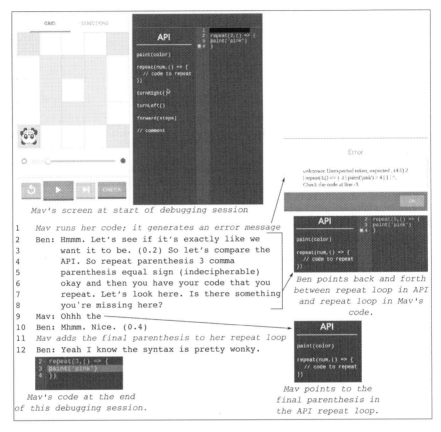

FIGURE 12.2 Modeling a critical thinking strategy: Comparing broken code with working code in the API.

In the second excerpt, we examine how an instructor *prompts* for a student to use a tool in the programming environment that facilitates critical thinking about logic errors: situations in which the program runs but results in output the student does not intend or want. Instead of directly pointing out a flaw in the student's reasoning, the instructor, Jad, prompts the student, Zoa, to use a tool to discover the underlying cause of the observable problem (see Figure 12.3). This example also illustrates how the goals students set in their coding journals can motivate the exploration of a debugging strategy.

In this example, an instructor offers debugging support by asking the student about her debugging goal for the day and drawing attention to her debugging statistics. Using these two reflective practices as a point of departure, the instructor then prompts for exploration of a critical thinking tool for debugging. The tool, known as a stepper, promotes the integration of a number of critical thinking strategies: *analyzing the argument* or logic in the code line by line, *evaluating* the relationship between that logic and the output of the program

Debugging for fostering reflection 221

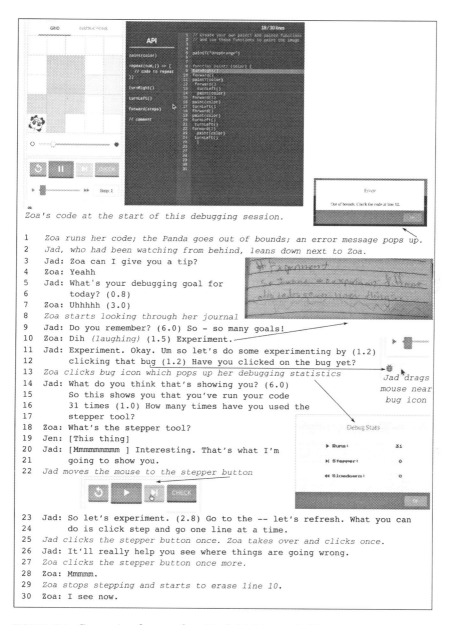

Zoa's code at the start of this debugging session.

```
1   Zoa runs her code; the Panda goes out of bounds; an error message pops up.
2   Jad, who had been watching from behind, leans down next to Zoa.
3   Jad: Zoa can I give you a tip?
4   Zoa: Yeahh
5   Jad: What's your debugging goal for
6        today? (0.8)
7   Zoa: Uhhhhh (3.0)
8   Zoa starts looking through her journal
9   Jad: Do you remember? (6.0) So - so many goals!
10  Zoa: Dih (laughing) (1.5) Experiment.
11  Jad: Experiment. Okay. Um so let's do some experimenting by (1.2)
12       clicking that bug (1.2) Have you clicked on the bug yet?
13  Zoa clicks bug icon which pops up her debugging statistics
                                                                Jad drags
14  Jad: What do you think that's showing you? (6.0)            mouse near
15       So this shows you that you've run your code            bug icon
16       31 times (1.0) How many times have you used the
17       stepper tool?
18  Zoa: What's the stepper tool?
19  Jen: [This thing]
20  Jad: [Mmmmmmmmm ] Interesting. That's what I'm
21       going to show you.
22  Jad moves the mouse to the stepper button

23  Jad: So let's experiment. (2.8) Go to the -- let's refresh. What you can
24       do is click step and go one line at a time.
25  Jad clicks the stepper button once. Zoa takes over and clicks once.
26  Jad: It'll really help you see where things are going wrong.
27  Zoa clicks the stepper button once more.
28  Zoa: Mmmmm.
29  Zoa stops stepping and starts to erase line 10.
30  Zoa: I see now.
```

FIGURE 12.3 Prompting for use of a critical thinking tool: The stepper.

(how the PixelBot moves and paints), and *self-correcting* by *drawing a conclusion* about a flaw in the code. Indeed, after prompting the student to try the stepper tool, the instructor in line 26 describes its value: helping the student to independently find ("help you see") the source of the problem ("where things are going wrong"). Without the instructor describing what has caused the problem,

FIGURE 12.4 Reflecting on critical thinking strategies after fixing a bug.

the student is nonetheless able to use the stepper to locate the trouble spot and start to repair it (line 29 in Figure 12.3).

Our third example (see Figure 12.4) documents how *reflection* on the critical-thinking process can incorporate debugging goals from students' journals and take place in conversation just after a bug fix. In the following exchange, the student, Lin, and the instructor, Teo, have already worked together to successfully repair her code when the instructor prompts for reflection.

In this exchange, the instructor prompts for post hoc analysis of prior critical thinking strategies immediately after the bug is fixed. The student provides a label (experiment) for a critical thinking strategy she used, and then the instructor and a peer synchronously highlight another critical thinking strategy (inspect). The group then discusses whether experimenting and inspecting advanced Lin's debugging goal for the day. Lin describes not meeting one of her goals: focusing. The instructor follows up by describing goal setting as a progressive practice, something we're "always working on." This interaction demonstrates how instructors and peers can

TABLE 12.3 Survey results about students' debugging skill level

	Question: How good are you at debugging code?			
	Pre Winter 2017	Post Winter 2017	Pre Summer 2017	Post Summer 2017
Terrible	6.12%	4.08%	11.90%	0%
Bad	14.29%	8.16%	13.01%	3.57%
Fine	48.98%	14.29%	35.71%	21.43%
Good	26.53%	63.27%	30.96%	59.53%
Extremely Good	4.08%	10.20%	8.33%	15.48%
	n = 49		n = 84	

collaboratively reify a set of actions into overarching descriptions of critical thinking strategies, and then evaluate whether those strategies advance students' debugging goals. This excerpt documents how collaborative reflection during coding can tie together, reify, and support the planning and enacting of critical thinking.

Overall results of instructional strategies

A number of interview and survey data sources used across our coding workshops suggest that the cumulative impact of our discourse and journaling/art making learning designs (core parts of all of our coding workshops) increased students' sense of their *debugging skill level*, their *confidence* with debugging, and their *awareness of debugging strategies*. With respect to skill level and confidence, students across three coding workshops (Tables 12.3 and 12.4) showed the same trend from pre to post survey data on a five-item Likert scale: fewer students reporting having low (terrible, bad, or fine) debugging skill/confidence and more students reporting having high (good, extremely good) debugging skill/confidence (with average gains, calculated by subtracting the pre-test Likert score (1-5) from the post-test Likert score (1-5) for each student, of .59 in winter 2017; .76 in summer 2017; and .41 in Spring 2018).

In addition, we narrowed our focus in Spring 2018 and asked students whether they believed they could create a helpful strategy for debugging (see Table 12.5). A similar trend emerged in which fewer students reported disagreeing with the statement that they could create debugging strategies and more students reported agreeing with this statement (leading to an average Likert scale gain of .48).

TABLE 12.4 Survey results about students' confidence with debugging

Question: How would you feel when you come across a problem with your code?		
	Pre Spring 2018	Post Spring 2018
Not at all confident that I can fix it.	0%	0%
Slightly confident that I can fix it.	16.67%	6.25%
Moderately confident that I can fix it.	47.92%	29.17%
Very confident that I can fix it.	22.92%	50.00%
Extremely confident that I can fix it.	12.50%	14.58%
		n = 48

TABLE 12.5 Survey results about students' capacity to create new debugging strategies

I can create a helpful strategy to find the problem with my code.

	Pre Spring 2018	Post Spring 2018
Not at all	4.17%	2.08%
Slightly	16.67%	2.08%
Moderately	37.50%	29.17%
Very	29.17%	50.00%
Extremely	12.50%	16.67%
	n = 48	

Apart from students reporting higher skill level/confidence in debugging and higher likelihood that they could invent debugging strategies, we also gathered evidence that students at the end of the summer 2017 2-week coding workshop could talk extemporaneously about a number of debugging strategies they had used throughout camp. During in-depth end-of-workshop interviews with 20 students, researchers asked: "What is your debugging process – how do you get rid of bugs?" Every student listed multiple debugging strategies. Overall, students discussed the strategies in Table 12.6.

The table of strategies ranges from specific tools in the coding environment (e.g., stepper tool) and approaches to reviewing code (reread my code) to methods for tinkering with code (e.g., experiment) and cognitive/affective states (e.g., focus and stay calm). The table suggests that students new to coding can start to consider a relatively wide range of critical thinking and affective practices they enact to debug code.

TABLE 12.6 Categorization of students' stated debugging strategies during an end of workshop interview

Percentage of students who described this strategy	List of strategies
5%	• Use what I learned • Check the most recent change • Stay calm • Slow down code • Figure it out myself • Classify the bug type
10%	• Comment out code • Focus
15%	• Use the stepper tool
30%	• Automatic Syntax Checker
40%	• Experiment • Look for common syntax errors
50%	• Ask for help • Look at/Re-read my code
60%	• Compare with working code

Discussion

Because breakdowns in learning naturally motivate reflection on a complex set of causes and possible resolutions (DeLiema, 2017; Heider, 1958; Herman, 2009; Weiner, 1985), they provide opportunities for communication about the critical thinking process. In this chapter, we described two instructional strategies designed to support communication about critical thinking: (1) student journaling and art making that focused on planning and examining critical thinking strategies and emotional experiences that surround failure; and (2) instructors modeling, prompting for, and reflecting on critical thinking strategies with students during failure to explore both expert debugging heuristics and students' own goals. These designs prioritized public reflection on and communication about the critical thinking process (Collins et al., 1989), both in stable artifacts (journals and artwork) and during coding. We argue that these teaching strategies are effective because they explicitly bridge *planning, reflecting,* and *enacting,* helping ensure that students and instructors actively pursue their plans for critical thinking during failure. Moreover, because this approach values reflection on the phenomenology of failure, or how it feels to encounter a breakdown (Jaber & Hammer, 2016; Sengupta, Dickes, & Farris, 2018), it makes possible conversations in the classroom about how emotion shapes students' selection of critical thinking strategies for failure, an insufficiently examined but important facet of problem solving.

Connections to deeper learning

Even though this chapter did not provide empirical evidence of the capacity of these teaching strategies to promote deeper learning, we would argue that fostering in students a capacity to think critically during failure, including by acknowledging affect and building students' confidence during failure, constitute key elements of pathways that foster high quality learning. To be more specific, pedagogical frameworks such as preparation for future learning (Schwartz & Martin, 2004) and productive failure (Kapur, 2008) have empirically documented the value of failure for long-term, robust learning. However, as Kapur (2008) notes, "learners' frustration thresholds and level of engagement in solving the problem, for example, may be particularly critical" (p. 414). Bringing experiences with frustration and other affective states out of the shadows and into public classroom discourse, whether through journaling or art making, invites *collective* approaches to understanding and supporting how emotion shapes critical thinking. In this way, deep learning may best emerge from failure when a community of teachers and students actively searches for ways to understand and communicate about emotion and critical thinking, rather than when students privately process breakdowns in learning. Moreover, explicitly working to build students' *authority* to debug (Engle & Conant, 2002), including by guaranteeing access to relevant resources, empowers *students themselves* to generate deeper learning from struggle.

Limitations and future work

There are a number of limitations to this work at its current stage. First, the link between the proposed teaching strategies and deeper learning is only hypothesized; future work should investigate whether communication about affect and critical thinking surrounding failure promotes robust learning. In a similar way, this study is limited by its focus on select moments of teaching and coverage of aggregate outcomes. More granular, longitudinal case studies, and systematic experimental work, could more meticulously document *how* and *under what conditions* these teaching strategies promote learning. In addition, even though we argued that failure provides a useful point of departure for communication about critical thinking, this assumption warrants inquiry. In particular, future research could explore these teaching strategies around moments of success in the learning process. Lastly, the data used in this study explored a limited dimension of time with respect to communication about failure. Journal reflections took place at the start and end of class, and interviews took place at the end of a 2-week workshop. Future work could explore whether and how student-driven communication about critical thinking strategies for failure, positioned at different points in the learning process (e.g., just before or just after a moment of failure), might promote more relevant or finer-grained planning with implications for the quality of learning.

Acknowledgement

This chapter is based on work supported by the National Science Foundation under Grant Nos. 1612660, 1612770, and 1607742.

References

Collins, A., Brown, J. S., & Newman, S. E. (1989). Cognitive apprenticeship: Teaching the crafts of reading, writing, and mathematics. In L. B. Resnick (Ed.), *Knowing, learning, and instruction: Essays in honor of Robert Glaser* (pp. 453–494). Hillsdale, NJ: Lawrence Erlbaum.

Dahn, M., DeLiema, D., & Enyedy, N. (in press). Art as a point of departure for understanding student experience in learning to code. *Teachers College Record*.

DeLiema, D. (2017). Co-constructed failure narratives in mathematics tutoring. *Instructional Science*, 45(6), 709–735.

Ducassé, M., & Emde, A. M. (1988). A review of automated debugging systems: Knowledge, strategies and techniques. In T. N. Nam (Ed.), *Proceedings of the 10th International Conference on Software Engineering* (pp. 162–171). Los Alamitos, CA: IEEE Computer Society Press.

Engle, R. A., & Conant, F. R. (2002). Guiding principles for fostering productive disciplinary engagement: Explaining an emergent argument in a community of learners' classroom. *Cognition and Instruction*, 20(4), 399–483.

Facione, P. A. (1990). *Critical thinking: A statement of expert consensus for purposes of educational assessment and instruction* (ERIC Document Reproduction Service No. ED 315 423). Retrieved from PhilArchive open access website: https://philarchive.org/archive/FACCTA

Fields, D. A., Searle, K. A., & Kafai, Y. B. (2016). Deconstruction kits for learning: Students' collaborative debugging of electronic textile designs. In P. Blikstein, M. Berland, & D. A. Fields (Eds.), *Proceedings of the 6th Annual Conference on Creativity and Fabrication in Education* (pp. 82–85). New York: ACM.

Flood, V. J., DeLiema, D., Harrer, B. W., & Abrahamson, D. (2018). Enskilment in the digital age: The interactional work of learning to debug. In J. Kay & R. Luckin (Eds.), *Rethinking Learning in the Digital Age: Making the Learning Sciences Count, 13th International Conference of the Learning Sciences (ICLS) 2018, Volume 3* (pp. 1405–1406). London, UK: International Society of the Learning Sciences.

Freeman, D. N. (1964). Error correction in CORC, the Cornell computing language. *AFIPS Conference Proceedings, Fall Joint Computer Conference, Volume 26* (pp. 15–34). Baltimore, MD: Spartan Books.

Glaser, B. G. (1965). The constant comparative method of qualitative analysis. *Social Problems*, *12*(4), 436–445.

Goodwin, C. (2018). *Co-operative action.* New York: Cambridge University Press.

Goldberg, P. D. (2005). Metacognition and art production as problem solving: A study of third-grade students. *Visual Arts Research*, *31*(2), 67–75.

Greiff, S., Wüstenberg, S., Csapó, B., Demetriou, A., Hautamäki, J., Graesser, A. C., & Martin, R. (2014). Domain-general problem solving skills and education in the 21st century. *Educational Research Review*, *13*, 74–83.

Haynes, A., Lisic, E., Goltz, M., Stein, B., & Harris, K. (2016). Moving beyond assessment to improving students' critical thinking skills: A model for implementing change. *Journal of the Scholarship of Teaching and Learning*, *16*(4), 44–61.

Heider, F. (1958). *The psychology of interpersonal relations.* Hillsdale, NJ: Lawrence Erlbaum.

Herman, D. (2009). *Basic elements of narrative.* Malden, MA: Wiley-Blackwell.

Hesslow, G. (1988). The problem of causal selection. In D. J. Hilton (Ed.), *Contemporary science and natural explanation: Commonsense conceptions of causality* (pp. 11–32). Brighton, England: Harvester Press.

Heyd-Metzuyanim, E. (2015). Vicious cycles of identifying and mathematizing: A case study of the development of mathematical failure. *Journal of the Learning Sciences*, *24*(4), 504–549.

Heyd, T., & Puschmann, C. (2017). Hashtagging and functional shift: Adaptation and appropriation of the #. *Journal of Pragmatics*, *116*, 51–63.

Hmelo-Silver, C. E. (2004). Problem-based learning: What and how do learners learn? *Educational Psychology Review*, *16*(3), 235–266.

Ingold, T. (2000). *The perception of the environment: Essays on livelihood, dwelling and skill.* Oxford, UK: Routledge.

Jaber, L. Z., & Hammer, D. (2016). Engaging in science: A feeling for the discipline. *Journal of the Learning Sciences*, *25*(2), 156–202.

Jordan, B., & Henderson, A. (1995). Interaction analysis: Foundations and practice. *Journal of the Learning Sciences*, *4*(1), 39–103.

Kapur, M. (2008). Productive failure. *Cognition and Instruction*, *26*(3), 379–424.

Katz, I. R., & Anderson, J. R. (1987). Debugging: An analysis of bug-location strategies. *Human-Computer Interaction*, *3*(4), 351–399.

Klahr, D., & Carver, S. M. (1988). Cognitive objectives in a LOGO debugging curriculum: Instruction, learning, and transfer. *Cognitive Psychology*, *20*, 362–404.

Ko, A., & Myers, B. A. (2009). Finding causes of program output with the Java Whyline. In D. R. Olsen & R. B. Arthur (Eds.), *Proceedings of the SIGCHI Conference on Human Factors in Computing Systems* (pp. 1569–1578). New York: ACM.

Koschmann, T., Kuutti, K., & Hickman, L. (1998). The concept of breakdown in Heidegger, Leont'ev, and Dewey and its implications for education. *Mind, Culture, and Activity, 5*(1), 25–41.

Langer, S. (1953). *Feeling and form: A theory of art.* New York: Charles Scribner's Sons.

Lewis, C. M. (2012). The importance of students' attention to program state: A case study of debugging behavior. In A. Clear, K. Sanders, & B. Simon (Eds.), *Proceedings of the Ninth Annual International Conference on International Computing Education Research* (pp. 127–134). New York: ACM.

Liu, Z., Zhi, R., Hicks, A., & Barnes, T. (2017). Understanding problem solving behavior of 6–8 graders in a debugging game. *Computer Science Education, 27*(1), 1–29.

Lin-Siegler, X., Ahn, J. N., Chen, J., Fang, F. F. A., & Luna-Lucero, M. (2016). Even Einstein struggled: Effects of learning about great scientists' struggles on high school students' motivation to learn science. *Journal of Educational Psychology, 108*(3), 314.

Metzger, R. (2004). *Debugging by thinking: A multidisciplinary approach.* Burlington, MA: Elsevier Digital Press.

Mohammad, S. M., & Kiritchenko, S. (2015). Using hashtags to capture fine emotion categories from tweets. *Computational Intelligence, 31*(2), 301–326.

Murphy-Hill, E., Zimmermann, T., Bird, C., & Nagappan, N. (2013). The design of bug fixes. In D. Notkin, B. H. C. Cheng, & K. Pohl (Eds.), *Proceedings of the 35th International Conference on Software Engineering* (pp. 332–341). Institute of Electrical and Electronics Engineers Press.

Oyserman, D., Terry, K., & Bybee, D. (2002). A possible selves intervention to enhance school involvement. *Journal of Adolescence, 25*(3), 313–326.

Palincsar, A. S., & Brown, A. L. (1984). Reciprocal teaching of comprehension-fostering and comprehension-monitoring activities. *Cognition and Instruction, 1*(2), 117–175.

Pelowski, M. J., & Akiba, F. (2011). A model of art perception, evaluation and emotion in transformative aesthetic experience. *New Ideas in Psychology, 29*(2), 80–97.

Perscheid, M., Siegmund, B., Taeumel, M., & Hirschfeld, R. (2017). Studying the advancement in debugging practice of professional software developers. *Software Quality Journal, 25*(1), 83–110.

Ripley, G. D., & Druseikis, F. C. (1978). A statistical analysis of syntax errors. *Computer Languages, 3*(4), 227–240.

Schön, D. A. (1983). *The reflective practitioner: How professionals think in action.* New York: Basic Books.

Schwartz, D. L., & Martin, T. (2004). Inventing to prepare for future learning: The hidden efficiency of encouraging original student production in statistics instruction. *Cognition and Instruction, 22*(2), 129–184.

Sengupta, P., Dickes, A., & Farris, A. (2018). Toward a phenomenology of computational thinking in STEM education. In M. S. Khine (Ed.), *Computational thinking in the STEM disciplines: Foundations and research highlights* (pp. 49–72). Cham, Switzerland: Springer International Publishing.

Suchman, L. A. (1987). *Plans and situated actions: The problem of human-machine communication.* New York: Cambridge University Press.

Weiner, B. (1985). An attributional theory of achievement motivation and emotion. *Psychological Review, 92*(4), 548–573.

Zeller, A. (2009). *Why programs fail: A guide to systematic debugging.* Burlington, MA: Elsevier.

PART 5
Training specific competencies

13

SHOWING WHAT IT LOOKS LIKE

Teaching students to use
diagrams in problem solving,
communication, and thinking

*Emmanuel Manalo, Yuri Uesaka, Ouhao Chen,
and Hiroaki Ayabe*

Summary

Cultivating the ability to use multiple representations is considered very important in 21st-century education. Students should be able to employ not only verbal representations but also visual representations such as diagrams to enable effective organization, understanding, and communication of information. However, despite this acknowledged importance, instruction in diagram use is rarely provided to students. In this chapter, we describe methods we have developed for the provision of such instruction and refer to evidence for their effectiveness, not only in improving students' spontaneity in using diagrams, but also in promoting deeper learning, communicative competencies, and critical thinking.

Introduction

The ability to use multiple representations of concepts and tasks is considered to be one of the key competencies that people need to develop in order to operate effectively in 21st-century environments (e.g., National Research Council, 2012). Multiple representations here pertain to the use of not only words, printed or spoken (i.e., verbal representations), but also diagrams, pictures, animation, and other forms of visual representations, as well as numerical, mathematical, scientific, and other forms of recognizable symbols and notations. In this chapter, we will use the term *diagrams* to broadly and inclusively refer to visual or graphic representations, including drawings, illustrations, tables and other arrays, flow charts, and graphs. When lines or arrows connect three or more words – thereby creating a flow or organizational chart – such a representation would also count as a diagram.

A number of authors have explained the efficacy of using diagrams. Perhaps one of the most well-known of these explanations is Larkin and Simon's (1987), in which they pointed out that diagrams have a computational advantage over sentential representations because they "group together all information that is used together" and thus "support a large number of perceptual inferences" (p. 98). In simple terms this means that, because diagrams group information together so that we can see connections and relationships much easier, they help us to draw inferences and to understand much more efficiently compared to when information is presented serially, like in sentences (where connections and relationships are usually not as immediately obvious because of spatial, and possibly temporal, distance).

When diagrams are used appropriately together with words in learning and communicative contexts, they can greatly enhance comprehension and learning outcomes because the combination facilitates the use of both the verbal and visual channels of working memory (e.g., Mayer, 2009; Mayer & Moreno, 1998, 2003). When diagrams are used in problem solving contexts, they help toward generating correct solutions because they translate the terms of the problem (usually given as verbal statements) into a representation that makes sense and is easier to understand (Beitzel & Staley, 2015; Hembree, 1992; Jitendra, Griffin, Haria, Leh, Adams, & Kaduvettoor, 2007; Tversky & Kessell, 2014).

Despite the generally acknowledged value of using diagrams in a wide range of learning and communicative contexts, the construction and use of diagrams is not usually taught explicitly in schools. Teachers may demonstrate the use of diagrams to students when explaining information or solving problems on the board, but they rarely go through the steps involved in diagram construction, or clarify the conditions that may apply in determining what diagrams to use and when they should be used. Much of formal education emphasizes the cultivation of verbal forms of expressing knowledge and ideas (i.e., the use of words, spoken and written), with the cultivation of the corresponding or complementary visual forms of expression largely neglected.

Perhaps not surprisingly, there are a number of problems that have been identified regarding student construction and use of diagrams. The most serious of these is lack of spontaneity in use (e.g., Dufour-Janvier, Bernarz, & Belanger, 1987; Manalo, Uesaka, Pérez-Kriz, Kato, & Fukaya, 2013; Uesaka & Manalo, 2017; Uesaka, Manalo, & Ichikawa, 2007; van Garderen, Scheuermann, & Jackson, 2012): unless required or prompted to use them, the majority of students tend not to use diagrams even in situations where diagram use would be deemed advantageous (e.g., solving difficult math word problems, constructing explanations of hard-to-imagine or complicated information for others). Because in most everyday life situations (outside of school) there are no requirements or prompts for using diagrams, this lack of spontaneity means that many students are likely to miss out on the potential benefits of using diagrams. Another serious problem is that when students do use diagrams, many fail to use the appropriate diagrams or to draw correct inferences from them (e.g., Cox, 1996; Uesaka & Manalo, 2006;

van Garderen et al., 2012). There are also problems relating to student use of diagrams that are provided to them: for example, Cromley, Snyder-Hogan, and Luciw-Dubas (2010) found that many students ignore or only superficially look over diagrams provided in their textbooks, suggesting that they are unlikely to fully benefit from those diagrams. However, in this chapter we will focus particularly on problems and issues relating to diagrams that students construct, rather than those provided to them.

Findings from our own research on the promotion of effective strategy use suggest that when two crucial conditions are missing, students do not manifest spontaneity in the use of such strategies. Those conditions are that they must *appreciate the value of employing the strategy,* and they must *possess adequate knowledge and skills in using that strategy* (e.g., Manalo, Uesaka, & Chinn, 2017; Uesaka & Manalo, 2017). In the following section, we will describe methods that teachers can use to address such deficits, and hence to promote the desired spontaneity – particularly in students' use of diagrams.

Descriptions of methods

Cultivating appreciation of the value of diagram use

Telling them the value

To get students to realize that using diagrams can benefit their work, teachers can directly tell them. For example, we found it effective to provide verbal encouragement to students who had failed to correctly solve a math word problem. We simply told them that they could have been more successful in solving that problem had they used an appropriate diagram: students who received such encouragement showed higher subsequent diagram use (Uesaka, Manalo, & Ichikawa, 2010). We also found it effective to provide a hint in the written feedback given to students for an explanation homework they completed. After receiving the hint that "including diagrams could make your explanations easier to understand," the students' rate of diagram inclusion in their subsequent homework significantly increased (Manalo & Uesaka, 2016). We should note that this increase occurred despite the fact that the students were aware that no specific grade points were allocated for diagram use in their homework.

Using interactive peer instruction

Teachers can also cultivate appreciation of the value of diagram use *indirectly* by getting students to work interactively with each other in peer instruction or explanation tasks. In a study involving mathematics word problem solving, we assigned pairs of junior high school students different problems to solve, and then afterward asked them to take turns at teaching each other how they solved the problem they had been assigned (Uesaka & Manalo, 2007). We found that many of the students not only used diagrams during the peer instruction session, but also in subsequent problem solving tasks that were given to them to solve individually. We found their use of diagrams to be significantly higher than students who were in a control group and received the exact same problems to solve, but not the opportunities for peer instruction. Our examination of the protocols generated during the peer instruction sessions suggested that, in such situations, verbal explanations alone often prove inadequate and students have to resort to using illustrations or other forms of visual explanations to clarify how they solved the problem. This kind of experience likely made them realize that constructing diagrams was helpful in explaining. Additionally, through being able to explain how to solve the problems more easily, the students may have come to realize the utility that diagram use brings to such problem solving.

We found similar effects in a study in which we asked students (university undergraduates this time) to take turns at explaining to each other the contents of a passage they had read (they were given different passages to read). Again, we found that when peer explanations were interactive, spontaneous diagram use was significantly higher compared to noninteractive peer explanations in which the students prepared and recorded their explanations for each other (Uesaka & Manalo, 2014). Our examination of the interactive explanation protocols revealed that students often received feedback from their interlocutors indicating that what they had said was not sufficiently understood, which made the explainers use illustrations and/or schematic diagrams to clarify details of what they were attempting to convey.

Cultivating knowledge and skills in diagram construction and use

Providing the necessary instruction

In teaching diagram construction and use to students, teachers need to facilitate the development of three kinds of knowledge: declarative (i.e., knowing *that*), procedural (knowing *how*), and conditional (knowing *when*) – as Paris, Lipson, and Wixson (1983) explained regarding the requirements of strategy use. For example, students need to *know that* constructing a table or equivalent array could be helpful when attempting to solve a math word problem in which there is a rule-bound or pattern-based change in quantities occurring and some future quantity needs to be calculated, or that including an illustration is helpful when the student needs to communicate how something appears, or where items or entities are located in relation to each other. Thus, in teaching diagram use for problem solving, students need to *know and understand that,* depending on the type of problem presented, a particular kind of diagram could help in solving it (e.g., Zahner & Corter, 2010). In a recent study that we conducted in a real classroom context (Ayabe & Manalo, 2018), we focused on the use of three kinds of diagrams: line diagrams, tables, and graphs. We used a good part of an entire class session to teach the use of each kind, first presenting examples of the corresponding types of problems and clarifying their requirements, next explaining how and why that kind of diagram in particular is helpful in solving such a problem, and then providing a demonstration of the steps taken in such solving.

In another study, which we also conducted in a real classroom context (Manalo & Uesaka, 2016), we provided instruction on the use of diagrams in written communication for other people. First, we explained the general reasons why diagrams can be helpful: we pointed out that diagramming the structure and organization of target information can clarify and confirm our understanding of it, as well as help us identify parts that we may not fully understand. We referred to research about using both verbal and visual channels of working memory when diagrams are used in combination with words (e.g., Mayer, 2009) – thus, including appropriate diagrams can make our explanations easier for other people to understand and learn. After that, we explained more specifically – and showed examples of – the kinds of diagrams that are helpful when we need to illustrate (e.g., the appearance of objects, spatial layout), to provide an overview or structure, to show process or cause-and-effect relationships, and to compare and contrast. Again, the aim was for students to *know and understand that,* depending on the purpose and content of the communication, the use of an appropriate kind of diagram can enhance the clarity and effectiveness of that communication (e.g., Novick & Hurley, 2001; Tversky, 2011; Xing, Corter, & Zahner, 2016).

Providing opportunities for practice

As noted, the development of procedural knowledge is also necessary. One intervention we have found effective for this purpose is to provide *guided* practice in the construction and use of each kind of diagram. Hence, in the Ayabe and Manalo (2018) study, following instruction in the use of each kind of diagram (e.g., line diagrams), the students were given practice in solving problems for which the use of that kind of diagram would be helpful. In the Manalo and Uesaka (2016) study, during the practice phase of the intervention, the students were not only given practice during class to use the kinds of diagrams they had received instruction in, they were also given homework that required them to look for information they had learned which could be explained more effectively with the use of each of those diagrams – and to construct the appropriate diagrams. The importance of practice was highlighted in the finding of this study that the student participants did not make sufficient improvements in the spontaneity of their diagram use until they had received opportunities for practice. This makes sense because even if students acquire declarative knowledge about diagrams and *know that* they could be helpful, they would be unlikely to use them unless they have sufficient procedural knowledge and confidence in *knowing how* to use them – which is exactly what the provision of practice promotes.

Cultivating procedural knowledge about *when to use* diagrams is also crucial, and such cultivation is usually embedded in teaching students about the kinds of diagrams and their applications, and in providing opportunities for practice. For instance, when teaching diagram use for math word problem solving, one important indicator that we should alert students to is when they cannot immediately conceptualize how to solve a given problem: this should serve as a signal to them that they should attempt alternative strategies such as constructing an appropriate diagram to re-represent the terms of the problem so that they would be able to gain insight about how to solve it. When instructing students about the different kinds of diagrams that are helpful in problem solving, that instruction should include explanations of *when* each kind may be appropriate to use. For example, constructing graphs may be helpful when two or more quantities are changing and some comparison or decision needs to be made based on those changes (e.g., Corter & Zahner, 2007; Zahner & Corter, 2010). Explaining how those conditions apply to the problems that students are given for practice is also crucial so that they can better appreciate and understand how those conditions appear and can be identified.

In teaching the use of diagrams for more effective communication of information to others, similar clarification of the conditions that would make particular kinds of diagrams helpful is important. For instance, in the Manalo and Uesaka (2016) study we mentioned previously, we explained to the students that diagrams depicting process or cause-and-effect relationships (e.g., flow charts) should be used when the reader of the information needs to understand how something works, the steps required in a particular procedure, or to identify/clarify the causes and/or the effects contained in the information being explained. We elaborated by explaining that such diagrams effectively address certain questions, which include: *What happens? How does it work? What causes it? What is the effect?*

Providing opportunities for active comparison

In an earlier study (Uesaka & Manalo, 2006), we found that the use of active comparison is effective in helping students correctly determine the choice of diagrams to use. Active comparison here pertains to an activity that was provided following students' problem solving sessions, during which they compared several kinds of representations (in this study: formulas, tables, graphs) they had used in solving different problems (the students conducted this activity mostly on their own, using worksheets provided by the teacher). The teacher asked them to consider when each kind of representation was most appropriate to use – and *why*, including the merits corresponding to each. The results of this study showed that students who received this additional activity constructed more appropriate diagrams in solving problems they were later administered. In a subsequent assessment of conditional knowledge, they also provided more abstract and detailed descriptions about the uses of diagrams in problem solving (e.g., "When looking for a rule about increasing values, using a table is effective"). These findings suggest that actively comparing several examples facilitates the formation of the necessary abstract rules, beyond each of the concrete examples dealt with.

Hence, students develop an understanding of *when* each kind of diagram might be effective to use (i.e., the conditional knowledge for use).

Evidence for effectiveness

In the previous section, we described methods we have designed and found effective for promoting student use of diagrams. While promotion of such use is in itself very much a worthwhile goal, an even more desirable goal is to demonstrate that such use in turn leads to beneficial learning outcomes. In this section, therefore, we describe evidence indicating that the promotion of diagram use leads to deeper learning, communicative competencies, and critical thinking.

Promotion of deeper learning

Deeper learning can be described as "the process through which an individual becomes capable of taking what was learned in one situation and applying it to new situations (i.e., transfer) … The product of deeper learning is transferable knowledge, including content knowledge in a domain and knowledge of how, why, and when to apply this knowledge to answer questions and solve problems" (National Research Council, 2012, pp. 5–6). Our research findings indicate that through the cultivation of students' appreciation of the value of diagram use, as well as their knowledge and skills in constructing and using such diagram, this kind of transfer occurs. Students not only evidence spontaneous use of diagrams in new situations, but their use of diagrams also comprises an integral part of their successful application of content knowledge (e.g., in mathematics, in education studies) to solve new problems and answer new questions. For example, in the Ayabe and Manalo (2018) study, following the provision of instruction and practice, not only did the students use diagrams more spontaneously in subsequent new problems, their correct answer rates also increased.

This kind of transfer was likewise demonstrated in the Manalo and Uesaka (2016) study, in which the focus of the intervention provided was on the use of diagrams to enhance the quality of written explanations *in homework tasks*. Following the interventions of providing a hint, an instruction session, and practice in diagram use, the student participants evidenced more spontaneous use of diagrams *in subsequent homework tasks*. Hence, they were able to effectively incorporate diagrams in constructing written explanations of *new topics* they were learning. However, further to this, the majority of the students also later evidenced transfer to an explanation task administered *in class* (i.e., not for homework – hence, a different task setting) and in a *final test* at the end of the semester. They were therefore incorporating diagrams in constructing written explanations in *different tasks* given in the course.

In Figure 13.1, we represent the components and steps involved in this kind of transfer. In the original learning situation, the intervention provided promotes students' diagram use competence and predisposition; this helps improve their

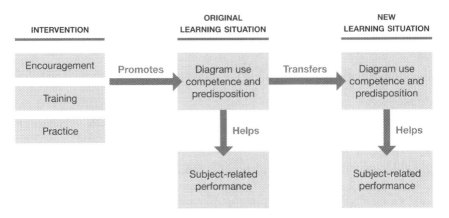

FIGURE 13.1 Transfer as evidence of deeper learning, achieved through promotion of diagram use competence and predisposition.

subject-related performance in that learning situation (e.g., they can more successfully solve math word problems, or more effectively explain information they have learned in their course). This successful application entails the integration of strategy knowledge (e.g., how to use diagrams) and content knowledge in a domain (e.g., how to solve word problems in math). Through this successful diagram application, students not only develop their knowledge about diagrams, they also get to appreciate their value. The diagram use competence and predisposition thus transfers to new learning situations; in other words, equipped with some knowledge about how to use diagrams – and presumably some appreciation of the associated benefits – the students use diagrams in new situations. As a consequence, they are able to improve their subject-related performance in those *new* learning situations (e.g., they can successfully solve new problems, explain different kinds of information, and complete other tasks that all have some degree of variation from what they had dealt with in the original learning situation).

Promotion of communicative competence

Our research findings indicate that with the use of diagrams, students are able to encode more of the key information in notes and explanations they construct. In one study (Chen, Manalo, & She, 2019), we found that junior high school students who were asked to draw a diagram to represent key points from scientific information they were given to read, managed to encode more of the key points compared to students who were asked to write a summary instead. In another more recent study we (first and third authors of this chapter, teacher collaborators) have been working on with undergraduate university students as participants, preliminary results indicate that when these students ($n = 45$) were asked to include at least one diagram in written explanations they produced of what they had been given to read, they were able to encode more of the key points from the reading materials

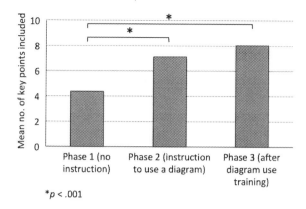

FIGURE 13.2 Mean number of key points students were able to include in written explanations they produced during the three phases of the study.

compared to baseline levels, during which they received no instruction to use a diagram. This result is shown in Figure 13.2, where phase 1 = "no instruction to use a diagram," phase 2 = "instruction to use at least one diagram," and phase 3 = "instruction to use at least one diagram, following training in how to use diagrams." The dependent variable is the number of key points from the reading materials the students were able to include in their written explanations (appropriate measures were taken to ensure equivalence and counterbalancing of the reading materials used). Analysis of variance revealed a significant phase effect, $F(2, 42) = 22.006$, $p < .001$, $\eta_p^2 = .51$; with the means in phases 2 and 3 being significantly higher than in phase 1, both at $p < .001$. These results suggest that when students are asked to incorporate diagrams in writing explanations of what they have read – even without training in how to effectively use diagrams for such purposes – their capacity for encoding important information can increase.

With training in how to appropriately use diagrams in explaining information, we found increases not only in the quantity of diagrams that undergraduate university students ($n = 19$) spontaneously included in written explanations but also in the variety of diagrams they were including (Manalo, Tsuda, & Dryer, in press). We found a significant phase effect for inclusion of each type of diagram (i.e., illustration, overview, process, and comparison diagrams) across four phases from baseline (no training) through to post-training-plus-practice [i.e., for illustration: $F(3, 60) = 7.19$, $p = .0003$, $\eta_p^2 = .27$; for overview: $F(3, 60) = 10.19$, $p = .001$, $\eta_p^2 = .34$; for process: $F(3, 60) = 26.96$, $p < .0001$, $\eta_p^2 = .57$; for comparison: $F(3, 60) = 4.89$, $p = .004$, $\eta_p^2 = .20$]. For all diagram types, the mean inclusion value at the post-training-plus-practice phase was significantly higher than at baseline, all at $p < .05$. In other words, following training and practice in how to use them, the students were using *more types* of diagrams in explaining. This is understandable, considering that training would have provided them with more knowledge about types of diagrams and when (for what purposes) to use them. Furthermore, we found that the number of diagrams the students included in their explanations negatively correlated with word count ($r = -.38$, $p = .056$) and verb-count ($r = -.43$, $p = .035$) in those explanations (both correlations indicate at least medium-size effects). This means that the more they used diagrams, the fewer words they used and the less complicated their sentence constructions tended to be (i.e., as indicated by the verb count, which can be used as one indicator of complexity in language production, cf. Manalo & Sheppard, 2016). However, a crucial point is that, despite the lower word and verb counts, the number of key points they included in their explanations *did not decrease*. This suggests that diagram use can promote efficiency in the construction of written explanations: if we include diagrams to convey what we want to communicate, we may not need to use as many words or to use structures that are as complex. This finding could have useful applications – which ought to be explored in future research – particularly in the cultivation of communicative competency in students who have some language use limitations (e.g., those who have to use a second or foreign language they are not so proficient in, those who have language-based learning disabilities such as dyslexia or dysgraphia).

Promotion of critical thinking

Where the promotion of critical thinking is concerned, research evidence shows that encouraging students to use diagrams can enable them to think more critically about information they are presented. More specifically, in Uesaka, Igarashi, and Suetsugu (2016), we found that junior high school students who received encouragement to use tables in generating and discussing arguments for and against controversial propositions (e.g., whether high school students should be permitted to hold part-time jobs) were subsequently better able to produce argumentation in which multiple perspectives about the proposition were effectively integrated, compared to students who received no such encouragement. This finding lends support to an earlier finding reported by Nussbaum (2008) that argumentation "vee diagrams" (a form of diagram that Nussbaum created) can promote argument-counterargument integration in students' reflective writing. However, our study additionally demonstrated that more ubiquitous diagrams – in this case, tables – can just as effectively serve the purpose of facilitating critical thought. Furthermore, in our study we were able to show that providing encouragement for and instruction in the use of tables for such a task can lead to significant increases in students' spontaneous decisions to use tables in a subsequent similar task (for which the students were able to freely choose whether to use a diagram or not).

We have also observed from classroom teaching situations that encouraging students to use diagrams can facilitate their ability to integrate various strands of information they are learning, and to draw inferences – both of which are important components of critical thinking (e.g., Facione, 1990). For example, in an undergraduate educational psychology course that the first author teaches, students are provided instruction on the basics of the brain structures and the

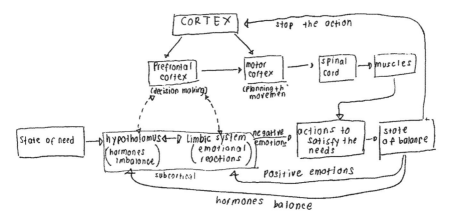

FIGURE 13.3 Example of student-generated diagram from a class exercise that required students to integrate and draw inferences from what they had learned.

functions generally attributed to different parts of the brain (e.g., the cortex and subcortical areas). They also learn about the maintenance of equilibrium and needs reduction, and how emotions/affect are also involved. But they need to make sense of how these different components are connected, so one class exercise they are given is to construct a diagram that would show the processes and connections from the emergence of "a state of need" to the satisfaction of that need in a socially acceptable way. To do this, they need to consider what happens when a human is in a state of need, and what follows after that – considering all the possibly relevant pieces of information they have learned. This is not an easy task for most students but, usually after several diagrammatic iterations, they are able to produce a diagram like the one shown in Figure 13.3. They therefore come to understand the basic mechanisms involved in this process of needs satisfaction in humans. We believe that constructing a diagram is crucial in facilitating this kind of understanding as it requires students to translate or re-represent what they know and what they have learned, as well as to clarify or make explicit what connections (e.g., arrows) might serve or mean in such representations.

Another example of a diagram produced by a student is shown in Figure 13.4. This one is from an undergraduate course in education studies, also taught by the first author. The students had received introductory lectures on comparative education and culture in the classroom and, during this particular class exercise, they were asked to consider how to connect or find relationships between the ideas those two topic areas contain. They were also asked to consider how those ideas might contribute to their own understanding of *what is important in the provision of education*, which is an issue discussed throughout the course. In this exercise, they were not explicitly asked to construct a diagram (many students, for example, simply jotted down bullet points), but this student spontaneously

242 Manalo, Uesaka, Chen, and Ayabe

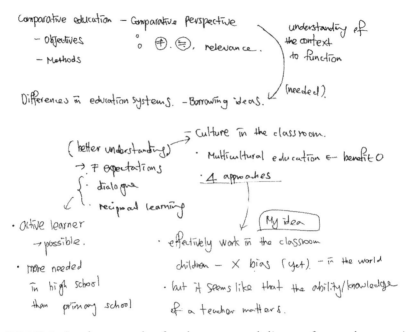

FIGURE 13.4 Another example of student-generated diagram from a class exercise that required students to consider connections between ideas and draw inferences from what they had learned.

constructed one. The diagram includes her own ideas (shown in the bottom part of the diagram): the inferences she had made about the possibility of developing more active learners (and how this may be needed more in high school), and how the introduction of culture in the classroom may be effectively undertaken because of children being – as yet – relatively unaffected by bias (but that the knowledge and ability of teachers would matter). We believe that this diagram – with the inferences drawn by the student – is another good example of how diagram use can be facilitative of critical thought. We frequently observe such facilitation when students diagrammatically represent what they have learned.

Conclusion: Abstracting, linking, clarifying

In this chapter, we have described research-based methods for promoting student use of diagrams. We have also summarized evidence indicating that these methods are effective for promoting spontaneity in diagram use, and that diagram use in turn can lead to the promotion of deeper learning, communicative competence, and critical thinking.

But why is diagram construction particularly beneficial for student learning? We believe that the answer to this question lies in diagram construction facilitating three mechanisms that are essential to meaningful learning: abstracting, linking, and clarifying. We mentioned earlier that in problem solving, the use of diagrams is helpful because it translates the terms of the problem into a form that is easier to understand (e.g., Beitzel & Staley, 2015; Hembree, 1992; Jitendra et al., 2007; Tversky & Kessell, 2014). However, to construct a useful diagram, the student needs to identify and select relevant components of the problem (and to discard irrelevant ones), and to recombine those relevant components in a way that makes sense and that would summarize the situation of the problem. In effect, therefore, the student has to *abstract,* or create a schematic representation (Barsalou, 2003; Tversky, 2011; Tversky & Kessell, 2014). Abstraction is necessary for meaning apprehension and construction and, as Saitta and Zucker (2013, p. 31) pointed out, "without abstraction no high level thinking would be possible." The important point here though is that *diagram construction by its very nature facilitates abstraction,* which must be one crucial reason why it promotes deeper learning.

The second reason is that diagram construction facilitates linking, or the establishment of connections between different parts of the issue under consideration. Here, both the process of constructing links and the resulting product of integrated (connected) parts are important. To be able to construct links, the student needs to understand the meaning and significance of the parts (otherwise, useful connections cannot be made) – hence that process directly contributes to the apprehension of meaning. But the resulting diagram in itself, with the parts arranged and connected to make sense, is valuable in terms of showing together all the parts that are to be used together – and thus, as Larkin and Simon (1987) noted, a diagram supports a large number of perceptual inferences. The important point here is that, through such linking, diagrams not only support the apprehension of meaning, they also support drawing of inferences – which is necessary for critical thinking (e.g., Facione, 1990).

The third reason we consider important in explaining why diagram construction is beneficial to student learning is that it clarifies the information under consideration. Through the use of a diagram, a student can for example clarify for another student how to solve a problem, or how something works (e.g., Uesaka & Manalo, 2007, 2014). But diagrams can also clarify information for oneself: as Manalo and Uesaka (2014) reported, students are more likely to spontaneously construct diagrams when making notes for their own use. This then raises the question of why diagrams clarify, and one simple answer to this – which has been mentioned earlier – is that adding a visual representation (the diagram) enables the use of the visual channel of working memory in combination with the verbal channel, where verbal information is processed (e.g., Mayer, 2009). To put this another way, instead of just hearing or reading about the information, we also get to see what it looks like – making it easier to understand. Thus, through the use of diagrams, students can improve their communicative competence: such use can enable them to more successfully convey the intended message to others, as well as to their own selves.

However, apart from enabling the use of both channels of working memory, diagrams also clarify by making abstract meanings and ideas more concrete (e.g., Tversky, 2011; Tversky & Kessell, 2014) – portraying how those meanings and ideas that previously lacked concrete form could look like or could be imagined. Tversky (2011) additionally pointed out that, not only do diagrams abstract and schematize by omitting what is deemed inessential, they also exaggerate and elaborate – in effect distorting the "truth" to make it clearer. Through such distortions (e.g., making important components bigger or more prominent; sharpening distinctions; adding arrows, labels, and other markers), diagrams repackage meanings and ideas for the consumption of human attention, which is known to be selective, ignoring much of incoming information (e.g., Schneider & Shiffrin, 1977). Hence, diagrams clarify the target information because they concretize and enhance salience of what requires attention.

Acknowledgement

The authors would like to thank Christoph Daniel Schulze for the construction of the diagram shown in Figure 13.1.

References

Ayabe, H., & Manalo, E. (2018, June). *Can spontaneous diagram use be promoted in math word problem solving?* Paper presented at Diagrams 2018: The 10th International Conference on the Theory and Application of Diagrams, Edinburgh, UK.

Barsalou, L. W. (2003). Abstraction in perceptual symbol systems. *Philosophical Transactions of the Royal Society B, 358,* 1177–1187.

Beitzel, B. D., & Staley, R. K. (2015). The efficacy of using diagrams when solving probability word problems in college. *Journal of Experimental Education, 83,* 130–145.

Chen, O., Manalo, E., & She, Y. (2019). Examining the influence of expertise on the effectiveness of diagramming and summarising when studying scientific materials. *Educational Studies, 45,* 57–71.

Corter, J. E., & Zahner, D. C. (2007). Use of external visual representations in probability problem solving. *Statistics Education Research Journal, 6,* 22–50.

Cox, R. (1996). *Analytical reasoning with multiple external representations* (Unpublished doctoral thesis). University of Edinburgh, UK.

Cromley, J. G., Snyder-Hogan, L. E., & Luciw-Dubas, U. A. (2010). Cognitive activities in complex science text and diagrams. *Contemporary Educational Psychology, 35,* 59–74.

Dufour-Janvier, B., Bernarz, N., & Belanger, M. (1987). Pedagogical considerations concerning the problem of representation. In C. Janvier (Ed.), *Problems of representation in the teaching and learning of mathematics* (pp. 110–120). Hillsdale, NJ: Erlbaum.

Facione, P.A. (1990). *Critical thinking: A statement of expert consensus for purposes of educational assessment and instruction: The Delphi Report.* Berkeley, CA: Academic Press.

Hembree, R. (1992). Experiments and relational studies in problem solving: A meta-analysis. *Journal for Research in Mathematics Education, 23,* 242–273.

Jitendra, A. K., Griffin, C. C., Haria, P., Leh, J., Adams, A., & Kaduvettoor, A. (2007). A comparison of single and multiple strategy instruction on third-grade students' mathematical problem solving. *Journal of Educational Psychology, 99,* 115–127.

Larkin, J. H., & Simon, H. A. (1987). Why a diagram is (sometimes) worth ten thousand words. *Cognitive Science, 11,* 65–99.

Manalo, E., & Sheppard, C. (2016). How might language affect critical thinking performance? *Thinking Skills and Creativity, 21,* 41–49.

Manalo, E., Tsuda, A., & Dryer, R. (in press). The effect of cultivating diagram use on the quality of EFL students' written explanations. *Thinking Skills and Creativity.*

Manalo, E., & Uesaka, Y. (2014). Students' spontaneous use of diagrams in written communication: Understanding variations according to purpose and cognitive cost entailed. *Lecture Notes in Artificial Intelligence, 8578,* 78–92.

Manalo, E., & Uesaka, Y. (2016). Hint, instruction, and practice: The necessary components in promoting spontaneous diagram use in students' written work? *Lecture Notes in Artificial Intelligence, 9781,* 157–171.

Manalo, E., Uesaka, Y., & Chinn, C. A. (Eds.) (2017). *Promoting spontaneous use of learning and reasoning strategies: Theory, research, and practice for effective transfer.* London and New York: Routledge.

Manalo, E., Uesaka, Y., Pérez-Kriz, S., Kato, M., & Fukaya, T. (2013). Science and engineering students' use of diagrams during note taking versus explanation. *Educational Studies, 39,* 118–123.

Mayer, R. E. (2009). *Multimedia learning* (2nd ed.). New York: Cambridge University Press.

Mayer, R. E., & Moreno, R. (1998). A split-attention effect in multimedia learning: Evidence for dual processing systems in working memory. *Journal of Educational Psychology, 90,* 312–320.

Mayer, R. E., & Moreno, R. (2003). Nine ways to reduce cognitive load in multimedia learning. *Educational Psychologist, 38,* 43–52.

National Research Council. (2012). *Education for life and work: Developing transferable knowledge and skills in the 21st century.* Committee on Defining Deeper Learning and 21st Century Skills, J. W. Pellegrino and M. L. Hilton (Eds.). Washington, DC: The National Academies Press.

Novick, L. R., & Hurley, S. M. (2001). To matrix, network, or hierarchy, that is the question. *Cognitive Psychology, 42,* 158–216.

Nussbaum, E. M. (2008). Using argumentation vee diagrams (AVDs) for promoting argument-counterargument integration in reflective writing. *Journal of Educational Psychology, 100,* 549–565.

Paris, S. G., Lipson, M. Y., & Wixson, K. K. (1983). Becoming a strategic reader. *Contemporary Education Psychology, 8,* 293–316.

Saitta, L., & Zucker, J.-D. (2013). *Abstraction in artificial intelligence and complex systems.* New York: Springer-Verlag.

Schneider, W., & Shiffrin, R. M. (1977). Controlled and automatic human information processing: I. Detection, search, and attention. *Psychological Review, 84,* 1–66.

Tversky, B. (2011). Visualizing thought. *Topics in Cognitive Science, 3,* 499–535.

Tversky, B., & Kessell, A. (2014). Thinking in action. *Pragmatics & Cognition, 22,* 206–223.

Uesaka, Y., Igarashi, M., & Suetsugu, R. (2016). Promoting multi-perspective integration as a 21st century skill: The effects of instructional methods encouraging students' spontaneous use of tables for organizing information. *Lecture Notes in Artificial Intelligence, 9781,* 172–186.

Uesaka, Y., & Manalo, E. (2006). Active comparison as a means of promoting the development of abstract conditional knowledge and appropriate choice of diagrams in math word problem solving. *Lecture Notes in Computer Science, 4045,* 181–195.

Uesaka, Y., & Manalo, E. (2007). Peer instruction as a way of promoting spontaneous use of diagrams when solving math word problems. In D. S. McNamara & J. G. Trafton (Eds.), *Proceedings of the 29th Annual Cognitive Science Society* (pp. 677–682). Austin, TX: Cognitive Science Society.

Uesaka, Y., & Manalo, E. (2014). How communicative learning situations influence students' use of diagrams: Focusing on the spontaneous construction of diagrams and student protocols during explanation. *Lecture Notes in Artificial Intelligence, 8578,* 93–107.

Uesaka, Y., & Manalo, E. (2017). How to address students' lack of spontaneity in diagram use: Eliciting educational principles for the promotion of spontaneous learning strategy use in general. In E. Manalo, Y. Uesaka, & C. A. Chinn (Eds.), *Promoting spontaneous use of learning and reasoning strategies: Theory, research, and practice for effective transfer* (pp. 62–76). London and New York: Routledge.

Uesaka, Y., Manalo, E., & Ichikawa, S. (2007). What kinds of perceptions and daily learning behaviors promote students' use of diagrams in mathematics problem solving? *Learning and Instruction, 17,* 322–335.

Uesaka, Y., Manalo, E., & Ichikawa, S. (2010). The effects of perception of efficacy and diagram construction skills on students' spontaneous use of diagrams when solving math word problems. *Lecture Notes in Artificial Intelligence, 6170,* 197–211.

van Garderen, D., Scheuermann, A., & Jackson, C. (2012). Examining how students with diverse abilities use diagrams to solve mathematics word problems. *Learning Disability Quarterly, 36,* 145–160.

Xing, C., Corter, J. E., & Zahner, D. (2016). Diagrams affect choice of strategy in probability problem solving. *Lecture Notes in Artificial Intelligence, 9781,* 3–16.

Zahner, D., & Corter, J. E. (2010). The process of probability problem solving: Use of external visual representations. *Mathematical Thinking and Learning, 12,* 177–204.

14

CLASS DESIGN FOR DEVELOPING PRESENTATION SKILLS FOR GRADUATE RESEARCH STUDENTS

Etsuko Tanaka and Emmanuel Manalo

Summary

A one-day workshop was designed to develop graduate research students' presentation skills. It comprised three components for cultivating competencies in constructing (i) a logical story, (ii) helpful slides, and (iii) an engaging conversation. Each component had three steps: instruction of key points, comprehension checking by analyzing an example presentation, and application of learning to own presentation. In addition, at the end of the workshop, students had an opportunity for self-reflection. To assess the usefulness of this workshop, students were asked to make pre- and post-workshop presentations. Evaluation of those presentations revealed that their quality significantly improved in terms of logical flow, usefulness of visuals, and audience engagement. Transfer of skills to a different kind of presentation was also evidenced.

Background

In the 21st century, graduate students need to develop a much broader set of skills. Doctoral and other graduate research degree holders are now expected not only to be competent in conducting various aspects of research but also to meaningfully contribute to the society they operate in beyond the confines of academia (see, e.g., Hyatt & Williams, 2011; McNair, 2010; Teijeiro, Rungo, & Freire, 2013). In the United Kingdom, for example, the Roberts Review (Roberts, 2002) pointed out the necessity of providing appropriate training for doctoral students to cultivate a broad set of general skills, such as interpersonal, communication, and management skills. In response, various training programs for early career researchers have been developed. In the Japanese context, MEXT (the Ministry of Education, Culture, Sports, Science and Technology) has increasingly been providing support to universities to promote qualitative and quantitative improvements in the provisions of graduate school education. For example, since 2012 MEXT has been funding a "Program for Leading Graduate Schools," aimed at developing global leadership skills in graduates and competencies in operating inside and outside of academia.

Developing skills for effectively presenting complex ideas to various audiences is essential in both academia and industry in virtually all disciplines (see, e.g., van Ginkel, Gulikers, Biemans, & Mulder, 2015). Such skills are, for example, considered necessary in many jobs: Bennett (2002) analyzed 1,000 job advertisements targeting new graduates and found that 15% of the employers mentioned presentation skills as a required skill. Reeves, Denicolo, Metcalfe, and Roberts (2012, p. 4), through a review of the pertinent literature, interviews, and consultation with stakeholders, constructed a framework of skills that researchers need to develop. In this framework, "engagement, influence, and impact" is one of the four domains that characterize excellent researchers, indicating that skills to work with others – ensuring a wider impact of research – are vital. In other words, it is crucial for researchers to develop the ability to communicate complex ideas in ways that would make those ideas accessible to different audience groups, including groups of nonexperts.

It is not difficult to find guidebooks and online materials for developing presentation skills, including some that are specifically designed for researchers and graduate students (e.g., Alley, 2007; Schwabish, 2016). Although these resources contain what would generally be considered sensible, practical, and useful advice about presenting research findings and other information to others, they rarely refer to actual research evidence that confirms the effectiveness of the methods they advocate. If anything, they simply refer to other authors who have expressed the same or similar views about what methods or procedures might be effective. One reason is that there are not many studies in the area of developing student competencies in making presentations.

Apart from a scarcity of evidence-based methods, there is also a limited number of studies that have considered what an effective class design might be for developing presentation skills. In their review of previous studies in this topic area, van Ginkel et al. (2015, p. 64) expressed the opinion that only an "incomplete and fragmented picture" of the learning environment for students to learn presentation skills has been revealed.

If effective instruction in presentation skills is to be provided to students, its construction needs to be guided by appropriate design principles, and its contents need to directly address the requirements of developing such skills. One set of research-based design principles comes from the van Ginkel et al. (2015) study mentioned previously. The study synthesized findings from 52 previous studies on the development of oral presentation competence for students at the tertiary level. Van Ginkel and his colleagues were able to derive seven design principles dealing with instruction, learning activities, and assessment strategy. The two principles concerning "instruction" are: clearly communicating objectives that are directly related to the criteria of oral presentations, and ensuring that presentation tasks are meaningful to students and relevant to their course of study or subject discipline. The two principles concerning "learning activities" are: providing students with opportunities to observe appropriate models of presentation, and to sufficiently practice their own oral presentations. Both the "instruction" and "learning activities" principles are aimed at enhancing self-efficacy (including reducing anxiety associated with presenting) and oral presentation skills. Finally, the three principles concerning "assessment strategy" are: paying attention to the quality of feedback given to students, involving peers in formative assessment processes, and facilitating self-assessment – all three geared toward the promotion of self-improvement.

In developing a course to cultivate the presentation capabilities of students, it would seem sensible to incorporate the seven design principles indicated by van Ginkel et al. (2015). However, the actual content that would promote the development of specific skills for oral presentation still needs to be determined. It would be important to inculcate understanding about the mechanisms of effective presentations, rather than simply providing students with lots of potentially useful but incongruous tips.

One crucial aspect that needs to be considered in determining the content of the course is the content of the presentation itself: in other words, attention needs to be placed on what the presenter might need to convey to his or her audience. That content needs to be understandable to the audience. In a study by Estrada, Patel, Talente, and Kraemer (2005), reviewers of scientific oral presentations were found to most frequently comment on the content: they considered it important that the key concepts are identifiable and relevance is clearly established. Likewise, criteria statements pertaining to "content" were included in a rubric instrument for assessing oral presentation performance that van Ginkel et al. (2017) designed and validated using an expert group of higher education professionals. These previous findings suggest that the speaker needs to construct a logical "story" that the audience would understand (where "story" pertains to the integrated content and the intended message of the presentation). Brophy and Guerin (2018) questioned the wisdom of the frequent omission of storytelling features in presentations that students make. They referred to previous research demonstrating that storytelling is a powerful tool for clarifying meaning, conveying opinions, and facilitating social interaction – all of which are important functions of presentations. Thus, a course on presentation skills would likely benefit from the inclusion of content that would inculcate the construction of logical story-threads to facilitate these functions.

Two other components that would appear indispensable in determining the content of a course on presentation skills are, firstly, the slides students use and, secondly, their style of presentation. In the previously mentioned study by Estrada et al. (2005), the researchers found that after content, presentation reviewers most frequently commented on these very aspects of presentations. Where "slides" were concerned, their comments focused on clarity, use of graphics, and readability, while "presentation style" (also referred to as "presentation delivery aspects" in the research literature, see, e.g., van Ginkel et al., 2015) comments drew attention to various aspects that included clarity, pace, voice, engagement with the audience, answering of questions, and eye contact. Other researchers have likewise noted the importance of slides and other visual aids that presenters use: perhaps the most important point that students need to understand is that the slides are used to help the audience follow the presentation, and hence they need to carefully consider the likely effect of the slides they construct on their intended audience (e.g., Živković, 2014). It should be noted, however, that there are presentation contexts where the use of slides or other visual aids are either not permitted or impractical, so presenters need to be aware of this possible constraint.

Where presentation style is concerned, the key point that students need to understand is that they have to effectively engage with their audience – to grab their attention and maintain it by keeping them involved in their presentation (e.g., Andeweg, de Jong, & Hoeken, 1998; Chou, 2011; Živković, 2014). A course on presentation skills should therefore include content that would develop students' understanding and competence in the use of slides and their engagement with their prospective audience.

In the study described in this chapter, the principles identified by van Ginkel et al. (2015) were used in addressing the three main competencies – construction of a logical story (content), helpful slides, and an engaging conversation (presentation style) – to develop a workshop on presentation skills aimed at Japanese and international graduate research students for whom English was a foreign language (EFL). The group of students targeted as participants in the study can be considered appropriate because the cultivation of EFL students' abilities to engage with other researchers in the global environment is a high priority not only in Japan but also in other countries. In the United States, for example, the number of international graduate students have been increasing (e.g., Anderson, 2013; Redden, 2013), drawing attention to the need to ensure that those students' skills development requirements are adequately met.

In conducting the workshop, strategies using the "thinking-after-instruction" approach to teaching (Ichikawa, 2004; Ichikawa, Uesaka, & Manalo, 2017) were employed. In this approach, which is intended to deepen students' understanding of what they learn, teacher instruction of key points is usually followed by activities for checking their understanding. Students are then given tasks that would require them to meaningfully apply what they have learned, and then to engage in self-evaluation and/or reflection about their learning experience. With reference to this approach, three steps within each component were designed: instruction of key points or steps, comprehension checking by analyzing an example presentation, and application and peer feedback. At the end of class, students were also given an opportunity to reflect on what they had learned.

The objective of the corresponding research was to evaluate whether this workshop's design and content effectively delivers some key requirements of

21st-century education – namely the promotion of communicative competence, deeper learning, and critical thought.

Method
Participants

The 16 students who comprised the participants of the present study were enrolled in a Japanese university, taking a graduate-level educational program that included the PhD. One of the aims of the program was to develop various competencies considered necessary for global leadership. All the students provided permission for their workshop data to be used by the first author (who was an instructor in the program) for the purposes of research and program improvement. Additionally, human participants research ethics committee approval was obtained by the first author for the conduct of the research described here.

At the time when the study was conducted, the students were in their first and second years at the Masters level, and their ages ranged from 22 to 36. Nine students were female and seven were male; five were Japanese and 11 were of various other nationalities (i.e., Chinese, Mongolian, Uzbekistani, and Vietnamese). Although all the students had studied English as a foreign language (EFL), they were sufficiently competent in using English for communication: their IELTS (International English Language Testing System; www.ielts.org) Academic scores ranged from 4.5 to 7.5. They were from different subject disciplines, which included economics, law, engineering, and physics.

Criteria for determining quality of a presentation

The first of the design principles that van Ginkel et al. (2015) derived from their research review was clearly communicating to students the presentation course objectives, which should be related to the criteria that will be used for evaluation. Thus, appropriate criteria for deciding the quality indicators of a good presentation were defined (Table 14.1). Note that, although the criteria used in the present study were decided independent of the rubric for oral presentation skills validated by van Ginkel et al. (2017), there are clear congruencies between these two sets of criteria.

In deciding the criteria to use in the present study, it was considered important to place equal emphasis on all three competencies: construction of a logical story, helpful slides, and an engaging conversation. Six criteria statements were defined for each of these competencies, based on the key points covered in the workshop (Figure 14.1a, b, c). For each of these key points, two criteria statements were formulated for determining whether a presenter had achieved that key point. For example, the first key point in the instruction provided for the "logical story" component was "Clarify the key message" (Figure 14.1a). The two criteria statements that corresponded to this key point were: "Key message

TABLE 14.1 Criteria of a good presentation

Logical story	Key message is clearly conveyed. The reason why the audience should pay attention to the topic of the presentation is communicated clearly. Sufficient, necessary information is provided to support the key message. There is no distracting, irrelevant information that makes it hard to understand the key message. Rather than a mere statement of information, the presentation has a "story." Appropriate time and slides are allocated to each item of content of the presentation.
Helpful slide	Amount of information contained on each slide is appropriate. Information on slides is congruent and supportive of presenter's speech. Each item of content is communicated in an appropriate way through the use of text, figure, table, and/or illustration. Slides do not include too much text. Design of slides is consistent in terms of color, font, and other visual aspects. Balance of information and use of white space on the slides help to make the content easily accessible.
Engaging conversation	Presenter uses appropriate techniques (e.g., sharing of feeling, familiar example, analogy, questioning) to generate audience interest. Presenter uses appropriate techniques (e.g., sharing of feeling, familiar example, analogy, questioning) to maintain audience interest. Presenter makes appropriate and regular eye contact with the audience. Presenter pauses at appropriate times to check on audience reaction and to ensure audience has sufficient time to comprehend and reflect on content. Presenter uses his/her voice effectively to deliver content of the presentation. Appropriate body language is used.

(a)

Logical story

Instruction	Comprehension check	Application and feedback
A lecturer shows the following key steps. Step1: Clarify key message – What message do you want to deliver to the audience? – What is interesting or valuable for the audience? Step2: Select information – What information does the audience need to get the message? Step3: Decide logical flow and emphasis – What flow is most understandable for the audience? – Which information should you spend more time on?	Watching a sample video of presentation, discuss the following questions. – What is the key message? – How is it different from an academic presentation for researchers in his area? – What can be improved in his presentation?	Students make their own logical story based on what you learned. As pair, students explain their own logical story and get feedback each other. Based on feedback students remake the logical story, explain toward a different partner and get feedback again.

FIGURE 14.1 a) Flow of class design, part 1, b) Flow of class design, part 2, and c) Flow of class design, part 3.

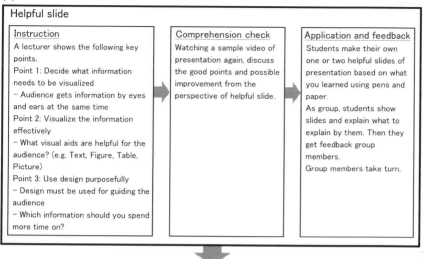

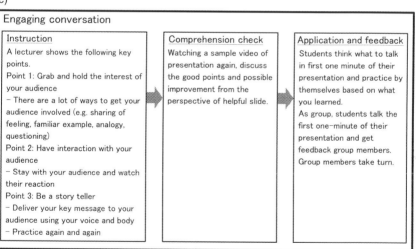

FIGURE 14.1 (*Continued*)

is clearly conveyed," and "The reason why the audience should pay attention to the topic of the presentation is communicated clearly" (Table 14.1).

Evaluating/scoring for each criteria statement was undertaken on a 5-point Likert-type scale where the ends were anchored as "1 = poor" and "5 = good."

This set of criteria was provided to the students at the start of the workshop, both as a guide to course objectives and expectations, and for evaluation of their own and others' presentations. As explained in the next sub-section, the workshop delivery focused on ensuring that students fully comprehended and were able to appropriately use this set of criteria. The same set of criteria was also used for instructor/researcher evaluation and scoring of the presentations made by the students (i.e., for teaching and research purposes).

Design and delivery of the workshop

Before the workshop, the participating students were asked to make two 5-minute presentations in English. One was to explain their own research to a nonspecialist audience (Research Presentation). The other was to introduce the educational program for graduate students that they belonged to (Program Presentation). The presentations were video recorded for the purposes of evaluation (described in more detail in the Results section) – both by the students (to evaluate their own Research Presentation, i.e., self-evaluation with a view to learning and making improvements), and by the researchers (to investigate whether there would be any detectable improvements as a consequence of the workshop provided).

The workshop was delivered one week later by the first author (the instructor). At the beginning of the workshop, the instructor explained that, for the purposes of the workshop, an essential quality of a good presentation would be audience-centeredness: the primary consideration in preparing a "good presentation" should be what the audience would understand, rather than what the presenter would say. Therefore, it would be necessary to prepare or make some adjustments to the presentation based on characteristics of the anticipated audience. For the workshop, the students were asked to assume/imagine that their audience would be people in the general public who were not specialists in the students' research field.

The instructor explained that an audience-centered presentation would pay particular attention to three components: a logical story, helpful slides, and an engaging conversation (Figure 14.2), and that the students would learn about each of these three components in the workshop.

Figures 14.1a–c shows the sequence used in providing instruction about these three components. All contents were taught using the three-step process:

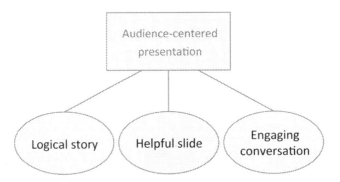

FIGURE 14.2 Three key components of a good presentation.

instruction of key points and methods, analysis of an example presentation, and application of learned key points to the individual Research Presentations and then providing/receiving peer feedback.

First, the instructor showed the key points on a slide and explained what those points meant. Then she showed a sample video of a presentation and asked the students to analyze it based on the key points they had just learned. The video was 3 minutes long, and the intended audience of the brief presentation it depicted was the general public. It satisfied some but not all of the key points that the students had learned. The students' task was to identify the presentation's shortcomings and to suggest possible ways of improving it. These were discussed in plenary with the instructor. Finally, the students were asked to apply what they had learned to their own presentations. They were then provided opportunities to work with each other in pairs or small groups, to critically evaluate each other's presentations (based on the key points learned) and to provide/receive feedback about what could be improved in those presentations.

At the end of the workshop, the students were given time to review what they had learned during the entire workshop (by going through the instructor-provided notes/materials for each part of the workshop, as well as any other notes they had taken) and to ask any questions they might have had at that point. This final part of the workshop was considered important to provide students with an opportunity to reflect on and check their comprehension of what they were supposed to have learned, and to address any questions or doubts that may occur to them.

After the workshop, students had about one month to improve their Research Presentation and Program Presentation. This length of time (one month) was considered appropriate by the management team overseeing the program that the students were enrolled in, which included the instructor.[1] The students had a lot of other study-related demands on their time, and it was considered important for them to have adequate time to reflect on what they had learned in the workshop, and to be able to implement any modifications to their presentations that they considered appropriate. The revised presentations they made were video recorded like their pre-workshop presentations, and were likewise evaluated using the same evaluation criteria described earlier and shown in Table 14.1.

Assessment of workshop impact

The students' self-evaluations of their own research presentations, before and after the workshop, were compared by two-way repeated measures ANOVA (3 components × 2 time periods). Also, third party evaluations of their own research and program presentations, before and after the workshop, were compared by two-way repeated measures ANOVA (3 components × 2 time periods). In addition, feedback comments from students were examined to gauge their perceptions about various aspects of the workshop.

Results: Evidence of effectiveness

Students' self-evaluation

To check the effect of the workshop, the students' self-evaluations of their own research presentations before and after the workshop were compared. Results revealed that, although the interaction was not significant [$F(2, 30) = 2.10$, $p = .14$], main effects due to components [$F(2, 30) = 15.54$, $p < .01$] and to time [$F(1, 15) = 16.03$, $p < .01$] were significant (Figure 14.3). These results indicate that the students evaluated their own presentation after the workshop higher than before the workshop. In evaluating their presentations in terms of the component parts, they also evaluated their "slides" the highest and their "conversation" the lowest. Multiple comparisons showed that their evaluations of each of these components were significantly different (i.e., slides > story > conversation).

Third-party evaluation

To check whether there were detectable improvements in the students' presentations apart from their own perceptions, "third-party" evaluations of the presentations before and after the workshop were undertaken by the second author who was not involved in delivery of the workshop and had not met or known any of the student participants. For that evaluation, the video recordings of the student presentations (both research and program presentations) were provided in a mixed up order, making it impossible to determine whether they were recorded before or after the workshop.

If changes in the evaluations of the students' research presentation could be detected, those could at least partly be attributed to the effects of the workshop, which dealt directly with improving such presentations. In contrast, the workshop did not directly deal with more general presentations (such as providing an introduction to a program). Therefore, if improvements in the students' program presentations could be detected, it can be considered as indicative of transfer of knowledge/skills they had acquired through the workshop.

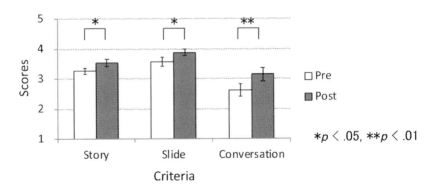

FIGURE 14.3 Self-evaluation scores of students' research presentation.

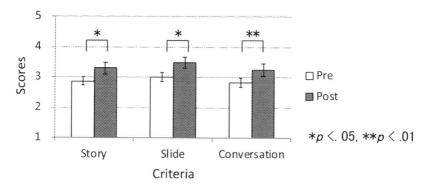

FIGURE 14.4 Third-party evaluation scores of students' research presentation.

In order to check inter-rater reliability, a graduate research student (not one of the students in the research described here) with experience in attending presentation skills workshops evaluated ten of the students' presentations using the same criteria. The correlations of the scores given by the second author and the graduate student for each component were calculated. Pearson's correlation coefficients for story, slide, and conversation components were $r = .64$ ($p = .05$), $.61$ ($p = .06$), and $.77$ ($p = .01$), respectively. These indicate that the two evaluations were not perfectly matched, but they were sufficiently similar (i.e., two components were significantly correlated and one was marginally so). The second author was deemed a more skilled presenter and understood the criteria more deeply, and therefore the decision was made to use his scores in subsequent analyses.

Regarding the research presentations, a two-way repeated measures ANOVA (3 components, 2 time periods) showed that interaction effect was not significant [$F(2, 30) = .15$, $p = .87$], but the main effects due to components [$F(2, 30) = 3.54$, $p = .04$] and time [$F(1, 15) = 7.25$, $p = .02$] were significant (Figure 14.4). The significant effect due to time indicates that the students improved in the quality evaluations of their presentations from the pre-workshop stage to the post-workshop stage. The significant effect due to components, indicates that some components were consistently evaluated more highly than others: multiple comparisons revealed that evaluations of the students' "slides" were significantly higher than their "conversation"; all other comparison results were not significant at the $p < .05$ level.

Regarding the program presentations, the main effect of time ($F(1, 15) = 11.55$, $p < .01$, and the interaction between components and time were significant [$F(2, 30) = 3.44$, $p = .05$], as shown in Figure 14.5. Simple main effect analysis revealed that improvements of all component were significant at the $p < .05$ level.

Feedback comments from the student participants

To further examine how the students perceived various aspects of the workshop, they were asked to complete a course evaluation questionnaire at the end of it.

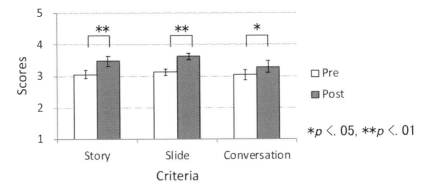

FIGURE 14.5 Third-party evaluation scores of students' program presentation.

The questionnaire included space where students could freely provide comments about their views and perceptions.

The student comments suggested that many of them found the way it was organized, with the three-component structure and three steps, easy to understand. Their comments regarding this aspect included: "I like the structure of the workshop, with three clear main points," and "I think it provides a systematic way to give a presentation and I can check if I make everything properly according to the materials provided in the workshop."

The students also appeared to have found the task of analyzing the video of a presentation helpful toward understanding what the key points meant. Examples of their comments included: "Through watching the example presentation several times, I could analyze it and think from a different perspective," and "I liked analyzing the TED presentation, through which I came to realize some presentation weaknesses similar to my own."

In addition, students' comments suggest they found it helpful to have the opportunity to apply what they had learned to their own presentation, and to provide feedback to each other. For example, students commented: "Although I tried to make my story understandable for other students, they could not understand it," and "Creating an improved slide and showing it to my group member was the most interesting part of today's workshop. By doing this, I could think more from the point of the audience and learned a lot of new ideas."

Discussion

As noted at the beginning of this chapter, developing competence in presenting complex ideas is considered essential for doctoral and other graduate research students operating in 21st-century environments. Such competence is required not only in academic settings but also in work that the students would likely undertake in their future careers. One concern, however, is that, although there are many methods available for the development of presentation skills, there is very little evidence available to indicate the effectiveness of those methods. Furthermore, most of them appear to be based mainly on opinions and intuition, and do not draw upon research-based design principles. In this chapter, effort was made to address these shortcomings by evaluating the effects of a workshop that utilized important components and design principles identified in previous research (e.g., Estrada et al., 2005; Ichikawa, 2004; van Ginkel et al., 2015).

The method described in this chapter appears to have been effective in improving students' research presentations, based on both the students' own presentation evaluations and a "third party" (blinded) evaluation. The students' presentations improved as far as conveying a logical story, presenting helpful slides, and providing an engaging conversation – the components that were addressed in the delivered workshop and evaluated in this research. There is also indication of successful transfer (which is one manifestation of deeper learning on the part of the students) in that, although skills for non-research presentations were *not* covered in the workshop the students' program presentations also evidenced some significant improvements (on the same components) in the students' second attempt. Furthermore, and perhaps most important in terms of possible application in real educational contexts, the research conducted and reported here had high ecological validity as it was conducted in a real educational setting, with graduate research students for whom the development of presentation skills was of genuine value and necessity. The students also worked on and prepared presentations on topics that were genuinely relevant to them (i.e., the research they were conducting, and the program they were enrolled in).

The workshop included getting the students to analyze and suggest possible ways to improve not only a sample pre-recorded video presentation but also each other's presentations. In this sense, they engaged in critical evaluation. Perhaps more importantly, the students appear to have found this activity of critical evaluation beneficial toward identifying and understanding ways they could improve their own presentations – as indicated by some of the comments they provided in the workshop evaluation questionnaire (examples of which were reported in the previous section). This finding is congruent with the importance that van Ginkel et al. (2015) placed on "self-assessment" as part of the "assessment strategy" component of their design principles. They noted evidence from previous research demonstrating that the incorporation of self-assessment in presentation skills courses has had positive effects on students' oral presentation competence, self-efficacy, confidence, and presentation-related attitudes and perceptions.

In considering why the workshop described in this chapter proved effective in improving students' presentations skills, the most likely reason is that it was designed and delivered using principles, content, and teaching methods that previous research indicates as being appropriate and effective for the task of cultivating such skills in students. As previously noted, the *design principles* used in the workshop – from van Ginkel et al. (2015) – were drawn from the synthesis of findings from 52 previous studies on the development of oral presentation skills in tertiary students. The *content* included in the workshop was based on what Estrada et al. (2005) found reviewers considered important when evaluating research presentations. And the *teaching method* utilized was based on Ichikawa's (2004) "thinking-after-instruction" approach, which has previously been demonstrated as effective in promoting not only deeper learning of content but also the use of effective strategies in students (e.g., Ichikawa et al., 2017).

The description of the workshop provided in this chapter ought to be sufficient for other instructors to apply with their students. Furthermore, the method is flexible enough for other content to be added if desired. For example, effective ways of responding to audience questions were not included in the workshop described here due to limited time. Effectively responding to questions was, however, identified in the Estrada et al. (2005) study as being one of the aspects that most reviewers pay attention to.

A number of other improvements could be made to the workshop described in this chapter. One of those is better addressing students' abilities in providing an "engaging conversation," which both the students themselves and the third-party evaluator felt was not improved as much as the other two aspects of telling a logical story and constructing/using helpful slides. Perhaps alternative methods of cultivating this ability and/or devoting more time to it could be considered in future provisions of this workshop.

Another possible improvement is that self-reflection could be included at the end of each session (i.e., at the end of the logical story, helpful slide, and engaging conversation component sessions). Previous studies have pointed out the importance of students reflecting on what they have learned and how their understanding changed through the instruction they have received. By describing learning in their own words, students' knowledge and skills could be developed more deeply to make them more likely to become transferable (e.g., Chi, De Leeuw, Chiu, & LaVancher, 1994; Tajika, Nakatsu, Nozaki, Neumann, & Maruno, 2007).

From a research perspective, there are also numerous aspects of the workshop that would need to be examined in future investigations. First and foremost, the workshop method used here – and variations of it – ought to be used and evaluated in instructing more groups of students, not only to verify its effectiveness but also to identify aspects that can be improved. Second, the validity and reliability of the presentation criteria used here should be examined more carefully. In this research, the correlations between the second author's and graduate student's score were not very high. Because we do not have one right answer for the question of what a good presentation ought to be like, it is difficult to suggest one set of criteria that would meet everyone's requirements. But we can compare different criteria and consider variations and conditions that could determine appropriateness.

Even though there are some possible improvements that could be made to the workshop for improving graduate students' research presentation skills described in this chapter, the workshop is already effective to some extent – as indicated by the students' own and the third party evaluations reported here. Furthermore, there were indications that through the workshop students were able to transfer knowledge and skills they had learned to the preparation and delivery of another, more general kind of presentation (hence, this is indicative of deeper learning, cf. Barnett & Ceci, 2002). Therefore, for instructors looking for an evidence-based method for developing their graduate students' presentation skills, the workshop design and content described here could be a good starting point. They could then make any adjustments and modifications to it according to the specific requirements of their students and their situations.

References

Alley, M. (2007). *The craft of scientific presentations: Critical steps to succeed and critical errors to avoid*. New York: Springer-Verlag.

Anderson, S. (2013, July 15). International students are 70% of EE grad students in U.S. *Forbes*. Retrieved September 26, 2018, from https://www.forbes.com/sites/stuartanderson/2013/07/15/international-students-are-70-of-ee-grad-students-in-u-s/#49b0ce69673e

Andeweg, B. A., de Jong, J. C., & Hoeken, H. (1998). "May I have your attention?": Exordial techniques in informative oral presentations. *Technical Communication Quarterly*, 7, 271–284.

Barnett, S. M., & Ceci, S. J. (2002). When and where do we apply what we learn? A taxonomy for far transfer. *Psychological Bulletin*, 128(4), 612–637.

Bennett, R. (2002). Employers' demands for personal transferable skills in graduates: A content analysis of 1,000 job advertisements and an associated empirical study. *Journal of Vocational Education and Training*, 54(4), 457–476.

Brophy, B., & Guerin, S. (2018). Stories in conversations and presentations – a comparative study. *Innovations in Education and Teaching International*, 55, 101–110.

Chi, M. T., De Leeuw, N., Chiu, M. H., & LaVancher, C. (1994). Eliciting self-explanations improves understanding. *Cognitive Science*, 18(3), 439–477.

Chou, M. (2011). The influence of learner strategies on oral presentations: A comparison between group and individual performance. *English for Specific Purposes*, 30, 272–285.

Estrada, C. A., Patel, S. R., Talente, G., & Kraemer, S. (2005). The 10-minute oral presentation: What should I focus on? *American Journal of the Medical Sciences*, 329(6), 306–309.

Hyatt, L., & Williams, P. E. (2011). 21st-century competencies for doctoral leadership faculty. *Innovative Higher Education*, 36, 53–66.

Ichikawa, S. (2004). *Improving learning motivation and skills: Requested strategies for improving academic achievement* [in Japanese]. Tokyo, Japan: Shogakukan.

Ichikawa, S., Uesaka, Y. & Manalo, E. (2017). Three approaches to promoting spontaneous use of learning strategies: Bridging the gap between research and school practice. In E. Manalo, Y. Uesaka, & C. A. Chinn (Eds.), *Promoting spontaneous use of learning and reasoning strategies: Theory, research, and practice for effective transfer* (pp. 195–210). London: Routledge.

McNair, D. E. (2010). Preparing community college leaders: The AACC core competencies for effective leadership and doctoral education. *Community College Journal of Research and Practice*, 34, 199–217.

Redden, E. (2013, July 12). New report shows dependence of U.S. graduate programs on foreign students. *Inside Higher Ed*. Retrieved September 26, 2018, from https://www.insidehighered.com/news/2013/07/12/new-report-shows-dependence-us-graduate-programs-foreign-students

Reeves, J., Denicolo, P., Metcalfe, J., & Roberts, J. (2012). *The vitae researcher development framework and researcher development statement: Methodology and validation report*. Cambridge, UK: Careers Research & Advisory Centre (CRAC) Ltd.

Roberts, G. G. (2002). *SET for success: The supply of people with science, technology, engineering and mathematics skills: The report of Sir Gareth Roberts' review*. Cambridge, UK: Careers Research & Advisory Centre (CRAC) Ltd.

Schwabish, J. (2016). *Better presentations: A guide for scholars, researchers, and wonks*. New York: Columbia University Press.

Tajika, H., Nakatsu, N., Nozaki, H., Neumann, E., & Maruno, S. (2007). Effects of self-explanation as a metacognitive strategy for solving mathematical word problems *Japanese Psychological Research*, *49*(3), 222–233.

Teijeiro, M., Rungo, P., & Freire, M. J. (2013). Graduate competencies and employability: The impact of matching firms' needs and personal and personal attainments. *Economics of Education Review*, *34*, 286–295.

Van Ginkel, S., Gulikers, J., Biemans, H., & Mulder, M. (2015). Towards a set of design principles for developing oral presentation competence: A synthesis of research in higher education. *Educational Research Review*, *14*, 62–80.

Van Ginkel, S., Laurentzen, R., Mulder, M., Mononen, A., Kyttä, J., & Kortelainen, M. J. (2017). Assessing oral presentation performance: Designing a rubric and testing its validity with an expert group. *Journal of Applied Research in Higher Education*, *9*, 474–486.

Živković, S. (2014). The importance of oral presentations for university students. *Mediterranean Journal of Social Sciences*, *5*(19), 468–475.

15
ONLINE WRITTEN ARGUMENTATION

Internal dialogic features and classroom instruction

Naomi Rosedale, Stuart McNaughton, Rebecca Jesson, Tong Zhu, and Jacinta Oldehaver

Summary

In this chapter, we draw from a study involving a 1:1 digital initiative in Auckland, New Zealand, to consider the impact of an Argumentation Tool (AT) on students' discussion board posts. We examine use of the AT, integrating Google Groups and competing text evidence, to support development of *internally dialogic* argumentation important for reasoning, critical thinking, and perspective taking. Cross-sectional data is analyzed from nine primary schools including 38 observations and 342 student posts by applying a profiling taxonomy. Use of the AT shows an emerging relationship between argumentation focused instruction and development of perspective integration in students' writing. Findings suggest the AT supports diagnostic assessment of internally dialogic argumentation and promotion of perspective taking as important 21st-century skills.

Introduction

A group of cognitive and social skills (perspective taking, collective problem solving, creativity and critical thinking) is claimed to be increasingly significant for successful living in the 21st century. Variously described as 21st-century skills (National Research Council, 2012) and key competencies (OECD, 2015), they are identified in many curricula round the world as important foci for national education systems (García, 2016; Voogt & Roblin, 2012).

There are several rationales for why we should focus on teaching these 21st-century skills, including the need for an informed and critically engaged civil society made more urgent in digital environments. Opinions can be manipulated through the rapid and extensive access to online information and the use of social media platforms. Self-perpetuating and reinforcing systems of knowledge can be created where misinformation, inaccuracies or untruths are taken as truth through repetition and support within social networks. For example, computational propaganda, with algorithms, automation, and human curation are being designed to purposefully distribute misleading information and increasingly influence popular decision making (Woolley, Philip, & Howard, 2017). Civic decisions, as well as judgments and complex health and science issues, are increasingly susceptible to these influences.

In keeping with the concept of being pertinent for the 21st century, there are also relationships between these skills and post-school outcomes such as the changing nature of work, although there are limitations in the evidence base of the degree to which we can attribute direct causal relationships (National Research Council, 2012). The relationships include benefits to the individual in terms of employability because skilled work now requires such skills and these skills contribute to mental health and well-being. Similarly, there are benefits to society from a more productive and cohesive citizenry (García, 2016; Roberts, Martin, & Olaru, 2015).

Argumentation, or critical reasoning, involves a set of knowledge and skills identifiable under the rubric of 21st-century skills and of critical importance in the development of higher-order thinking. Along with critical thinking and critical literacy, argumentation provides a means to make reasoned judgments (Rapanta, García-Mila, & Gilabert, 2013), but has wider significance, including assisting students to conceptualize and filter information, make connections across contexts, enhance their abilities to communicate knowledge (Kuhn, 1991, 2005) and integration of alternative viewpoints.

Developing expertise in argumentation necessarily implies perspective taking and aspects of cognitive and emotional empathy, but there is less evidence for these assumed generalized impacts on social and emotional skills. However, there are experimental demonstrations of building practices for a "community of learners" in argumentation and collaborative reasoning which include these skills in different subject areas such as science (Rapanta et al., 2013), and English language arts (Brown, 2016). These instructional designs include a focus on the *inter*personal and *intra*personal skills necessary to engage effectively in the practices of face-to-face communities. Less is understood about how argumentation impacts cognitive and social skills in online environments and the notion of *internal dialogism*: features necessary for attending to and integrating alternative perspectives to inform belief and decision making. Kuhn and colleagues (2014) make a distinction between the skills required for individual argumentative writing and dialogic argumentation between individuals "personified by a flesh-and-blood other." Advocating for student development of *dialogic focus* the authors maintain that effective thinking involves internal integration of others' positions, such as counter arguments and taking into account "the framework of alternatives" (Kuhn, Hemberger, & Khait, 2014, p. 43).

Thinking with a dialogic focus is arguably far more complex and challenging for young people not least because alternative positions have to be imaginatively conjured, held in creative tension (Wegerif, 2013) and reasoned independently. In online contexts such as forums, blogs and instant messaging (IM), argumentation with dialogic focus is an increasingly important skill when participating in uncensored global communities, for maintaining well-being and contributing or consuming content. The intellectual skills of counter, rebuttal, acknowledging alternative evidence and self-correction are features of an internalized awareness of "other" ways of knowing and the incomplete nature of personal knowledge. To formalize the notion of dialogic focus (in the absence of a conversation partner), we will refer to these features as *internally dialogic* markers within written argumentation.

Incorporating the use of digital tools in classrooms, such as communication platforms and diagnostic applications, offers opportunities to investigate the internally dialogic nature and development of student argumentation for improved thinking and communicating. For example, Kuhn and Crowell (2011) report dialogic argumentation with middle-schoolers using online IM, citing much improved direct counterargument over 3 years. One of the observed benefits of using IM applications was the ability to engage reflectively with transcripts of the written exchanges. Saltarelli and Roseth (2014) showed that cooperation can be enhanced in a digital version of "constructive controversy," a cooperative learning procedure involving dialogic argumentation which has the goal of reaching and raising awareness of an integrated position. However, incorporating argumentation with classroom curriculum is said to require thoughtful planning (Howell, Butler, & Reinking, 2017) and found to present pedagogical challenges, which include use of multi-modal evidence (Hutchison & Reinking, 2010) and teacher emphasis on internet inquiry skills over engagement with other viewpoints (Purcell, Heaps, Buchanan, & Friedrich, 2013).

The development of internally dialogic argumentation: Function and profile

To examine the developmental features of argumentation, Kuhn and Crowell (2011) have developed a taxonomy of functional moves children can make. The framework is based on idea units: essentially a statement that carries a single claim supported by a reason. Each idea unit has one of four functions, namely: support one's own position, counter an alternative position, acknowledge weakness in one's own position, and acknowledge or consider the strengths in an alternate position. The development of ideas can be examined in two ways. One is to look at the sheer number of these different forms across ages. A second is to consider each child's overall argument in terms of three developmental profiles (Kuhn & Crowell, 2011). A *Single* profile only contains ideas that support one's own position. A *Dual* profile has these types of ideas but also contains one or more ideas that critique positions other than one's own. The third profile represents arguments that are *Integrated*; they contain ideas that consider the merits of other positions, and/or the weakness in one's own with the purpose of weighing

TABLE 15.1 Descriptions of Argumentation Profile by Argumentation Function

Profile	Functions of argumentation
Single profile	ideas that advance **own** position only, i.e., one direction
Dual profile	ideas that include critique of **alternative** positions, i.e., critique often aims to advance own position by identifying drawbacks in the other position
Integrated profile	ideas that integrate the **strength** in an alternate position(s) or a **weakness** of own position

these up in drawing conclusions. For clarity, Table 15.1 outlines each of the three profiles in order of progression alongside the associated functions:

In a three-year longitudinal study, the taxonomy was used to determine profiles of 6th-8th grade students' written argumentation (Crowell & Kuhn, 2014; Kuhn & Crowell, 2011). The majority of students participating in a dialogic argumentation curriculum began to make dual perspective arguments by the end of the first year but integrated arguments did not emerge until the third year. By contrast, comparison-group students, in an essay-style, whole class discussion condition, showed no evidence of gains in either respect. Earlier research supports these findings, that without intervention, young adolescents typically concentrate attention on exposition of their own claims, ignoring other positions (Kuhn & Udell, 2003; Kuhn, Goh, Iordanou, & Shaenfield, 2008). In other words, it is likely students are either uninformed of the value of perspective taking in their communication or are constrained by the context, including social norms of the classroom.

Teaching dialogic argumentation skills

Much of what we know about the teaching of argumentation comes from science-based fields that promote learning through evidence-based claims (Song, Deane, Graf, & van Rijn, 2013). Rapanta et al. (2013) distinguish between an "arguing to learn" approach premised upon the idea of content learning resulting from engagement in argumentation and a "learning to argue" approach which focuses on the development of argument skills. Both approaches have been widely employed. Much less is understood of how to develop dialogic focus, particularly in online discourse, where the critical integration of perspectives and alternative evidence require targeted practice and instruction.

Recent research on classroom designs to increase argumentation and reasoning indicate that dialogue intensive pedagogy can contribute to valued student outcomes, such as comprehension, perhaps better than other instructional designs (Wilkinson & Son, 2010; Reznitskaya et al., 2001). The design of Collaborative Reasoning focuses on learning from each other in the process of arguing and the development of argument schema. The dialogic forms go beyond adversarial and coalescent forms because they are embedded in activities in which positions are modified in light of the arguments.

Given the need for deliberate socialization, it is not surprising to find low levels of argumentation and weak skills reported across grade levels and disciplines (Kuhn, Wang, & Li, 2011). Litman and Greenleaf (2017) identified just 24 argumentation tasks in 40 lessons with 18 volunteer teachers, all of whom had been recruited as experienced in developing disciplinary literacy and had been long term partners in a design-based research project in argumentation. Nevertheless, the majority of the tasks had incipient forms of productive argumentation in which students worked collaboratively to identify and evaluate possible meanings or positions.

Research design

We designed an argumentation tool (AT) as part of a wider project *Developing in Digital Worlds*[1] to better understand how school-wide digital environments might promote 21st-century skills. The 4-year project is located in a 1:1 digital initiative in primary and secondary urban schools ($n = 16$) in New Zealand, serving mostly Māori (indigenous) and Pasifika (from Pacific Islands) families from low socioeconomic status (SES) communities. Schools employ a range of digital tools, to achieve valued student outcomes and the pedagogy promotes "digital citizenship" inside and outside of the classroom.

We developed the AT as a classroom instructional resource and an assessment instrument. In what follows we describe its development and provide evidence of argumentation instruction in classrooms including how the AT can establish a link between instruction and the development of student perspective taking (the internally dialogic features of student written argumentation).

Data were collected at two time points 18 months apart. These provided independent samples of teachers in different classrooms using the AT. Alternate forms of the AT were used at these times to test the flexibility of the tool and how it could be used for reliably coding features of argumentation in different forms. We could also check its sensitivity to instructional focus of the teachers. Thirty-eight classrooms in the primary schools participated.

Description of the method

The Argumentation Tool (AT): Providing a context for internally dialogic argumentation

The AT positioned students as first responders to a Google Groups discussion board. Students were required to adopt an independent, but dialogic focus in response to the topic provocation and hyperlinks to corresponding media resources. The topic provocation emulated the "voice" of a would-be discussant, and the hyperlink to contradictory online evidence. This was embedded in a teacher resource which included a PowerPoint presentation introducing the provocation, activity instructions and hyperlinks to the evidence documents and discussion board.[2]

The first form of the AT proposed an issue related to a recent event in New Zealand online media. The issue was considered highly topical for young people at the time and concerned a visiting celebrity, and a local production crew filming a music video at a local beach. Bethels Beach has a protected area for native Dotterels, an endangered bird species, which is controlled by the New Zealand Department of Conservation and requires a permit regulating use of the beach. The local film company were reported to have disregarded the regulations, transporting equipment and personnel (including the famous song star) in 12 vehicles instead of the mandated two. The online discussion board topic stated: "Taylor Swift should have treated the beach with more respect."

The second featured a different environmental issue. The New Zealand government's Predator Free 2020 campaign seeks to eradicate all animal and insect pests (e.g., rats, stoats, feral cats, possums) considered a threat to native wildlife. The targeted pests are listed on the Department of Conservation website and contain some species of potential concern such as eradication of certain introduced horse breeds and wild hares. Extreme Predator Free groups are calling for the long-term ban on cats and interim curfews. Figure 15.1 provides a screenshot of the second version of the discussion board which states: "Predator Free groups should treat 'pests' with more respect."

A slide presentation with the activity instructions was read out to the students by the teacher and a copy was shared with students via email (or a class website). The assignment guidelines given to teachers included reading through the instructions with the whole class, answering any questions and being on hand to give support with reading comprehension. Teachers were required to share with the class any questions raised in their one-on-one interactions, so that all students benefitted equally from any advice.

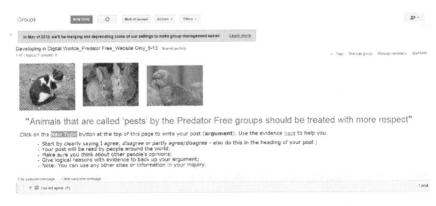

FIGURE 15.1 Discussion board with link to evidence document at Time 2.

Source: "Creative Commons Gato callejero en Madrid 02.jpg, Wild Rabbits at Edinburgh Zoo.jpg and (1)Rainbow Lorikeet 074a.jpg" used under the CC Attribution-Share Alike 2.0 Generic license / Desaturated from originals.

After reading the evidence sheet, students were given thirty minutes to post their response to the Google Groups discussion board. While composing their individual response, they were unable to see any of the other responses as Google Groups opens a separate window instance during composing, and the discussion thread is not updated until after selecting the "Post" option. Teachers were encouraged to invite students to read and respond to one another's responses, in a subsequent lesson. Students were not permitted to edit their contribution once posted to the discussion board, but editing could be undertaken prior to final posting.

All of the classrooms were given the same prompt posted by a fictitious discussant (e.g., *MusicBot; Naturelover*). Students were asked to post their written response supported by guidelines including: "Start by clearly saying – I agree, disagree or partly agree/disagree; remember that your post will be read by people around the world; make sure you think about other people's opinions when you reply; give good reasons and think logically; you can use other sites or information on the Internet to help you."

Reference material in the form of a hyperlink to an evidence sheet provided brief summaries of the event from four different sources: a national newspaper (the *New Zealand Herald*), Department of Conservation, *YouTube*, and *Kiwi Kids News* (an online news website for young New Zealanders). Each source offered confirmatory or conflicting evidence. The evidence document and assignment instructions were composed to ensure age appropriate readability and the original source texts could be accessed if students followed up with an online search.

Classroom observations

We also observed practices in classrooms. The 38 teachers (20 at Time 1 and 18 at Time 2) were observed teaching a nominated "21st-century skill" and nine of the teachers specifically nominated argumentation. We observed the teacher interacting with students in a 3-minute interval and alternated that with checking what the students were doing, singly or together with their devices (3 minutes) as they worked away from the teacher. Observers recorded field notes for one minute after the teacher focus (3 minutes) and student focus (3 minutes) for a total of 8-minute intervals. Each classroom observation totaled 48 minutes (6 intervals). The observation schedule coded each interval for the presence of argumentation sub-skills such as a claim, warrant, evidence, and conclusion.[3] We analyzed 132 intervals at Time 1 and 89 intervals at Time 2. In observations using two observers we determined inter-rater reliability was above 90% at each time point.

The observations enabled us to identify classrooms where there was a relatively high explicit focus by the teacher on the sub-skills involved in argumentation (a focus on any one of the sub-skills was explicitly observed in at least one interval; $n_{T1} = 8$, $n_{T2} = 9$) or a relatively low explicit focus on argumentation skills (no explicit focus was observed $n_{T1} = 12$, $n_{T2} = 9$).

Data analysis

Google Groups offers a downloadable summary of written posts, including date and time stamp, email identity of the correspondent and content of the individual responses posted to the discussion thread. Each classroom audit from Google Groups was checked against the online discussion board and used to transfer written responses into an Excel database.

Written posts by students were each subjected to a word count, segmented into idea units, and units classified into one of four categories from Kuhn and Crowell's (2011) scheme. Each idea unit was blind coded by its function; M+ (idea supporting one's own position), O- (idea that critiques alternate position), M- (acknowledges weakness in own position), O+ (acknowledges strengths of an alternate position). Verbatim examples are provided in Table 15.2.

In addition, each student's developmental profile was categorized as one of the three argumentation profiles according to the set of their argumentation functions (as described in Table 15.1). An *Integrated* profile featuring M- idea units are rare phenomenon, considered developmentally challenging even for adults (Kuhn et al., 2014).

Existing practices

Students' online argumentation

A total of 470 and 716 idea units were coded at Time 1 and 2 respectively. As explained earlier, we coded each idea unit by its function and in turn determined student argumentation profiles.

The distributions of the four types of function in idea units are shown in Figure 15.2. Almost three quarters of the idea units ($n = 1186$) were *Single* (M+), adopting a position and supporting that position (74.3% at Time 1 and 71.1% at Time 2). 11.7% (Time 1) and 8.8% (Time 2) of the idea units were coded *Dual* in that they provided a critique of an alternate position (O-). Shifts in percentages of ideas in *Single* and *Dual* profiles resulted in increased *Integrated* profiles, ideas recognizing the worth of the alternative position (O+) and/or the weakness of one's own (M-). Chi-squared test of independence indicated that changes in the distributions of ideas by argumentation function and profile were statistically significant at 5% [$\chi^2(2, n = 1186) = 9.20, p < .05$].

The *Single* profile follows a curvilinear pattern across age, increasing to a point of inflection at 10 years (Year 6) and at an average number of almost three ideas. Students' *Integrated* profiles also have a curvilinear pattern with a change in growth curve at 10 years, similar to the development of single perspective but at a much lower average frequency; close to one idea unit on average (see Figure 15.3). Although the *Dual* profile has a similar pattern, emerging at the same age as the *Integrated*, the number of ideas per post are far less (much lower than one idea unit on average). Therefore, even though change in development of perspective taking profile occurs at the same age

TABLE 15.2 Coding scheme for the AT discussion board posts

Argument type	Agrees. Taylor Swift Should Have Treated the Beach with More Respect	Disagrees. Taylor Swift Treated the Beach with Respect
No argument	"Taylor should have treated the beach with more respect." Year 3 student (age 7)	"I disagree because she treated the beach just fine." Year 4 student (age 9)
Own-perspective only (includes only positives of preferred option): *Single* profile	"I agree because Taylor Swift was told to come with 2 vehicles but her crew came with 12 vehicles so she disrespected New Zealand by not listening [M+1]." Year 8 student (age 11)	"I agree that Taylor should have treated the beach with more respect when she was making her video at the beach in New Zealand because her crew was only allowed to take two trucks but instead she took 12 trucks [M+1] and could damage the rare bird, the dotterels and their nests [M+2]." Year 4 student (age 9)
Dual perspective (includes negatives of other option): *Dual* profile	"She could have said something to the film people [O-1]. The trucks would have upset the creatures [M+1]." Year 5 student (age 9)	"I disagree that Taylor swift did not respired [sic] our country and the beach because she was complementing it and saying that it was the best beach that she has ever been to [M+1] … If Taylor swift did not respect our beach then she would not have posted the music video [O-1]." Year 7 student (age 11)
Integrative perspective (includes positives of other option or negatives of preferred option): *Integrated* profile	"Taylor Swift messed up the beach by bringing too many cars because her crew damaged bird nests with all their trucks [M+1]. She should have known better [O-1]. But she did get a video out to the world that shows off our beach [O+1] and maybe she didn't even know about the contract [O-1]." Year 8 student (age 12)	"I'm in the middle because I think that yes it was bad about that she might have scared the birds [M+1]. And she brought 12 cars when she was only allowed 2 [M+2]. But she did promote NZ beaches [O+1] and our film company [O+2]. Since she prompted [sic] us tourists will come so that's a positive O+3." Year 6 student (age 10)

(10 years), the *Single* profile dominates such that ideas incorporating critical thinking (*Dual*) are unlikely to reach the same level as for a single idea unit without instructional intervention.

Teachers' practices

Nine teachers volunteered a lesson specifically illustrating the teaching of argumentation. Overall the design of their lessons mirror practices identified by Kuhn (2015), only one of which could be considered to promote dialogic perspectives.

272 Rosedale, McNaughton, Jesson, Zhu, and Oldehaver

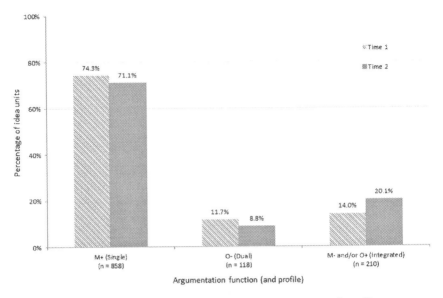

FIGURE 15.2 Distribution of ideas by argumentation function and profile.

There was *Coalescent* practice in which the goal was consensus building through discussion to achieve synthesis and common ground (*"We discuss the answers until we are happy"*; *"Choose whose is the best strategy"*). A second practice was *Adversarial*, persuading and outperforming others, for example by winning a debate (*"So how*

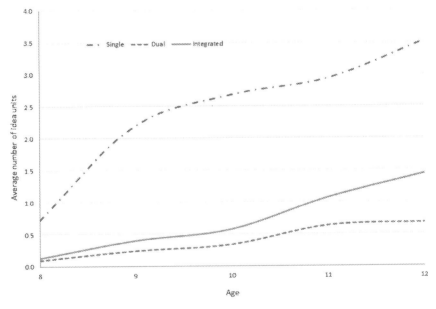

FIGURE 15.3 Trends of average number of ideas across student age by argumentation profile.

do you win an argument?"). A mixed *Coalescent* and *Adversarial* form was observed which involved persuading and deciding on a best solution through a democratic process such as students using a voting protocol to gain agreed position (*"Majority wins"*). There was one lesson that was clearly focused on dialogic argumentation where the objective was to develop a considered position or solution (*"Be open to having your mind changed"*). Across all the 38 lessons there were: few instances of explicit teaching to learn sub-skills of arguing or collaboration; little evidence of explicit discussion or deliberate reference to varying perspectives; and limited pushing of student reflection and quality of justifications or positions.

Sensitivity to classroom practices

The sensitivity of the AT to classroom practices was examined by looking at the association between the proportion of integrated idea units in a classroom and the instructional focus in that classroom. There was a clear association as shown in Figure 15.4. The proportion of integrated idea units was significantly higher in high instructional focus classrooms (p_{T1} = 33.9%, p_{T2} = 47.7%) compared with low instructional focus classrooms (p_{T1} = 18.2%; p_{T2} = 30.3%).

The differences in proportion of *Integrated* profile was significant at each time point as determined by Chi-square tests of independence (see Table 15.3). At both time points, the odds of students having a dialogic perspective (an integrated idea unit) was more than 2 times higher in high focus classrooms.

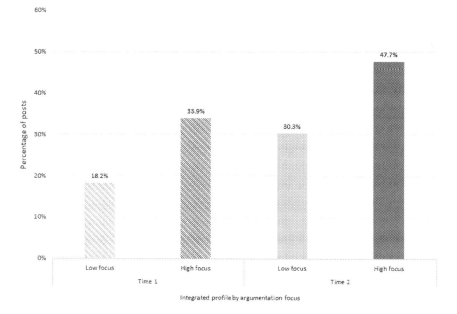

FIGURE 15.4 Percentage of *Integrated* profile by level of teaching instruction on argumentation skills.

TABLE 15.3 Chi-squared tests of independence: Level of students' integrated views in online posts and level of instructional focus in classrooms

Statistics	Time 1	Time 2
Odds ratio	2.31 [1.09, 4.91]*	2.10 [1.15, 3.82]
χ^2	4.88	5.97
P-value	0.03	0.01

*95% confidence interval in square brackets.

Interestingly, the percentage of *Integrated* profile improved between Time 1 and Time 2 for both high and low focus classrooms. The result of a *t*-test of two sample proportions showed that improvement in classrooms with low frequency of teaching argumentation were statistically significant at 5% ($t(197) = 2.01$, $p = .045$). We have not reported here how the results from Time 1 were fed back to teachers in the schools, nor how especially designed professional development was used to develop the overall teacher resource using the AT. We are currently using case studies of teachers for whom we have data in common at both time points and for whom we have information about their exposure to professional development to answer the question of what the change over time can be attributed to.

Evidence for effectiveness

We designed the AT to achieve two purposes. One was to reliably assess the internal dialogicity of student argumentation and its development over the primary years. The second was as part of a teacher resource for promoting argumentation. For the latter, we needed to know if the tool as an assessment was sensitive to pedagogy. In this chapter, we have focused on the assessment question and the sensitivity question.

Developmental and diagnostic functionality

Use of the two versions of the AT two time points offers provisional evidence of the tools' diagnostic functionality related to the *Hi-Hi and Lo-Lo* patterns (high instruction focus in classroom associated with high integrated perspectives in students' posts). Firstly, replication of the *Hi-Hi and Lo-Lo* patterns across the two time points suggests evidence of integration in student online argumentation is sensitive to argumentation instruction in classrooms. Both time points demonstrate consistency of integrated student argumentation profiles with higher frequencies of argumentation instruction in classrooms.

Although the pattern is not surprising, given argumentation involves proposing and supporting propositions, it is our view that the AT is purpose built to engage with multiple perspectives, and therefore offers opportunities to stimulate student perspective integration. Teachers would be able to diagnostically evaluate their instructional sufficiency in impacting student perspective via the argumentation profiles, particularly in identifying evidence of *Integrated* profile in student discussion posts. Secondly, the AT (including coding framework and the task) demonstrates consistency in that the two different versions yielded the same pattern of *Hi-Hi and Lo-Lo* association between instruction and students' *Integrated* profile. Therefore the AT can be applied with different topics and learning contexts to reliably gauge the sensitivity of student perspective integration to argumentation instruction.

Influence of multiple texts

Additionally, central to the AT approach is "dialogic" provision of multiple sources of textual evidence, thereby offering a multiplicity of "voices" to stimulate student perspective taking and informed argumentation. Therefore, aside from the discussion board topic that sets up a provocation, one of the key features of the AT design is careful selection of diverse perspectives to fuel attention to alternative evidence and positions. Half of the evidence sources (two texts) confirm or support the perspective of the topic statement, and the balance (two texts) contradict or challenge this view. Students who only demonstrated a single perspective profile bypassed these differences, indicating limitations in their ability to attend to and negotiate the complexity of the issue. On the other hand, inclusion of multiple texts could support (and perhaps prompted) other students to consider the "framework of alternatives," including any dilemmas in reasoning, reliability of source and provision of scientific evidence. The AT is effective in promoting attention to alternatives and therefore more advanced, internally dialogic forms of argumentation.

Discussion

The early developmental profiles of own position stance in students' argumentation was predicted and aligns with the findings of other studies (Kuhn & Crowell, 2011). Attention to other perspectives, and counterargument is known to place considerable demand on cognitive capabilities, particularly for younger children, though even young adolescents have been found to concentrate attention on exposition of their own claims, ignoring alternative perspectives, and disconfirming evidence (Kuhn, 2001). That said, the developmental trends in our data reflect some differences from previous studies in the earlier emergence of integrated perspectives, although mainly to consider the merits of other positions, rather than as a critique of one's own position.

This finding of earlier emergence is significant for at least two reasons. The first aligns with Cavagnetto and Kurtz's (2016) view that students may not be as deficient in knowledge of argumentative reasoning skills as prior research suggests (Kuhn, 1991; Kuhn & Crowell, 2011). The authors maintain that students "argumentative reasoning is heavily influenced by how they interpret the task" and this influences the knowledge they bring to bear in response (Kuhn & Crowell, 2011, p. 628). Our working hypothesis is that the authentic, social context of the AT's discussion board offered students the opportunity to draw on everyday knowledge of argumentative interaction, where attending to the merits of other's views can be both socially validating and informing.

The second reason, is the possibility of digital tools creating developmental pathways to more sophisticated argumentation. Contrary to Kuhn and Crowell's (2011) findings, that a *Dual* profile (critique to strengthen own view) precedes and may offer a bridge to integration (revise own view), our data suggests the possibility of an alternative progression. It may be that first attending to the strengths in another's position, may offer a bridge to uncovering weaknesses in one's own, or alternatively, confirmation of its strengths. The sequence and focus of attention may be of importance epistemically. For example, the primary goal of an adversarial approach is to first *undermine* an *opponent's* position in support of one's own (Walton, 1989), which might be considered epistemically inflexible. Students may be more open to arguing for the purposes of reaching a "better truth" (Wegerif, 2013) where alternative views are negotiated in less "hostile" terms, and critiqued in the service of informed decision making and for co-furthering knowledge. In a New Zealand context, the opportunity for multiple developmental pathways toward more sophisticated argumentation positions is likely to resonate with culturally responsive instructional designs (Berryman, 2013). For example, classroom routines for engagement with digital formats where multiple perspectives are posed will need to take into account the ways family and socio-cultural values influence students' engagement with critique. The consistently low levels of criticality across our student data (e.g., identifying weakness in my or other's reasoning) may be suggestive of wider norms constraining critical forms of engagement. On the other hand, longstanding school practices that promote adversarial debate and persuasive public speaking will undoubtedly have exerted a strong influence on students' argumentation schema as persuasive rhetoric.

The AT, coupled with guided support, offers an effective means to develop students' awareness of the limitations of single perspective argumentation in online contexts, where respectful engagement with difference and healthy forms of intellectual skepticism are 21st-century necessities.

Notes

1 https://developingindigitalworlds.blogs.auckland.ac.nz/
2 https://developingindigitalworlds.blogs.auckland.ac.nz/tools/online-argumentation/
3 https://developingindigitalworlds.blogs.auckland.ac.nz/teachers/

References

Berryman, M. (2013). Culturally responsive pedagogies as transformative praxis. *Waikato Journal of Education*, *18*(2), 3–10.

Brown, A. C. (2016). Classroom community and discourse: How argumentation emerges during a Socratic circle. *Dialogic Pedagogy: An International Online Journal*, 4. Retrieved from http://dpj.pitt.edu/ojs/index.php/dpj1/article/view/160

Cavagnetto, A. R., & Kurtz, K. J. (2016). Promoting students' attention to argumentative reasoning patterns. *Science Education*, 100(4), 625–644.

Crowell, A., & Kuhn, D. (2014). Developing dialogic argumentation skills: A three-year intervention study. *Journal of Cognition and Development*, 15(2), 363–381.

García E. (2016). The need to address non-cognitive skills in the education policy agenda. In M. S. Khine, & S. Areepattamannil (Eds.), *Non-cognitive skills and factors in educational attainment. Contemporary approaches to research in learning innovations* (pp. 31–61). Rotterdam, The Netherlands: Sense Publishers.

Howell, E., Butler, T., & Reinking, D. (2017). Integrating multimodal arguments into high school writing instruction. *Journal of Literacy Research*, 49(2), 181–209.

Hutchison, A., & Reinking, D. (2010). A national survey of barriers to integrating information and communication technologies into literacy instruction. *Fifty-ninth yearbook of the National Reading Conference* (pp. 230–243). Milwaukee, WI: National Reading Conference.

Kuhn, D. (1991). *The skills of argument*. New York: Cambridge University Press.

Kuhn, D. (2001). How do people know? *Psychological Science*, 12, 1–8.

Kuhn, D. (2005). *Education for thinking*. Cambridge, MA: Harvard University Press.

Kuhn, D. (2015). Thinking together and alone. *Educational Researcher*, 44(1), 46–53.

Kuhn, D., & Crowell, A. (2011). Dialogic argumentation as a vehicle for developing young adolescents' thinking. *Psychological Science*, 22, 545–552.

Kuhn, D., Goh, W., Iordanou, K., & Shaenfield, D. (2008). Arguing on the computer: A microgenetic study of developing argument skills in a computer-supported environment. *Child Development*, 79, 1310–1328.

Kuhn, D., Hemberger, L., & Khait, V. (2014). *Argue with me: Argument as a path to developing students' thinking and writing*. Bronxville: NY: Wessex.

Kuhn, D., & Udell, W. (2003). The development of argument skills. *Child Development*, 74, 1245–1260.

Kuhn, D., Wang, Y., & Li, H. (2011). Why argue? Developing understanding of the purposes and value of argumentive discourse. *Discourse Processes*, 48, 26–49.

Litman, C., & Greenleaf, C. (2017). Argumentation tasks in secondary English language arts, history, and science: Variations in instructional focus and inquiry space. *Reading Research Quarterly*, 53(1), 107–126.

National Research Council (2012). *Education for life and work: Developing transferable knowledge and skills in the 21st-century. Committee on defining deeper learning and 21st-century skills.* Pellegrino, J. W. & Hilton, M. L. (Eds.). Washington, DC: National Academies Press.

OECD (2015). *Skills for social progress: The power of social and emotional skills*. OECD. Retrieved from https://read.oecd-ilibrary.org/education/skills-for-social-progress_9789264226159-en#page1

Purcell, K., Heaps, A., Buchanan, J., & Friedrich, L. (2013). How teachers are using technology at home and in their classrooms. *Washington, DC: Pew Research Center's Internet & American Life Project*. Retrieved from http://www.looooker.com/wp-content/uploads/2013/05/PIP_TeachersandTechnologywithmethodology_PDF.pdf

Rapanta, C., García-Mila, M., & Gilabert, S. (2013). What is meant by argumentative competence? An integrative review of methods of analysis and assessment in education. *Review of Educational Research*, 83(4), 483–520.

Reznitskaya, A., Anderson, R. C., McNurlen, B., Nguyen-Jahiel, K., Archodidou, A., & Kim, S. Y. (2001). Influence of oral discussion on written argument. *Discourse Processes*, 32(2–3), 155–175.

Roberts, R. D., Martin, J., & Olaru, G. (2015). *A Rosetta Stone for noncognitive skills: Understanding, assessing, and enhancing noncognitive skills in primary and secondary education.* New York: Asia Society and ProExam.

Saltarelli, A. J., & Roseth, C. J. (2014). Effects of synchronicity and belongingness on face-to-face and computer-mediated constructive controversy. *Journal of Educational Psychology, 106*(4), 946.

Song, Y., Deane, P., Graf, E. A., & van Rijn, P. (2013). Using argumentation learning progressions to support teaching and assessments of English language arts. *R&D Connections, 22*, 1–14.

Voogt, J., & Roblin, N. P. (2012). A comparative analysis of international frameworks for 21st-century competences: Implications for national curriculum policies. *Journal of Curriculum Studies, 44*(3), 299–321.

Walton, D. N. (1989). Dialogue theory for critical thinking. *Argumentation, 3*(2), 169–184.

Wegerif, R. (2013). *Dialogic: Education for the Internet age.* London: Routledge.

Wilkinson, I., & Son, E. (2010). A dialogic turn in research on learning and teaching to comprehend. In M. Kamil, P. Pearson, E. Moje, & P. Afflerbach (Eds.), *Handbook of reading research* (pp. 360–387). New York: Routledge.

Woolley, S. C. & Howard, P. N. (2017). Computational propaganda worldwide: Executive summary. In S. Woolley & P. N. Howard (Eds.), *Working paper 2017.11.* Oxford, UK: Project on Computational Propaganda. Retrieved from http://comprop.oii.ox.ac.uk/wp-content/uploads/sites/89/2017/06/Casestudies-ExecutiveSummary.pdf

16

CULTIVATING PRE-SERVICE AND IN-SERVICE TEACHERS' ABILITIES TO DEEPEN UNDERSTANDING AND PROMOTE LEARNING STRATEGY USE IN PUPILS

Tatsushi Fukaya and Yuri Uesaka

Summary

Twenty-first-century skills education attempts to deepen understanding and promote effective learning strategies use among pupils. To accomplish this goal, we need to elucidate ways to enrich teachers' competencies. In this chapter, we introduce two practices to develop pre-service and in-service teachers' competence in promoting pupils' understanding and use of effective learning strategies. In the first practice, trainees in a university educational methods course experienced one-on-one tutoring (*cognitive counseling*) to assess and support learners who had difficulty in studying. In the second practice, elementary school teachers engaged in a new type of class called *Thinking After Instruction* (TAI) and lesson studies. We examined how these practices changed the teaching approaches employed by the in-service and pre-service teachers.

Introduction: Two components of deeper learning

One of the important goals of education in the 21st century is to foster a set of student educational outcomes collectively called *deeper learning*. This chapter focuses on deeper learning from two perspectives. In one aspect, deeper learning refers to profound understanding of learned concepts in a variety of disciplines. Structured content knowledge has long been recognized as an important component of academic ability which allows people to solve problems or make judgements efficiently and effectively (Bransford, Brown, & Cocking, 1999).

In addition, recent educational research emphasizes the importance of helping students acquire competencies which are broader and more practical in society. This trend emerged in such concepts as *key competencies* (Rychen & Salganik, 2003) and the *21st-century skills* (Griffin, McGaw, & Care, 2012). In this chapter, we focus on learning strategy as one of the important competencies. We chose to focus on learning strategy because the use of effective strategies promotes the acquisition of structured knowledge (Ainsworth, Prain, & Tytler, 2011), and developing students' ability to learn by themselves is especially important to life in changing societies (Rychen & Salganik, 2003).

Importance of teacher education

To promote students' deeper learning, we must address the following question: how can we foster teachers' abilities to deepen understanding and promote use of effective learning strategies in pupils? According to Darling-Hammond and Baratz-Snowden (2005), teacher education is an issue that must be addressed in order to practice effective teaching, and teachers' knowledge has been a point of interest as a factor which enables teachers to perform high quality teaching. In that context, *pedagogical content knowledge* (PCK), introduced by Shulman (1986), has been an important addition to research on professional teaching.

Shulman (1987) defined PCK as a "special amalgam of content and pedagogy that is uniquely the province of teachers, their own special form of professional understanding" (p. 8). Two components proposed by Shulman (1986) have been influential in this area (Depaepe, Verschaffel, & Kelchtermans, 2013): *knowledge of instructional representations* and *knowledge of learners*. The former means knowledge used to explain subject contents effectively with analogies, illustrations, examples, or demonstrations. The latter refers to knowledge about students' procedural bugs and misconceptions. It also includes the knowledge used to judge whether students learn specific contents with ease or difficulty.

However, while PCK has successfully conceptualized teachers' ability to impart subject contents effectively, it seems to be failing to capture teachers' expertise to help pupils acquire more generic competencies such as learning strategy use. To solve this problem, Fukaya and Uesaka (2018) proposed *knowledge of instructing learning strategy* as a new component of teachers' knowledge. This corresponds to the base of teachers' knowledge to support students in mastering learning strategies through teaching specific subject content. On the basis of acknowledging the importance of cultivating children' generic competencies as mentioned above, we need to develop ways to assess and enrich teachers' knowledge to promote not only deep understanding, but also pupils' ability to use learning strategies.

The framework of this chapter

To develop teachers' competency in promoting pupils' understanding and use of learning strategies, we have to enrich the quality of teacher education both for pre-service and in-service teachers. Recent educational research and policies assume that teachers develop their professional ability all through their work life (e.g., OECD, 2005). We assume that engaging in practical teaching activities based on educational theories during both pre-service and in-service stages is effective to promote lifelong learning in teachers. Therefore, we conducted practices for pre-service teachers (Practice 1) and for in-service teachers (Practice 2). It is also important to note that although two practices were conducted for different participants (pre-service teachers, and in-service teachers) in different contexts (a university methods course and elementary school classes), both practices attempted to improve teaching methods focusing on students' deep understanding and effective learning skills.

Practice 1 explored the effects of learning and experiencing *cognitive counseling* in a university course (details of this study were reported in Fukaya & Uesaka, 2017). Cognitive counseling is a research activity in which counselors (usually educational researchers or school teachers) assess clients' (usually students) problems in learning and teach the client to solve those problems thorough individual consultations (Ichikawa, 2005). Cognitive counseling has a basis in cognitive theory; that is why counselors focus on students' problems from the perspective of understanding, metacognition, and learning skills. Although we usually conduct individual consultations from five to ten times or more in cognitive counseling, it is difficult to provide university students with such opportunities in a regular educational method course. Therefore, we required students to conduct a counseling session only once as a homework assignment.

On the other hand, Practice 2 focused on in-service teachers. In Practice 2, teachers in a public elementary school in Japan engaged in practices to improve math classes over a period of two years, introducing a teaching approach called *Thinking after Instruction* (TAI); this practice was reported in Fukaya, Uesaka, Ota, Koizumi, & Ichikawa, 2017. TAI is intended to promote students' deep understanding and learning strategy use through changing teachers' ways of designing classes. To achieve this aim, our research group worked with teachers together to design lesson plans and did *lesson studies* (explained in detail in a later section).

Practice 1

Description of the practice

This practice examined the effects of learning cognitive theory and experiencing cognitive counseling on pre-service teachers' knowledge of teaching. The participants were 102 students in a pre-service teacher training program who attended an educational methods course at a national university in Japan and provided consent for study participation. The course consisted of 15 class sessions. Because this course addressed educational methods for elementary and secondary education in general, we handled a variety of subjects like mathematics, science, and social studies. The first half of the course (first to eighth class sessions) was directly related to cognitive counseling. We describe that below, dividing the contents into three parts.

Initial stage of the practice

The purpose of the initial stage of the course was to understand an educational goal: attaining deep understanding and mastering learning strategies. For example, the class sessions dealt with topics like *understanding* (in the second class session), *metacognition* (third class session), and *motivation* (fourth class session). In the first class session, the teacher (first author) explained the course goal: to acquire knowledge and skills to support pupils' learning in a variety of contexts based on cognitive theory. The students would be required to conduct one-on-one tutoring as an opportunity to practice what they were learning, and to write a report summarizing the outcomes as a homework assignment.

The theme of the second class session was types of knowledge. Students first learned the distinction between rote memorized knowledge and deeply understood knowledge. Research in cognitive theory demonstrates that understanding a principle or meaning behind a procedure or rule promotes memory, knowledge transfer, and motivation (e.g., Bransford et al., 1999), while rote memorized knowledge is easy to forget and difficult to apply in other contexts. In the class, students participated in actual memory experiments as demonstrations. Students then discussed how they would explain concrete subject contents if they were teachers trying to promote pupils' understanding.

In the third class session, students learned about metacognition, particularly focusing on *conceptions of learning* and *learning strategy*. To explain conceptions of learning, we emphasized that it is important for students to have conceptions that are understanding (not rote) oriented, process (not result) oriented, and quality (not quantity) oriented (e.g., Ichikawa, 2005). Students were also instructed in three types of learning strategies (cognitive strategy, metacognitive strategy, and external resource strategy; cf. Pintrich, Smith, García, & McKeachie, 1993) with examples or demonstrations in various disciplines. Finally, they discussed in groups how they could help junior high school students learn effectively.

Middle stage of the practice

During this stage, the pre-service teachers learned how they could enhance students' academic ability. We particularly focused on the basic skills of cognitive counseling in the fifth and sixth classes, and students conducted an actual counseling session outside of the class.

The topic of the fifth class was the basic procedures of cognitive counseling. In cognitive counseling, three perspectives of assessment for pupils' difficulty with learning a subject were emphasized: knowledge, learning strategy, and conceptions of learning. To effectively assess a pupil's difficulty, four counseling techniques were introduced: a) asking pupils to explain their thoughts, b) explaining concepts with diagrams, c) requiring pupils to explain what they learned (checking their comprehension), and d) prompting pupils to extract important points (lesson induction; e.g., Ichikawa, 2005). The teacher then showed a brief report of an actual case in which a fifth-grade pupil incorrectly solved the problem of "What is the area of 20 m^2 in cm^2?" (her answer was 2,000 cm^2). After students discussed what difficulty she faced and how to support her if they were counseling, the teacher summarized the important points: teachers should assess pupils' difficulty not only at the knowledge level (i.e., she confused area with length), but also at the learning strategy level (i.e., she did not draw a diagram spontaneously), and support strategy use by, for example, requiring the pupil to explain their thoughts with diagrams or promoting their awareness of strategy use as a resource for understanding.

Final stage of the practice

Students conducted an individual counseling after the fifth class and submitted a brief report in the seventh class. In the eighth class, a representative student gave a presentation about her report, in which she conducted a counseling session with a 10th-grade high-school girl who incorrectly solved a word problem involving a quadratic function. After the representative student presented her report, the class discussed what was good in the report and how she could improve her counseling session. They then considered how they might improve their own counseling session and written report. Because they could again realize the importance of deep understanding and strategy instruction through the representative report, they made comments such as "I should emphasize the meaning of the formula, not only giving the knowledge" and "I should ask my student after solving the problem what he should do to avoid the same mistake."

Measurements

We conducted a pre test in the first class and a post-test in the eighth class through a tutoring scenario method. In this method, a description was provided of a girl who had difficulty in understanding and incorrectly solved a concrete mathematical problem (Fukaya & Uesaka, 2018). Students described how they would respond to the hypothetical tutoring situation. The scenarios consisted of two types of material; the first one was addition of fractions (the pupil's incorrect answer was 1/2 + 1/3 = 2/2 = 1), and the second one was calculating the area of complex circles (see Fukaya & Uesaka, 2017, for details). Participants who worked on the fraction problem at pre-test worked on the circle problem at post-test, and vice versa. Both tests were conducted during the class.

Post-tests included additional questions to check the meaning of what participants described. We hypothesized that the number of descriptions about comprehension checking and strategy instruction would increase. Therefore, we asked the following additional two questions and had students write responses as concretely as possible: a) "How do you confirm the pupil's understanding after you counsel her?" and b) "What kind of points do you want her to write if you ask her to extract lessons from this problem?" The first question concerned the level of checking (understanding of mathematical procedures or concepts) and the second concerned the level of lessons (lessons on knowledge or learning strategy).

Results and discussion

Coding procedure

The number of participants who responded to the fraction problem was 51 at pre-test and 53 at post-test, and those who responded to the circle problem were 51 at pre-test and 46 at post-test. The data of seven participants were excluded from the data analysis, because they erroneously responded to the same task at pre- and post-tests.

All descriptions were classified into corresponding categories according to the following perspectives: *assessment, explanation, comprehension checking,* and *strategy instruction*. With respect to assessment, for example, the descriptions were classified into four categories: *no assessment, abstract description, questioning,* and *analyzing*. The first author coded all descriptions based on the schema. Then, after training, a graduate student majoring in educational psychology also coded all data. We computed kappa coefficients with respect to each perspective and deemed inter-rater agreement satisfactory ($M = .81$).

We then defined effective assessing and teaching strategies based on specific criteria. Assessment was considered effective when the student intentionally assessed the cause of the pupil's mistake (*questioning* and *analyzing*). We deemed *conceptual explanation* (explaining to the pupil the meaning of the mathematical procedure) effective when the student explained the concept or reason behind the procedure that the pupil had misunderstood. Comprehension checking was classified effective when the student required the pupil to explain the problem to confirm whether they understood the meanings behind the procedures (*requiring explanation*). Strategy instruction was deemed effective when those descriptions included statements to promote use of learning strategies in students (*explicit instruction* and *inducing lessons*).

Comparison between pre- and post-tests

A Mann-Whitney U test was conducted on each problem and perspective, in which time (pre- or post-test) was treated as an independent factor. With the fraction problem, we found significant differences in assessment ($z = 3.20, p < .01$), comprehension checking ($z = 4.84, p < .01$), and strategy instruction ($z = 3.52, p < .01$), indicating that participants provided more effective descriptions at post-test than they did at pre-test (Figure 16.1). For conceptual explanation, the difference between pre- and post-tests did not reach statistical significance. The same analysis was conducted with the circle problem. Those results showed that the post-test ratios of effective descriptions were higher than the pre-test ratios on assessment ($z = 3.46, p < .01$), comprehension checking ($z = 5.75, p < .01$), and strategy

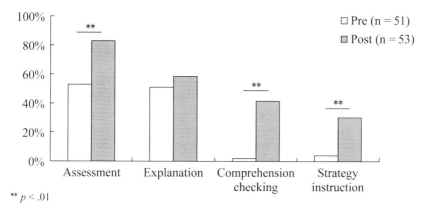

FIGURE 16.1 Ratios of descriptions representing effective teaching in fraction problem.

instruction ($z = 4.44$, $p < .01$) (Figure 16.2). Although the post-test ratio on conceptual explanation was higher in descriptive terms, the difference did not reach statistical significance ($z = 1.66$, $p = 0.97$).

Even though the pupil's answer clearly indicated that she did not understand the rationale of the solution to the problem, pre-service teachers did not at first make inferences or ask what she misunderstood; however, throughout the course, they seemed to increasingly pay attention to pupils' deep understanding. In fact, we found that the post-test ratio of effective assessment was higher than the pre-test ratio by almost 30%. We also found that almost none of the pre-service teachers provided effective descriptions of comprehension checking and strategy instruction in the pre-test. However, after learning in the course and experiencing cognitive counseling outside of class, effective descriptions of comprehension checking and strategy instruction increased greatly at the post-test.

On the other hand, we did not find any significant difference in conceptual explanation. This might be due to the fact that participants would need more

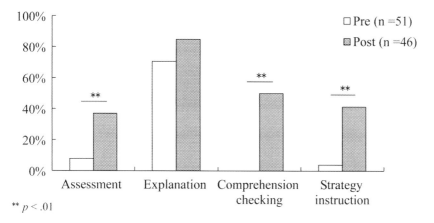

FIGURE 16.2 Ratios of descriptions representing effective teaching in circle problem.

subject expertise to provide conceptual explanations compared to other perspectives (Inoue, 2009). However, the post-test ratios in conceptual explanation were higher as descriptive values than the pre-test ratios in both tasks, so that students could possibly provide conceptual explanations with longer term training. Further research should be carried out to investigate whether pre-service teachers can acquire the ability to explain the meaning behind mathematical procedure by training in cognitive counseling.

In practice 1, pre-service teachers not only learned a variety of concepts in cognitive theory and procedures of cognitive counseling but also performed actual cognitive counseling outside of the class as an opportunity to practice what they learned in the course. In addition, they learned from actual cases including a report presented by a representative student and reflected on how they could improve their own counseling and reporting. The results of the tutoring scenario method suggest that participants acquired skills to assess a pupil's state of knowledge and promote understanding and learning strategy use, although these results, which did not evaluate actual teaching behavior, were preliminary in nature.

Practice 2

Description of the practice

Pupils' deep understanding and acquisition of effective learning strategies could be achieved mainly through daily classes in schools. Therefore, it is important to provide training for in-service teachers to improve the quality of lessons. In this practice, we introduced an approach centered on *Thinking after Instruction* (TAI). TAI, proposed by Ichikawa (2004), is a framework used to design classes in a variety of subjects, in which direct instruction from a teacher and discovery learning of pupils are combined with activities to promote pupils' metacognition (Fukaya, Uesaka, & Ichikawa, 2018; Ichikawa, Uesaka, & Manalo, 2017).

TAI consists of four phases: (a) teacher's instruction, (b) comprehension checking, (c) deepening understanding, and (d) self-evaluation. First, teachers give direct instruction on basic content focusing on meanings or principles, which enable pupils to elaborate facts, concepts, or formulas. Even after a teacher provides direct instruction, however, pupils might not understand the concepts. In comprehension checking, pupils are required to check their understanding by, for example, working in pairs to explain what the teacher explained. In the third step, the teacher provides a task to deepen pupils' understanding. The task is designed to require them to apply what they had learned in the class or resolve their remaining misconceptions, and pupils try to discover those solutions in collaborative groups with other classmates. In self-evaluation, pupils reflect on what they understood and what they did not understand in the class.

One of the characteristics of TAI is an emphasis on pupils' deep understanding. Direct instruction from a teacher must focus on meaning, rationales, or relationships, not just pronouncing isolated facts or formulas (Ichikawa et al., 2017).

After instruction, pupils are required to check their comprehension by explaining the teacher's lesson in their own words. The explanation activities make them aware of whether they really understand the material (Fukaya, 2013). In deepening understanding, pupils engage in solving more advanced problems. This is important because pupils often do not fully understand the content or fail to apply knowledge in other contexts (e.g., Renkl, Mandl, & Gruber, 1996).

Another important characteristic of TAI is that teachers elaborate explanations and set activities to promote pupils' use of effective learning strategies (Ichikawa et al., 2017). For example, one such learning strategy is to draw diagrams. Although many studies have demonstrated that drawing diagrams is an effective strategy to solve problems or learn concepts efficiently (e.g., Ainsworth et al., 2011), some pupils have difficulty in using diagrams spontaneously and effectively (e.g., Uesaka & Manalo, 2017). In TAI, teachers set up opportunities to prompt pupils to use diagrams in classes. For example, teachers give direct instruction using diagrams to represent the structure or meaning of the problems as a model for explanation. In the following phases, such as comprehension checking and deepening understanding, pupils are required to use diagrams actively when they solve problems and explain their thoughts to others.

In practice 2 (reported in detail in Fukaya et al., 2017), teachers in a public elementary school in Japan adopted TAI on a daily basis to design mathematics classes for two years. In this school, other interventions such as lesson study, a three-way review, and corroboration with external researchers (i.e., the authors) were also implemented as detailed below. The wide range of interventions used in this educational practice made it difficult to specify with certainty which of those interventions affected the dependent variables. However, it was important to investigate if these interventions, centered on TAI, improved pupils' academic ability and teachers' skills at teaching, especially in general terms (i.e., not limited to specific topics). Of course, we were not expecting that the effects of the interventions would transfer to other subjects in an unlimited manner (cf. Barnett & Ceci, 2002), but we predicted that teachers could design effective TAI classes dealing with mathematical topics, which some of them do not teach directly in their classes, after the interventions.

Email exchanges preceding a lesson study class

Teachers in each grade in the school conducted lesson study once a year. Lesson study is an educational method of improving teaching quality conducted widely in Japanese schools. In lesson study, a representative teacher conducts a class, and other teachers, including the school principal and external participants (in this case, the authors) observe. Afterward, teachers and participants get together and discuss the class in an open format (see Lewis, Perry, & Murata, 2006, for more detail about lesson study).

Prior to a lesson study, teachers and researchers exchanged emails to explain the details of the practice. Although TAI is assumed to be a powerful framework for designing classes that promote pupils' understanding and use of effective learning strategies, at first, the quality of the lesson plans that teachers made was not good enough. For example, a lesson in sixth-grade in the first semester of the first year concerned the topic of x times and proportion. The problem in the textbook was like this: *A pupil played basketball. Her number of successful shots in three games increased from 30 in 5th-grade to 50 in 6th-grade. How many times is the number of successful shoots in 6th-grade compared to the number in 5th-grade?* At first, teachers planned to show a formula for "the amount compared ÷ the amount referred = proportion (x times)" and explain how to apply the formula to the problem.

Via email, both the first and second authors separately pointed out that the plan did not seem to emphasize pupils' understanding of the meaning behind the formula. The first author pointed out, "In the plan, it seems that the teachers are just showing the formula and having pupils put the problems into that formula. I am worried that pupils will learn the procedure without understating the meaning through that explanation." We also proposed alternative ideas to teachers. The second author suggested the following idea: "The important point of this topic is the idea of viewing the amount referred to as a referential part. ...If I were a teacher, I would show three lengths (10 m, 50 m, and 25 m), and explain that if I view 10 m as a referential part, then 50 m is 5 times and 25 m is 2.5 times, but if I view 50 m and 25 m as a referential part, then 10 m is 1/5 and 10/25 (2/5) times more, respectively..."

Of course, teachers did not have to adopt our ideas, but, through discussions, we (teachers and researchers) gradually shared the goals which TAI aims to achieve. In actual classes, teachers changed their plans and carefully explained the point of reference using diagrams.

An example of lesson study and discussions

We also briefly showed an example of a lesson study and subsequent discussions. In the 6th-grade class in the second year, a lesson study on *speed* was conducted. In the lesson study class, the teacher used the following task: *which is faster, a red car driving 300 km in 3 hours or a blue car driving 250 km in 2 hours?* The teacher first explained that we can compare speeds by distance per hour. In his explanation, the relationships between speed, time, and distance were emphasized using two blocks representing two cars' distance and hours, not just telling pupils the formula. In comprehension checking, pupils solved similar problems by drawing number lines, and explained their thoughts in pairs using the drawn diagrams. In deepening understanding, three types of problems were shown: a) a problem asking about speed, b) a problem asking about distance, and c) a problem asking about time. Pupils drew number lines and explained, in groups, how they could work out the answer.

After the class, all the teachers got together and had group discussions using a three-way review approach. In the three-way review, teachers in small groups (three to six participants in each group) reflected on the class from three perspectives: a) good points, b) points for improvement, and c) points that could be used in other units or subjects (Uesaka, Fukaya, & Ichikawa, 2017). Each group then presented their summarized comments to share ideas. In the discussions, several groups pointed out that while the teacher's instruction using diagrams was effective to help pupils understand the relationship between speed, time, and distance, some pupils have difficulty in drawing and explaining the diagrams in the following phases. The external researchers commented that teachers should demonstrate a model of explanation by, for example, showing pupils how to represent and explain number lines. Through these discussions, teachers understood the concepts of deep understanding and learning strategy and how to design effective TAI classes.

Measurements

To verify the effects of the interventions, we collected three kinds of data (two for pupils and one for teachers) in the first semester of each year. Although the effects of interventions would emerge most strongly in the final semester in the second year, we had to report the results at a school conference in November in the second year, so we conducted investigations in the first semester (rather than the second semester) of that second year.

The first set of data was taken from the National Assessment of Academic Ability, which is conducted annually for sixth-grade pupils in Japanese elementary schools. This test consists of mathematics and Japanese, so we examined if test performance in the second year improved only in mathematics, not in Japanese (see National Institute for Educational Policy Research, 2013, 2014 for actual test items). The second set of data was from a learning strategy test, which examined the degree to which pupils used diagrams while solving word problems. Two test sets were prepared. In each set, four word problems were shown with space under each problem. In the space, we required pupils to write their thoughts in words, formula, and/or diagrams. In the third data set, teachers' knowledge was examined through lesson plan tasks. Teachers wrote a lesson plan for an hour on *the formula of the area of a trapezoid* or *line symmetry* based on TAI. With a copy of a textbook, about half of the teachers made a plan for teaching the trapezoid material in the first year, and a plan for teaching the line symmetry material in the second year (and vice versa). The data were taken from all teachers who teach mathematics. The total number of participants was 100 6th-grade pupils and 20 teachers in the first year, and 111 pupils and 17 teachers in second year.

Results and discussion

National Assessment of Academic Ability

First, we computed z scores based on national average scores in each year. There were also two types of problems (A or B); while type A consisted of basic problems, type B comprised applied problems. We analyzed each type of test. We conducted

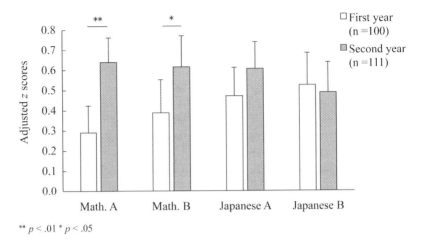

FIGURE 16.3 Test performance of national assessment of academic ability. Error bars represent 95% confidence intervals.

ANCOVAs with two variables as covariates (self-reported pre-achievement on report cards and whether they go to cram school). The results in Figure 16.3 show that the effects of time (first versus second year) were statistically significant only in mathematics, demonstrating that test scores in the second year were higher than those in the first year ($t(207) = 3.64$, $p < .001$ in mathematics A, $t(207) = 1.96$, $p < .05$ in mathematics B). In addition, the degree of SD (a measure of spread or variation) in the second year in mathematics A ($SD = .60$) was smaller than that in the first year ($SD = .88$) ($F(1, 209) = 5.54$, $p = .02$), indicating that differences between individuals in math test performance decreased in the second year. In contrast, the differences in scores on the Japanese test were not statistically significant.

Learning strategy test

The first author scored answers and coded whether pupils drew diagrams. Inter-rater reliabilities with a trained undergraduate student were high both in test scores (95%) and use of diagrams (89%). We conducted an ANCOVA to examine the effects of time and task set with two covariates. For the number of problems with incorrect answers without diagrams, the effect of time was statistically significant ($F(1, 199) = 12.65$, $p < .001$). There was no other significant main effect or interaction. For the number of problems of correct answers with diagrams, the effect of time was also statistically significant ($F(1, 199) = 9.31$, $p < .01$). Again, there was no other significant main effect or interaction. As shown in Figure 16.4, the results demonstrate that while the number of problems with incorrect answers *without diagrams* in the first year was higher than that in the second year, the number of problems with correct answers *with diagrams* in the second year was higher than that in the first year. The results suggest

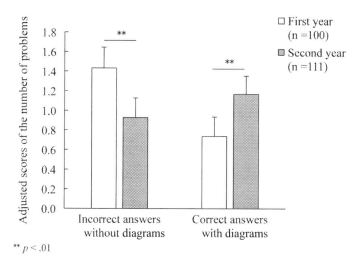

FIGURE 16.4 The number of problems with incorrect answers without diagrams and correct answers with diagrams. Error bars represent 95% confidence intervals.

that pupils in the second year more often drew diagrams spontaneously when solving word problems, which helped lead them to correct answers, compared to pupils in the first year.

Lesson plan task

One hypothesis to explain the increase of academic performance in pupils is that teachers' way of designing mathematics classes had changed. Teachers in the second year might have designed more effective TAI than those in the first year. To verify this hypothesis, we examined if there were differences between lesson plans in the first and second years. In the analysis, we coded descriptions of teachers' instruction, comprehension checking, and deepening understanding. Based on previous research and practices (e.g., Depaepe et al., 2013), we coded the existence of descriptions representing effective teaching in each phase. For example, we coded whether teachers explained rationales of formulae or relationships between concepts and gave instructions that took pupils' misconceptions into account. Comprehension checking and deepening understanding were also measured by, for instance, noting whether the tasks focused on rationales of relationships or pupil's misconceptions and whether teachers set opportunities for pupils to explain their thoughts in pairs or groups.

To compare total average scores of the lesson plan task between the first and second years, we conducted an ANOVA with the difference of academic year and task (trapezoid or line symmetry) as independent variables and coded scores of lesson plans as a dependent variable. The results showed that while the task had a significant effect ($F(1, 33) = 22.71$, $p < .01$), the difference of academic year showed only a marginally significant effect (F (1, 33) = 3.35, p = .08). Although the difference of academic year did not reach significance due to the limited sample size, the scores on the lesson plan task in the second year were higher than those in the first year in both types of problems (for area of trapezoid, M = 5.80 in the first year and M = 6.43 in the second year; for line symmetry, M = 7.10 in first year and M = 8.30 in second year).

Practice 2 examined whether interventions centered on TAI have an impact on pupils' academic ability and teachers' mathematics classes. Here, we discussed how these interventions might have changed teachers' ways of teaching, and pupils' ways of learning. First, the results of the lesson plan task indicated that teachers developed an ability to design effective TAI classes. For example, the descriptions about setting pair or group work in comprehension checking and deepening understanding increased from 48% (first year) to 59% (second year) in total. Setting pair or group work possibly enhanced pupils' diagrams use, because using diagrams is effective for pupils to communicate their thoughts in pair and group work. In fact, Uesaka and Manalo (2017) argued that explanation activities in pairs or groups promote subsequent spontaneous use of diagrams during individual problem solving. The results of the learning strategy test, which demonstrated pupils could use diagrams as tools to grasp meanings and structures of mathematical concepts in the second year, also support this conjecture.

Second, the results of analyzing the teachers' lesson plan task suggest that teachers came to emphasize conceptual meanings behind procedures and take into account pupils' misconceptions in their instructions and task setting in the second year. As we described in the section on "Description of the practice," teachers at first designed lesson plans which focused on procedural memorization rather than conceptual understanding of what's behind the procedure. But they gradually realized how they could promote mathematical understanding and resolve misconceptions in pupils. These changes in classes likely led to pupils' acquisition of structured, usable knowledge. In fact, the results of the National Assessment of Academic Ability demonstrated that pupils in the second year attained higher achievement on basic and applied knowledge tests in mathematics. Individual differences in the type A mathematics test also decreased in the second year. As such, teachers' changes in designing TAI mathematical classes could possibly influence pupils' use of learning strategies and knowledge acquisition.

General discussion

As described at the beginning of this chapter, it is important for learners to acquire both structured subject knowledge and more generic competencies in 21st-century environments. These competencies include, for example, learning strategies. Students need to master how to learn effectively though school education because, in rapidly changing societies, they have to keep their knowledge updated after they graduate from schools. It is, therefore, important to cultivate teachers' competencies to promote not only deep understanding of contents but also acquisition of effective learning strategies in pupils. This chapter introduced two practices aimed at enhancing teachers' knowledge of teaching strategies. Although the two practices we introduced were different in contents, participants, and approaches, they shared an emphasis on the same educational goals and methods for strengthening pupils' knowledge base and competencies (e.g., setting up explanation activities with diagrams).

One of the distinctive features of the two practices is their conceptualization of knowledge about instructing learning strategies as knowledge that pre-service and in-service teachers must develop. Previous research on teachers' knowledge such as PCK has focused on *knowledge of instructional representations* and *knowledge of learners* (Depaepe et al., 2013; Shulman, 1986, 1987). Of course, these components are still important to help pupils become aware of their own misconceptions and lack of knowledge, and to effectively support knowledge acquisition. If teachers, however, can successfully impart subject knowledge to pupils, it does not mean that they can successfully help pupils acquire the ability to learn by themselves. Although many interventions using PCK have been conducted, those interventions mainly concerned knowledge for teaching specific subject matter (see Depaepe et al., 2013, for a review). Considering the increasing recognition of the importance of generic skills (Griffin et al., 2012; Rychen & Salganik, 2003), teacher education focusing on nurturing pupils' generic skills has also been emphasized in this study.

Although two practices reported in this chapter demonstrated the effects of interventions based on cognitive counseling and TAI, several important issues remain unanswered. First, in both practices, teachers' knowledge for teaching was evaluated using paper-based assessments (tutoring scenario method in practice 1, and lesson plan task in practice 2). We assume that these assessments partly reflect actual teaching behavior, but more rigorous and multifaceted verifications would be needed to capture more accurate data about teachers' knowledge for teaching. In actual teaching situations, teachers would need to check and flexibly adjust to pupils' responses, so it is not guaranteed that teachers could conduct their teaching as they planned. Therefore, further research should be conducted to examine how classroom teaching using teachers' knowledge changes in practice, for example, by observing actual mathematics classes.

Second, because pre-service teachers had limited experience of cognitive counseling in practice 1, long-term commitment in actual cognitive counseling would be needed in future research. In actual cognitive counseling, we conducted individual tutoring sessions for a higher number of sessions (usually five to ten times) in order to cultivate pupils' acquisition of knowledge and learning skills (Ichikawa, 2005). In an ongoing research project in Hiroshima University, we have provided opportunities for pre-service teachers to conduct cognitive counseling to elementary school pupils over a longer term. In that project, about 40 pre-service teachers learned cognitive theory and are practicing cognitive counseling for four years. Thus, we plan to examine how the long-term practice of cognitive counseling influences knowledge for teaching of pre-service teachers in a future study.

Third, the findings of practice 2 were based on a limited sample and measurements. Participants were only 6th-grade pupils, and the practice was conducted in only one school. Furthermore, we have to verify whether interventions based on TAI have impact on learning strategies other than drawing diagrams. For example, pupils in pairs check their comprehension by explaining what a teacher instructed in comprehension checking in TAI. This explaining activity may strengthen pupils' awareness of the effectiveness of the explanation strategy, because they realize that they can check their own understanding by explaining what they learned to others. Hence, TAI research targeting a variety of learning strategies would be an interesting direction in future research.

References

Ainsworth, S., Prain, V., & Tytler, R. (2011). Drawing to learn in science. *Science, 333*, 1096–1097.

Barnett, S. M., & Ceci, S. J. (2002). When and where do we apply what we learn? A taxonomy for far transfer. *Psychological Bulletin, 128*, 612–637.

Bransford, J. D., Brown, A. L., & Cocking, R. (1999). *How people learn: Brain, mind, experience, and school.* Washington, DC: National Academy Press.

Darling-Hammond, L., & Baratz-Snowden, J. C. (2005). *A good teacher in every classroom: Preparing the highly qualified teachers our children deserve.* San Francisco, CA: Jossey-Bass.

Depaepe, F., Verschaffel, L., & Kelchtermans, G. (2013). Pedagogical content knowledge: A systematic review of the way in which the concept has pervaded mathematics educational research. *Teaching and Teacher Education, 34*, 12–25.

Fukaya, T. (2013). Explanation generation, not explanation expectancy, improves metacomprehension accuracy. *Metacognition and Learning, 8*(1), 1–18.

Fukaya, T., & Uesaka, Y. (2017). Kobetsu shien no jissen taiken wo toriireta kyoin yousei katei no jyugyo jissen (Educational practice to enhance teacher trainees' practical abilities for learning support through the experience of Cognitive-Counseling). *Japan Journal of Educational Technology, 41*, 157–168.

Fukaya, T., & Uesaka, Y. (2018). Using a tutoring scenario to assess the spontaneous use of knowledge for teaching. *Journal of Education for Teaching, 44*, 431–445.

Fukaya, T., Uesaka, Y., & Ichikawa, S. (2018). Investigating the effects of Thinking after Instruction approach: An experimental study of science class. *Educational Technology Research, 41*, 1–11.

Fukaya, T., Uesaka, Y., Ota, Y., Koizumi, K., & Ichikawa, S. (2017). Tishiki no syutoku, katsuyo, oyobi gakusyu houryaku ni shouten wo ateta jygyo kaizen no torikumi (Improving students' performance in an elementary mathematics class: Focusing on students' knowledge acquisition, utilization, and learning strategies using a "Thinking After Instruction" Approach) [In Japanese with English abstracts]. *The Japanese Journal of Educational Psychology, 65*, 512–525.

Griffin, P., McGaw, B., Care, E. (2012). *Assessment and teaching of 21st century skills.* Dordrecht, The Netherlands: Springer.

Ichikawa, S. (2004). *Manabu iyoku to sukiru wo sodateru (Fostering motivation and skill to learn: Strategies for improvement in academic ability).* Tokyo, Japan: Shogakukan.

Ichikawa, S. (2005). Cognitive counseling to improve students' metacognition and cognitive skills. In D. W. Shwalb, J. Nakazawa, & B. J. Shwalb (Eds.), *Applied developmental psychology: Theory, practice, and research from Japan* (pp. 67–87). Greenwich, CT: Information Age.

Ichikawa, S., Uesaka, Y., & Manalo, E. (2017). Three approaches to promote spontaneous use of learning strategies. In E. Manalo, Y. Uesaka, & C. A. Chinn (Eds.) *Promoting spontaneous use of learning and reasoning strategies: Theory, research, and practice for effective transfer* (pp. 195–210). London: Routledge.

Inoue, N. (2009). Rehearsing to teach: Content-specific deconstruction of instructional explanations in pre-service teacher training. *Journal of Education for Teaching, 35*, 47–60.

Lewis, C., Perry, R., & Murata, A. (2006). How should research contribute to instructional improvement? The case of lesson study. *Educational Researcher, 35*, 3–14.

National Institute for Educational Policy Research. (2013). Heisei 25 nendo zenkoku gakuryoku gakusyu jyokyo chosa no chosa mondai, seitou rei, kaisetsu siryo ni tsuite (Test items, examples of correct answer, and commentaries of national assessment of academic ability in 2013). Retrieved from http://www.nier.go.jp/13chousa/13chousa.htm

National Institute for Educational Policy Research. (2014). Heisei 26 nendo zenkoku gakuryoku gakusyu jyokyo chosa no chosa mondai, seitou rei, kaisetsu siryo ni tsuite (Test items, examples of correct answer, and commentaries of national assessment of academic ability in 2014). Retrieved from http://www.nier.go.jp/14chousa/14chousa.htm

OECD (2005). *Teachers matter: Attracting, developing and retaining effective teachers*. Paris, France: OECD.

Pintrich, P. R., Smith, D. A., García, T., & McKeachie, W. J. (1993). Reliability and predictive validity of the Motivated Strategies for Learning Questionnaire (MSLQ). *Educational and Psychological Measurement, 53*, 801–813.

Renkl, A., Mandl, H., & Gruber, H. (1996). Inert knowledge: Analyses and remedies. *Educational Psychologist, 31*, 115–121.

Rychen, D. S., & Salganik, L. H. (Eds.). (2003). *Key competencies for a successful life and well-functioning society*. Cambridge, MA: Hogrefe & Huber.

Shulman, L. S. (1986). Those who understand: Knowledge growth in teaching. *Educational Researcher, 15*, 4–14.

Shulman, L. S. (1987). Knowledge and teaching: Foundations of the new reform. *Harvard Educational Review, 57*, 1–23.

Uesaka, Y., & Manalo, E. (2017). How to address students' lack of spontaneity in diagram use. In E. Manalo, Y. Uesaka, & C. A. Chinn (Eds.), *Promoting spontaneous use of learning and reasoning strategies: Theory, research, and practice for effective transfer* (pp. 62–76). London: Routledge.

Uesaka, Y., Fukaya, T., & Ichikawa, S. (2017). Strategies for achieving deep understanding and improving learning skills: New approaches to instruction and lesson study in Japanese schools. In Yip, M. (Ed.), *Cognition, metacognition and academic performance: An East Asian perspective* (pp. 101–121). New York: Routledge.

PART 6
Program/course teaching

17
CULTIVATION OF A CRITICAL THINKING DISPOSITION AND INQUIRY SKILLS AMONG HIGH SCHOOL STUDENTS

Takashi Kusumi

Summary

The project described in this report examined the effects of critical thinking instruction and project-based inquiry learning on high school students' critical thinking disposition, inquiry skills, learning competence, and self-efficacy in science courses. One thousand 10th- to 12th-grade students of a Super Science High School in Japan participated in the study. The curricula in this school are constructed using a mixed approach regarding critical thinking: a general approach to critical thinking instruction and practice in special classes is combined with an infusion approach in each subject (e.g., critical-logical thinking instruction in STEM) as well as an immersion approach in cooperative inquiry and project-based learning. The results of three studies show that these learning activities are able to improve students' critical thinking disposition and inquiry skills.

Introduction

Middle school education in Japan has concentrated on cultivating subject knowledge and skills, rather than thinking skills. However, international educational reform movements from about the year 2000 (e.g., OECD, ATC21S [Assessment and Teaching of 21st-Century Skills], and Partnership for 21st-Century Skills in the US [P21]) have been emphasizing the cultivation of generic skills. Critical thinking is considered as one of the most crucial skills among these generic skills.

Japan's Ministry of Education, Culture, Sports, Science and Technology (MEXT) launched educational reforms in 2002 in response to globalization and the country's shift to a knowledge-based society. To promote science education to develop students' abilities in STEM (Science, Technology, Engineering, and Math) as well as their generic skills (e.g., critical thinking, creativity, communication, and collaboration), MEXT has designated about 200 high schools throughout Japan as Super Science High Schools (SSH). SSHs are upper secondary education institutions that focus on science and math, and receive support from the Japan Science and Technology Agency (JST) (JST, 2011; MEXT, 2003) (Figure 17.1). SSHs develop enriched curriculum and teaching methods and materials on science and mathematics in cooperation with universities and research institutes. The educational programs of these schools include inquiry-based learning, advanced STEM classes, English for use in scientific contexts, international learning activities with foreign high schools and universities, special programs conducted in cooperation with universities and academic institutions, research activities using regional characteristics to promote students' critical thinking skills, creativity with high-level abilities in STEM, and global mindsets for developing next-generation human resources in science and technology. High schools that apply to be designed as SSH are required to present their curriculum and a five-year plan in their applications.

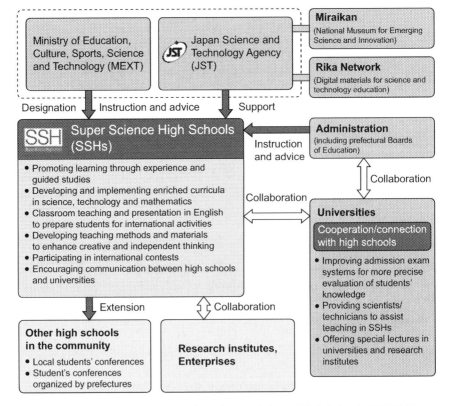

FIGURE 17.1 Collaborative relationship of Super Science High Schools (SSHS) (Japan Science and Technology Agency (JST), 2011).

The budget for each SSH is about US$140,000 per year. The acceptance rate varies between 22% and 74% according to fluctuations in the number of schools that apply each year. Surveys of graduates of SSH show that the rate at which SSH students enter higher education in the natural sciences is about two to three times higher than the national average (Kobayashi, Araki, & Ono, 2015).

This paper concentrates on critical thinking, which has been studied since at least the 1910s when John Dewey first published his landmark book, *How We Think* (1910). Based on Dewey's conceptualization, critical thinking is analogous to metacognition or thinking about one's thinking. Critical thinking is (a) reasonable and reflective thinking focused on deciding what to believe or do (Ennis, 1987); (b) logical, and unbiased thought based on criteria and evidence (Kusumi, 2018b); and (c) skilled and active interpretation and evaluation of observations and communications, information, and argumentation (Fisher & Scriven, 1997).

Critical thinking is divided into two parts: cognitive and affective components (e.g., Ennis, 1987). First, cognitive components are skills and knowledge, especially domain-general skills and knowledge; for example, clarification, evaluation of the reliability of information, inference, and decision-making. Note that in contrast, examples of domain specific knowledge include scientific methodology and knowledge for understanding health information. Second, the affective components of critical thinking are disposition and attitude. Critical thinking is not conducted using one's cognitive abilities alone; disposition is also important. For example, critical thinking disposition is an important factor in being able to draw correct conclusions from contrary pieces of evidence and avoid succumbing to the influence of belief biases (Hirayama & Kusumi, 2004).

It is important to cultivate critical thinking skills and disposition through a systematic curriculum that utilizes a mixed approach (Ennis, 1987), combining a general approach (e.g., general critical thinking instruction in special classes) with infusion (e.g., critical thinking instruction in STEM subjects) and immersive approaches (e.g., project-based learning). Metanalyses of the teaching of critical thinking indicate that the mixed approach significantly outperforms all other single approaches (Abrami et al., 2008).

We conducted three surveys concerning critical thinking skills, disposition, and learning competence at a Super Science High School, which is a top-ranked public high school located in the Kansai region in Japan.

This high school aims to arouse students' intellectual curiosity and cultivate their critical thinking skills through its educational programs (Zeze High School, 2018). Students participate in a project-based learning class (see Tables 17.1 and 17.2), special classes (e.g., humanity and social science, environmental science, life science, and medical science) presented by Kyoto University and Shiga University of Medical Science, international learning activities (e.g., visiting high schools in the United States and UK), and regular classes (e.g., STEM, English for use in scientific contexts, and history) based on systematic curricula that foster students' logical-critical thinking skills, international awareness, and sense of curiosity.

TABLE 17.1 Project-based learning class (one or two hours per week) for 10th- to 12th-grade students

Objectives
1. Cultivating students' dispositions on learning and thinking, active and creative problem solving and inquiry skills, and encouraging students to reflect on their lives and careers.
2. Cultivating students' competence and ability to find and solve problems, learn, and make decisions.

10th-grade students
First semester
Cultivating individual inquiry skills through lectures and individual project-based learning

a. Lectures and practice on problem finding, inquiry learning, critical thinking, and ICT skills (e.g., searching for information using the Internet) for students' research projects.
b. Conducting research projects individually (identifying research questions, conducting research, and writing papers).

Second semester
Cultivating individual inquiry skills through lectures, reflection on students' projects and project-based learning in groups.

a. Lectures and project-based learning involving ICT skills (e.g., computation using Excel) for the group project.
b. Reflecting on individual research projects in a group (reading fellow group members' reports and providing critical comments).
c. Conducting a group research project (identifying a research question, conducting research).

Third Semester
Presenting the outcomes of the group projects and engaging in a critical discussion.

a. Writing reports and posters.
b. Presenting posters and conducting discussions critically.

11th-grade students
First semester
Cultivating individual inquiry skills through lectures and individual project-based learning.

a. Lectures and practice on inquiry learning, critical thinking, presenting posters, and writing papers.
b. Conducting individual research projects (identifying research questions, conducting research, and writing papers).
c. Developing academic English skills for preparing a poster presentation in English.

Second semester
Cultivating individual inquiry and critical skills through lectures, reflections on students' projects, and group project-based learning.

a. Lectures and project-based learning in groups.
b. Reflecting on students' research projects in a group (reading fellow group members' reports and providing critical comments).
c. Conducting a group research project using ICT (e.g., conducting questionnaire, data analysis).
d. Preparing a poster presentation in English in the school and presenting a poster at a university in the US (ten-minute presentation and five-minute discussion).

(continued)

TABLE 17.1 Project-based learning class (one or two hours per week) for 10th- to 12th-grade students (*Continued*)

Third Semester
Conducting a final individual research project.

a. Planning and conducting the final research project.
b. Reflecting on progress on research projects.

12th-grade students
First semester
Cultivating individual inquiry and critical skills through project-based learning.

a. Lecture and practice on oral presentations using Power Point and writing papers.
b. Continuing the final research project (conducting research and writing a paper).
c. Presenting papers in an oral session in school.

Second semester
Cultivating individual inquiry and critical skills by preparing for university studies.

a. Researching admissions policies and preparing studies for students' chosen universities.
b. Presenting and discussing the results of research in the group.

TABLE 17.2 Process of project-based learning in the SSH

1. Planning research project
   i. Idea generation (e.g., generating topics of interest using 10 × 10 cell tables)
   ii. Clustering ideas (e.g., sorting the 100 ideas-cards into several piles)
   iii. Clarifying research topics (e.g., naming the piles of clustered topics)
   iv. Reviewing previous research
2. Collecting empirical evidence
   i. Selecting a research method and planning
   ii. Conducting an experiment
   iii. Analyzing data
3. Presenting results
   i. Writing a paper in Japanese
   ii. Comments on the paper by peers in small groups
   iii. Preparing posters and practicing presentations in a group
   iv. Preparing and practicing oral presentations in Japanese and in English

Examples of research projects
  Changes in birds' bills due to environmental changes
  Production of antibiotics by soil bacteria
  Ecosystem changes related to water pollution
  Is it possible to stop desertification?
  The benefits and harms of the volcano
  An evaluation of "complexity" via fractal dimension: An illustration of stone walls
  Relationship between superabsorbent polymers and deodorization
  An analysis of bubble transformation
  Research on coil with Gauss accelerator

This school uses a mixed approach to teach critical thinking (Ennis, 1989), combining a general approach (e.g., critical thinking instruction and practice in special classes), an infusion approach in each subject (e.g., critical-logical thinking instruction in STEM and English for use in scientific contexts), and an immersion approach through project-based learning (Krajcik & Shin, 2014; Thomas, 2000). Metanalyses have indicated that mixed-approach and project-based leaning improves students' critical thinking skills (Abrami et al., 2008).

We had previously explored the relationships between critical thinking disposition, reflective predisposition, and perceived academic competence in elementary school students (5th- and 6th-graders) and junior high school students (7th–9th graders) in Japan using a two-wave questionnaire survey (Kusumi, Murase, & Takeda, 2011). A simultaneous path analysis revealed that during each wave, (i) reflective predisposition influenced critical thinking disposition in general (CT-G); (ii) critical thinking disposition in general (CT-G) affected critical thinking disposition during study in class (CT-S); and (iii) critical thinking disposition during study (CT-S) affected perceived academic competence. However, there are few studies that examine the kinds of learning activities that might improve critical thinking in high school. Abrami et al. (2008) reviewed 158 empirical studies on the teaching of critical thinking skills in post-elementary education published between 1960 and 2005. There were only eight studies (5%) concerning high school students (16–18 years of age) and their effect size ($g+$) was .10 ($SE = .06$, 95% CI [−.03, .22], $Z = 1.56$, ns). In contrast, the number of studies concerning undergraduate postsecondary students was 80 (51%) and the effect size ($g+$) was .25 ($SE = .02$, 95% CI [.21, .29], $Z = 12.30$, $p < .05$). Therefore, in the investigations we report here, we decided to explore critical thinking education at the high school level.

In the following section, we will describe methods of our three surveys conducted in the Super Science High School that, among other things, aimed at improving critical thinking disposition and inquiry learning skills in its students.

Methods employed in the SSH to cultivate critical thinking

The curriculum in the school consists of three main parts: (1) learning in regular classes (e.g., learning STEM knowledge and research methods), (2) project-based learning classes, and (3) visiting research institutions and universities in Japan and the United States (e.g., attending lectures and seminars, and presenting papers).

The project-based learning class was divided into three parts (Table 17.1, Table 17.2): (i) improving inquiry and critical thinking skills through lectures and practice (the author conducted a lecture on critical thinking for students in the 10th- and 11th-grades [Table 17.3] as part of this section); (ii) conducting research projects individually, writing papers, and engaging in discussions in groups of four students; and (iii) conducting advanced group research projects,

TABLE 17.3 Content of lecture on critical thinking

1. Definition and importance of critical thinking (e.g., Ennis, 1987)
2. Critical thinking skills for inquiry learning
   - Clarification, basis of inference, inference (induction, deduction, analogy, value judgment), behavioral decision (career decision) based on Ennis's (1987) framework
   - Practice concerning scientific literacy (e.g., hidden assumptions, 2×2 matrix, control group, the reliability of scientific evidence, credibility of information, over-generalization)
3. Critical thinking disposition (e.g., Kusumi, Murase, & Takeda, 2011)
4. How to cultivate your critical thinking skills

presenting posters in Japanese and English, and writing papers in Japanese (Zeze High School, 2010).

Evidence for the effectiveness of the approach used in the high school

Study 1: The effect of learning activities on critical thinking and other skills: Cross-sectional data

This study addressed three research questions: (i) Are there any improvements in critical thinking disposition by grade? (ii) What types of learning activities promote critical thinking disposition? (iii) What factors affect learning competence and satisfaction in school?

Method

We conducted a questionnaire survey of all students of the SSH. There were 1,141 students (629 boys, 512 girls), comprised of 371 10th-graders (187 boys, 184 girls), 395 11th-graders (243 boys, 152 girls), and 375 12th-graders (199 boys, 176 girls). The questionnaire had six parts: (a) Critical thinking disposition in general (CT-G: 10 items) and during study (CT-S: 10 items [Kusumi, Murase, & Takeda. 2011]). The CT-G scale is a modified version of Hirayama and Kusumi's (2004) critical thinking scale (Manalo, Kusumi, Koyasu, Michita, & Tanaka, 2013) that is based on the California Critical Thinking Disposition Inventory (CCTDI; Facione & Facione, 1992). (b) Reflective-impulsive scale (5 items) (Takigiku & Sakamoto, 1991). (c) Learning competence scale (10 items, 4-point scale) (Sakurai, 1992). (d) Participation in learning activities (7 items, 6-point scale, e.g., a project-based learning class, club activity). (e) Learning time at home and in a study hall (time spent per day). (f) Satisfaction with school life (5-point scale).

Results and discussion

The critical thinking disposition in general scale (CT-G) items are divided into four factors: inquisitiveness (e.g., search for multiple options and consider all

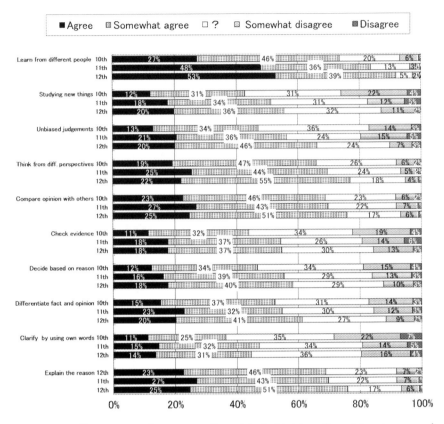

FIGURE 17.2 Percentage of responses for critical thinking disposition in general (CT-G) (Study 1).

situations with open-mindedness), objectivity (e.g., use reliable sources of information), reliance on evidence (e.g., decide based on evidence and reason), and logical thinking disposition (e.g., seek clear assertions and reasons). Figure 17.2 shows the percentage of "*agree*" and "*mildly agree*" responses in the self-evaluation of critical thinking disposition in general. Examples are, "I want to meet different kinds of people, and to learn a lot from them" (inquisitiveness), "studying new things all my life would be wonderful" (inquisitiveness), "I try to make unbiased judgments" (objectivity) and "I try to think from different perspectives" (objectivity). These responses and the total mean score increased with the number of years spent in school. The differences among 10th-, 11th-, and 12th-graders were significant (Ms = 3.54, 3.73, 3.83, respectively; F = 23.0, p < .001).

The critical thinking disposition during study (CT-S) items are divided into three factors: elaboration, thinking in class, and actively listening to others' opinions. Figure 17.3 shows the percentage of "*agree*" and "*mildly agree*" responses in the self-evaluation of critical thinking disposition during study. For example, "I try to relate new information to everyday life and society" (elaboration),

Cultivation of a critical thinking disposition **307**

FIGURE 17.3 Percentage of responses for critical thinking disposition during study (CT-S) (Study 1).

"I am thinking of what the important point in the topic is" (thinking in class), and "I am checking the bias and prejudice in others' opinions" (active listening), increased with the number of years spent in school. The total mean score increased significantly between 10–12th grades in school (Ms = 2.78, 2.80, 3.02, respectively; F = 14.5, $p < .001$).

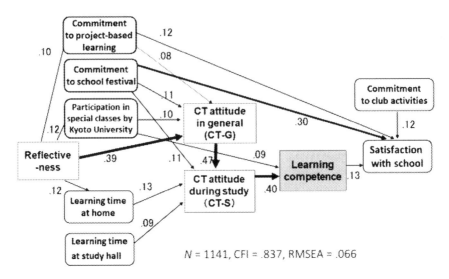

FIGURE 17.4 The effects of learning activity on learning competence via critical thinking. Standardized coefficients for path analysis (Study 1).

Figure 17.4 shows the effects of learning activity on learning competence via critical thinking. All path coefficients are significant. The application of path analysis to the above data revealed the following: (i) Students' reflectiveness affected their critical thinking disposition in general (CT-G). Highly reflective students committed more to engaging in the project-based learning and the special classes provided by Kyoto University, and then, developed their critical thinking disposition in general (CT-G). (ii) Students' critical thinking disposition in general (CT-G) strongly affected their critical thinking disposition during study (CT-S), which was affected by learning times (amount) at home and in the study hall. (iii) Critical thinking disposition during study (CT-S) affected learning competence. (iv) Students' satisfaction with school was affected by learning competence, commitment to school festivals, the project-based learning, and club activities.

These results indicate that: (i) critical thinking disposition in general (CT-G) and during study in class (CT-S) improved by grade level, (ii) project-based learning activities and the special classes by Kyoto University promoted critical thinking disposition (CT-G, CT-S), (iii) critical thinking disposition during study (CT-S) affected learning competence, and school activities then affected satisfaction with school.

We found critical thinking disposition by grade—using cross-sectional data—increased among students in the school. In the next study, we conducted a two-wave questionnaire study to explore more precisely the causal effect of the project-based learning program on critical thinking disposition and inquiry skills development. We also explored the effects of critical thinking skills on inquiry learning skills, self-efficacy and interest in science, and learning competencies.

Study 2: The effect of critical thinking and other skills: Two-wave data

We concentrated on inquiry learning in Study 2 and developed an inquiry learning skills scale for this study. This study addressed two research questions: (i) Do critical thinking disposition, inquiry learning skills, and other variables improve from the beginning to the end of the school year by learning activities? (ii) What factors affect learning competence and satisfaction at school?

Method

We conducted a two-wave questionnaire survey with 10th- and 11th-grade students of the SSH at the beginning and at the end of the school year. There were 837 students (457 boys, 361 girls, 19 undetermined [did not respond to the question about gender]), comprised of 439 10th-graders (250 boys, 176 girls, 13 undetermined) and 398 11th-graders (207 boys, 185 girls, 6 undetermined).

The questionnaire had six parts: (a) Inquiry learning skills (11 items, 5-point scale, Cronbach's αs = .80, .82), which are based on three phases of inquiry learning: planning of research project; collecting empirical evidence; and presentation of results). (b) Critical thinking disposition in general (10 items, αs = .78, .78) and during study (10 items, αs = .78, .81) (Kusumi, Murase, & Takeda, 2011). (c) Reflective-impulsive scale (5 items, αs = .70, .71) (Takigiku & Sakamoto, 1991). Both (b) and (c) were the same as in Study 1. (d) Learning competence scale (10 items, 4-point scale, αs = .78, .78) (Sakurai, 1992). (e) Self-efficacy in science (4 items, 4-point scale, αs = .68, .76, e.g., identify the better of two explanations for the formation of acid rain). (f) Interest in science (5 items, 4-point scale, αs = .84, .85, e.g., "I enjoy acquiring new knowledge in natural science"). Both (e) and (f) were used in PISA 2006 (Programme for International Student Assessment, 2007).

Results and discussion

As previously noted, the inquiry learning skills scale items comprised the three phases of planning research, collecting empirical evidence, and presenting results. Figure 17.5 shows the percentage of responses on the 5-point scale in students' self-evaluation of their inquiry learning skills. The percentage of "*agree*" and "*mildly agree*" of all items of inquiry learning skills increased between Time 1 and Time 2. For example, "I define my research topic based on my

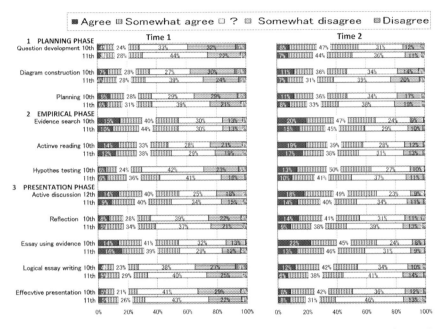

FIGURE 17.5 Percentage of responses for inquiry learning skills at time 1 and time 2 (Study 2).

interests and develop a precise research question" (planning research and presenting results phases) (from Time 1 [agree + mildly agree] 28% (10th grade) and 31% (11th grade) to Time 2 [agree + mildly agree] 55% (10th grade) and 51% (11th grade), respectively); "I test hypotheses based on empirical evidence" (collecting empirical evidence phase) (from 30%, 42% to 63%, 51%); "I write essays logically based on evidence" (presenting results phase) (from 27%, 34% to 56%, 34%) increased from time 1 (the beginning of the school year) to time 2 (the end of the school year).

Table 17.4 indicates that the mean scores in the three subscales of inquiry learning skills (planning research; collecting empirical evidence; and presenting results) in 10th- and 11th- grade students increased significantly from time 1 to time 2.

Furthermore, the critical thinking disposition in general and during study in class, self-efficacy and interest in science, and learning competence in the 10th and 11th grades also increased significantly from time 1 to time 2.

Figure 17.6 shows the effects of critical thinking disposition on learning competence via inquiry skills in Time 1 and Time 2. The path analysis of two-wave data results indicates that: (a) reflectiveness affected critical thinking disposition in general (CT-G) and during study in class (CT-S); (b) CT-G affected CT-S and inquiry skills; (c) CT-S affected inquiry skills, learning competence, interest, and self-efficacy in science; (d) CT-S and inquiry skills affected self-efficacy in

TABLE 17.4 Means (SDs) for critical thinking and inquiry skills and outcome measures in time 1 and time 2 (Study 2)

		Time 1		Time 2			
Scale	Grade	M	SD	M	SD		
Reflectiveness[a]	10th[c]	3.14	(.74)	3.17	(.71)	0.75	
	11th[d]	3.17	(.71)	3.24	(.72)	1.92	+
Critical thinking disposition	10th	3.66	(.55)	3.85	(.51)	7.57	**
in general[a] (CT-G)	11th	3.67	(.54)	3.80	(.50)	5.28	**
Critical thinking disposition	10th	3.10	(.58)	3.15	(.63)	1.59	
during study[a] (CT-S)	11th	2.94	(.55)	2.98	(.57)	1.11	
Inquiry skills[a]	10th	3.16	(.57)	3.57	(.51)	14.76	**
	11th	3.22	(.53)	3.41	(.53)	6.64	**
Planning[a]	10th	2.97	(.79)	3.41	(.68)	10.19	**
	11th	3.05	(.68)	3.30	(.69)	5.43	**
Empirical[a]	10th	3.29	(.76)	3.68	(.68)	9.20	**
	11th	3.35	(.67)	3.50	(.71)	3.44	**
Presentation[a]	10th	3.11	(.76)	3.58	(.70)	12.16	**
	11th	3.22	(.71)	3.41	(.66)	4.56	**
Self-efficacy in science[b]	10th	2.53	(.50)	2.70	(.51)	6.80	**
	11th	2.57	(.50)	2.70	(.52)	4.39	**
Interest in science[b]	10th	3.10	(.56)	3.22	(.54)	4.54	**
	11th	2.97	(.57)	3.06	(.59)	2.93	**
Learning competence[b]	10th	2.44	(.51)	2.52	(.56)	3.31	**
	11th	2.36	(.55)	2.47	(.57)	4.54	**

Note. [a]5-point scale, [b]4-point scale, [c]$n = 396$, [d]$n = 291$, **$p < .01$, +$p < .10$.

science; (e) self-efficacy affected interest in science; (f) learning competence was affected by CT-S and interest in science; (g) the variables in Time 1 strongly affected the same variables in Time 2; (h) the causal relationship in Time 1 was structurally mapped onto Time 2; and (i) the differences between the 10th- and 11th-grade students in coefficients were small.

Using two-wave data of 10th- and 11th-grade students, we found improvements in critical thinking disposition, inquiry-learning skills, self-efficacy and interest in science, and in learning competence from the beginning to the end of the school year. We also discovered the effects of critical thinking disposition on study in inquiry learning skills, self-efficacy and interest in science, and learning competencies.

In the next study, we explored more precisely the effect of the critical thinking lecture on the students' image of critical thinking and their critical thinking disposition in general and in writing.

Study 3: The effect of the critical thinking lecture on the image of critical thinking

We concentrated on the effects of the critical thinking lecture on students' image of critical thinking in Study 3. "Critical thinking" is often misunderstood by

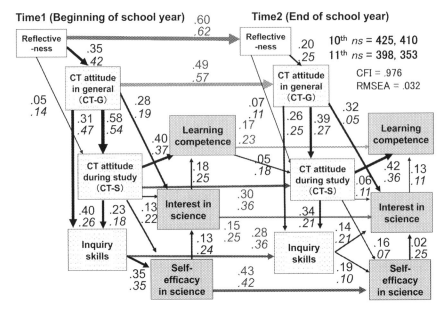

FIGURE 17.6 The effect of critical thinking disposition on learning competence via inquiry skills. Standardized coefficients for path analysis using two-wave data. CT = Critical thinking.

students; critics of critical thinking may claim that it is aggressive and confrontational rather than collegial and collaborative (Bailin & Siegel, 2003). Students tend to have a negative image of critical thinking and critical thinkers, believing that they must be aggressive and uncooperative. For example, Japanese students conceive of critical thinkers as unamicable people (Hirooka, Ogawa, & Motoyoshi, 2000). Rather than being aggressive, however, critical thinking is in fact cooperative. We instruct students that critical thinking is logical, reflective, and cooperative thinking that they can use in their studies and everyday life through cooperative project-based learning, which is not confrontational.

We also focused on writing, which is an important inquiry learning skill in the research presentation phase. Writing is important for developing and assessing critical thinking (Wade, 1995). Students are required to write a report on their research project at the end of both the spring and fall semesters. This third study addressed two research questions: (i) Do lectures on critical thinking change students' conception of "critical thinking" from negative to positive? (ii) Do logical and cooperative images of critical thinking affect students' critical thinking disposition in general and in their writing?

Method

We conducted a one-hour lecture on critical thinking for project-based learning (e.g., definition, purpose, skills, disposition, and practices) and a pre-lecture and

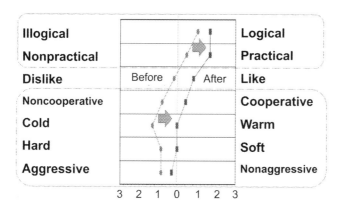

FIGURE 17.7 The change of meaning in "Critical thinking": Before and after the lecture using semantic differential scale (Study 3) (N = 424).

post-lecture questionnaire survey of 424 10th-grade students (247 boys, 177 girls) of the high school. These students were participants in Study 2.

The questionnaire had three parts: (a) semantic differential scale (seven pairs of bipolar adjectives, 7-point scale; e.g., *warm-cold, aggressive-non aggressive, logical-illogical*, see Figure 17.7); (b) critical thinking disposition as displayed in their own writing (nine items, Stapleton, 2002, e.g., "It is important to state my opinion clearly, even if the topic is controversial," "It is not important to mention the opinion of those who disagree with me as long as I write my own opinion clearly") (α = .58); (c) critical thinking disposition in general (10 items, αs = .78, 78) and during study (ten items, αs = .78, 81) (Kusumi, Murase, & Takeda, 2011), as used in Study 1.

Results and discussion

Figure 17.7 shows the effect of the critical thinking lecture on the students' image of critical thinking. The profiles indicate the mean ratings of "critical thinking" from before (left) to after the lecture (right) based on the mean ratings of the semantic differential scale.

The mean scores of "logical" and "practical" were changed from "*somewhat*..." to "*quite*..." (Cohen's ds = .53, .97). The mean score of "like-dislike" was changed from neutral to "somewhat like" (d = .86). Conversely, the mean score of "non-cooperative," "cold," "hard," and "aggressive" were changed from "*somewhat (negative)*" to "neutral" (ds = .97, 1.22, .89, .51).

The bipolar items were divided into two subscales "logical-practical image" (2 items) and "cooperative image" (4 items), which were indicated in the two dotted line boxes in Figure 17.7. These two subscales were based on factor analysis (method of maximum likelihood, Promax rotation) which extracted the two factors (62.6% of the variance).

TABLE 17.5 Correlations for the image of critical thinking and critical thinking disposition as a function of the lecture (Study 3)

	After lecture[a]		End of the school year[b]		
Image of Critical thinking (CT)	CT disposition in writing (CT-W)	CT disposition in general (CT-G1)	CT disposition in general (CT-G2)	CT disposition during study (CT-S)	Inquiry skills
Before lecture					
Logical image (L1)	.22***	.22***	.22***	.13*	.08
Cooperative image (C1)	−.04	.02	.00	−.04	−.16**
After lecture					
Logical image (L2)	.37***	.29***	.26***	.20***	.14**
Cooperative image (C2)	.10	.08	.03	.02	.01
Difference					
Logical image (L2-L1)	.14**	.06	.03	.07	.06
Cooperative image (C2-C1)	.11*	.04	.02	.05	.14**

Note. [a]N = 389–401, [b]N = 356–366, *p < .05, **p < .01, ***p < .001.

Table 17.5 shows the correlations between the two images of critical thinking (before and after the lecture) and critical thinking (CT) disposition in writing (CT-W) and in general (CT-G1). The correlation between the logical-practical image of CT (L1,L2) and CT disposition in writing (CT-W) (before .22, after .37) and in general (CT-G1) (before .22, after .29) increased after the lecture. Differences in the logical-practical image before and after the lecture (L1, L2) were slightly correlated with CT disposition in writing (CT-W) (.14). Concerning the long-term effect (four-month interval), the logical-practical image after the lecture (L2) was correlated with CT disposition in general (CT-G1) (.29), during study (CT-S) (.20), and at the end of the school year (CT-G2)(.26). These correlations were higher than the logical-practical image before the lecture (L1).

Figure 17.8 indicates the causal effects of the logical-practical image of critical thinking (CT) after the lecture on CT disposition in general and in writing. CT disposition in general (CT-G1) and in writing's (CT-W) effect on CT disposition in general (CT-G2) at the end of the school year are then depicted. CT disposition in general after the lecture (CT-G1) also affected CT disposition during study (CT-S) and inquiry skills. The image of CT before the lecture (L1) affected the image after the lecture (L2) but did not directly affect CT disposition at the end of the school year (CT-G2, CT-S). Conversely, the cooperative image of CT did not affect CT disposition in general and in writing. The reason for this is that the cooperative image of CT

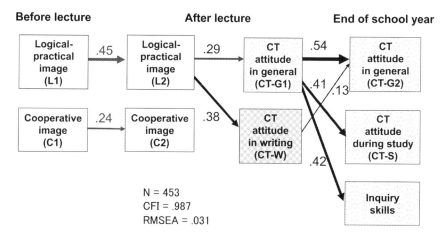

FIGURE 17.8 The effect of the logical-practical image of critical thinking after the lecture (L2) on CT disposition in general (CT-G1) and in writing (CT-W). Standardized coefficients for path analysis using pre- and post-lecture and data four months later. CT = Critical thinking.

was related to CT disposition during discussion and in group work, but not in writing and other individual situations.

Figure 17.9 shows the test of mediation of the logical-practical image of CT after the lecture (L2). The mediation occurs when the significant relationship between the logical-practical image of critical thinking after the lecture (L1) and the dependent variables (Figure 17.9a: CT-G1; Figure 17.9b: CT-W), reliably decrease. Confirmation was found for the mediator role of L2: both the mediation effect (range from .10 to .19, and from .06 to .18 not including zero in the 95% CI) and the Sobel test ($ps < .001$) were significant.

These results indicate that the lecture enhanced the perception of the logical-practical aspects of "critical thinking." Conversely, the meaning of the aggressive aspects was decreased by the lecture. The image of "critical thinking" became an image of something more logical-practical and cooperative. The logical-practical image of critical thinking after the lecture affected critical thinking disposition in general and in writing.

General discussion and conclusion: Cultivating critical thinking dispositions and inquiry skills in high school education

In this chapter, we examined the effects of learning activities on cultivating critical thinking disposition and inquiry skills in a high school. We have described three studies using cross-sectional data of 10th- to 12th-grade students, two-wave data of 10th- and 11th-grade students, and pre-post lecture data of 10th-grade students. The three main results are reported in the following paragraphs.

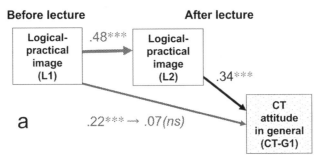

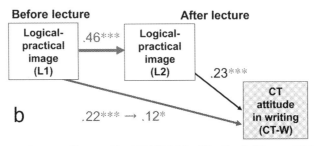

FIGURE 17.9 Results from mediation analysis of the logical-practical image of critical thinking (CT) after the lecture (L2) on the effects before the lecture (L1) for CT disposition a) in general (CT-G1) and b) in writing (CT-W). Standardized coefficients are as shown. ***$p < .001$, *$p < .05$ ($N = 453$).

First, we found that (i) critical thinking disposition in general and during study improved by grade, (ii) various learning activities (e.g., project-based learning) promoted critical thinking disposition, and, (iii) the critical thinking disposition during study affected learning competence.

Second, we found that critical thinking disposition, inquiry-learning skills, self-efficacy and interest in science, and learning competence improved from the beginning to the end of the school year. We also determined the effects of critical thinking disposition during study on inquiry learning skills, self-efficacy and interest in science, and learning competencies.

Third, we discovered that the logical-practical image of critical thinking was enhanced after the lecture, while the aggressive image of it decreased. The logical-practical image of critical thinking after the lecture affected critical thinking disposition in general and in writing.

This enhancement of the logical-practical image of critical thinking is most likely due to the mixed approach to the teaching of critical thinking that was used, combining a general approach (e.g., critical thinking practice in special class), an infusion approach in each subject (e.g., critical-logical thinking instruction in STEM, English for preparing presentations), and the immersion approach in cooperative inquiry and project-based learning (e.g., Krajcik & Shin, 2014).

These results are consistent with the findings of meta-analytic studies that have indicated that a mixed approach (e.g., Abrami et al., 2008), project-based inquiry learning, and collaborative learning (e.g., Ten Dam & Volman, 2004) improve students' critical thinking disposition and abilities. The three components of the mixed approach used to cultivate students' critical thinking disposition and inquiry skills are (i) the general approach to critical thinking instruction and practice utilizing group work, in which students reflect on their own thinking by interacting with group members; (ii) the infusion approach in each subject (e.g., critical-logical thinking instruction in STEM, including scientific research methods and knowledge), which promotes students' critical thinking disposition and inquiry skills in STEM for scientific research; and (iii) the immersion approach in project-based learning (e.g., Barron, & Darling-Hammond, 2010; Krajcik & Shin, 2014; Thomas, 2000), which promotes students' critical thinking dispositions and inquiry skills for problem solving in science and everyday life. Students also acquired cooperative critical thinking disposition and inquiry skills by preparing presentations and papers for group projects.

Previous studies on inquiry-based and cooperative learning in undergraduates (e.g., Ahern-Rindell, 1998; Gokhale, 1995) as well as in elementary and high school students (e.g., Adams & Hamm, 1996) have also indicated the effectiveness of cultivating students' critical thinking. Therefore, these essential elements in the instructional method (the mixed approach combining a critical thinking practice, an infusion approach in each subject, and an immersion approach in project-based learning) can be applied to other high schools, junior high schools, and elementary schools in Japan and in other countries.

There are several constraints on conducting surveys, engaging in educational interventions, and collecting performance data in high schools. These constraints have placed limitations on this study that will need to be addressed in future work. First, students' critical thinking disposition and inquiry learning skills increased over their years spent in school. However, this has not been compared with a control group. Second, students' critical thinking dispositions affected their learning competence, self-efficacy, and interest in science. These results relied only on students' self-reports of their critical thinking disposition and competencies. In future work, students' performance tests, academic grades, achievement tests, and behavior concerning critical thinking dispositions and inquiry skills should be considered.

The following are a few important research questions for future studies.

- Are there any differences in the improvement of critical thinking disposition between the intervention group (e.g., Super Science High Schools) and the control group (e.g., students of non-Super Science High Schools or students in other courses in the same school)? We are conducting this type of comparative study in a different high school, studying a science course and another course (Kusumi, 2018a).

- Can improvements in critical thinking abilities be measured by standardized tests or performance tests? We are developing a standardized critical thinking test (Kusumi, Taira, Hasegawa, 2016) and performance tests using critical questions (Browne & Keely, 2007; Kusumi, 2017).
- Does critical thinking education affect academic achievement (e.g., in STEM and other subjects) via critical thinking disposition and inquiry skills? We are conducting a longitudinal study of this topic using standardized academic achievement tests and academic grades in STEM subjects and inquiry-based learning classes (Kusumi, 2018a).

This chapter described three surveys conducted at the school level. The school in question has an active learning environment using project-based collaborative learning and instruction on cultivating critical thinking and inquiry skills. Through various learning activities, students can improve their critical thinking dispositions and inquiry skills. We believe that the research-oriented characteristics of the school culture and school organization are also important contributors to cultivating students' critical thinking at the school level (e.g., Ten Dam & Volman, 2004).

References

Abrami, P. C., Bernard, R. M., Borokhovski, E., Wade, A., Surkes, M. A., Tamim, R., & Zhang, D. (2008). Instructional interventions affecting critical thinking skills and dispositions: A stage 1 meta-analysis. *Review of Educational Research*, *78*(4), 1102–1134.

Adams, D., & Hamm, M. (1996). *Cooperative learning: Critical thinking and collaboration across the curriculum*. Springfield, IL: Charles C. Thomas.

Ahern-Rindell, A. J. (1998). Applying inquiry-based and cooperative group learning strategies to promote critical thinking. *Journal of College Science Teaching*, *28*(3), 203–207.

Bailin, S., & Siegel, H. (2003). Critical thinking. In N. Blake, P. Smeyers, R. D. Smith, & P. Standish (Eds.), *The Blackwell guide to the philosophy of education* (pp. 181–193). Oxford, England: Blackwell.

Barron, B., & Darling-Hammond, L. (2010). Prospects and challenges for inquiry-based approaches to learning. In H. Dumont, D. Istance, & F. Benavides (Eds.), *The nature of learning: Using research to inspire practice* (pp. 199–255). Paris, France: OECD Publishing.

Browne, M. N., & Keeley, S. M. (2007). *Asking the right questions: A guide to critical thinking*. Upper Saddle River, NJ: Pearson Education.

Dewey, J. (1910). *How we think*. Boston, MA: DC Heath.

Ennis, R. H. (1987). A taxonomy of critical thinking dispositions and abilities. In J. B. Baron, & R. J. Sternberg (Eds.), *Teaching thinking skills: Theory and practice* (pp. 9–26). New York: W. H. Freeman.

Ennis, R. H. (1989). Critical thinking and subject specificity: Clarification and needed research. *Educational Researcher*, *18*(3), 4–10.

Facione, P., & Facione, N. (1992). *The California critical thinking dispositions inventory and the CCDI test manual*. Millbrae, CA: California Academic Press.

Fisher, A., & Scriven, M. (1997). *Critical thinking its definition and assessment*. Norwich, UK: Centre for Research in Critical Thinking.

Gokhale, A. A. (1995). Collaborative learning enhances critical thinking. *Journal of Technology Education*, 7(1), 22–30.

Hirayama, R., & Kusumi, T. (2004). Effect of critical thinking disposition on interpretation of controversial issues: Evaluating evidences and drawing conclusions. *Japanese Journal of Educational Psychology*, 52, 186–198.

Hirooka, S., Ogawa, K., & Motoyoshi, T. (2000). An exploratory study of measurement of "the orientation toward critical thinking." *Bulletin of the Faculty of Education, Mie University (Educational Science)*, 51, 161–173.

Japan Science and Technology Agency (JST). (2011). *Support for Super Science High School*. Retrieved from http://rikai.jst.go.jp/eng/e_about/e_sshs.php

Kobayashi, Y., Araki, H. & Ono, M. (2015). Overview and verification of effect of Super Science High School. [Discussion Paper (National Institute of Science and Technology Policy (NISTEP), No. 117, Ministry of Education, Culture, Sports, Science and Technology (MEXT), Japan). Retrieved from http://data.nistep.go.jp/dspace/bitstream/11035/3047/5/NISTEP-DP117-FullJ.pdf

Krajcik, J. S. & Shin, N. (2014) Project-based learning. In R. K. Sawyer (Ed.), *The Cambridge handbook of the learning sciences* (pp. 275–297). NY: Cambridge University Press.

Kusumi, T. (2017). Cultivating inquiry learning skills and critical thinking disposition in Super Global High School (2): A two year longitudinal study. *Proceedings of the 59th Annual Meeting of Japanese Educational Psychology* (p. 127). Nagoya, Japan: Nagoya University.

Kusumi, T. (2018a). The effect of inquiry learning skills on academic ability in a super science school. *Proceedings of the 60th Annual meeting of Japanese Educational Psychology* (p. 503). Yokohama, Japan: Keio University.

Kusumi, T. (2018b). Critical thinking: Approaches in cognitive sciences. *Cognitive Studies*, 25(4), 461–474.

Kusumi, T., Murase, M., & Takeda, A. (2011). Measurement of critical thinking attitude in fifth- through ninth-graders: Relationship to reflective predisposition, perceived academic competence and the educational program. *Japanese Journal of Educational Technology*, 40, 33–44.

Kusumi, T., Taira, T. & Hasegawa, Y. (2016). Development of assessment for transferable abilities for high school students. *Proceedings of the 32nd Annual meeting of Japanese Educational Technology* (pp. 803–804). Osaka: Osaka University.

Manalo, E., Kusumi, T., Koyasu, M., Michita, Y., & Tanaka, Y. (2013). To what extent do culture-related factors influence university students' critical thinking use? *Thinking Skills and Creativity*, 10, 121–132.

Ministry of Education, Culture, Sports, Science and Technology (MEXT) Japan. (2003). *How human resources in science and technology should be fostered and secured*. White Paper on Education, Culture, Sports, Science and Technology 2003. Retrieved from http://www.mext.go.jp/b_menu/hakusho/html/hpag200301/hpag200301_2_019.html

Programme for International Student Assessment (2007). *PISA 2006: Science competencies for tomorrow's world* (Volume 1, Analysis). Paris, France: OECD.

Sakurai, S. (1992). The investigation of self-consciousness in the 5th- and 6th-grade children. *Japanese Journal of Experimental Social Psychology*, 32, 85–94.

Stapleton, P. (2002). Critical thinking in Japanese L2 writing: Rethinking tired constructs. *ELT Journal*, 56(3), 250–257.

Takigiku, K., & Sakamoto, A. (1991). The reliability and validity of cognitive deliberative-impulsive scale. *Proceedings of 39th Annual meeting of Japanese Group Dynamics Society* (pp. 39–40). Sendai, Japan: Tohoku Fukushi University.

Ten Dam, G., & Volman, M. (2004). Critical thinking as a citizenship competence: Teaching strategies. *Learning and Instruction, 14*(4), 359–379.

Thomas, J. W. (2000). A review of research on project-based learning. San Rafael, CA: Autodesk Foundation. Retrieved from http://www.bobpearlman.org/BestPractices/PBL_Research.pdf

Wade, C. (1995). Using writing to develop and assess critical thinking. *Teaching of Psychology, 22*(1), 24–28.

Zeze High School. (2010). *Annual report of research and development on Super Science High School* (The fifth year). Ohtsu, Japan: Zeze High School.

Zeze High School. (2018). *Zeze High School*. Retrieved from http://www.zeze-h.shiga-ec.ed.jp/

18
USING TASK-BASED LANGUAGE TEACHING IN THE SECOND LANGUAGE CLASSROOM
Developing global communication competencies

Chris Sheppard

Summary

English as a foreign language needs to be taught so that it is useful in practice. However, currently, in the Japanese education system the approach is often to teach only the logical grammatical structure of English. Even though the Japanese Ministry of Education recognizes that English needs to be taught as a practical skill, beyond requiring that teachers improve their students' second language proficiency, it offers very little guidance on what should be done in the classroom. In this chapter, task-based language teaching (TBLT) is introduced as a method which can be used to develop English as a second language skills beyond grammatical knowledge. Three studies, which demonstrate how language learning tasks can be used to develop three dimensions of language skill (accuracy, complexity, and fluency), are offered as evidential support that this approach is effective.

Introduction

Arguably, the focus of education needs to change to skills required for the 21st century. One of the most important of these skills is the ability to communicate effectively in relevant communities (Ananiadou & Claro, 2009). Traditionally, these communities have been local, and individual's native languages were sufficient. However, increasingly, individuals have become members of global communities, which require the use of a second language – very often English (Phillipson, 2008). Japan is no exception. Today, Japanese individuals often find themselves in situations where English is the common language of the communities they participate in.

In recognition of these changes, recent reforms in Japan have attempted to refocus English education. College graduates are now expected to be able to use English to participate in the global economy (MEXT, 2003), and there has been some limited success in developing the English skills of native Japanese. For example, Super English High Schools where the classes are conducted in English, have furthered the communicative abilities of their students. Unfortunately, these successes have largely not extended to the general Japanese population (Nishino & Watanabe, 2008).

There are numerous reasons for such limited success, but two stand out. The first is that there are dual purposes for English education in Japan, and the second is the government's resourcing of English teaching. Although the government has attempted to refocus on teaching English as a communicative skill through various initiatives, it is often still taught as an academic skill directed towards entrance examinations (Butler & Iino, 2005). These examinations are often perceived to be designed to test English grammatical understanding and comprehension of complicated reading texts which are understood through grammar-translation. (However, Seki et al., 2011, rebuts this perception.)

Entrance examinations have a washback effect on the Japanese education system. In spite of being required to focus on the development of English as a communication skill, teachers at secondary level must also focus on students' examination preparation (Allen, 2016). The more schools move away from "teaching to" entrance exams and attempt to develop communication skills, the more students participate in what has been called "shadow education," or the after-school *juku*, which, in 1997, 75% of public junior high school students attended (Højlund Roesgaard, 2006). Many of these *juku* teach solely towards entrance examinations. One key purpose for learning English, then, is to acquire discrete grammatical knowledge and grammar-translation skills, while the second communication purpose gets less attention.

The second reason for limited success is lack of government resourcing. In its 2003 document, the Ministry of Education, Sport, Science, Culture and Technology (MEXT) focused on the development of teachers by requiring improvements in their English proficiency, not by training them how to develop their students' communication skills. MEXT stated that "almost all English teachers will acquire high English skills" (2004, p. 4) and set a goal of 550 points in the Test of English as a Foreign Language (TOEFL, https://www.ets.org/toefl) for new teachers. This approach to English education is also apparent in their action plans, which aim to "increase the use of Assistant Language Teachers" (unqualified native or near-native English speakers) and to use "local personnel who are proficient in English" (in Butler & Iino, 2005, p. 34).

This ignores the professional component of English education, and it makes the common assumption of nonexperts in Japan: to be a good language teacher only subject proficiency is necessary. However, appropriate tools and professional development could transition teaching content from the academic knowledge required by the entrance examinations to tasks which develop second language communication skills.

This chapter introduces task-based language teaching (TBLT), which aims to develop second language as a communication skill. Its purpose is to provide a framework which can be applied by teachers at any curriculum level to their language classrooms. First, theoretical support for the skill-based learning, on which TBLT is based, is presented. This is followed by an introduction to TBLT. The final section gives evidence for the utility of this approach. Although this chapter frames the use of TBLT in Japanese English language education, it is effective in any educational context which aims to teach language for communication.

Learning language as a skill

For adult learners, the skill-based learning of a second language requires the development of implicit knowledge (Ellis, 2004). Similar to Anderson's (2015) procedural knowledge in his Adaptive Control of Thought-Rational (ACT-R) model, it is an unconscious knowledge of both the linguistic structure of a language and also the ability to use this information to communicate. Using Ellis' (2017) example, a native-English-speaking 3-year-old is able to apply the rules of the language, effortlessly and unconsciously, while speaking, but she will be unable to verbally explain them because she has an implicit knowledge of the language, not an explicit one.

Implicit knowledge is represented in the brain by connectionist networks (Roberts, 1998), reflecting the neurobiological reality of the neurons linked by a network of synaptic connections. Interestingly, Rumelhart and McClelland (1986) researched the utility of connectionism as a metaphor for language knowledge in the 1980s and demonstrated that a Parallel Distributed Processing network was able to "learn" and "represent" the regular and irregular past tense of English verbs from the input alone.

It may be useful, at this point, to contrast implicit knowledge with explicit knowledge (known as declarative knowledge in Andersen's ACT-R model). Explicit knowledge is the knowledge of how to do something (Ellis, 2004). In language learning, it might be the knowledge of a grammatical rule. One characteristic of explicit knowledge is that it is accessible consciously and can be verbalized. An outcome of adult language education in many countries is explicit knowledge, which is useful but insufficient for actual communication.

DeKeyser (2007), drawing on Anderson (2015), explains that one way to develop second language production skills is through repetitive practice in three stages: cognitive, associative, and automatic (which Anderson calls autonomous). The first cognitive stage of skill learning starts under conscious control, usually by the application of explicitly known grammatical rules and vocabulary. This conscious process creates an implicit exemplar of the rule (i.e., a single application of the rule in context). Once several such exemplars are created, the learning moves to the next step. This conscious process is taxing on our cognitive resources and requires time.

The second, associative stage of learning involves the partial activation of the exemplars. The context of the communication activates associations related to one or more of the exemplars and, hence, they are recalled. However, as the connections are weak, exemplars may be slow to activate, or fail altogether. In this case, the conscious process takes over and creates a new exemplar. When a previous exemplar is partially activated, the new exemplar is then associated with it. Thus, the associative stage is a process of creating linked contextualized exemplars. Another form of associative learning occurs when there is partial or full activation of the exemplar which is consciously manipulated to better match the communicative purpose of the production. This process also creates a new exemplar, which is likewise connected to the original (see Logan, 1988). These exemplars make up procedural knowledge.

In the last, automatization stage, the context will activate the interconnected network of exemplars and autonomously produce a new exemplar which matches the communicative context. The more exemplars produced, the greater the levels of activation and the faster the production becomes. This further develops the procedural knowledge network.

For successful language learning, the teacher needs to create an environment which will guide students through this process from explicit to implicit knowledge. According to DeKeyser (2007), three conditions need to be fulfilled for this. The first is that the learning should be fully contextualized through meaningful communication. The process of learning is the creation of new exemplars connected to an existing knowledge network. Without this connection, while new exemplars may be created, it will be more difficult to access them.

The second condition for effective skill learning is repetition. Second language acquisition follows "the same power function learning curve as the acquisition of other cognitive skills" (DeKeyser, 1997, 2007), and so to attain automaticity the learner needs contextualized repetition. In his experiment, DeKeyser found that learning morpho-syntactic rules in context could be modeled by this power law. (The power law describes the relationship between practice and learning, often measured by reaction time. The first few repetitions result in great gains in performance, and thereafter each repetition results in a diminishing return in improvement.) This was also true for reaction times and for accuracy rates in receptive and productive tasks. A considerable amount of repetition was required to achieve automaticity on a picture selection comprehension task. It took a total of 15 hour-long sessions over a period of 8 weeks.

The third condition for skill-based learning is to have sufficient processing capacity available for the learning to occur. The conscious components of language skill learning take place in working memory (Baddeley, 2003), a cognitive system with a limited capacity that is responsible for temporarily holding information available for processing (Miyake & Shah, 1999). Activated knowledge from our long-term memory is linked to auditory and visual sensory inputs in working memory (Baddeley, 2015). Limited capacity in working memory means that activated memories decay quickly and the executive systems lose access to them. Likewise, the auditory and visuo-spatial loops which hold perceptual auditory and visual information respectively are also limited, as is our ability to attend to activated information.

Second language learning taxes a student's available processing capacities. If the processing requirements exceed the resources available, learners will prioritize the meaning over the form of the language (VanPatten, 1990). This is counterproductive if the primary aim of a learning event is to encode a new exemplar of the form of the language.

Description of the method

Teaching language as a skill: Task-based language learning

Second language education requires a systematic method which will enable the teacher to ensure that the three necessary conditions – contextualization, repetition, and sufficient capacity – are met to enable learners to develop their second language for communicative purposes. This section describes task-based language teaching (TBLT). It defines language learning tasks and describes how they can be organized into a pedagogic syllabus.

What is a task?

Though there are many different definitions of a language learning task (Ellis, 2003) the following definition from Van den Branden (2006, p. 4) is useful. He suggests "a task is an activity in which a person engages in order to attain an objective, and which necessitates the use of language." For example, imagine being in a store and unable to find an item. Finding that item is the objective. One choice is to use language and ask the shop attendant for help. The attendant's response will likely be an explanation of where the item is. The successful outcome to this task would be locating the item after following the instructions the attendant provided. So, a language learning task is one used with the goal of developing language skills in the process of achieving an objective.

Many classroom learning activities lack such a purpose. Their objectives include learning by using the language in some noncommunicative way. Examples are completing textbook exercises which require learners to change a verb from the present tense into the past tense, or translating a sentence from Japanese to English, or mimicking sentences spoken by the teacher. In each of these cases, the learning goal is to accurately use the language and the successful outcome of the language learning exercise is assessed by how accurate the use of the target language is.

What sets a language learning task apart from other learning activities, is that it has a dual purpose. The first purpose is achieving the communicative outcome.

In the example above, this was finding the item in the shop. The second is the language learning goal of the task. This can be as general as developing a learner's holistic language proficiency, or as specific as learning to apply the past-tense to verbs. In the shopping task above, the language learning goals could be achieving skill in making requests for information, or in understanding directions, depending on how the teacher designed the task.

The easiest way to determine if the learning activity is a task or an exercise is to question whether the learning goal and the outcome of the activity are the same. If the outcome and the goal of the activity are the same, then it is a language learning exercise. For example, if the goal is to produce the past-tense, and the outcome of the activity is to have changed the verbs in a sentence from the present tense to the past tense, then the goal and the outcome are the same. On the other hand, if the outcome and goal are different, then it is a language learning task. For example, if the outcome of a learning activity was to have used language to successfully locate a product in a shop but the language learning goal was to accurately comprehend instructions, then the goal and the outcome are different.

Another characteristic of tasks is their authenticity. Authenticity is the degree to which a classroom task is reflective of a real-world task (Gilmore, 2007). For example, if the learner is required to phone and order a pizza, then a successful task outcome would be to have a pizza delivered to the classroom. A less authentic task has no such real-world correspondence. An example might be a picture story task, where one student describes a series of pictures, while the other student listens and puts the same jumbled pictures into time order. Most people are unlikely to find a real-world application for this kind of task.

Some TBLT practitioners suggest that all tasks ought to be authentic to best foster language development (Long, 1985). However, complete authenticity in the classroom is difficult. In Japan, where English is a foreign language, for example, there is little opportunity to create truly authentic tasks – the restaurant staff will answer the phone in Japanese. Ellis (2003) suggests that for tasks to be of pedagogic value, they need only be authentic in their ability to foster authentic communication between the task participants. In other words, if the task elicits language which is able to create contextualized exemplars, then it is sufficient for the purposes of language learning. Students who are role playing restaurant staff can respond to other students who in turn are role-playing customers.

What does the use of tasks achieve?

One of the criticisms aimed at TBLT is that while doing language tasks, learners are able to use any language and strategic resource they have to achieve the set outcome (Ellis, 2003). Sato (2010), for example, found that the university participants in his task-based study did not use the target structure, in his case, the present perfect, at all. This suggests that teachers will find it difficult to use tasks to focus on one grammatical feature at a time, as is currently common.

Skehan (1998) believed that, in addition to designing tasks which elicit the communicative use of grammatical features, teachers should aim to develop complexity, accuracy, or fluency. Also due to the learners' limited processing capacity, a task should focus on improving only one of these dimensions at a time. Housen, Kuiken, and Vedder (2012) demonstrated that these three dimensions of language can be independently taught. Basing tasks on each of these dimensions in turn is also a practical way to organize language learning and language curricula.

Accuracy focuses on the correct use of the language. Accuracy-focused tasks are aimed at building a repertoire of linguistically correct exemplars which can be drawn on later.

Complexity can be lexical or grammatical. Lexical complexity pertains to the production of language with a greater variety of vocabulary items. Grammatical complexity refers to the level of sophistication of expressions of language "rules" and structure. Consider, for example, the number of clauses in a sentence. More clauses make it longer and grammatically more complex. Tasks developing complexity direct the learner's attention to expressing more involved content and ideas during their performance. The intention is that by doing so the learner will be able to build on and expand their existing linguistic knowledge in new contexts, often by using the grammatical structures learned explicitly. This process can be linked to the associative stage of skill learning.

Fluency indicates the speed at which someone can process language. Tasks which focus on fluency require learners to process content and use familiar language as quickly as possible without losing much accuracy. The goal of fluency development is to activate previously acquired knowledge, and thus strengthen and increase the connections in the brain, as occurs in the automatizing stage of skill learning.

Using tasks in the classroom

When tasks are used in the classroom, the learner's attention should be oriented to aspects of language use which will meet the required outcomes and language goals most effectively, either through the design of the task itself, or through the design of the individual lessons.

Task design features

Ellis' (2003) general task framework describes several ways to design tasks. The features of task design that he differentiates are: the input, the conditions, the cognitive processes, and the outcomes. The input includes how information is provided to the learners; pictorially, orally, or in written form, for example. The task conditions will describe how the information will need to be shared between the students in order to achieve the outcome. Do the students have different information, or the same information? Does all the information come from one student, or is the information shared? The cognitive processes refer to the function of the communication: an exchange of information, opinion, or an explanation. Finally, in what form will the outcome be expressed: pictorially, orally, or written? (See Skehan, 2018, for a more recent classification).

Task procedures

In addition to identifying the task type, teachers can direct learner attention through the design of the lesson, beginning with the pre-task phase, during the task phase, and in the post-task phase (Ellis, 2003). The pre-task phase prepares the learners. It will usually include an explanation of the communicative purpose and the criteria for successful completion. It may include, for example, providing a model exemplifying the required performance. It could also be an explicit reminder to the learners of a grammatical form which would assist them in the completion of the task. During the task itself, the teacher controls such things as materials and resources available, who gets what information, the time available, and the number of participants. In the post-task session, for example, the teacher could provide successful examples of the same task the learners had just completed for comparison, and give feedback to the students on their performance. Alternatively, the teacher could ask the students to evaluate their own performance based on the outcomes and learning goals of the tasks.

The task-based curriculum

Tasks can be central to a curriculum, as in task-based language teaching, or peripheral elements such as in task supported language teaching (Ellis, 2018). In order to use tasks successfully in either approach, they need to be selected and ordered effectively (Nation & Macalister, 2010).

Students' needs should be paramount and task selection should depend on how and why students will use the target language in the future. As explained previously, one need for many Japanese students is to pass the university entrance examination. Other Japanese students, for example graduate engineering students, have more specific needs, like being required to present their research at international conferences and write papers for conference proceedings in English. Only relevant tasks leading to proficiency in these areas should be selected for them.

Learners may have a need to use English to present research, but such authentic tasks are very complex and successful outcomes are unlikely. A task-based curriculum will therefore need to gradually build up skills starting from students' current levels and ending at a point where they can perform the target tasks. This is done by gradually increasing task complexity (Robinson, 2001). (Task complexity is a characteristic of the task and is different to the complexity described above which is a feature of the language used while performing a task). Cognitive complexity results from the degree to which the structure of a task demands resources in order to successfully achieve the outcome. To illustrate, a task with more components is more complex; i.e., a picture story with ten frames is more complex than a picture story with five frames. In summary, designing tasks to gradually increase fluency, accuracy, and complexity is key to a TBLT curriculum.

The argument here is that the task is an effective unit of design in a classroom focused on developing language as a communicative skill. It provides a framework to contextualize communication and enables learners to make the necessary exemplars and connections to develop increasingly complex language skills. In other words, a task-based curriculum provides teachers with a way to organize the development of a learner's language from their current level to their target levels.

Evidence for effectiveness

This section introduces evidence from three studies conducted by the author that suggests tasks, alone and as part of a curriculum, are effective in improving the accuracy, complexity, and fluency of second language learners. The first study examines how feedback during task performance can improve accuracy. The second study describes how gradually increasing task complexity develops the linguistic complexity of written output. The third study examines the limits of task repetition as a means of developing fluency.

Developing accuracy

TBLT provides teachers with mechanisms to focus on the forms of language and the accuracy of its production. Feedback may be one such mechanism. Although often eschewed in communicative language teaching as being ineffective and even detrimental to the learning process (Krashen, 1985), a more recent meta-analysis of research examining the efficacy of feedback has shown it to have a positive effect on learning (Li, 2010). Sheppard (2006, 2016) demonstrated that feedback, in the form of recasts, was an effective way to improve the accuracy of learner output.

As mentioned, a problem with task-based language production is that learners can use any resources they have available to attain the outcome of the task, making it difficult to predetermine a focus on any grammatical feature. In addition, there is a lower likelihood that learners will notice and respond to any feedback. VanPatten (1990) also pointed out that learners will focus on meaning first, and then only if any processing resources remain, the form of the language.

Swain's (1995) output hypotheses, however, provides for a mechanism in language production through which learners shift from a focus on meaning to form, which she called "noticing the gap." According to Levelt's (1989) Speech Production Model, this is the point during production where the learner notices that they are unable to formulate a conceptualized message. Sheppard (2006, 2016) attempted to determine if noticing the gap would lead learners to be oriented to feedback which was aimed at filling this gap and result in increased accuracy in production in subsequent task performance.

To investigate this, 40 Japanese university students were recruited and placed into either a control group or a repair group. Both groups repeated a ten-frame picture story task three times (time 1, time 2, and time 3) and then a new task of the same type (time 4). Upon completion of the first task (time 1), the repair group underwent a stimulated recall procedure where the participants watched a video of their own performance and responded to questions about "what they were thinking" any time the video showed pauses, repetitions, or reformulations during their oral task output. Whenever the participants indicated that they had "noticed a gap," a recast, or a phrase to fill the gap, was provided. The control group, on the other hand, participated in a general conversation about content unrelated to the task for an equivalent amount of time.

The results for the accuracy of production, as measured by the percentage of error-free clauses, are shown in Figure 18.1. The performance accuracy of the repair group increased significantly at time 2 when compared to that of the control group, and the accuracy of the performance on a new task stayed significantly higher at time 4.

These results show that feedback aimed at filling noticed gaps assists learners to produce more accurate language. The change is probably due to a combination of incorporating language contained in the feedback, thus creating new exemplars, and to more attention being focused on accurate performance, reformulating existing exemplars. This study demonstrates that tasks can be designed to increase accuracy.

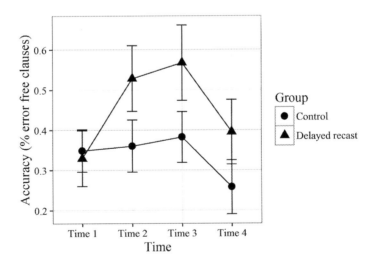

FIGURE 18.1 Oral task production accuracy by group of three task repetitions (time 1, time 2, and time 3) and a new task of the same type (time 4).

Developing complexity

As described above, tasks can be ordered based on complexity. The next study described set out to demonstrate that increasing task complexity over 3 years results in performance improvements (Sheppard & Ellis-Tanaka, 2011). The study was conducted within a large-scale English for Specific Purposes (ESP) program in the science and engineering faculty of a Japanese university. This program aimed to develop the communication skills the learners would need to participate in the international community as researchers in the fields of science, technology, engineering, and mathematics (STEM). One goal of the program was to develop the ability to report research findings in written form in conference proceedings. The curriculum was built around repeating tasks, which gradually increased in complexity.

The first rotation was completed in the first year during two courses called Academic Lecture Comprehension 1 and 2 (ALC 1 and ALC 2). Learners completed a series of note-taking tasks requiring a one-way information transfer from the teacher to the students. The information was presented in lecture form, and the tasks were varied by increasing the complexity of the information structures. Each task represented the structure of the various sections of a research paper. For example, the course began with process-structured lectures, and finished with a research presentation using an Introduction-Method-Results-and-Discussion structure (see Sheppard, 2019).

The second rotation of the cycle was executed in the first semester of the second year in Concept Building and Discussion 1 (CBD 1). The information structures were the same; however, this time the tasks were two-way, the information was shared between students. Again, the task complexity was gradually increased by varying the information structures. An example of a task used here is "listen and draw," where information was provided orally to complete a graph or a table (see Anthony, Rose, & Sheppard, 2010).

The third rotation increased the complexity in two ways in Concept Building and Discussion 2 (CBD 2). The first required individual students to generate the content of the task, through completing the individual steps of a research project. The task content was also linked so that subsequent task content was dependent on the outcomes of the previous tasks. The task order followed the steps of an empirically based research project: introduction, method, results, and then discussion. An example is an opinion-gap task, where the students discussed their opinions of the answer to a shared research question using their data as supporting evidence. The desired outcome was to reach an agreement between the participants (see Rose & Anthony, 2010).

Finally, Technical Writing 1 (TW 1) followed a project-based approach, rather than a task-based approach. The students were required to complete a research project following the same steps as in the third repetition. However, this time, the content needed to be related to their field of study, thus increasing the complexity.

The program was evaluated in terms of the development of grammatical complexity in writing over a 3-year period. Samples of paragraph summaries from the first part of the first rotation, and multiple-paragraph summaries from the second part were analyzed. The second rotation samples came from written summaries of oral tasks. The written samples from the third rotation were four-page IMRAD research reports. Similarly, the written samples from the final rotation were the final reports which simulated conference proceedings papers. The target sample, for comparison purposes, was taken randomly from chemistry and engineering IEEE conference proceedings published in 2010. Nine samples were taken from each level.

Complexity was measured in three ways: the average length of the sentences in words, verbs per sentence, and words per clause. The data was taken from intact classes taught by the researcher over several years. However, as the design was not longitudinal, each data set represented a completely different group of students.

The results are displayed in Figure 18.2, Figure 18.3, and Figure 18.4. The sentence length (Figure 18.2) and the clauses per sentence (Figure 18.3) demonstrate a development towards the target. However, the average number of words per clause (Figure 18.4) does not show improvement.

It is also clear that the proficiency of the class could have affected these results. The class representing the second part of the first rotation (ALC 2) averaged TOEIC-IP scores of more than 750 points, much higher than other classes' scores. This higher student proficiency may account for the higher complexity of written production apparent in the results for ALC 2.

Overall, the results show that using task complexity to order tasks in a task-based curriculum does appear to improve the written complexity of Japanese

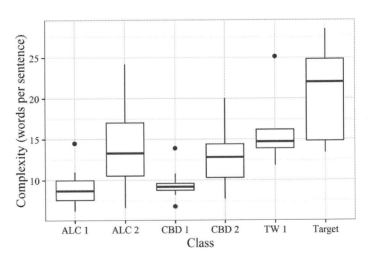

FIGURE 18.2 The complexity (words per sentence) of written production by class.

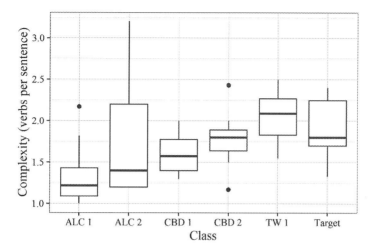

FIGURE 18.3 The complexity (verbs per sentence) of written production by class.

STEM students' writing, with the number of clauses per sentence even reaching the target standard. However, this improvement does not extend to all dimensions of complexity (i.e., not in the average words per clause). The reason for the improvement is most likely from a combination of task-demands, which required more complexity in the written expression to achieve the expected task outcome, and proficiency improvements gained through participating in a task-based curriculum. It should be reiterated here that as each of the class groups were very different and that because the tasks themselves were very different, the improvement in the complexity of writing was also affected by other factors.

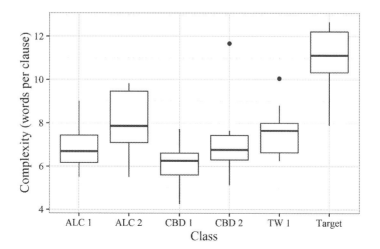

FIGURE 18.4 The complexity (words per clause) of written production by class.

Developing fluency

The final study described here, reported in Sheppard and Ellis (2018), demonstrates that task-repetition is effective for developing oral fluency on performance of the same task but does not extend to performance on the same task-type. Meaningful repetition is central to the development of autonomous skills (Anderson, 2015), that is, the ability to use a second language fluently (DeKeyser, 1997). Thus, repeating the same task many times would likely have an effect of improving spoken fluency (Bygate, 2001).

The study reported here looked at the spoken performance of participants in two groups who completed a picture story task. (The data came from the same data set, but from different groups as in the accuracy study reported in the previous section.) The first group just repeated the task, whereas the second group completed the same stimulated recall procedure as described previously, but there was no further intervention. Fluency was measured in terms of the pruned words per minute, where reformulations and repetitions, including fillers were deleted before calculating the speech rate. The first ten-frame picture story was repeated three times. Time 1 and time 2 took place within 30 minutes of each other, while time 3 was two weeks later. The fourth repetition (time 4) was of the same task-type (a ten-frame picture story), but with new content.

The results are shown in Figure 18.5. The fluency of production increased for both groups in time 2. Although this improvement was marginal for the task-repetition group, it was much greater for the stimulated recall group. The improvement was maintained for the two groups two weeks later, but the speech rate of the stimulated recall group dropped back to that of the task-repetition group in the new task.

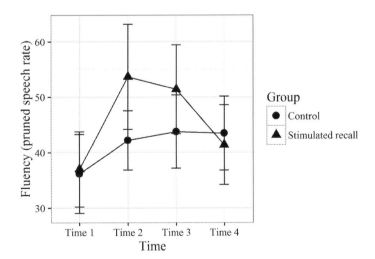

FIGURE 18.5 The oral fluency by group of three task repetitions (time 1, time 2, and time 3) and a new task of the same type (time 4).

Overall, the results show that while task-repetition is marginally beneficial initially, this improvement is not backed up by further task repetitions. There are two possible reasons for this which will impact on how task-repetition can be used to improve spoken fluency in the classroom. The first is that 2 weeks between tasks is likely too long to foster fluency development. This is because the memory activations gained through the first repetitions are lost, so the exemplar network is not developed. The second is that the amount of repetition is likely to be insufficient. According to the DeKeyser (1997) study reported previously, 15 hour-long sessions over 8 weeks were necessary for improvement. The study here only had three repetitions separated by 2 weeks. Ahmadian (2011) demonstrated improvements in fluency from mass task-repetition (11 times) transferred to a new task. Further evidence for a possible effect of increasing the number of repetitions comes from the superior improvement of the stimulated recall group. It is likely that the stimulated recall procedure acted as further repetition. The opportunity to view their video and consider their performance further maintained the mental activations, resulting in improved fluency. Thus, in order to further improve fluency, larger amounts of meaningful repetition, with smaller intervals between repetitions may be necessary.

Conclusion

Second language teachers, including those in Japan, need the tools required to teach language for practical communication. One such tool is TBLT. Tasks in TBLT require the learner to focus on the form and the meaning of the language simultaneously during communicative task performance. They have been shown to develop the accuracy, complexity, and fluency of language which make up the individual components of the knowledge and skills required to communicate in a second language.

The TBLT teacher is able to manipulate tasks in several ways to teach communicative skills. Tasks can be designed differently depending on, for example, the distribution of information, the outcome required, and the conditions under which the tasks are completed to help learners focus on both the form and the meaning of the language simultaneously. For example, the complexity study described in this chapter demonstrated that tasks which require the one-way passage of information are likely to elicit less complex language than a two-way task.

The task procedures can also be manipulated. Teachers can design pre-task, during-task, and post-task interventions to assist the learners to focus on the required performance. Task repetition is one procedure that has been shown to have the potential for developing fluency. The accuracy study demonstrated that the provision of feedback to learners when they were aware of a gap helped improve the accuracy of their performance.

Teachers also control the ordering of tasks in a TBLT curriculum. Task-complexity can be used both to classify tasks and order them in a curriculum.

The complexity study showed that by increasing the complexity of the tasks over a 3-year period, STEM students were able to develop more sophisticated written production, finally achieving target proficiency in one of the measures. While TBLT is not suitable for all situations and all contexts, this chapter has introduced how TBLT can successfully be used to develop the communicative language skills of students.

References

Ahmadian, M. J. (2011). The effect of 'massed' task repetitions on complexity, accuracy and fluency: Does it transfer to a new task? *The Language Learning Journal, 39*(3), 269–280.

Allen, D. (2016). Japanese cram schools and entrance exam washback. *The Asian Journal of Applied Linguistics, 3*(1), 54–67.

Ananiadou, K., & Claro, M. (2009). *21st Century Skills and Competences for New Millennium Learners in OECD countries. OECD education working papers, No. 41.* Paris, France: OECD.

Anderson, J. R. (2015). *Cognitive psychology and its implications* (8th ed.). New York: Macmillan.

Anthony, L., Rose, R., & Sheppard, C. (2010). *Concept building and discussion: Foundations* (2nd ed.). Tokyo, Japan: DTP.

Baddeley, A. (2003). Working memory and language: An overview. *Journal of Communication Disorders, 36*(3), 189–203.

Baddeley, A. D. (2015). Working memory in second language learning. In Z. Wen, M. B. Mota, & A. McNeill (Eds.), *Working memory in second language acquisition and processing* (pp. 17–28). Bristol, UK: Multilingual Matters.

Butler, Y. G., & Iino, M. (2005). Current Japanese reforms in English language education: The 2003 "action plan". *Language Policy, 4*, 25–45.

Bygate, M. (2001). Effects of task repetition on the structure and control of oral language. In M. Bygate, P. Skehan, & M. Swain (Eds.), *Researching pedagogic tasks* (pp. 33–58). Essex, UK: Routledge.

DeKeyser, R. (1997). Beyond explicit rule learning: Automatizing second language morphosyntax. *Studies in Second Language Acquisition, 19*(2), 195–221.

DeKeyser, R. (2007). Skill acquisition theory. In B. VanPatten & J. Williams (Eds.), *Theories in second language acquisition: An introduction* (pp. 97–114). Mahwah, NJ: Routledge.

Ellis, N. C. (2017). Implicit and explicit knowledge about language. In J. Cenoz & D. Gorter (Eds.), *Language awareness and multilingualism. Encyclopedia of language and education* (pp. 113–124). Boston, MA: Springer.

Ellis, R. (2003). *Task based language learning and teaching*. Oxford, UK: Oxford University Press.

Ellis, R. (2004). The definition and measurement of L2 explicit knowledge. *Language Learning, 54*, 227–275.

Ellis, R. (2018). *Reflections on task-based language teaching*. Bristol, UK: Multilingual Matters.

Gilmore, A. (2007). Authentic materials and authenticity in foreign language learning. *Language Teaching, 40*(2), 97–118.

Højlund Roesgaard, M. (2006). *Japanese Education and the Cram School Business: Functions, Challenges and Perspectives of the Juku*. Copenhagen, Denmark: NIAS Press.

Housen, A., Kuiken, F., & Vedder, I. (Eds.). (2012). *Dimensions of L2 performance and proficiency: Complexity, accuracy and fluency in SLA*. Amsterdam, The Netherlands: John Benjamins.

Krashen, S. D. (1985). *The input hypothesis: Issues and implications*. London, UK: Longman.

Levelt, W. (1989). *Speaking: From intention to articulation*. Cambridge, MA: MIT Press.
Li, S. (2010). The effectiveness of corrective feedback in SLA: A meta-analysis. *Language Learning*, 60(2), 309–365.
Logan, G. D. (1988). Toward an instance theory of automatization. *Psychological Review*, 95(4), 492–527.
Long, M. H. (1985). A role for instruction in second language acquisition: Task based language teaching. In K. Hyltenstam & M. Pienemann (Eds.), *Modelling and assessing second language acquisition* (pp. 77–99). Clevedon, UK: Multilingual Matters.
MEXT. (2003). *Eigo ga tsukaeru nihonjin no ikusei no tameno koudoukeikaku* [An action plan to cultivate Japanese with English abilities]. Retrieved from www.mext.go.jp/b_menu/shingi/chukyo/chukyo4/007/gijiroku/03032401/009.pdf
Miyake, A., & Shah, P. (Eds.). (1999). *Models of working memory: Mechanisms of active maintenance and executive control*. Cambridge, UK: Cambridge University Press.
Nation, I. S. P., & Macalister, J. (2010). *Language curriculum design*. New York: Routledge.
Nishino, T., & Watanabe, M. (2008). Communication-oriented policies versus classroom realities in Japan. *TESOL Quarterly*, 42(1), 133–138.
Phillipson, R. (2008). The linguistic imperialism of neoliberal empire. *Critical Inquiry in Language Studies*, 5, 1–43.
Roberts P. (1998). Implicit knowledge and connectionism: What is the connection? In K. Kirsner, C. Speelman, M. Maybery, A. O'Brien-Malone, M. Anderson, & C. L. Macleod (Eds.), *Implicit and explicit mental processes* (pp. 119–132). Mahwah, NJ: Lawrence Erlbaum.
Robinson, P. (2001). Task complexity, cognitive resources, and syllabus design: A triadic framework for examining task influences on SLA. In P. Robinson (Ed.), *Cognition and second language instruction* (pp. 285–318). Cambridge, UK: Cambridge University Press.
Rose, R. & Anthony, L. (2010). *Concept building and discussion: Applications*. Tokyo, Japan: DTP.
Rumelhart, D. E. & McClelland, J. L. (1986). On learning the past tenses of English verbs. In J. L. McClelland & D.E. Rumelhart (Eds.), *Parallel distributed processing: Vol. 2. Psychological and biological models* (pp. 216–271). Cambridge, MA: MIT Press.
Sato, R. (2010). Reconsidering the effectiveness and suitability of PPP and TBLT in the Japanese EFL classroom. *JALT Journal*, 32(2), 189–200.
Seki, S., Kato, K., Chamoto, T., Nagakura, Y., Miura, T., & Watari, Y. (2011). To what degree can the grammar-translation classroom cope with contemporary college-entrance English examinations? *Journal of the Chubu English Language Education Society*, 40, 315–322.
Sheppard, C. (2006). *The effect of instruction directed at the gaps second language learners noticed in their oral production* (Unpublished doctoral dissertation). University of Auckland, Auckland, New Zealand.
Sheppard, C. (2016, September). Instructional intervention in between task repetitions and second language development. In Shintani, N. (Chair), *Impact of task repetition on L2 learning: Multiple perspectives*. Colloquium conducted at the Pacific Second Language Research Forum 2016, Chuo University, Tokyo, Japan.
Sheppard, C. (2019). *Academic lecture comprehension*. Tokyo, Japan: CELESE.
Sheppard, C., & Ellis, R. (2018). The effects of awareness-raising through stimulated recall on the repeated performance of the same task and on a new task of the same type. In M. Bygate (Ed.), *Learning language through task repetition* (pp. 171–192). Amsterdam, The Netherlands: John Benjamins.
Sheppard, C., & Ellis-Tanaka, N. (2011, November). *The evaluation of a task-based curriculum for EST*. Poster presented at the Fourth International Task-Based Language Teaching Conference, Auckland University, Auckland, New Zealand.
Skehan, P. (1998). *A cognitive approach to language learning*. Oxford, UK: Oxford University Press.

Skehan, P. (2018). *Second Language Task-Based Performance: Theory, research, assessment*. New York: Routledge.
Swain, M. (1995). Three functions of output in second language learning. In G. Cook & B. Seidlhofer (Eds.), *Principle and practice in applied linguistics: Studies in honour of H. G. Widdowson* (pp. 125–144). Oxford, UK: Oxford University Press.
Van den Branden, K. (Ed.). (2006). *Task-based language education. From theory to practice*. Cambridge, UK: Cambridge University Press.
VanPatten, B. (1990). Attending to form and content in the input: An experiment in consciousness. *Studies in Second Language Acquisition, 12*(3), 287–301.

19
COLLECTIVE REASONING IN ELEMENTARY ENGINEERING EDUCATION

Christine M. Cunningham and Gregory J. Kelly

Summary

Properly designed engineering curricula can engage students in the engineering design process to foster creativity, problem solving, and communicative competence. This chapter examines how curricula can be designed to provide learning opportunities for students as they propose, communicate, modify, and evaluate multiple solutions within and across small group and whole class conversations to optimize their engineering designs. By making the criteria and constraints, prototypes, and proposed solutions available for public scrutiny, students can hold themselves and each other accountable across discourse events in classrooms. In the illustrative case of elementary engineering presented in this chapter, students analyze data collected by themselves and classmates and use the results to make evidence-based decisions about engineering solutions in an iterative engineering design process.

Introduction

Humans in modern society spend 98% of our time interacting with the *human-made*, or engineered, world. For example, we use toothpaste, bicycles, bandages, stairs, and smartphones. Traditionally, school has primarily included study of the *natural* world through science. Recently, however, in the United States, engineering has become part of K-12 science education; the *Next Generation Science Standards* (NGSS Lead States, 2013) and many state standards now include engineering. The discipline of engineering offers interesting possibilities for engaging students in ill-structured problems set in social contexts that differ from science. These stem in part from the purposes of the two disciplines (Cunningham & Carlsen, 2014). Science aims to describe, understand, and predict the natural world. Ultimately its goal is to articulate encompassing theories or descriptions. Engineering aims to create technologies (objects, systems, or processes) that solve problems (Cunningham, 2018). It strives to optimize solutions given certain resources and constraints. These possible solutions to a problem can be numerous and varied and depend on the client, the situation, and the criteria and constraints – multiple satisfactory outcomes can exist. For example, the best design for a bridge crossing a small stream in rural Pennsylvania is quite different than that which spans San Francisco Bay. People wear different types of footwear depending on what they are doing (dancing at a party, hiking up a mountain, relaxing in the park), the shape and needs of their feet, and their personal preferences. The open-ended nature of engineering offers possibilities in classrooms for stimulating new opportunities for students to think and reason. Instead of working toward a singular answer, students should consider and evaluate a number of designs.

Because engineering is a fairly new subject in K-12 classrooms, there is a need to create activities, challenges, and curricula for this area. As we do so, it is important to think about how to represent engineering concepts and practices in an age-appropriate manner. To ensure that all children can participate and learn, engineering materials should be developed so they include all students (Cunningham & Lachapelle, 2014) and provide scaffolds so students are learning from and with each other. Fifteen years ago, one of the authors (Cunningham) founded the Engineering is Elementary (EiE) program to tackle the challenge of creating engineering curricula for all children. She and her team created three school-based engineering curricula for the preschool, kindergarten, and elementary levels as well as two for afterschool and summer camp settings— one for the elementary and one for the middle school level. Overall, the team created 69 award-winning engineering units for preK-8. These are rooted in a theory of learning that situates students in social contexts where disciplinary knowledge is constructed in the service of solving problems (Hutchins 1995; Kozulin 2003; Vygotsky, 1978). This view of learning suggests that students need opportunities to engage in purposeful activity to develop conceptual understanding through discourse processes (reading, writing, speaking) (see Kelly, McDonald, & Wickman, 2012; Reveles, Kelly, & Durán, 2007). As we as developers created materials, we thought deeply about how to design engineering challenges and instructional supports that would engage students in authentic tasks and foster problem solving, innovation, and critical thinking. This led us to articulate and refine design principles for the development of engineering activities (Cunningham, 2018; Cunningham & Lachapelle, 2014; Lachapelle & Cunningham, 2014). Overall, three sets of frameworks to anchor the creation of the engineering curricular materials were developed.

Conceptual frameworks

A mission to include and retain *all* students, particularly those students traditionally underserved or underrepresented in STEM disciplines, led Cunningham to articulate a set of 14 inclusive design principles (Cunningham & Lachapelle, 2014; Cunningham, 2018). For example, engineering challenges should be set in a narrative context that highlights how engineering can help people, animals, society, or the environment; should assume no previously familiarity with materials, tasks, and terminology; and should develop challenges that require low-cost, readily available materials.

Fifteen years ago when we began this work, engineering for elementary-aged students was a radical idea. We asked ourselves what high-quality engineering would look like in the classroom. We also read studies of engineering work in professional settings (Bucciarelli, 1994; Johnson, 2009; Petroski, 2006; Vincenti, 1990). From these, we distilled a set of 16 practices of engineering (Cunningham & Kelly, 2017a). For instance, these include: envisioning multiple solutions, making tradeoffs between criteria and constraints, making evidence-based decisions, and communicating effectively. We considered what age-appropriate manifestations of these might be.

Development processes and cycles

Creating curricular materials that were innovative but that worked with the realities of classrooms today was also a guidepost of the project. To develop high-quality materials, the EiE team followed an iterative process of development. Critical to this was close collaboration with practicing classroom teachers as advisors and as field testers of the materials. Hundreds of teachers provided feedback about the lessons and materials to ensure that conceptual bases were translated into the realities of classroom life. The development process has allowed the program to scale—EiE materials have reached over 20 million children and 200,000 educators.

Systems approach

Finally, the work recognized the interdependence of three domains: curriculum, professional development, and evaluation and research. As we developed resources, we considered how these areas mutually support one another and developed all domains in tandem.

This chapter examines how carefully designed curricular units can provide opportunities to learn disciplinary knowledge in engineering and science. By considering these opportunities in detail, we document the ways that engaging students in the engineering design process (EDP) (Figure 19.1) fosters creativity, problem solving, and communicative competence, while adhering to the constraints of recognized knowledge in the fields of engineering and science. This paper explores how engineering challenges and instructional supports can be designed to support students in this kind of work. To illustrate what this looks like in an elementary classroom, we draw from one representative curricular unit of the EiE curriculum.

The Engineering Design Process

FIGURE 19.1 EiE's elementary engineering design process.

Description of the method

In this section, we explore some principles that underlie the development of engineering challenges that support creativity, problem solving, and communicative competence in children. Overall, the strategies focus on engaging students in purposeful activity, asking them to draw from current and constructed knowledge to develop solutions, and providing a social basis for the evaluation of the solution by inviting them to share the evidence they collected and analyzed within their student group and with the larger class. To illustrate what this looks like, we offer examples from one EiE unit, *Lighten Up: Designing Lighting Systems* (EiE, 2011a). This unit introduces students to optical engineering by having them explore how to use their science knowledge related to the properties of light (reflection, refraction, and intensity) as they design a lighting system using a flashlight and mirrors to illuminate hieroglyphics on the inside of a model Egyptian tomb.

Provide a context

Children are more motivated when they can situate what they are learning in the real world (Hmelo-Silver, 2004). We believe engineering challenges should begin with a context that helps students to understand why the work they will undertake matters and, hopefully, motivates them to tackle the challenge. Connecting classroom activities to the real world through a narrative can help children see it as relevant. There are many ways to do this; the media and method will vary. For example, we use a puppet to introduce challenges for preschoolers, illustrated storybooks kick-off units for elementary students, and short videos highlight how professional engineers are solving the same problems as middle school students. In each of these media, connections are made to topics of potential interest for the students. In the example below, we describe how optical engineering ties to tombs in Egypt.

In the first lesson of the Lighten Up unit students read a storybook, *Omar's Time to Shine* (EiE, 2011b). In the book, Omar, a boy in Egypt, is involved in a school dance performance. His brother, an optical engineer, works at the Valley of the Tombs in Egypt. While visiting him, Omar learns about how a system of mirrors had been used many years ago to reflect the sun's rays and illuminate the artwork deep inside the chambers. Omar puts this knowledge to use when a brownout occurs during his dance performance. He uses the engineering design process and what he knows about light and optical engineering to save the show. After they read the book, students in the class tackle a similar challenge.

Scaffold the problem-solving process

One core engineering concept is the use of a structured engineering design process. This systematic and iterative process guides the development of new technologies. To help students move beyond tinkering and to orient students to the goal of the activity at hand, an explicit engineering design process is valuable. We created an age-appropriate, five-step process for elementary students (Ask – Imagine – Plan – Create – Improve) (Figure 19.1), a three-step process for preschoolers, and an eight-step process for middle schoolers. But regardless of the number of steps, what is important is that the process focuses students' work so they are engaging in reflective problem-solving, not just doing crafts or following a set of steps. The process should ask them to think and plan, reflect and evaluate their designs against a goal, and use what they learn to improve their technology. This goal directed activity allows students to apply creativity to their solutions, while holding such solution accounts to a public standard of success.

Our engineering design process (EDP), centers around a goal. For the Lighten Up unit, the goal is "to design a lighting system for a tomb that lights up as many hieroglyphs as possible with the greatest possible intensity" (EiE, 2011a, p. 119). The "hieroglyphics" (an image of a vulture) are taped on six locations on the inside walls of a copy paper box. Using a flashlight that they shine through an opening in the wall, the students design ways to position mirrors that reflect the light to illuminate the vultures. Figure 19.2 is a photograph of students building their lighting system in the box. A mirror in the lower left is held by a student. Images of the vulture ("hieroglyphics") are taped on the walls at specified locations (a constraint on the system). Notice the students are coordinating across the modes of representation – their notebook sketch on the left and the grid of the box ("tomb").

Our five-step engineering design process devotes three of the steps to work that is often done before students begin physical construction. Professional

FIGURE 19.2 Students working on the optimal engineering design challenge.

engineers usually create detailed plans, backed by knowledge, tests, and data, before the actual building of a technology (such as an airplane or auditorium) begins. Students, too, should recognize that activities such as identifying the question, drawing on previous knowledge, brainstorming possible solutions, considering materials and other constraints and criteria, and creating a detailed plan are important work for engineers. These problem-solving strategies, while contextualized to this challenge, can also be generalized and applied to other situations. The technologies students construct will be better if they spend some time learning and thinking about them.

For some students, the task of engineering a solution might initially seem daunting. Outlining a process, with steps that each have questions that guide students' work for that day, can make the work much more approachable. For example, when students are engaged in the "Ask" phase, they are prompted to consider: What's the problem? What have others done? What are the constraints? (EiE, 2011a, p. 4–1).

Articulate criteria and constraints

Optimizing a design entails understanding the limitations and specifications that the design must meet. Challenges should articulate these criteria (requirements of the design) and constraints (limits that restrict the design such as materials, cost, or space) early in the process. Students and professional engineers create better designs if they understand what their guidelines are. Working with students to develop a list, posted at the front of the classroom, that outlines the challenge's criteria and constraints creates a public record for review throughout the design and testing processes. Some of the criteria and constraints will likely be clear at the outset of a challenge; others might arise during an activity and can be added. Students will need to balance the tradeoffs between these as they optimize their solutions.

Elementary engineering education **345**

One consideration in creating engineering challenges for young students is that they are challenging but not overwhelming. Students should be able to reach the criteria eventually but not immediately. The parameters for success should leave room for improvement as they motivate students to improve their technologies. And, as the next section discusses, they should afford a range of possible designs. In large part, these variables depend on the criteria and constraints of the challenge. To establish ones that are reasonable for and attainable to students, curriculum development teams should test many, many possibilities to inform the final choices.

In the optical engineering unit, the students engage in a lesson designed to help them learn more about the properties of light and the criteria and constraints of the challenge at hand. Based on the activities they have done in science class and a set of activities designed to help them see that light travels in straight lines and can be reflected, students generate a "What We Know About Light" list. Through their investigations they conclude:

- Light travels in a straight line until it hits another object.
- Light can be absorbed.
- Light can be reflected.
- The angle of incidence is always equal to the angle of reflection.
- The shorter the distance from a light source, the more intense the light.
- The greater the distance form a light source, the less intense the light. (EiE, 2011a, p. 111)

In this case, some of the properties of light also serve as constraints, and in this manner students learn science (properties of light) through the investigations. Additionally, the students work with their teachers to construct a list of the criteria and constraints for this challenge (see Figure 19.3). The teacher provides

Criteria and Constraints for our Lighting System	
Criteria	Constraints
• You need to light up as many of the hieroglyphs as possible. **Intensity** • The light shining on the hieroglyphs should be as intense as possible so that the artists can see enough details to copy them accurately.	• There is only one light source in the southeast corner of the tomb and it cannot be moved. • The tomb cannot be changed—you can't change its size or cut openings into it. • The hieroglyphs cannot be moved. • Cost should be low.

(EiE, 2011a, p. 112)

FIGURE 19.3 Criteria and constraints for the lighting systems generated by students.

a "price sheet" for the components that the students have access to when they create their designs (different sized mirrors, index cards, craft sticks, tape). The teacher also demonstrates the method the class will use to measure the intensity of the light that reaches each of the six hieroglyphics the students are trying to illuminate. The students need to balance multiple variables – it is complicated, so they gather data and create records that document how to achieve solutions within the given constraints.

Structure activities with multiple solutions

Engineering problems in the real world are open-ended – there are many ways to solve them and engineers continually develop new solutions. In the classroom, too, students should engage in challenges that afford multiple possible solutions. The opportunity to design a solution that is unique is something that is highly motivating to students, as it allows them to apply their own creativity and insight. As mentioned above, in designing or selecting engineering challenges, reviewing whether they encourage a diversity of solutions is an important consideration.

One way to encourage a range of ideas is to provide students with a number of different kinds of materials. In the lighting challenge, students have mirrors of two sizes to choose from. They will need to figure out how many mirrors they will use and where and how in the box to position them. The angle of reflection is one variable they will consider. But they also will consider how to mount the mirrors. Index cards, craft sticks, binder clips, string, tape, and pipe cleaners are available. Students design how they will prop, hang, or adhere the mirrors, and at which heights within the box. Encouraging students to exercise their creativity often results in novel solutions. Some of their solutions will work well and some will not – those that do not may prompt another innovative approach.

Develop students' shared knowledge, experiences, and resources

Professional engineering teams have shared knowledge that grounds their conversations and decisions. Such common understandings permit deeper, more probing interactions (Cunningham & Kelly, 2017b). To allow students to engage in meaningful discussions that push ideas in new but relevant directions, engineering experiences should establish common understandings and protocols that students can reference. It permits students to ask much more insightful questions of their team and class members. And it opens up possibilities for cross-pollination of ideas that are rooted in knowledge. Including time for all members of the class to engage in common experiences and sense making ensures that all class members benefit from such knowledge and enter the challenge on a more equal footing, thus potentially alleviating some of the disparities that might exist between students with respect to their previous access to related resources and activities.

Starting with a defined set of materials for an engineering challenge can allow students to gain familiarity with them, their properties, and how they function. Before students start thinking about how to use the materials to solve a problem, they should explore them. They should touch and manipulate them, learn their names, and conduct scientific tests that build their understanding of which might work best to meet certain challenges. Because the types of materials are limited and common to all students (each group does not use different materials), all students develop familiarity and have experiences with them. Thus, they can engage in conversations and questioning across groups. This helps build up the students' repertoire of technical terms, labels for engineering processes, and descriptions of possible solutions.

For example, before students begin brainstorming possible designs for their lighting system, they investigate the mirrors they will use. They undertake a series of experiments designed to help them understand how mirrors work. They learn, through exploration and class conversation, what reflection, refraction, angle of incidence, and intensity are. Through these shared experiences, students develop shared understandings and a common language.

The engineering design experiences also introduce and hold students accountable to common rubrics, data tables, and testing protocols. These are set out in worksheets and students review them as a class to understand what to do and how to do it. This allows students to share and reason as a group and as a class. Students in the Lighten Up unit use additional shared resources as they begin the challenge. A common protocol for calculating the cost of their solution and a class protocol for measuring the intensity of the light, allow students to share their ideas and results. Figure 19.4 shows the worksheet that students will complete to assess their lighting system design solutions. During the Create phase of the engineering design process students build their solution for lighting the hieroglyphic images, while trying to optimize the light intensity (criteria) and minimizing the costs (constraints)—see Figures 19.2 and 19.3. The scoring process is tabulated on the form presented in Figure 19.4. In this case, the students are able to calculate the total score of the engineering design by using quantifiable measures of costs and light intensity. These are important considerations in engineering—while there can be multiple solutions, and creativity is encouraged, any given solution is held accountable to imposed criteria and constraints. This common forum for calculating ways to optimize proposed solutions allows students to compare across groups and learn from each other.

Make data and discussions a shared resource

As mentioned above, one of the principal reasons for fostering shared experiences, using shared procedures, and reporting mechanisms is that students can learn with and from each other. A critical part of such interactions is having students share the results of their work and what they have learned with each other. This allows students the opportunity to engage in discourse practices relevant

| Name: _____ Date: _____ | A |

| Design # | **Designing a Lighting System**
 Engineering Design Process:
 Create! | |

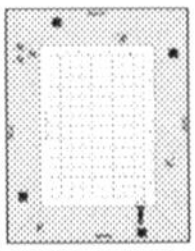

Directions: Complete the chart below with each of the scores for your lighting system design. Add all of your scores together to get your Total Score.

Cost Score	
The cost of our lighting system is $ _____	Our Cost Score is: _____

Score	Cost
1	More than $7.51
2	$6.51 to $7.50
3	$5.51 to $6.50
4	$4.51 to $5.50
5	$3.51 to $4.50
6	less than $3.50

Intensity Score	
What was your total Intensity Score on Intensity Score {4-11}?	_____

Total Score	
Add your Cost Score and your Intensity Score to get your Total Score. *Remember, a **HIGHER** score is better.*	_____

EiE: Designing Lighting Systems
© Museum of Science, Boston
Duplication Permitted

4-6

Lesson 4: Designing a Lighting System

FIGURE 19.4 Student worksheet for assessing design solutions.

to learning the disciplinary knowledge (Kelly, 2016). They learn by articulating their views and listening to others.

Using common materials, engaging in common protocols for testing, gathering similar data, and reporting it in similar forms, enables students to pool their data, analyses, and reflections. In some classrooms, students engage in public testing of their designs – classmates watch the testing of the technologies. By observing the performance of their and others' designs, students come to consider how the parameters interact. In other classrooms, students share the data they have created to generate a master data table that includes information from all groups' designs or that tallies the results of shared tests. Perhaps most importantly, the sharing of testing and data permits a period of shared reflection in which students can look across the designs of all groups and distill principles about what variables might influence how the technologies behave.

After students have designed their tomb illumination system and have scored it on the cost and intensity rubric to create a total score, they engage in a class discussion. Each group describes its lighting system to the class – what materials they used and how. The group explains which parts of the system its members believe worked well and which did not. The public conversations allow the teacher to ask students to reflect upon relationships like distance and intensity and the number of mirrors and their placement, to open a discussion that could inform the redesign of their technology. Because the entire class is privy to the conversation, all members and groups can draw on what they learn. Such knowledge informs students' next design and makes them smarter about light and optics.

Ensure engineering is an iterative process

Throughout history, humans have improved technologies to better suit their needs. Many first designs often do not function or function well. Fortunately, students (and engineers) look forward to redesigning them to make them better. Engineering challenges should include time for students to iterate and create another version of their design. Such redesign can be informed by students, the teacher, or the class asking what worked well, what could be improved, and then permitting them to design, create, and test another version. Comparing the performance of the new version with the original one allows students to see if their changes improved the design. If given the chance, most students welcome the opportunity to redesign and redesign.

After sharing their data with the class, groups doing the optical engineering challenge make tweaks to their design and recalculate their cost and intensity scores. They share these new data again with the class – sometimes on the same data table so they can assess whether the changes positively impacted the outcome. By engaging in these authentic practices of engineering, students build affiliation and academic identity.

Evidence for effectiveness

There is emerging evidence of the effectiveness of the learning theory and curriculum design supporting the learning opportunities described in this chapter. In the optical engineering example described previously, we identified how, by providing avenues for multiple solutions and mutual learning, students were able to apply creativity to solve problems. Across the five steps of the iterative engineering design process, students engaged in a number of discourse practices supporting engineering and science learning. The students' abilities to engage in practices of engineering entailed not only taking actions, but also listening, speaking, drawing, writing, and interpreting multiple forms of communication. This is an important part of the learning approach. Our research about the value of the engineering design process and engagement in engineering practices, draws from discourse analysis – the study of language-in-use. We applied discourse analysis across a set of educational research studies to make sense of the students' emerging communicative competence in these technical discourses (Hymes, 1972; Wallat & Piazza, 1988). Discourse analysis refers to the study of language-in-use in some setting (Bloome, Carter, Christian, Otto, & Shuart-Faris, 2005; Cazden, 2001; Green & Castanheira, 2012). In the three studies described below we considered the ways that everyday life in the classrooms shaped and was shaped by the discourse processes. Discourse includes verbal exchanges, contextualization such as gesture, written texts, signs and symbols, and other semiotic resources (Gumperz, 2001). Importantly, the moment-to-moment interactions that create everyday life through discourse are situated in social and cultural practices of a relevant speech community and thus over-time analysis is required to understand the meaning of instances of talk and action (Kelly & Green, 2019). These studies were all conducted in classrooms using EiE engineering units; thus, they follow the same curricular design principles as those described in the optical engineering unit.

The engagement of students in engineering practices involves not only carefully designed and tested curricula, but also informed instructional practices. In the first study, Cunningham and Kelly (2017b), we examined how a 4th-grade teacher and her students constructed a set of classroom norms and expectations for "talking" engineering and science in an aerospace engineering unit. In this study, the analysis of the classroom discourse demonstrated a set of teacher moves that support student engagement in engineering practices. For example, the teacher posed questions, revoiced student responses, and modeled ways of thinking about data analyses. In this way, the classroom community developed common foci around science concepts and engineering processes and held each other accountable to common standards of quality in engineering work. This common knowledge provided a basis for evaluation of the engineering designs and a means for students to learn to improve design from sharing of data and results. The development of students' competence in these discourse practices was supported by the teachers' uses of metadiscourse – talk about the ways they were talking about engineering and themselves as engineers.

In this first study (Cunningham & Kelly, 2017b), the teacher's discourse moves supported a learning community. In another study of elementary engineering, the prominence of students' written engineering notebooks was evident. Hertel, Cunningham, and Kelly (2017) took an ethnographic perspective to study the role of the engineering notebook in organizing, facilitating, and documenting the work of finding solutions to engineering design challenges across four different EiE units (package, electrical, geotechnical, and environmental engineering). In this study, the teachers provided the students with an engineering notebook – a set of bound worksheets from the curriculum designed to scaffold the students' work and reflections about the engineering challenge. The notebooks included schematics, data tables, rubrics, and spaces for drawing designs. Such supports allowed for common ways of engaging in productive discussion related to the disciplinary practices such as predicting, justifying decisions, and communicating solutions. In this manner, the notebooks allowed for students to creatively solve problems, and also provided common means for sharing and communicating results. The study documented how the notebooks scaffolded student activity and supported engagement in the practices of engineering. Thus, the communicative competence of the students was facilitated by the written and spoken discourse used in conjunction to support engaging in engineering practices.

The framing of the disciplinary knowledge through metadiscourse and the uses of written discourse in engineering notebooks both supported student communicative competence as they appropriated disciplinary knowledge and fostered identity work—the ways that the students use discourse to come to view themselves. Kelly, Cunningham, and Ricketts (2017) applied a sociolinguistic perspective to show how engagement in engineering builds the potential for students to see themselves differently as learners and students of aerospace and materials engineering. In the two units examined, the teachers and students engaged in engineering practices and subsequently called their actions "engineering," leading to development of student affiliation and identity with engineering. This was accomplished through the talk action of engaging in engineering practices, and publicly recognizing and acknowledging such engagement as engineering. Much like the Lighten Up unit described in this chapter, the two units provided multiple opportunities to use the engineering design process to propose unique and creative solutions to ill-structured problems. The students not only referred to their work as engineering and themselves as engineers, they also envisioned future work and possibilities for engineering in their lives. In these and other engineering units, the identity work was the result of talk about the purposeful activities of the classrooms.

Discussion

The curricular design features of and the enacted discourse practices of the classrooms described in this paper demonstrate ways that children can be supported to develop creativity, problem solving, and communicative competence. Across the curricular units and the examples provided in this chapter, a number of strategies supported this development. We review three ways that the curriculum and classroom discourse work together to support student learning: (a) engaging students in purposeful activity, (b) constructing knowledge to support solutions with evidence, and (c) providing a social basis for dialogue around the evaluation of solutions. These three ways of supporting learning build on and develop communicative competence and support reasoning.

First, central to developing creative problem solving is engaging students in purposeful activity. The EiE curricular units are composed of four lessons that provide a thematic approach to the study of engineering that includes providing a context, developing awareness about the disciplines of engineering, learning science relevant to the design challenge, and completing the engineering design challenge. This orientation has the benefit of building coherent lessons across the unit that provide motivation, encourage multiple solutions, and include multiple iterations of design, testing, and redesign. Across the four lessons constituting the engineering unit, the students reason through problems using the engineering design process. This fosters the development of reasoning skills related to the disciplinary knowledge (in the hieroglyphics example, properties of light) and engineering practices (such as improving through iteration). The design solutions depend on knowing about light propagation, reflection, and intensity, and only through reasoning through the multiple angles of incidence and reflection are the student groups able to illuminate the vulture images. Similarly, they need to learn from iterative design (their own group's and that of other student groups) to improve over time, thus reasoning through the engineering entailed in such optimization.

Second, the students' activities are goal-directed and aligned with the learning goals. Building a learning context for solving problems needs to include a number of important dimensions. In the engineering units, the students' problem solving was informed by relevant knowledge and evidence constructed in and through the classroom activities. To support this work, the curricular units built in scaffolding processes. Throughout the lessons, the engineering design process was introduced, evoked, employed, and reviewed to organize and support the student work. This design process served as a framework to draw in relevant knowledge to inform decisions made in the classrooms about the science, engineering, and processes for decision making. Such decision making depended on the use and evaluation of relevant evidence. Evidence in engineering design can take multiple forms, and often spans different modes of communication. Students use evidence to make meaning across modes in engineering. Such modes include using everyday discourse to communicate ideas; evoking science concepts to provide the basis for a decision; illustrating a process through written, symbolic, or gestural communication; or employing the materiality of the engineering design itself as an instantiation of knowledge. In this way, the articulation and interpretation of evidence supports the development of communicative competence (Hymes, 1972; Mishler, 1972). The students come to learn how to employ the discourse features of technical knowledge (reflection of light, properties of materials) and to do so in ways that are consistent with the local speech community (adhering to the norms for data sharing and discussion). In the examples from the designing lighting systems unit, the students were asked to consider how to create solutions through deliberative processes in small groups and whole class conversations.

Third, engaging in purposeful activity to solve problems with evidence advances student thinking about the science and engineering involved in the lessons. This third way that student learning was supported concerns the basis for dialogue around the evaluation of solutions. Each of the engineering design challenges provided criteria and constraints, structured activity to support multiple solutions, and engaged the students in an iterative process. These activities get students actively involved in constructing knowledge. But this is not enough. In addition to constructing knowledge claims and proposing solutions, the engineering designs need to be tested, evaluated against criteria, refined, redesigned, and rebuilt. Discourse around the assessment of the knowledge and solutions is important to assess the merits of different proposed designs and compare across designs to learn from differences. Thus, the organization of the curricular units and associated classrooms discourse provide a social basis for dialogue around the evaluation of solutions. Dialogues of this sort expand the students' communicative competence beyond just knowing concepts, to using concepts, inventing solutions, and saliently engaging in the discourse of evaluating their own and others' work. This social basis for decision making within and across student groups, and in the whole class, makes participating and learning a collective endeavor. Thus, reasoning is situated in social processes and the local cultural practices of the relevant speech community (the classroom members). The epistemic agent in such cases is the collective – individual reasoning and contributions may be valued, but become candidates for knowledge through the discursive work of classroom members in the varying social configurations of the activities.

In the illustrative examples we provide, support for creativity, problem solving, and communicative competence are interconnected. We offer examples of how allowing for multiple solutions (while adhering to criteria and constraints) encouraged creative design solutions. There are multiple ways to solve the posed problem. By opening up the problem space, and allowing creative solutions, students are situated in social contexts where decisions about engineering designs need to be adjudicated with evidence. By holding students accountable to the criteria and constraints and to each other, the discussions around problem solving become opportunities to employ discourse processes. Because decisions needed to be made with evidence through deliberation, the activities foster communicative competence among the participating students.

References

Bloome, D., Carter, S., Christian, B., Otto, S., & Shuart-Faris, N. (2005). *Discourse analysis and the study of classroom language and literacy events: A microethnographic approach.* Mahwah, NJ: Lawrence Erlbaum.

Bucciarelli, L. L. (1994). *Designing engineers.* Cambridge, MA: MIT Press.

Cazden, C. (2001). *Classroom discourse: The language of teaching and learning* (2nd ed.). Portsmouth, NH: Heinemann.

Cunningham, C. M. (2018). *Engineering in elementary STEM education: Curriculum design, instruction, learning, and assessment.* New York: Teacher College Press.

Cunningham, C. M., & Carlsen, W. S. (2014). Precollege engineering education. In N. Lederman (Ed.), *Handbook of research on science education* (pp. 747–758). Mahwah, NJ: Lawrence Erlbaum.

Cunningham, C. M., & Kelly, G. J. (2017a). Epistemic practices of engineering for education. *Science Education, 101*(3), 486–505.

Cunningham, C. M., & Kelly, G. J. (2017b). Framing engineering practices in elementary school classrooms. *International Journal of Engineering Education, 33*(1B), 295–307.

Cunningham, C. M., & Lachapelle, C. P. (2014). Designing engineering experiences to engage all students. In S. Purzer, J. Strobel, & M. Cardella (Eds.), *Engineering in pre-college settings: Synthesizing research, policy, and practices* (pp. 117–142). Lafayette, IN: Purdue University Press.

Engineering is Elementary. (2011a). *Lighten up: Designing lighting systems*. Boston, MA: Museum of Science, Boston.

Engineering is Elementary. (2011b). *Omar's time to shine*. Boston, MA: Museum of Science.

Green, J. & Castanheira, M. L. (2012). Exploring classroom life and student learning: An interactional ethnographic approach. In B. Kaur (Ed.), *Understanding teaching and learning: Classroom research revisited* (pp. 53–65). Rotterdam, NL: Sense.

Gumperz, J. J. (2001). Interactional sociolinguistics: A personal perspective. In D. Schiffrin, D. Tannen, & H. E. Hamilton (Eds.), *Handbook of discourse analysis* (pp. 215–228). Malden, MA: Blackwell.

Hertel, J. D., Cunningham, C. M., & Kelly, G. J. (2017). The roles of engineering notebooks in shaping elementary engineering student discourse and practice. *International Journal of Science Education, 39,* 1194–1217.

Hmelo-Silver, C. E. (2004). Problem-based learning: What and how do students learn? *Educational Psychology Review, 16,* 235–266.

Hutchins, E. (1995). *Cognition in the wild*. Cambridge, MA: MIT Press.

Hymes, D. (1972). On communicative competence. In J. Pride & J. Holmes (Eds.), *Sociolinguistics: Selected readings* (pp. 269–293). Harmondsworth, G. B.: Penguin.

Johnson, A. (2009). *Hitting the brakes: Engineering design and the production of knowledge*. Durham, NC: Duke University Press.

Kelly, G. J. (2016). Methodological considerations for the study of epistemic cognition in practice. In J. A. Greene, W. A. Sandoval, & I. Braten (Eds.) *Handbook of epistemic cognition* (pp. 393–408). New York: Routledge.

Kelly, G. J., Cunningham, C. M., & Ricketts, A. (2017). Engaging in identity work through engineering practices in elementary classrooms. *Linguistics & Education, 39,* 48–59.

Kelly, G. J., & Green, J. (Eds.). (2019). *Theory and methods for sociocultural research in science and engineering education*. New York: Routledge.

Kelly, G. J., McDonald, S., & Wickman, P. O., (2012). Science learning and epistemology. In K. Tobin, B. Fraser, & C. McRobbie (Eds.), *Second international handbook of science education* (pp. 281–291). Dordrecht, The Netherlands: Springer.

Kozulin, A. (2003). Psychological tools and mediated learning. In A. Kozulin, B. Gindis, V. S. Ageyev, & S. M. Miller (Eds.), *Vygotsky's educational theory in cultural context* (pp. 15–38). Cambridge, UK: Cambridge University Press.

Lachapelle, C. P., & Cunningham, C. M. (2014). Engineering in elementary schools. In S. Purzer, J. Strobel, & M. Cardella (Eds.), *Engineering in pre-college settings: Synthesizing research, policy, and practices* (pp. 61–88). Lafayette, IN: Purdue University Press.

Mishler, E. (1972). Implications of teacher strategies for language and cognition: Observations in first-grade classrooms. In C. B. Cazden, V. P. John, & D. Hymes, (Eds.), *Functions of language in the classroom* (pp. 267–298). New York: Teachers College Press.

59–60, 67, 82, 106–110, 177–180, 183, 185, 187, 190, 209, 238, 242–243, 251, 339, 341–342, 350–353; repertoires 84, 86, 89, 92–93, 98
community 20, 29, 75, 84–90, 94–101, 117, 146, 178, 180, 185, 189, 219, 225, 265, 300, 331, 350, 352–353; of inquiry 17, 20–21, 28–29
Compare and Discuss instructional method 48, 50–51, 57, 60
comparison 48–50, 52–61, 77–78, 169, 236, 328; active 236
competencies 2–3, 6, 8–12, 36, 76, 82, 101, 151–153, 156, 161, 193–194, 197, 201, 231, 237–238, 247–248, 250–251, 258–259, 262–263, 279–280, 292–293, 299–305, 308–312, 316–318, 350
complexity 12, 101, 203, 240, 275, 303, 321, 327–329, 331–336
computer: based assignments 142; science (CS) 178–182, 184, 210, 216; teachers' pedagogies 177
conceptual: knowledge (*see* knowledge, conceptual); understanding 26, 32, 35–36, 87, 94, 292, 340
conditional knowledge (*see* knowledge, conditional)
confidence 27–29, 101, 164, 168–170, 180, 182, 209–210, 215–218, 223–225, 235, 259
constraints 204, 317, 339–341, 344–347, 353
construction of knowledge (*see* knowledge, construction of)
constructive feedback (*see* feedback, constructive)
content unrelated questions (*see* question, content unrelated)
context 6–8, 18, 26, 37–38, 49, 60–61, 68, 70, 74, 76, 79–80, 85, 87, 89, 92–95, 101–109, 111, 134, 143–144, 165, 179, 183–185, 188, 198–199, 201, 203, 209, 232, 234–235, 242, 247, 250, 264–267, 275–276, 280, 282, 287, 300–301, 304, 323–324, 336, 339–342, 352–353
contextual learning (*see* learning, contextual)
contextualization 11, 141, 152, 156, 325, 350
cooperative learning (*see* learning, cooperative)
creative thinking 9, 39, 42, 74, 189
creativity 6, 8, 11–12, 141, 152, 156, 178, 187, 217–218, 263, 300, 339–343, 346–347, 349, 351, 353
criteria 19–20, 27, 201, 249, 251–253, 255, 257, 260, 284, 301, 328, 339, 341, 344–345, 347, 353
critical thinking 1–5, 8–12, 19–20, 23, 29, 56, 59, 67, 75–76, 141, 152, 156, 177–180, 183–185, 187, 189–190, 193–195, 197, 200–201, 204, 209–211, 214–216, 218–226, 231, 237, 240, 242–243, 263–264, 271, 299–305, 308–309, 311–318, 340; definition 1, 8, 19–20, 152, 194, 301; disposition 12, 299, 301, 304–309, 311–314, 316–318; image of 312, 314–317; practices 179–180, 184, 317; skills 9–10, 17, 19–21, 123, 130, 177–179, 182, 193–194, 200–201, 204, 300–301, 304–305, 309
criticality 276
culture 7, 12–13, 17, 22, 29, 68, 89–90, 92, 98, 108–109, 196, 241–242, 318; of inquiry 10, 84–86, 89–93, 95, 101
curriculum 18–19, 21, 25–29, 37, 44, 48, 57, 59–61, 116–117, 149, 265–266, 300–301, 304, 323, 328–329, 331–333, 335, 341, 345, 349, 351

debugging 11, 209–220, 222–225; strategies (*see* strategies, debugging)
declarative knowledge (*see* knowledge, declarative)
deep approaches to learning (*see* learning, deep approaches to)

358 Index

deeper: comprehension 134; structure 67–68, 71, 73, 78–82; understanding 11, 36, 46, 48, 108–109, 115–116, 134, 139, 165, 167

deeper learning 1, 2, 4–7, 9–12, 34, 48, 76–77, 82, 84, 100, 105–108, 160–162, 169–172, 178, 195, 209–210, 225–226, 231, 237–238, 242–243, 251, 259–261, 279–280; definition 6, 77, 237

design: instructional 85–88, 101, 135, 264, 266, 276; principles 211, 214, 248–249, 251, 259, 340–341, 350; solutions 347–348, 352–353; task 92, 327

design-based research 24, 267

diagram: construction 232, 234, 242–243; definition 231; method of instruction 233–237

diagram use: problems or difficulties in 232–233; practice in 235, 237, 239; value of 233, 237

dialogic 32–37, 41–46, 263–267, 271, 273, 275; argumentation (see argumentation, dialogic); education 35, 43, 46; focus 264–267; learning (definition) 1, 7; talk 37, 40, 45; teaching 10, 32–34, 37, 40, 43–44

dialogue 1, 7–8, 10, 17, 32–46, 185, 242, 266, 351, 353; collaborative 10, 17, 24; facilitation of 41; transformation of the self through 45

digital: interactive map 144, 148; tools 265, 267, 276

direct instruction (see instruction, direct)

disciplinary knowledge (see knowledge, disciplinary)

discourse 339–340, 347, 349–353

discovery learning 286

discursive strategies (see strategies, discursive)

discussion 50, 52, 56, 59–61; board 263, 267–271, 275–276; skills 21, 29

diverse students (see students, diverse)

domain: specific knowledge 301; general skills 301

ecological validity 259

educational: method course 281; reforms 3, 299; technologies 141

effective strategies (see strategies, effective)

emotion 68, 73, 138, 187, 200, 209–214, 216–219, 225, 241

engagement 9, 11, 45, 130, 132–133, 178, 180–183, 187, 199, 225, 247–248, 250, 265–266, 276, 350–351

engineering design process 339–343, 347–352

English as a foreign language (EFL) students' abilities 250

ethnographic perspective 86, 88–89, 100–101, 106–107, 109, 116, 350; interactional 89, 105, 107, 109, 110, 115–116

everyday thinking 67, 69, 74, 80

evidence-based intervention tools 196

exemplar 57, 71, 74, 216–217, 323–330, 335

explanation 55–59, 61, 233–240

explanatory power 67–69, 78–80

exploratory talk 37, 40, 44–45

facilitation of dialogue (see dialogue, facilitation of)

failure 36, 85, 209–211, 214, 218–219, 225–226

feedback 60, 81, 144, 148, 152, 154–156, 223, 234, 249–250, 255, 257–258, 328–330, 335, 341; constructive 148, 156

first year college students (see students, first year college)

flexibility 8, 49, 52, 267; procedural (see procedural, flexibility)

fluency 12, 321, 327, 329, 334–335

Four Cs (4Cs: critical, caring, collaborative, and creative thinking) 38–39, 42

generic skills 293, 299–300
ground rules 32, 34, 37–41, 44–45
group work 39, 41, 82, 94, 186, 281, 292, 315, 317

higher-order: knowledge network 160, 164; thinking 155–157, 193, 264
high-quality questions (*see* question, quality)
history learning 161, 163–164
homework 160–161, 171–172, 186, 198, 233, 235, 237, 281–282
humor 11, 177–183, 185–190

identity: academic 98, 349, 351
image of critical thinking (*see* critical thinking, image of)
immersion approach 299, 317
incorrect strategies (*see* strategies, incorrect)
information and communications technology (ICT) literacy 11, 141, 148, 152–153, 156–157, 203
inquiry: based 29, 85, 88–89, 139; learning skills 12, 304, 309–313, 317; practices 92–93, 179
inquiry-based learning 123, 128, 139, 143, 300, 317–318
instruction: diagram method of (*see* diagram, method of instruction); direct 56, 161, 286–287; mathematics (*see* mathematics instruction); peer 233–234
instructional: design (*see* design, instructional); materials 4, 57, 142; method 48, 50–51, 57, 59–60, 62, 139, 317
interactional ethnography 89, 105, 107, 109; perspective (*see* ethnographic perspective, interactional)
intercontextual 89, 93, 95

interdisciplinary 101, 105–108
internal dialogism 264
interpretive principles and practices (of literary texts) (*see* practice, interpretive principles and)
inter-rater reliability 151, 257, 269
intertextual links 107, 115
iteration 24, 26–27, 29, 110, 241, 352

Japan's Ministry of Education, Culture, Sports, Science and Technology (MEXT) 247–248, 299–300, 321–322
journals 4, 24, 211, 215–217, 220, 225–226
joy 177–183, 185, 187–190

knowledge: accountability to 43; background 126–128; clash hypothesis 125, 127; conceptual 53, 58; conditional 198, 236–237; construction of 7, 142; declarative 197–198, 202–203, 235, 323; deficit hypothesis 125; disciplinary 3, 35, 42, 88, 110, 340–341, 348, 351–352; in pieces 80; of instructing learning strategies 198, 280, 293; of instructional representations 280, 293; of learners 280; pedagogical (*see*, pedagogical, knowledge); prior 58, 61, 77, 80, 127, 139, 161–162, 164, 166, 169–172, 217–218; procedural (*see* procedural, knowledge)

lack of spontaneity in strategy use (*see* strategy, spontaneous use)
languaculture 88, 95, 108
learner-generated questions (*see* question, learner-generated)
learners worldwide 141
learning: beliefs about 162, 165, 169; collaborative 5, 142, 144, 146, 171, 317; communities 141–142, 350; contextual 155; cooperative 171, 265, 317; deep approach to 203;

deeper (*see* deeper learning); dialogic (*see* dialogic learning); discovery (*see* discovery learning); in context 143; inquiry-based (*see* inquiry-based learning); linking of 45, 102, 242–243; meaningful 161–170, 243; new learning environments 142–143; opportunities for 86, 88, 101, 108; preparatory 11, 160–163, 170, 172; process 24, 61, 87, 101, 143, 196, 199, 204, 209, 226, 329; project-based 299, 301–305, 308–309, 313, 316–317; related beliefs 162; self-regulated (*see* self-regulated learning); skills 12, 161, 198, 281, 293, 304, 309–313, 316–317; skills-based 323–324; strategies (*see* strategies, learning); strategy (*see* strategies, learning); vicarious 197–198
lesson: plan task 289, 291–293; study 287–288
Letters from Gervase 11, 193, 196, 199–201
linking of learning (*see* learning, linking of)
listening skills 18–19
literary interpretation 113, 115
location-based: platforms 142; questions (*see* question, location-based)

materials 2, 4–6, 18, 24, 29, 38, 51, 57–61, 74, 114, 123–130, 134–139, 142–143, 157, 160–161, 181, 194, 201, 209, 214, 238–239, 248, 255, 258, 269, 283, 287, 289, 300, 323, 340–341, 344, 346–349, 352
math word problems 232, 234, 236, 238
mathematics: instruction 49; learning 48, 170
meaningful learning (*see* learning, meaningful)
metacognition 37, 39, 40, 194–195, 199, 212, 281–282, 286, 301
metacognitive: awareness 45; processes 157, 195

metadiscourse 92–94, 98, 101–102, 107–108, 110, 116, 350–351
mixed approach 299, 301, 304, 317
modeling 11, 115, 142, 197, 200, 209–210, 214–215, 219–220, 225
motivation 3, 44, 109, 124, 129, 142, 157, 169, 170, 171, 195, 197, 199–200, 203, 282, 352
multimedia-rich questions (*see* question, multimedia-rich)
multiple: perspectives (*see* perspective, multiple); representations 231; solutions 48, 58, 339, 341, 346–347, 349, 352–353; strategies (*see* strategies, multiple)

narrative-based approach 193
new learning environments (*see* learning, new learning environments)
new pedagogy 141
Next Generation Science Standards (NGSS) 339
nonverbal reasoning 44

obstacle + goal hypothesis 125–126
opportunities for learning (*see* learning, opportunities for)
oral presentation competence 248, 259

pattern 6, 19, 22, 67–69, 71–82, 97, 114–115, 234; of practice (*see* practice, pattern)
pedagogical: approach 21, 185, 210; content knowledge (PCK) 280, 293; knowledge 106; practices 180, 189; tool 182
pedagogies of humor and joy 177–183, 185, 187–190
peer: assessment 146, 148–149, 151–152, 154, 156; instruction (*see* instruction, peer)
perceptual inference 232, 243
perspective: multiple 110, 195, 201, 204, 240, 274, 276; taking 11, 263, 266, 267, 270, 275

philosophical: discussion 25; question (*see* question, philosophical)
Philosophy for Children (P4C) 37–38
Philosophy with Children 17, 23, 26, 28
plan 23, 38, 43, 50, 57, 59, 110, 129, 138, 183, 190, 214–216, 225, 281, 288–289, 291–293, 300, 322, 343–344
playfulness 179, 185, 189
Playground of Ideas 10, 17, 21–24, 26–29
practice 340–341, 347, 349–353; classroom (*see* classroom, practices); critical thinking (*see* critical thinking, practices); in diagram use (*see*, diagram, use, practice in); in strategy/diagram use (*see* diagram, use, practice in); inquiry (*see* inquiry, practices); interpretive principles and 106–107, 111; pattern of 92; pedagogical (*see* pedagogical, practices); principles of 84, 102; reflective 32, 38–39, 220
preparation 11, 105, 160–172, 218, 225, 260, 322
preparatory learning (*see* learning, preparatory)
presentation skill 11, 247–251, 258–261
principles: guiding 84, 86, 94, 101 102; of practice (*see* practice, principles of)
prior knowledge (*see* knowledge, prior)
problem solving 2, 5, 9, 11, 12, 49, 58–59, 90, 200, 218, 225, 231–236, 243, 263, 292, 302, 317, 339–342, 351–353
procedural: flexibility 58, 60; knowledge 52, 54, 58, 150, 153, 198, 235, 323–324
productive: discussion 18, 61, 351; talk 18–19
project-based learning (*see* learning, project-based)
prompting 11, 197, 209–210, 214, 219, 221, 225, 282
purposeful activity 340, 342, 351–352

question: based Instruction (QBI) 11, 123, 127–129, 133–134, 138–139; content unrelated 138; generating activities 143, 155; generating taxonomy 149–151, 153–154, 156; learner-generated 123, 139; location-based 141, 149; multimedia-rich 11, 141, 144, 150–151, 153, 156–157; philosophical 23–26; quality 127, 134, 136, 139
questioning: skills 123–126; stems 124–125; strategy (*see* strategy, questioning)

reflect (also reflecting, reflection) 10–11, 18, 24, 28, 37–42, 45, 48, 50, 52, 56, 60, 70–71, 75–76, 82, 87, 105, 107, 111, 113, 185, 187, 194–204, 209–219, 222–226, 247, 250, 252, 255, 260, 273, 286, 302–303, 310, 317, 323, 343, 348–349, 351; self (*see* self-reflection)
reflective practice (*see* practice, reflective)
reflectiveness 308, 311
reflexive (process) 84, 86, 88, 90, 94–96, 98, 100–102, 105, 107
reflexivity 87, 106, 109
repertoires. communicative (*see* communicative, repertoires); of action 89, 94
review 41, 57, 124, 165–167, 172, 255, 344, 347
rich points 109, 114–115, 117
rubric 249, 251, 264, 347, 349, 351

science: class 68, 142, 345; computer (*see* computer, science); education 141–144, 151, 153, 299, 339
scientific: conceptions 67–68, 78; theory-building 67–68; thinking 76, 156, 157; understanding 10, 67, 143, 153
self-assessment 249, 259
self-efficacy 12, 169, 197, 202, 249, 259, 299, 309, 311–312, 316–317

self-evaluation 250, 254–256, 286, 306–307, 309
self-reflection 196, 199, 247, 260
self-regulated learning 11, 161, 193–195; story-tool to improve 193; strategies 195; Zimmerman model 179
sense-making 61, 74, 76
signal words 124
skill-based learning (*see* learning, skills-based)
social cognitive framework 197
solving problems (*see* problem solving)
speaking skills 27
spontaneous strategy use (*see* strategy, spontaneous use)
STEM (Science, Technology, Engineering, and Math) 157, 178, 190, 299–301, 304, 317–318, 331, 333, 336, 340
story-tool to improve self-regulated learning (SRL) (*see* self-regulated learning, story-tool to improve)
strategies: debugging 211–212, 215–220, 223–224; discursive 105, 107–108; effective 4, 45, 162–163, 169, 219, 233, 260, 280, 287; incorrect 50, 52–53; learning 3–4, 12, 195–199, 201–202, 204, 279–284, 286–290, 292–294; multiple 48–50, 52, 57–59, 61; self-regulated learning (*see* self-regulated learning, strategies)
strategy: inquiry-based teaching (*see* inquiry, practices); learning (*see* strategies, learning); practice in (*see* diagram, use, practice in); questioning 124; spontaneous use 171, 232, 234, 237, 242–243, 291–292; test learning 289–290, 292
students: diverse 84–86, 100–102, 190; English as a Foreign Language (EFL) (*see* English as a Foreign Language (EFL) students' abilities); first year college 202; underrepresented 180, 188
Super Science High Schools 299–301, 304, 318

task 1, 7–9, 11–12, 22, 29, 41, 69, 71–72, 74, 80, 90, 92, 144, 152, 156, 160–161, 163, 165, 177, 185, 193, 195, 197–198, 200–201, 213, 231, 233–234, 237–238, 240–241, 249–250, 255, 258–259, 267, 275–276, 284, 286, 288–293, 321, 323–336, 340–341, 344; complexity 328, 329, 331–332; design features 327; procedures 328, 335; based curriculum 328–329, 333
task-based language teaching (TBLT) 321, 323, 325–326, 328–329, 335–336
teacher: practice 180; professional development 60; training 28, 281
textbook analysis 49
theoretical turn-of-mind 67–68, 76, 82
theory building 67–69, 71–77, 79, 80–82; scientific (*see* scientific, theory-building); discussion 72, 74–75, 79–81
Thinking after Instruction 279, 281, 286, 294
Thinking Together 10, 32–33, 36–41, 44–46
Think-Pair-Share 52, 56, 59
third-party evaluation 256–258
tracing 108, 111
transfer 6, 56, 197–201, 237–238, 247, 256, 259–260, 282, 287
transformation of the self through dialogue (*see* dialogue, transformation of the self through)
tutoring scenario method 282, 286, 293
twenty-first century challenge in education 2
twenty-first century skills 2, 4–5, 7, 9, 141, 156–157, 263–264, 267, 269, 279, 299

underrepresented students (*see* students, underrepresented)
understanding: conceptual (*see* conceptual, understanding); deeper (*see* deeper, understanding); scientific (*see* scientific, understanding)

value of diagram use (*see* diagram, use, value of)
vicarious learning (*see* learning, vicarious)
visual representation 213, 231, 243

web-based: platforms 141; technologies 141–142
worked examples 49, 52–54, 57–58
workshop 11, 211, 216, 223–226, 247, 250, 251, 253–261

writing 20, 56–57, 59–60, 75, 79, 81, 85, 87–89, 93–95, 98–99, 128, 145, 170, 214, 216, 218–219, 239–240, 263, 302–303, 305, 310, 312–317, 331–333, 340, 350
written argumentation (*see* argumentation, written)

zone of proximal development 179

Taylor & Francis eBooks

www.taylorfrancis.com

A single destination for eBooks from Taylor & Francis with increased functionality and an improved user experience to meet the needs of our customers.

90,000+ eBooks of award-winning academic content in Humanities, Social Science, Science, Technology, Engineering, and Medical written by a global network of editors and authors.

TAYLOR & FRANCIS EBOOKS OFFERS:

- A streamlined experience for our library customers
- A single point of discovery for all of our eBook content
- Improved search and discovery of content at both book and chapter level

REQUEST A FREE TRIAL
support@taylorfrancis.com

Printed in the United States
by Baker & Taylor Publisher Services

NGSS Lead States. (2013). *Next Generation Science Standards: For states, by states.* Washington, DC: The National Academies Press.

Petroski, H. (2006). *Success through failure: The paradox of design.* Princeton, NJ: Princeton University Press.

Reveles, J. M., Kelly, G. J., & Durán, R. P. (2007). A sociocultural perspective on mediated activity in third grade science. *Cultural Studies in Science Education, 1,* 467–495.

Vincenti, W. G. (1990). *What engineers know and how they know it.* Baltimore, MD: Johns Hopkins University Press.

Vygotsky, L. (1978). *Mind in society: The development of higher psychological processes.* Cambridge, MA: Harvard University Press.

Wallat, C., & Piazza, C. (1988). The classroom and beyond: Issues in the analysis of multiple studies of communicative competence. In J. L. Green & J. O. Harker (Eds.), *Multiple perspective analyses of classroom discourse* (pp. 309–341). Norwood, NJ: Ablex.

INDEX

abstract (*see* abstraction)
abstraction (of meaning) 6, 67, 71, 79, 81–82, 180, 242–244
accountability to knowledge (*see* knowledge, accountability to)
accuracy 12, 321, 324, 327, 329–330, 334–335
active comparison (*see* comparison, active)
advanced organizer 161–162, 170
agency 196, 198
algebra 48–50, 57–60
analogical reasoning 68, 73
appropriation 45
argumentation 8, 9, 11, 194, 240, 263–267, 269–276, 301; dialogic 264–267, 273; profile 266, 270, 272, 274–275; tool 263, 267; written 263–267
art 11, 110, 209, 211–214, 216, 218–219, 223, 225, 343
associative stage 324, 327
AugmentedWorld 142, 144–148
automatization stage 324

background knowledge (*see* knowledge, background)
beliefs about learning (*see* learning, beliefs about)

bilingual 84, 101
brainstorming 70, 93, 344, 347
breakdowns 209–210, 215, 225
broadening participation in computing 179

capabilities 1, 3–5, 7–12, 151, 249, 275
classroom: discourse 10, 86, 100, 105–117, 216, 225, 350–351; practices 5, 10, 17, 106–107, 273; talk 19, 21, 34, 36–37, 105, 107, 109, 111
co-construction (of knowledge and understanding) 45, 88
cognitive: beliefs 162; counseling 279, 281–282, 285–286, 293–294; gaps 126, 128; stage 323
collaboration 6–7, 18, 273, 300, 341
collaborative: approach 28; dialogue (*see* dialogue, collaborative); inquiry 29, 86; learning (*see* learning, collaborative); thinking 17, 29
collective reasoning 45
communication skills 130, 134, 184, 202, 322–323, 331, 329, 335
communicative: approach 36, 41, 43; competence 10, 12, 21, 46, 48, 56,